# THE LOOPHOLE IN LSAT LOGICAL REASONING

Published by Elemental Prep

Author: Ellen Cassidy

Editor: Dave Killoran

Printed in Canada

09 01 20 21

# Table of Contents

## ANSWER CHOICE STRATEGY   TIME-SAVING TRICKS FOR FUN AND PROFIT   413

**Chapter Breather   ADVANCED TRANSLATION DRILL**   419

## FULL LOGICAL REASONING SECTION PRACTICE   423

## EPILOGUE   444

## APPENDIX A   REAL LSAT PRACTICE EXTRAVAGANZA   446

## APPENDIX B   A LIST OF ALL THE REAL LSAT QUESTIONS IN THIS BOOK   455

## APPENDIX C   YOUR WRONG ANSWER JOURNAL   456

# INTRODUCTION

me: I'm so excited you're finally here. This is going to be awesome.

you: Hi. You're excited I'm reading an LSAT prep book? I have an unnerving mix of fear and anxiety.

me: No, really I am so excited! There is not one thing I wish I could be doing other than helping you with the LSAT. I could have done a ton of other things; I'm helping you with the LSAT because I freaking love it.

you: You love the LSAT? But that's like physically impossible. Who *are* you?

me: Well, first, my name is Ellen Cassidy, and I was kind of crafted in a lab to teach the LSAT. I studied language at Stanford University and Oxford University. At 23, I was one of the youngest lecturers in the history of the Rutgers University English Department. I love two things: words and teaching, mostly teaching about words. I even spent a few years as an actor and creative writer, so I can write stuff that's (hopefully) fun to read.

you: How'd you end up taking the LSAT then?

me: I decided to take the LSAT super randomly. My friend dragged me to a party where I heard a funny story about being a public defender. I was so deep in my quarter-life crisis that I started researching LSAT prep methodologies on my phone before I even left the party. As soon as I started prepping, I felt more mentally alive than I had in my entire life. I loved working with the test for those two months; it felt like someone was finally speaking to me in my native language. As I got into the car after taking the LSAT, I literally said out loud, "I wish I could just do the LSAT forever."

you: Did you end up going to law school?

me: After I got the score, I figured, "This is a pretty awesome score. I guess I might as well apply to law school?" (This is not a good reason to apply to law school.) I was admitted to Harvard Law School and deferred three times before turning them down. I taught my first LSAT class shortly after I was admitted to Harvard, and I immediately knew I loved helping people learn to reason far more than I could ever love being a lawyer.

you: Dangggggg. That's crazy. But wait, this is a standardized test, not something actually fun. Seriously, what's so great about the LSAT?

me: What *isn't* great about the LSAT? But since this is a Logical Reasoning book, let's start there first. I love the skills that Logical Reasoning tests, and I believe our world would be better off if more people had those skills regardless of whether they go to law school.

you: What skills does Logical Reasoning test?

me: Logical Reasoning tests your ability to do two things:

| | |
|---|---|
| **Read intently** | You have to pay attention to every word. If you don't *really* understand what you're reading, you can't answer the question. The LSAT is the incorruptible skimming police. |
| **Question authority** | You have to question the claims the author makes in Logical Reasoning. Many students just say, "Sounds good…" after they're done reading because the LSAT is intimidating. Don't be such a pushover! Get critical. Get mean. Get your nitpick on. |

Those two skills are the core of Logical Reasoning. And they're the two things you're going to be rocking out on by the end of this book.

you:    What's different about this book versus all the other LSAT prep solutions out there? There are a lot of choices and I just want whatever's going to get me the highest score.

me:    I want you to get the highest score possible too. That's why I spent five years perfecting the new techniques outlined in this book.

Experts do Logical Reasoning entirely differently than what's typically taught in courses and written in books. We do the questions intuitively. This is a book designed to lead you — from wherever you happen to be starting — into doing Logical Reasoning like an expert, like the mythical "naturals." Some people are lucky enough to come into LSAT preparation with the critical intuition the expert has — the inclination toward skepticism, side eye, and Loopholes. I'm one of those people. We're naturally judgmental.

you:    So I have to be more judgmental to do better in Logical Reasoning?

me:    Yes, and this book contains a system designed to help you do just that. The methods in this book are based on the critical intuition experts use to complete Logical Reasoning questions quickly. But to teach critical intuition, you have to break it down into concrete steps so students know exactly what to do. Once students practice these steps enough, they fade into the background and one fluid, subconscious process takes the steps' place. That process is critical intuition. For years, I have tested this system with many students at many different levels to verify that it *will* build that intuition in students at all levels. It does.

you:    How does it work?

me:    Chapters 1-3 teach you how to read and understand arguments. This section culminates in the Basic Translation Drill, which is responsible for more student improvement than anything else I've ever created.

Chapters 4-8 lay the foundation for the skeptical stance with arguments. You'll learn what's wrong with arguments and put that knowledge into practice with the CLIR Drill at the end of Chapter 8. This is where you learn to predict the answer to the majority of Logical Reasoning questions without even knowing the question type.

Chapters 9-12 focus on the question types and answer choices. You'll learn about the Powerful-Provable Spectrum, which massively simplifies answer choice selection. This section caps off with two real Logical Reasoning practice sections.

Basically, we lay the foundation together in each chapter, and then put it into practice at the end of each section. The same principle applies to the book as a whole: Chapters 1-8 lay the foundation that is applied in Chapters 9-12.

you:    Woah, that's a lot of stuff.

me:    YES. It is a lot of stuff. Treat it like a textbook even though it's friendlier than that. Read slower than you feel like you have to. Take active notes, highlight, actually write in answers to the drills instead of "doing them in your head." You *can* get significantly better at Logical Reasoning. I know it. I've seen it. I believe in you, reader.

Don't worry if you don't know what terms like CLIR and Powerful-Provable mean right now. You'll learn what they mean soon.

# The Anatomy of a Logical Reasoning Question

Every Logical Reasoning (LR) question consists of the same three parts: the stimulus, the question stem, and the answer choices. We'll tackle each of these parts one at a time throughout this book.

## THE STIMULUS

First, we'll focus on the stimulus, the most important part of an LR question. **The answer to the question isn't in the answer choices; it's in the stimulus.**

Stimuli come in four flavors: Arguments, Premise Sets, Debates, and Paradoxes. Arguments are the most common stimulus type, so the bulk of your

Always read the stimulus first. Always read the whole stimulus.

> Game show host:   Humans are no better than apes at investing, that is, they do not attain a better return on their investments than apes do. We gave five stock analysts and one chimpanzee $1,350 each to invest. After one month, the chimp won, having increased its net worth by $210. The net worth of the analyst who came in second increased by only $140.  — Stimulus
>
> Each of the following describes a flaw in the game show host's reasoning EXCEPT:  — Question Stem
>
> (A) A conclusion is drawn about apes in general on the basis of an experiment involving one chimpanzee.
> (B) No evidence is offered that chimpanzees are capable of understanding stock reports and making reasoned investment decisions.
> (C) A broad conclusion is drawn about the investment skills of humans on the basis of what is known about five humans.
> (D) Too general a conclusion is made about investing on the basis of a single experiment involving short-term investing but not long-term investing.
> (E) No evidence is considered about the long-term performance of the chimpanzee's portfolio versus that of the analysts' portfolios.
>  — Answer Choices

Logical Reasoning score will depend on your ability to analyze arguments. The beginning of this book will help you build the analytical foundation to do this like a boss. We'll examine each of these stimulus types in detail soon.

## THE QUESTION STEM

Once you're familiar with the question types, you'll see that the tasks they ask you to perform are pretty simple.

Next, we'll take our stimulus-based strategy and apply it to the question types. You'll learn what each question wants from its correct answer. Spoiler: Every correct answer on the LSAT is either powerful or provable, so we split our question types according to whether they're seeking a powerful correct answer or a provable correct answer.

The question stem lets you know which of the question types you're dealing with. It's the most predictable part of an LR question; there are only so many question types and they all have reliable indicators. It's crucial to know your question types, so you can make the task of the question simple and predictable.

## THE ANSWER CHOICES

Finally, we'll head to the answer choices, by far the trickiest part of an LR question. But we can break the answer choices down into powerful and provable types too! It's simplicity in the chaos.

The answer choices are crafted to seduce and destroy you. They play to the most common errors in reasoning; they play you. This is why you need to know what you want before you start reading the answer choices. That confidence inoculates you against temptation. This is also why you have to read all the answer choices all the way through. The LSAT is too good at crafting deceptive wrong answers for it to be safe to move on without reading *every* word of *every* answer.

# How to Study

> Read the chapters of this book in order.

This book is crafted to be read in order and if you don't read the beginning, you will not be as well served as you could be. Obviously, you bought the book and you can use it however you want: It can be a coaster, a doorstop, or even kindling (yeah, I know what people do with LSAT books after they're done studying). But it's literally my job to tell people how to study, so here's my advice: **Don't skip ahead.**

Let's think through a situation where you might be tempted to skip ahead. Say you know you struggle with Necessary Assumption questions. It seems efficient to jump to the Provable Questions Chapter, read only the Necessary Assumption section, and close the book, assuming there's nothing else to help you. But this would not be the best way to get better at Necessary Assumption questions. Like did you know there's a whole chapter just on Assumptions & The Loophole? And a couple chapters preceding that chapter to prepare you for the work that's going on there? And a chapter before that on how to read the difficult language on the LSAT (which is another reason you could be getting that question type wrong)? There's more to LR than the question types and these foundational chapters fill in the gaps you don't know are there.

I get that your time is limited and you want to get as much improvement as you can as quickly as possible. But **your time is better spent reading the foundational chapters of this book (1-8) than skipping to the chapters that look more like other Logical Reasoning books.**

### THE WRONG ANSWER JOURNAL

> Keep track of your wrong answers in a Wrong Answer Journal.

Your wrong answers are your greatest asset. They are the evidence you need to get a higher score. Each wrong answer implies at least one error in your reasoning that needs to be remedied in order to get a similar question right in the future. Your wrong answers show you your weaknesses, which is great! Your weaknesses are what you have to address to get a higher score. **The time you spend reviewing your wrong answers is the most productive time in your entire prep process.** Your Wrong Answer Journal will keep all your wrong answers in one neat, organized place.

**To all the skimmers out there:**

You may feel like you can skim this book because it reads like a distant cousin of a Buzzfeed article. You may not even know you're skimming! But fight the urge. Read it methodically. I know you want to be done as fast as possible, but if you skim this book, you will have to read it twice to increase your score. It is much more content-dense than it feels.

One of my favorite students, Anna, is a consummate skimmer or "fast reader." She's also brilliant, so this isn't some diss against skimmers. She "read" this book once, but she could tell me almost nothing about it. She improved slightly after "reading" the book, but she still missed 7 or 8 per LR section. She stagnated for months at that level, thinking she was stuck. She read the book for real after another student convinced her she left a lot of content on the page. After that, she missed 0-1 per section. She got a 178 on her real LSAT. All she did was delay her progress by making a half-hearted attempt at "reading" this thing.

Have questions like "How is the LSAT scored?" or "When is the LSAT given?" Check out the Meet the LSAT FAQ at elementalprep.com/bonus

A blank Wrong Answer Journal is waiting for you at the back of this book! Start recording your progress on page 456.

Never check your answers in the middle of practice sections.

Here's an example of how Nicole, a real student, filled in her Wrong Answer Journal.

| TEST.SECTION.# | STIMULUS TYPE | QUESTION TYPE | REASON MISSED | SOLUTION |
|---|---|---|---|---|
| 62.4.24 | PS → I | Fill In | Didn't understand stimulus, went into answers blind | Translate stimulus, break it down. What is it saying and what does that mean? |

To create your own Wrong Answer Journal, ask the following two questions:

| QUESTIONS | EXAMPLE RESPONSES |
|---|---|
| 1. "Why did I choose the wrong answer?" | **BAD RESPONSE** — I messed up. |
| | Yeah, but how did you mess up? What exactly did you do? |
| The answer to this question goes in the **Reason Missed** column of your Wrong Answer Journal. You have to go deep on what motivated you in analyzing these mistakes. | **GOOD RESPONSE** — I misread the answer choice. |
| | This is great! It's concrete and specific. |
| 2. "What can I do in the future to not make this same mistake again?" | **BAD RESPONSE** — Don't misread. |
| | Yeah, but how are you not going to misread? Come up with a plan, man. |
| The answer to this question goes in the **Solution** column of your Wrong Answer Journal. Write in precise, concrete changes. | **GOOD RESPONSE** — Don't rush the answer choices. I'll tap each word with my pencil to force myself to read every word. |
| | This is awesome because you can keep this in mind on future sections. You'll know whether you did it or not. It's a real plan. |

**Review your Wrong Answer Journal before you start studying each day** to make sure that you're in the right mindset to remedy your persistent errors. **Getting a question wrong isn't a failure and ignoring your wrong answers doesn't make you stronger.** Dive deep into your wrong answers. That's how you'll improve.

Before you start any LR prep, **take a blind diagnostic now.** We're going to use both of the Logical Reasoning sections from the June 2007 exam in the Basic Translation Drill, CLIR Drill, and practice sections. **If you would like to use the June 2007 test as a full practice test, take that test now as your blind diagnostic.** You can reuse the LR questions for all the drills in this book, even if you've seen them before. It's seriously no worries. You'll be using the questions entirely differently in the drills.

# TRANSLATION & CLUSTER SENTENCES

This, my friends, is the problem:

> *Wanting to pursue the life of the mind since she allowed herself to end her gymnastics career, Chimera, as a result of her childhood dream to get off the mat and read more Plato, which gave her a sense of mental acuity that she had never previously encountered and which she only rediscovered after her second Olympics when she almost missed her balance beam routine by getting so engrossed in The Republic, finally decided it was the right moment to take that next step.*

Just like the paragraph above, the LSAT is hard to read. It's poorly written. And they do this on purpose. They could write the test much more clearly; they choose not to.

Remember all those things your English teachers used to write on your essays? Stuff about awkward word combinations and how you need to get to the point? The writing on the LSAT makes you realize exactly why English teachers make those comments. The purpose of writing is one thing: conveying information to the reader skillfully enough to make it easy for them. This chapter is about sentences that do the opposite: They *try* to make the reading difficult for you. The test writers purposefully write poorly. They purposefully hide their points in difficult language. In doing so, they create monsters called **cluster sentences**.

The examples in this book are... fantastical. Some might say they're weird, crazy, surreal. And that's on purpose. We're emulating the *structure* of LSAT writing, but the content is a little more likely to keep you awake. You'll see examples about koalas teaching children, pretzels eating people, and building cake towers. Weirdly enough, this is the best way to prepare you for the writing on the LSAT. You need to focus on the structure of the language at first, not worry about boring content. Once you've got the linguistic (and argumentative) structures down, we will add more layers of difficulty, including real LSAT examples. Once we build your foundation, we'll work with real LSAT stimuli exclusively.

Cluster sentences test your ability to read convoluted language. They don't put cluster sentences on the LSAT just to be sadistic. To succeed in law school, you have to be able to decode cluster sentences. But this may not come easily to you right now. That's ok. That doesn't mean you're dumb. It means you're going to have to work to build the skills the LSAT (and the legal profession) want you to have.

**The first thing you have to do is stop giving up on sentences you find difficult.** You must stop the vicious cycle of zoning out, getting frustrated, blaming the test for being difficult, and never looking at a confusing sentence again because it makes you upset. This cycle is what keeps students from improving their skills. By engaging with the cluster sentence (instead of pretending it doesn't exist), you have a shot at figuring out what it means. This is key. You won't get the question right if you don't know what the stimulus means. The good news: Once you translate a difficult stimulus, the rest of the question will be dramatically easier.

Don't worry. I'm not going to bore you with a ton of formal grammar. You don't need to know all that stuff to understand cluster sentences. In fact, many of those who decode intuitively have forgotten 8th grade English entirely. I skipped middle school English, so I couldn't bore you with it, even if I wanted to. We'll go over as much grammar as you need to figure these sentences out and nothing more.

*If you actually read that whole paragraph at the top, congrats! You have the heart of an ox and the spirit of a hummingbird. Most students don't read it fully.*

*Most LSAT preparation tools don't touch sentence-level comprehension. That's because it's very difficult to fundamentally change how well someone reads in a few short months. However, I'm not going to attempt to make you a better reader in this chapter. I'm going to turn you into a detective by giving you a few tools automatically used by those who decode these sentences intuitively.*

# What Are Sentences Really

If you remember anything from elementary school, you'll probably say a sentence is "a complete thought." This rule falls a bit on the shady side of the truth. Yes, basic sentences represent a complete thought, but, in general, a sentence represents *at least one* complete thought. Cluster sentences usually compress several thoughts into one not-so-neat package, and the reason you're having trouble with them is precisely because they are not conveying *a* complete thought. They're conveying several compressed, contorted thoughts. To understand cluster sentences, you have to break them down, recognizing the many complete thoughts in each sentence. Then, you will see the individual ideas in the sentence, instead of the jumbled mess those ideas create.

## SPECIFIERS: WHAT MAKES CLUSTER SENTENCES A CLUSTER

**Specifiers are those little words that glue bigger words to explanations.** This seems innocuous, right? Who doesn't like things explained to them? The clustering comes in when they've got a thing; they decide to explain it (cool so far), then they explain part of the explanation (ok, maybe fine), then they explain a part of the explanation of the explanation (aghhhhhhhhh). It is this over-explaining that makes cluster sentences difficult to read. By the time you're done reading the explanation of the explanation of the explanation, you forget what the beginning of the sentence was even about. This is called bad writing. As a reader, you are completely within your rights to call the author out for being a bad writer. As an LSAT test taker, you are called to action.

Specifiers here are not referring to the real part of speech.

### SPECIFIERS

| by | in | on | which | until |
|----|----|-----|-------|-------|
| since | in addition to | that | for | when |
| as | because | of | although | while |
| if | after | around | between | who |

This is not a complete list of every specifier that ever specified, but it's enough to give you an idea of the type of words we're looking for.

→ used to *expand on an idea by providing further detail*

Let's talk through how a cluster sentence uses specifiers to compress many ideas into one sentence:

> *The box, which was red since it came up on our red-sensor that was developed by Alex and Jordan, who happened to enjoy color spectroscopy, was empty.*

Now, let's make a list of all the ideas in this sentence. To make the list, I'll stop at every comma or specifier and jot down a complete thought from what I've found so far:

First, I see "the box" and then a comma, which cuts into the middle of the complete thought about the box. So I salvage my knowledge of those first two words by jotting down the only complete thought I can get out of the words "the box":

**There is a box.**

Second, I pass the comma and "which was red." Then I stop at the word "since" because it's a specifier. I want to translate "which was red," so I ask myself, "What's red?" and work backwards to find "the box." Now, I have a complete thought:

**The box was red.**

Next, I read "since it came up on our red-sensor" and stop when I hit the "that" since I have enough for a complete thought. I have to translate a little, just to remember what the "it" is. Looking back at the sentence, I see that the "it" is the box, so I've got my complete thought:

**The box came up on our red-sensor.**

Now, I read through "that was developed by Alex and Jordan" and stop both because I hit the comma and because I need to remember what the "that" is. "Red sensor" is right next to "that" in the sentence, so I have the complete thought:

**Our red-sensor was developed by Alex and Jordan.**

Proceeding past the comma, I read "who happened to enjoy color spectroscopy" and stop at the comma. I look for a person right before the "who" and see Alex and Jordan. So, I have my complete thought:

**Alex and Jordan enjoyed color spectroscopy.**

Finally, I pass the comma and see "was empty." This is where things get weird. You've got this lonely verb and really no idea what it links to when you read the sentence quickly. I run through a few quick possible combinations, working from what is closest to "was empty." Is color spectroscopy empty? The red-sensor? No, it's the box from all the way back at the beginning of the sentence. How do I know it's the box? Well, it's the only noun in the whole sentence that could realistically be empty, but, beyond that, the commas after "the box" and before "was empty" pair up nicely to show me that everything in between them is optional (more information on how this works soon). If I delete everything between the commas, I end up with a nice and simple complete thought:

**The box was empty.**

> That's six sentences in one! No wonder this cluster sentence is hard to read. It's compressing a huge amount of information.

**Divorcing the sentence's main noun ("box") from its verb ("was") is a classic cluster sentence trick.** In this case, "box" is really far away from "was," which makes this sentence hard to understand. It's super difficult for our brains to remember the noun we read 23 words ago when we've been given a bunch of information since then.

Just to review, let's look at one more example of a sentence with a separated main noun and verb:

> The five-cent **nickel**, which in reality is composed of approximately 75% copper, **came** into circulation in the late 19<sup>th</sup> century.

> A noun is a person, place, or thing. A verb is an action.
>
> Nouns and verbs are the essential building blocks of every sentence.

Check out that gap between "nickel" (the noun) and "came" (the verb)! The larger the gap, the easier it is to lose track of the sentence. This leads us to our greatest cluster sentence ally, the comma. The easiest way to overcome the difficulty of separated nouns and verbs is with awesome comma tricks.

# Commas Are Your Friend

Commas are your friend because they tell you when to pause. Pauses may not seem important, so you should try telling a story to a friend without any pauses between words. The story will be hard to listen to. Commas are the visual equivalent of a breath in that story. We shouldn't talk without pauses, and we need comma pauses to make our writing understandable too.

You may not have had any punctuation mark friends until now, so congratulations on branching out.

Check out this example:

**12 COMMAS**

Once upon a few months ago, Killian, a lowly mole rat in Modesto, changed everything. In the midst of his daily grind, foraging for Fritos and the like, he smelled his way into a modest suburban home. The split-level compound, purchased by Joseph, a retired Army Ranger, in 2003, was desolate. In his solitude, Joseph valued little beyond his video games. When Killian entered Joseph's living room, he heard something, a sound he'd never heard before.

**NO COMMAS**

Once upon a few months ago Killian a lowly mole rat in Modesto changed everything. In the midst of his daily grind foraging for Fritos and the like he smelled his way into a modest suburban home. The split-level compound purchased by Joseph a retired Army Ranger in 2003 was desolate. In his solitude Joseph valued little beyond his video games. When Killian entered Joseph's living room he heard something a sound he'd never heard before.

Ahhhhhhhhhh. A life without commas is a sad time.

See what I mean about using commas to catch your breath? Punctuation is to written sentences as intonation is to spoken sentences. Because of this, **you should be happy when you see a long sentence on the LSAT with a bunch of commas, as opposed to a long sentence without a bunch of commas.** Commas are awesome. They have rules that you can learn and use to your advantage.

## CORE ELEMENTS & OPTIONAL ELEMENTS

> Commas indicate that something on either side of the comma is an optional element.

A **core element** is a part of the sentence that cannot be removed without destroying all grammatical sense of reason. It has the sentence's main noun and verb in it.

*what is contained within the commas*

An **optional element** is a piece of the sentence that can be removed without any bad grammatical consequences. It's specifying things that happen in the core of the sentence or (unfortunately) in other optional elements.

**You can figure out which piece of the sentence is optional by looking at it by itself and seeing if it's a complete thought.** If the piece makes sense as a full sentence on its own, you've zeroed in on the core element. If it does not make sense, you've found an optional element.

Everything about commas in this section applies to pretty much all commas, except those used to separate items in a list. Understanding lists is pretty intuitive, so you don't need much instruction on how to do that.

*Don't discard the "optional" info*

Remember, optional elements are *grammatically* optional, not meaning optional. The information contained in optional elements could be essential to your understanding of the stimulus.

Check out these two sentences:

*Upon arriving at our destination, I immediately collapsed.*

*The forest ranger, a man with kind eyes, put out our illegal fire.*

These two sentences are using commas in different ways in formal grammar terms, but you can use the same trick on both of them. Something on either side of the comma is optional; you just need to figure out which side it is.

Let's look at our first sentence in detail:

*Upon arriving at our destination, I immediately collapsed.*

So, can "upon arriving at our destination" stand on its own as a complete sentence? No, it doesn't make sense by itself. It's an optional element. Can "I immediately collapsed" be a full sentence? Yeah, definitely. From this, we can see that "upon arriving at our destination" is an optional element, which specifies the core of the sentence. It's telling us more information about how the "I immediately collapsed" occurred.

Let's examine the second sentence. We're expanding our comma toolkit here, so hold off on decoding this one yourself:

*The forest ranger, a man with kind eyes, put out our illegal fire.*

Even though we have two commas, the same rule holds: Something on either side of these commas is optional. For the first comma, we can choose between "the forest ranger" and "a man with kind eyes." For the second comma, we can choose between "a man with kind eyes" and "put out our illegal fire." Notice how "a man with kind eyes" comes up twice! **The way the middle of the sentence comes up both times tells me that it is either the most important or least important part of the sentence.** We're going to work from the middle out.

So can I make a complete sentence out of "a man with kind eyes"? No. That lets me know that "a man with kind eyes" is our optional element. We can delete it, and the sentence will still make sense. If I delete it, I can combine the two outer pieces of the sentence into one core element. I end up with "the forest ranger put out our illegal fire," a perfectly acceptable sentence.

## MIDDLE-OUT

**When you have two or more commas in a sentence, use middle-out. All you have to do is see if the middle piece can be a complete sentence by itself.** If the middle can be a complete sentence, both outer pieces are optional. If the middle piece can't be a complete sentence, it's just specifying. We can delete it and read the core outer pieces back to back to clarify our understanding of the sentence. Check out a couple examples:

*[handwritten: 2 and therefore optional]*

| | | |
|---|---|---|
| **Optional Middle Element** | Hannah, an entertainment mogul, **ran for governor in Montana.** | "An entertainment mogul" is specifying Hannah, but we can read this sentence with just the bolded outer elements. They're the core. |
| **Core Middle Element** | In addition to winning the race, **Jared completed his first year at ASU**, a fine university in the American southwest. | "Jared completed his first year at ASU" is a complete thought. It works on its own as a sentence, so the two outer elements are optional. "In addition to winning the race" is specifying Jared, and "a fine college in the American southwest" is specifying ASU. |

Sometimes, parts of the sentence are both core *and* optional. Here's an example of how this works:

I like jade, and I like holograms.

Both sides of the comma could stand on their own as full sentences and could be removed without bad grammatical consequences.

Anybody ever seen the season one finale of HBO's *Silicon Valley*? If you have, then no, the name of this technique is not coincidental.

All of these optional elements are, for the most part, specifiers. Meaning, you have to treat them as chances to break the sentence down into smaller pieces. **The commas setting off these optional elements are little specifier flags telling you to notice that not all the information in this sentence has to be here.** Optional elements, the words that don't have to be there, can be filtered out when you're first trying to figure out what the sentence could possibly mean. Return to the optional elements to get the sentence's full meaning once you've identified the core.

## WHAT IF THERE ARE 3+ COMMAS IN A SENTENCE?

I'm glad you asked! Cluster sentences often contain 3+ commas, so it's important to know how to handle them. Let's return to our favorite cluster sentence:

> *The box, which was red since it came up on our red-sensor that was developed by Alex and Jordan, who happened to enjoy color spectroscopy, was empty.*

We've got three commas here. But **even though three is an odd number, we're still going to look at each pair of commas and use middle-out.** We'll take this sentence apart two commas at a time, reusing commas to create pairs as needed. First, let's look between the first two commas and see if "which was red since it came up on our red-sensor that was developed by Alex and Jordan" is a complete thought. It's not. OK, we've got that checked off as an optional element. Next, let's look between the second and third comma and see if "who happened to enjoy color spectroscopy" stands on its own as a complete thought. No way. Alright, so the whole big middle of this sentence is optional. That means the very beginning and the very end are the core. Let's string them together:

> *The box was empty.*

The core of the sentence is so simple! All of that stuff in the middle was just optional elements that we needed to filter out to see what's going on. Now, we can look at how the whole sentence, optional elements and all, works together. The first optional element ("which was red since it came up on our red-sensor that was developed by Alex and Jordan") was specifying "the box." I know this because the comma came right after "the box" and specifiers tend to specify things directly on the other side of their comma. Our second optional element ("who happened to enjoy color spectroscopy") was specifying "Alex and Jordan."

And we can represent this specifier relationship visually!

Remember how both sides of the comma could potentially be optional elements? This is especially important when there are 3+ commas in a sentence. These sentences go down the rabbit hole of specifying specifiers.

## Cluster Trees    A VISUAL TRANSLATION

Don't worry; I'm not asking you to draw cluster trees. I'm drawing them for you to help you mentally break sentences apart into distinct, visual pieces.

Cluster trees visually represent how specifiers work in sentences. The complexity of the tree corresponds to the complexity of its associated sentence. Cluster trees look complicated, but drawing them only requires following one simple rule: I'll branch down at every specifier. I'll keep branching until the specifying stops. When it does, I'll go back up and continue writing the sentence normally.

Cluster trees are a visual translation. They neutralize the visual mess of cluster sentences, a key part of their power. Throughout this chapter, I'll draw cluster trees for you, just to show how modular sentences really are.

Let's look at a simple example first:

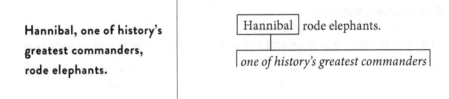

**Hannibal, one of history's greatest commanders, rode elephants.**

The middle piece of this sentence is optional and it's specifying "Hannibal." We can branch this specification down off of "Hannibal."

Now let's return to our earlier example to deconstruct something a little more complicated:

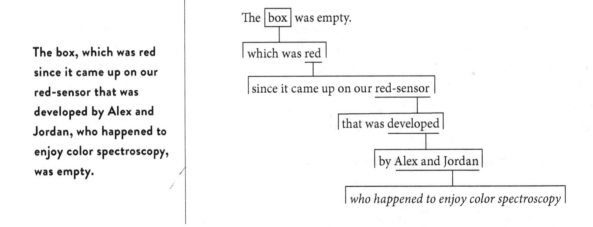

**The box, which was red since it came up on our red-sensor that was developed by Alex and Jordan, who happened to enjoy color spectroscopy, was empty.**

The cluster tree breaks our box cluster sentence apart into easier-to-digest parts!

# When You're Abandoned by Your Friend, the Comma

Most of the time, the test makers will use commas and everything will be cool. But sometimes, they are less kind and choose to go down the specifying rabbit hole without commas. We're going to build your intuitive sense of where specifying occurs, so you'll still be able to sense the specifying without your comma friends.

Let's return to our list of common specifiers from earlier and check out some examples:

| SPECIFIER | EXAMPLE |
|---|---|
| by | She broke his heart **by** going off into the meadow. |
| in | She broke his heart **in** her own cruel fashion. |
| on | She broke his heart **on** top of everything else. |
| which | She broke his heart **which** was already beyond repair. |
| since | She broke his heart **since** he had already done the same to her. |
| in addition to | She broke his heart **in addition** to his mind. |
| that | She broke his heart **that** had broken so many buildings. |
| for | She broke his heart **for** without breaking she was lost. |
| as | She broke his heart **as** had been done to her long ago. |
| because | She broke his heart **because** she wanted admission to the club. |
| of | She broke his heart **of** stone and steel. |
| between | She broke his heart **between** chem lab and her yoga class. |
| until | She broke his heart **until** she realized her culpability. |
| when | She broke his heart **when** she found out. |

Instead of memorizing these specifiers, focus on what they have in common in terms of meaning. It's not enough to just recognize these specific words in context. You have to clue into what they're *doing* in the sentence.

## MORE INFO PLEASE

Each of these specifiers glues on an explanation of "she broke his heart." Specifiers let me give more information about the heart, the breaking, or the one doing the breaking. **It's like these words clicked all the "more info" links for you** and then inserted all that extra information into the middle of what you were reading.

Let's experiment with how specifiers work, starting with a simple sentence:

*Pretzels eat people.*

This is a really basic sentence with a great story to tell. Let's specify:

| | | |
|---|---|---|
| **Maybe I want to know more about the pretzels?** | *Pretzels* ***by*** *the seaside eat people.*<br><br>*Pretzels* ***that*** *can't control themselves eat people.*<br><br>*Pretzels* ***in*** *Philadelphia eat people.* | [Pretzels] eat people.<br>*by the seaside / that can't control themselves / in Philadelphia* |
| **How about the eating?** | *Pretzels eat people* ***after*** *attending the city council meeting.*<br><br>*Pretzels eat people* ***because*** *we deserve it.*<br><br>*Pretzels eat people* ***while*** *playing the mandolin.* | Pretzels [eat] people.<br>*after attending the city council meeting / because we deserve it / while playing the mandolin* |
| **But what if I just want more information about the people?** | *Pretzels eat people* ***who*** *disobey their orders.*<br><br>*Pretzels eat people* ***who*** *eat with their mouths open.*<br><br>*Pretzels eat people* ***who*** *have messy handwriting.* | Pretzels eat [people.]<br>*who disobey their orders / who eat with their mouths open / who have messy handwriting* |

All of these newly specified sentences are pretty easy to read. That's because I'm specifying one thing per sentence. If we combine two of the specifiers into one sentence, it looks like this:

*Pretzels in Philadelphia eat people who have messy handwriting.*

*Pretzels that can't control themselves eat people while playing the mandolin.*

*Pretzels eat people who disobey their orders because we deserve it.*

These aren't *that* bad. They're starting to become confusing, but they aren't terrible. Notice how adding just one more specifier to the sentence made it about twice as difficult to read. That's because the core of the sentence ("Pretzels eat people.") is getting drowned out. Let's make it worse by combining all three specifiers into one sentence:

*Pretzels by the seaside eat people who eat with their mouths open after attending the city council meeting.*

Now that we specified all three words, the sentence is legit cumbersome. It's also become unclear what exactly "after attending the city council meeting" is referring to. This is the muddy nonsense that happens when too many specifiers are stacked in one sentence. Triple-specifying is exceedingly common on the LSAT.

# Cluster Drill

## INSTRUCTIONS

*Bracket the three optional elements in each of these triple-specified sentences. Identify the core of the sentence and write it below.*

**1.** Chris [as a member of the Paper Clan] folds [with gusto] paper planes [that may have malevolent intentions.]

CORE     Chris folds paper planes

**2.** The LEGO [who had finally attained sentience] assembled [without incident] Johnny [who had just been studying.]

CORE     The LEGO assembled Johnny

**3.** The mango [from the conference room] fought [with great vigor] the CLIF Bars [that Michael pretended he made.]

CORE     The Mango fought the CLIF Bars

**4.** The Guild [from the Land of Teal] opened talks [which changed Colorland forever] [that fateful day.]

CORE     The Guild opened talks that day

**5.** Generators [of thermovoltaic designation] convert [with minimal energy loss] heat [into electricity.]

CORE     Generators convert heat

**6.** Crosswalks [at heavily-trafficked intersections] prevent accidents [that could have resulted in fatal injury] [by encouraging caution.]

CORE     Crosswalks prevent accidents

*Check out an example:*

Robots [that appear human] fly [with an unknowable alien element] home [to their little metal families.]

CORE     Robots fly home.

**Triple specifying like this is always hard to understand.** The good news is that it's hard for everybody, even those who decode these sentences intuitively.

*Where's the answer key?*

You'll find the answer key at the end of the chapter on page 28.

The Loophole in Logical Reasoning | 17

# The Importance of Translation on the LSAT

> To master Logical Reasoning, you need to master its language. Translation is how you will overcome the LSAT's difficult language. On the day of the test, you'll automatically translate every stimulus.

Translation is what allows us to work through difficult stimuli quickly. The next few pages and the Basic Translation Drill will train you to translate like a pro.

As humans, we're good at listening to a story and telling it to others. We don't repeat the exact words of the story we've heard; we make it our own first. **Translating turns the stimulus into a story you can tell.** It's necessary because our brains don't intuitively internalize complex jargon and non-ideal word order, trademarks of LSAT writing. We internalize stories. Once you put the stimulus in your own words, it's much more likely to mentally stick; this improves your memory and enables you to get the question right more quickly.

*[handwritten note: Read Stimuli as though you will have to explain it to someone]*

## HOW TO TRANSLATE

1.  Read and understand each sentence piece by piece.

2.  In the beginning of your prep, cover up the stimulus with a Post-It after you're done reading.

3.  Say what you just read in your own words. Use practical, easy-to-remember, casual words. Make it sound like something you would actually say in real life.

*Covering up the stimulus before you translate trains you to remember what you read. This step will be skipped when you start doing timed sections and full practice tests.*

**In LR, you have to know what the stimulus says in order to answer any question correctly.** Once you know what the stimulus says, analyzing it usually isn't that hard. When you don't really know what the stimulus means, analyzing it is nearly impossible. When you're answering questions later on, if you need to refer back to the stimulus, definitely go for it. But most of the time you'll work through the stimulus' translation, design your CLIR, and know the answer. Translation is the first step toward that future.

## THE THREE COMMANDMENTS OF TRANSLATION *[handwritten: → telling the story]*

1.  **You must translate every LSAT stimulus.**

    If you can't translate the stimulus, you don't understand it well enough to answer the question and you will get the question wrong.

2.  **Translating is the opposite of skimming.**

    Translation is not "getting the gist." It's something you do after you have a lot more than the gist.

3.  **At first you will have to translate consciously. It will quickly become subconscious with practice.**

    When I do Logical Reasoning myself, I translate every stimulus. But I was translating long before I realized I was doing it. Before, I somehow "just knew" everything the stimulus said from reading it. That's the goal. You will get there too, but you have to stay disciplined until it becomes that automatic.

Let's translate a couple cluster sentences from real LSAT stimuli together!

## Real LSAT Translation  GYPSY MOTHS

*16.2.21*

> Several years ago, as a measure to reduce the population of gypsy moths, which depend on oak leaves for food, entomologists introduced into many oak forests a species of fungus that is poisonous to gypsy moth caterpillars.

Look! Our first real LSAT stimulus!

The full question attached to each solo LSAT stimulus is in the back of the book in Appendix A, unless the full question is used somewhere else in the book. This way, we can use just the stimulus for our dedicated purpose (in this case, translation), and you can still use the rest of the question for extra practice later.

This first example uses commas! Huzzah! Read it now and we'll work through it together.

There are three commas in total, so we should use middle-out. "As a measure to reduce the population of gypsy moths" is between the first and second commas. Can it stand on its own as a complete thought? No! It's flagged as an optional element. The next middle piece comes between the second and third commas: "which depend on oak leaves for food." Can that stand on its own as a sentence? No! Another optional element. We're out of commas, so the first and the last pieces of this sentence must be the core elements.

Every real LSAT stimulus has a citation right above it. These citations contain the PrepTest number, section number, and question number in that order. This gypsy moth stimulus, for instance, is from Preptest 16, Section 2, and is #21.

If we string the core elements together and forget about the specifiers, we're left with:

> *Several years ago entomologists introduced into many oak forests a species of fungus that is poisonous to gypsy moth caterpillars.*

That makes sense! Now that we have the core, let's return to the specifiers in the optional elements and see if they're giving us any interesting information.

**Optional Element One** | as a measure to reduce the population of gypsy moths

We need to figure out what that's talking about. Let's look on the other side of the comma. Is it specifying "several years ago"? Eh, that doesn't make sense. We need to look farther away from the comma. Is it specifying "which depend on oak leaves for food"? No, that's not really a thing that can be a measure either. We'll keep going into the core: "entomologists introduced into many oak forests a species of fungus that is poisonous to gypsy moth caterpillars." Does that sound like something that could be a measure to reduce the population of gypsy moths? Yes! OK, so they put this fungus in the forests in order to reduce the population.

> Several years ago entomologists [introduced] into many oak forests a species of fungus that is poisonous to gypsy moth caterpillars.
>
> *as a measure to reduce the population of gypsy moths*

**Optional Element Two** | which depend on oak leaves for food

What depends on oak leaves for food? Let's look on the other side of the comma. "Gypsy moths" is right on the other side of the comma. It makes total sense that a bug would depend on oak leaves for food, so it seems like "gypsy moths" are being specified here.

Several years ago entomologists | introduced | into many oak forests a species of fungus that is poisonous to gypsy moth caterpillars.

       | as a measure to reduce the population of gypsy moths |

           | *which depend on oak leaves for food* |

Now, translate this whole cluster sentence into something readable. Compare your translation to mine afterwards. Don't be afraid to use more than one sentence in your translation.

Here's the whole cluster sentence again:

> *Several years ago, as a measure to reduce the population of gypsy moths, which depend on oak leaves for food, entomologists introduced into many oak forests a species of fungus that is poisonous to gypsy moth caterpillars.*

TRANSLATION   *a poisnus fungus was introduced by entomologrsts in oak forces to reduce gypsy moth the oak reaf eating gypsy moth populasus* [1]

*After* you translate the sentence yourself, look at the bottom of the page for my translation.

It's totally cool if your translation puts the ideas in a different order than the stimulus or my translation.

Your translation should contain the ideas in the sentence, but with less fanciness. No one says, "as a measure to" in real life, so that kind of thing shouldn't be in your translation either. You have to make it your own.

Next, let's look at a legendarily difficult LSAT stimulus in its entirety.

---

1. **Translation:** Years ago, the entomologists wanted to get rid of the gypsy moths and so they poisoned the oak leaves, their food source.

*12.1.24*

Until recently it was thought that ink used before the sixteenth century did not contain titanium. However, a new type of analysis detected titanium in the ink of the famous Bible printed by Johannes Gutenberg and in that of another fifteenth-century Bible known as B-36, though not in the ink of any of numerous other fifteenth-century books analyzed. This finding is of great significance, since it not only strongly supports the hypothesis that B-36 was printed by Gutenberg but also shows that the presence of titanium in the ink of the purportedly fifteenth-century Vinland Map can no longer be regarded as a reason for doubting the map's authenticity.

Blahhhhhhhhh, that's a lot of words. Let's take these sentences apart one by one.

LSAT experts agree that this stimulus is one of the most difficult of all time. I wanted to use the most challenging example here to show you that translation works (and thrives) on even the hardest LR stimuli. Most LR stimuli are not this difficult.

**Cluster Sentence One** | Until recently it was thought that ink used before the sixteenth century did not contain titanium.

So what did this mean? There aren't a ton of specifiers here, so let's try to translate this sentence all in one go. Read the sentence again, then cover it up with your hand, and translate it for yourself. Repeat the story of the sentence as though you're telling a friend about it. No fancy language allowed. When you're done, check your translation against mine.

TRANSLATION _____ *people used to think there was no titanium in ink* _____
_____ *before the 18th century* _____ [1]

After you translate the sentence yourself, look at the bottom of the page for my translation.

Notice how I condensed "ink used before the sixteenth century" into "pre-16th century ink." Getting rid of all those connector words makes the sentence easier to remember. Also, morphing "it was thought that" into "they thought" makes the sentence more natural-sounding. It's *almost* like something a real person would say.

**Cluster Sentence Two** | However, a new type of analysis detected titanium in the ink of the famous Bible printed by Johannes Gutenberg and in that of another fifteenth-century Bible known as B-36, though not in the ink of any of numerous other fifteenth-century books analyzed.

We've got two commas in this sentence so we'll use middle-out. Check out the middle piece of this sentence:

---

1. **Translation:** Until recently, they thought pre-16th century ink didn't use titanium.

| **Core Middle** | a new type of analysis detected titanium in the ink of the famous Bible printed by Johannes Gutenberg and in that of another fifteenth-century Bible known as B-36 |
|---|---|

This is a complete thought! It's the core of our cluster sentence. But even the core of this sentence is difficult to understand; let's explore why that is. We'll start by breaking down the pieces of the core. The beginning is simple. Analysis detected titanium in the ink, awesome. But then we start specifying:

*…of the famous Bible printed by Johannes Gutenberg…*

**So they found titanium ink in a Gutenberg Bible.** Cool. There are two specifiers in this piece of the sentence, "of" and "by." We're heading down the rabbit hole of specifying specifiers. "Of the famous Bible printed" is specifying "ink," so I'm going to branch that down off of ink. Then "by" is specifying who printed the Bible. I will branch "printed by Johannes Gutenberg" off "Bible." But we have even more to go:

*…and in that of another fifteenth-century Bible known as B-36…*

**So they found titanium ink in this other 15th century Bible too!** They've stopped specifying along the Gutenberg branch, so I'll head back to the top of our cluster tree. Since they found titanium ink in this other Bible too, I'll branch "and in that of another fifteenth-century Bible" off "ink," just like I did with the Gutenberg Bible piece. "Known as" is specifying the other Bible, so I'll branch "known as B-36" down off of "Bible":

A new type of analysis detected titanium in the ink.
- of the famous Bible
  - printed by Johannes Gutenberg
- and in that of another fifteenth-century Bible
  - known as B-36

Finally! That piece of the sentence is done! Now let's translate all that jazz. Here's the core again for your translating convenience:

| **Core** | A new type of analysis detected titanium in the ink of the famous Bible printed by Johannes Gutenberg and in that of another fifteenth-century Bible known as B-36. |
|---|---|

TRANSLATION 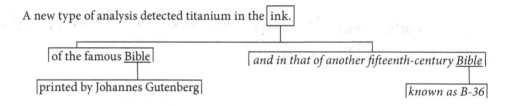 *A new method found titanium in Gutenberg bible and the B-36 Bible, both from 15th century* [1]

Let's examine the (much easier) first and last pieces of this sentence now that we have the core out of the way.

*However … though not in the ink of any of numerous other fifteenth-century books analyzed.*

Take a second to notice that I just wrote a whole page on how to understand 30 words. This stuff is complicated. You shouldn't beat yourself up or call yourself dumb for not getting it on the first pass.

---

1. **Translation:** They found titanium in the ink of two 15th century Bibles, the Gutenberg Bible and B-36.

The "however" before the first comma just indicates that we're about to say something contrary to the first sentence. Cool. The last piece of the sentence, "though not in the ink of any of numerous other fifteenth-century books analyzed," is more interesting. This optional element doesn't make it clear what wasn't in the other books' ink, but the core only talks about titanium being in ink, so you can assume they're still talking about titanium. So what does this optional element really mean? Try your own translation first, then check it against mine:

TRANSLATION  *In the many other 15th century books no titanium was found*
_____
[1]

Now, it's up to you to put it all together! Translate the whole cluster sentence into a couple of easier-to-understand sentences and check your work against mine.

For reference, here is the full cluster sentence again:

| **Cluster Sentence Two** | However, a new type of analysis detected titanium in the ink of the famous Bible printed by Johannes Gutenberg and in that of another fifteenth-century Bible known as B-36, though not in the ink of any of numerous other fifteenth-century books analyzed. |
| --- | --- |

TRANSLATION  *found titanium in two 15th century bibles, Gutenberg's & B-36, but none in the many other 15th century works tested*
_____
[2]

Awesome! Now on to the last sentence of the stimulus.

| **Cluster Sentence Three** | This finding is of great significance, since it not only strongly supports the hypothesis that B-36 was printed by Gutenberg but also shows that the presence of titanium in the ink of the purportedly fifteenth-century Vinland Map can no longer be regarded as a reason for doubting the map's authenticity. |
| --- | --- |

There's only one comma in this cluster sentence. First, check both sides of the comma for optional elements. On the left side of the comma we have "this finding is of great significance," which works as a complete thought! The other side of the comma starts with a "since," a classic specifier. There's a whole lot of sentence still waiting behind the "since," but let's translate this initial piece of the cluster sentence first, just to get our bearings and remember what this "finding" is.

What "finding" are they talking about here? It must be what we discovered in the last sentence, that titanium ink is in the Gutenberg Bible, B-36, and no other 15th century books. Let's translate this core before we move forward. As always, try your own translation before looking at mine.

TRANSLATION  *~~the very~~ discovery of titanium is very important*
_____
[3]

Cool, now we're about to see why the finding is important. I'll set "this finding is of great significance" at the top of my cluster tree and get ready to branch the "since" phrase.

_____

1. **Translation:** They didn't find titanium ink in the other 15th century books.
2. **Translation:** However, they found titanium ink in two 15th century Bibles, the Gutenberg Bible and B-36. They didn't find titanium ink in any of the other 15th century books.
3. **Translation:** It's important that we found titanium ink in the books.

*...since it not only strongly supports the hypothesis that B-36 was printed by Gutenberg...*

**So it's important because it supports B-36 being by Gutenberg.** The "since" phrase is specifying why the finding was important, so I'll branch down off the whole core. "That B-36 was printed by Gutenberg" is telling us about the "hypothesis," so I'll branch it off of "hypothesis." Now, let's keep moving into the rest of the sentence.

*...but also shows that the presence of titanium in the ink of the purportedly fifteenth-century Vinland Map...*

**So the finding is also important because it tells us something about the titanium ink in this map.** It's important to view this piece of the sentence in light of what came before it — it makes a lot more sense that way. This branch just shows us another reason why the finding is important. I'll branch down off "shows" since the rest of the phrase is specifying what's being shown. But then we have another specifier! "Of the purportedly fifteenth-century Vinland Map" tells us more about this ink. I'll branch this piece down off "ink." Let's keep going.

*...can no longer be regarded as a reason for doubting the map's authenticity.*

**So the titanium ink is no longer a reason to doubt the map.** Interesting. On my cluster tree, I'll place "can no longer be regarded as a reason" right next to "ink" to make it clearer that the ink is what can't be a reason. Then we hit "for doubting the map's authenticity," which specifies "reason." I'll branch it off "reason." Check out this monster!

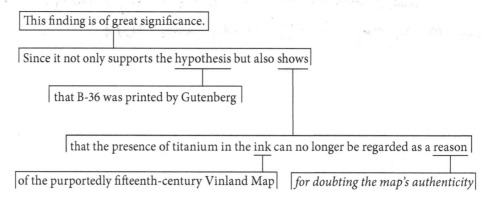

Awesome. Now let's put this whole cluster sentence together. Take the whole thing apart and tell me what it means.

Here's the whole sentence again:

| **Cluster Sentence Three** | This finding is of great significance, since it not only strongly supports the hypothesis that B-36 was printed by Gutenberg but also shows that the presence of titanium in the ink of the purportedly fifteenth-century Vinland Map can no longer be regarded as a reason for doubting the map's authenticity. |
| --- | --- |

TRANSLATION *The discovery of the titanium ink is important b/c it shows B-36 was printed Gutenberg and confirms the authenticity of the Vinland map*

---

1. **Translation:** Finding the titanium in the Bibles matters for two reasons. First, it makes us think B-36 was probably Gutenberg's. Second, it makes the titanium ink in the Vinland Map not a problem for its authenticity anymore.

Now for the whole stimulus. I'll combine all of my translations:

**Whole Stimulus Translation**

> Until recently, they thought pre-16th century ink didn't use titanium. However, they found titanium ink in two 15th century Bibles, the Gutenberg Bible and B-36. They didn't find titanium ink in any of the other 15th century books. Finding the titanium in the Bibles matters for two reasons. First, it makes us think B-36 was probably Gutenberg's. Second, it makes the titanium ink in the Vinland Map not a problem for its authenticity anymore.

It's almost like you can understand it now!

**BUT THIS SEEMS HARD. HOW WILL I USE IT?**

You're right. This is hard. Granted, I chose one of the hardest stimuli of all time for our last practice run together. Hopefully, now you get the importance of breaking cluster sentences down into smaller, manageable pieces. This stuff is hard! Most stimuli will feel easy after our deep dive into titanium ink.

The only thing that makes reading complex language less hard is practice. **Never give up when you're reading a stimulus**, and translate piece by piece when you get confused. You can do this.

---

**TRANSLATION & CLUSTER SENTENCES GAME PLAN**

- Recognize cluster sentences in stimuli. Choose not to panic.

- Look for your friend, the comma. If commas are present, deploy our comma tricks.

- When you get confused, translate small, manageable chunks of the sentence one at a time. Before you know it, you'll understand the whole thing.

- Translate everything! Use your translations as you work through each question.

---

There's a ton of translation practice coming your way soon! After a couple chapters on arguments, the Basic Translation Drill is waiting to put everything you've learned so far into action with real LSAT stimuli.

Could they have just written that simpler version? Yeah, they totally could have. Why didn't they? Because you have something to prove. **They want to know that you can understand complicated writing.**

## Quiz 1   TRANSLATION & CLUSTER SENTENCES

There will be a review quiz at the end of every chapter. These quizzes make sure you're absorbing the material in each chapter. If you don't know the answers to the quiz questions, there's more in the chapter for you to learn.

The quizzes are designed to be low-effort and require a basic minimum comprehension of the ideas discussed in the chapter. If you can't complete the quiz, you need to reread the chapter.

### INSTRUCTIONS

*Answer these questions based on your knowledge of the chapter. Attempt to answer without looking back at the chapter first. If you don't know the answer, circle the question number and go find the answer in the chapter. Study the sections of the chapter that you couldn't remember at first.*

### Word Bank

| | | |
|---|---|---|
| core(s) | optional element(s) | core element(s) |
| ~~middle-out~~ | ~~sentence~~ | ~~specifier~~(s) |
| ~~translation~~ | studying | cluster sentence(s) |

*Use the word bank to answer the fill-in-the-blank questions. Some words will not be used and others may be used more than once.*

**1.** A(n) _____Sentence_____ contains *at least* one complete thought.

**2.** _____Specifiers_____ are those little words that glue bigger words to explanations.

**3.** To tackle a cluster sentence with two or more commas, use _____middle-out_____.

**4.** _____Translation_____ is the one skill you need to master Logical Reasoning.

*Circle the correct answer to the following questions.*

**5.**     **TRUE OR FALSE**     A core element is a piece of the sentence that can be removed without any bad grammatical consequences.

**6.**     **TRUE OR FALSE**     Commas indicate that something on either side of the comma is a core element.

**7.**     **TRUE OR FALSE**     The test writers purposefully write poorly.

**8.**     Seek and find!     Circle only the specifiers in the word cloud.

| after | them | who | interrogatory |
|---|---|---|---|
| long | since | comma | ostentatious |
| when | cluster | for | that |

*Where's the answer key?*

You'll find the answer key at the end of the chapter on page 29.

## Cluster Drill  ANSWER KEY

**1.** Chris [as a member of the Paper Clan] folds [with gusto] paper planes [that may have malevolent intentions.]

 CORE            *Chris folds paper planes.*

**2.** The LEGO [who had finally attained sentience] assembled [without incident] Johnny [who had just been studying.]

 CORE            *The LEGO assembled Johnny.*

**3.** The mango [from the conference room] fought [with great vigor] the CLIF Bars [that Michael pretended he made.]

 CORE            *The mango fought the CLIF Bars.*

**4.** The Guild [from the Land of Teal] opened talks [which changed Colorland forever] [that fateful day.]

 CORE            *The Guild opened talks.*

**5.** Generators [of thermovoltaic designation] convert [with minimal energy loss] heat [into electricity.]

 CORE            *Generators convert heat.*

**6.** Crosswalks [at heavily-trafficked intersections] prevent accidents [that could have resulted in fatal injury] [by encouraging caution.]

 CORE            *Crosswalks prevent accidents.*

**Q**
**U**
**I**
**Z**

**1.** A **sentence** contains *at least* one complete thought.

**2.** **Specifiers** are those little words that glue bigger words to explanations.

**3.** To tackle a cluster sentence with two or more commas, use **middle-out**.

**4.** **Translation** is the one skill you need to master Logical Reasoning.

**5.** False. An *optional* element is a piece of the sentence that can be removed without any bad grammatical consequences.

**6.** False. Commas indicate that something on either side of the comma is an *optional* element.

**7.** True.

**8.** You should have circled the following specifiers and no other words: after, who, since, when, for, that.

# OMMMM.

chapter one. done and done.

## CHRIS

1.   Don't take the test until you feel you are really ready.

2.   Keep a Wrong Answer Journal from day one.

3.   Don't do more questions when you're consistently getting them wrong. Spend time understanding why you got them wrong before attempting another question.

4.   Games are fun.

5.   Find someone to talk through your work. It's a great way to make sure you understand what you're doing (and good, fun moral support).

We'll always take a quick Breather between the chapters of this book.

Breathers come in many flavors! Sometimes they're drills; sometimes they're explanations of frequent LR stimulus topics. Other times Breathers contain advice from former students. Sit back and enjoy.

## LAUREN

1.   While prepping for the LSAT, you actually learn and develop valuable skills (like reading comprehension), which will be useful beyond the LSAT.

2.   Hating the LSAT is not going to make it any easier. Embrace the experience and challenge.

3.   It's crucial to take practice exams in public.

4.   Figure out how much studying per day works for you, and don't overdo it or cram.

5.   Start reading more complex literature about various topics early in prep.

These are quotations from real LSAT students! These former students were in your shoes not too long ago, and they wanted to share a few key takeaways from their prep experiences.

## VEENA

1.   Be smart with your usage of the material! Don't waste questions by half-heartedly doing them just so you can tell yourself you did questions. It's better to wait until you're committed to give 100%.

2.   The LSAT isn't the make-or-break of your entire legal career, so don't act like your life depends on it.

3.   Mindset prep for the LSAT is just as important as understanding logic better.

4.   Learning all of this material takes time. More than 3 months for most people.

5.   The LSAT doesn't have to be something you do 24/7.

Hey, beloved reader! Here's a quick pro tip to keep in mind before your desire to skim costs you valuable LSAT points:

**Read Chapter 12.** It's called The Answer Choices. Students tend to skim this chapter because it's at the end and they're eager to finish the book as quickly as possible. I get you, but **Chapter 12 is full of shortcuts that will help you get faster right answers**. If you're worried about finishing LR sections in time, Chapter 12 is *essential* study material. But don't skip there right now! Read it last! Chapter 12 requires knowledge of all the concepts outlined in Chapters 1-11.

THE STIMULUS FRAMEWORK

# The Stimulus-Based Approach

Want to know the biggest secret in Logical Reasoning?

The answer is in the stimulus, not in the answer choices.

This is why reading is so important. You have to know what happened in the stimulus in order to complete the question.

Imagine you're taking a math test. You all took math at one point and have the scars to prove it. Imagine you've got a big messy equation and a bunch of possible answers to choose from. Do you think you'd give the equation a quick skim and run down to the answer choices, hoping that something about **A** will just look better than **B**? No, that makes no sense. You would stay with the equation until you really understood what it said. You would take it apart and simplify it. You would do whatever needed to be done to put yourself in a position to know the right answer. That's what anyone would do with a math test.

So why don't we do that here? Why doesn't anyone have an analogous system for the stimuli in LR? What is so different about verbally-based testing that we feel we can just "get the gist" of the stimulus before "figuring out" which answer is "better" for that specific question type? I would guess it's because a lot of us have gotten by in school skimming for as long as we can remember. We haven't had to *really* read anything deeply in order to do well enough in our classes. The LSAT requires a lot more from us, and so will law school.

Since the answer to the question is in the stimulus, you can guess that the stimulus is pretty important. Luckily, **there are only four types of stimuli** on the LSAT. Let's take a moment to introduce each of them.

## THE FOUR STIMULUS TYPES

The purpose of this book is to provide you with the toolkit to understand and analyze each of these four stimulus types. Mastering the stimulus will allow you to predict the correct answer to Logical Reasoning questions before even reading the question type.

| STIMULUS TYPE | DESCRIPTION |
|---|---|
| **Argument** | Premises and conclusions |
| **Premise Set** | Non-contradictory premises |
| **Paradox** | Contradictory premises |
| **Debate** | Two speakers |

Let's briefly talk through each stimulus type and check out a few examples. **Don't worry if you don't understand some of these concepts right now.** We're purposefully not going into depth in this section. We want to show you where you're headed and keep the purpose of the next few hundred pages at the forefront of your mind. We will go into depth with each of these types throughout the book, starting with Arguments and Premise Sets in Chapter 2.

## ARGUMENTS

*June 2007.2.4*

Consumer:  The latest Connorly Report suggests that Ocksenfrey prepackaged meals are virtually devoid of nutritional value. But the Connorly Report is commissioned by Danto Foods, Ocksenfrey's largest corporate rival, and early drafts of the report are submitted for approval to Danto Foods' public relations department. Because of the obvious bias of this report, it is clear that Ocksenfrey's prepackaged meals really are nutritious.

Most LSAT stimuli are Arguments. These stimuli consist of premises and conclusions. Premises are facts and conclusions are the interesting/tenuous opinions based on those facts. Together, premises and conclusions make an Argument, the cornerstone of both the LSAT and the legal profession. The next six chapters of this book are designed to prepare you to understand and analyze Arguments.

## PREMISE SET

*June 2007.3.22*

If the price it pays for coffee beans continues to increase, the Coffee Shoppe will have to increase its prices. In that case, either the Coffee Shoppe will begin selling noncoffee products or its coffee sales will decrease. But selling noncoffee products will decrease the Coffee Shoppe's overall profitability. Moreover, the Coffee Shoppe can avoid a decrease in overall profitability only if its coffee sales do not decrease.

Premise Sets are the second-most prevalent stimulus type on the LSAT. They're made up of *just* the premises, no conclusion. They're a bunch of facts waiting for you to add them up. Chapter 2 discusses premises in detail.

## PARADOX

*June 2007.3.2*

After replacing his old gas water heater with a new, pilotless, gas water heater that is rated as highly efficient, Jimmy's gas bills increased.

Paradoxes are a specific type of Premise Set. The premises in a Paradox contradict one another, creating a stimulus that doesn't make sense. Paradoxes provoke an eyebrow raise. They make you ask, "How is that possible?" Paradoxes will be discussed in detail in Chapter 8, The CLIR.

## DEBATE

*June 2007.3.3*

Carolyn:  The artist Marc Quinn has displayed, behind a glass plate, biologically replicated fragments of Sir John Sulston's DNA, calling it a "conceptual portrait" of Sulston. But to be a portrait, something must bear a recognizable resemblance to its subject.

Arnold:  I disagree. Quinn's conceptual portrait is a maximally realistic portrait, for it holds actual instructions according to which Sulston was created.

Debates are two-speaker stimuli. Basically, two people have an exchange, and at least one of them will likely make an argument. The two speakers will argue the truth or falsity of a specific point. Debates will also be discussed in detail in Chapter 8, The CLIR.

Don't worry if you aren't super clear on premises and conclusions yet; you'll learn a ton about them in just a few pages.

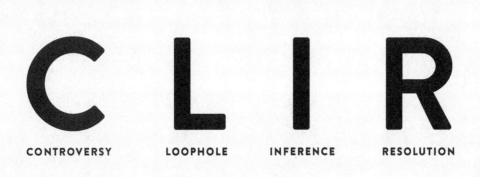

Now that you know the stimulus types, let me give you a sneak preview into how you'll analyze each type. Keep in mind that this will be explained in far more detail (once you have the necessary foundation to enact the methodology; that's what Chapters 2-7 are for) in Chapter 8, The CLIR.

**When you're doing an LR section (untimed or timed), you will always detect the stimulus type and perform an analytical task associated with that stimulus type; these tasks are collectively called the CLIR.**

The CLIR will very often give you the correct answer to the question that follows the stimulus. Here is how the stimulus types map to their associated tasks in the CLIR:

- **Debate ⟶ Controversy**

- **Argument ⟶ Loophole**

- **Premise Set ⟶ Inference**

- **Paradox ⟶ Resolution**

CLIR is an acronym to help you remember the tasks for each stimulus. In Chapter 2, we will begin discussing Loopholes and Inferences, the L and the I of the CLIR. **Pay special attention to Loopholes and Inferences in the next few chapters.** Loopholes and Inferences are not just concepts you have to understand well enough to continue reading; these are tasks you are going to be performing frequently when you start designing your own CLIRs. Loopholes and Inferences are associated with the most common stimuli types in LR; **45 out of 51 LR stimuli on a randomly selected recent LSAT were Arguments or Premise Sets**. So you need a mastery-level understanding of Arguments and Premise Sets, along with Loopholes and Inferences. That's what the next few chapters are here for!

It may seem like there are a lot of pages in this book until we get to "really doing LSAT" (the question types purposefully do not start until Chapter 9). I can assure you that every minute you spend reading this book is "really doing LSAT"; you need the foundation we're about to build. *Every single word* **of this book is devoted to getting you the absolute highest LSAT score you're capable of.**

For instance, when you see an Argument stimulus, you will immediately design a Loophole and then proceed to the question stem.

Don't worry about Controversies and Resolutions for now. They won't appear until we go into detail with them in Chapter 8.

ARGUMENTS
& INFERENCES

# So, an Argument   THE CENTERPIECE OF LOGICAL REASONING

In Logical Reasoning, arguments are the single most important concept you need to understand on an in-depth level. We will spend a lot of this book talking about different mistakes in argumentation. We will learn to manipulate arguments. But first, you have to have a crystal clear understanding of what an argument is.

## ARGUMENTS ARE PREMISES AND CONCLUSIONS

Arguments are quite simple at their core. An argument is made up of two things: premises and conclusions.

The most common type of stimulus in Logical Reasoning is the Argument. The second most common stimulus is the Premise Set. You will learn the tools to handle both of them in this chapter.

**PREMISES SUPPORT CONCLUSIONS.**

Premises are the evidence.

**That's it.** Arguments are just premises and conclusions. They have a lot of complicated baggage that we'll introduce soon, but at their core, arguments are always this simple.

**CONCLUSIONS RELY ON PREMISES.**

Conclusions are the claim.

## HARK, A SIMPLE ARGUMENT

Imagine you're building a table made of blocks to keep a delicious piece of cake off the floor (you live a very interesting life in this example).

Your blocks are **solid**. They aren't going anywhere. These are your **premises**.

Your cake is squishy and **fragile**. It needs to be held up off the floor because it can't fend for itself. This is your **conclusion**.

{CAKE}          ⟵ Conclusion (squishy claims)

[BLOCK] [BLOCK]   ⟵ Premises (solid facts)

The cake is only safe from the floor because you arranged your blocks *exactly* right. Conclusions are worthless and delicious like this too. They can't keep themselves off the floor. If left to their own devices, conclusions would run amok on the floor and we'd never get anything done. **Conclusions need to be supported by premises to be worth anything.**

Let's dive into premises and conclusions. Make sure this sinks in. If you don't understand premises and conclusions, you won't be able to follow the rest of this book or succeed at LR.

# Premises   STATEMENTS OF FACT

Premises are just the facts, the evidence. They describe how the world is. We accept premises. We don't question their truth.

| THINGS PREMISES ARE | THINGS PREMISES ARE NOT |
|---|---|
| Premises are the building blocks that allow us to make interesting claims about the world. | Premises are not questionable. |
| Premises are the infrastructure of arguments. | Premises are not dependent on the conclusion or one another. |
| Premises do the argument's heavy lifting. | Premises don't need anything to support them. |

In the real world, we often argue by attacking the truth of our opponent's premises. For instance:

> *"You said that we won't be late to the bonanza **because** you've never been late before and there's no traffic. But there is traffic! And you were late to another bonanza last week!"*

This example questioned the truth of two premises, being late before and no traffic. While this is fine to do in real life, the LSAT doesn't let you off that easy; it's way more awesome than that. **If you want to get the questions right, don't worry about debating the truth of the premises.** The correct answer almost never questions the truth of a premise. Instead, you should focus on how the premises fit together. That's what will lead you directly to the correct answer. Premises are defined by their *relationship* to the conclusion.

These words typically introduce premises:

| PREMISE INDICATORS | | | | |
|---|---|---|---|---|
| *because* | *for* | *since* | *as* | *given that* |

**Memorize this list.**

## Conclusions   CLAIMY JUDGMENTS THAT ARE USUALLY WRONG

Conclusions are the judgments the author makes. They are the main event. Conclusions are built upon the arrangement of premises.

**THINGS CONCLUSIONS ARE**

Conclusions are where the author goes out on a limb. The author takes what's been given in the premises and infers something new in the conclusion.

Conclusions are based on premises. They rely on the premises.

**Conclusions are the part of the argument you question.** They are where things get interesting.

**THINGS CONCLUSIONS ARE NOT**

Conclusions are not necessarily ironclad. **The premises are usually not arranged well enough to prove the conclusion.**

Conclusions can't just live on their own. They are dependent on the premises.

**REMEMBER!**   *Arguments are all about the **relationship** between the conclusion and its premises.*

These words typically introduce conclusions:

**CONCLUSION INDICATORS**

| | | | |
|---|---|---|---|
| *therefore* | *accordingly* | *consequently* | *so* |
| *thus* | *hence* | *it follows that* | |

**Memorize this list.**

Here are a few examples of how the premise and conclusion indicators function:

*Monica claimed to have caused the extinction of the dinosaurs and everything Monica claims is always true. **Therefore**, Monica is responsible for the extinction of the dinosaurs.*

***Since** Monica claimed to have caused the extinction of the dinosaurs and everything Monica claims is always true, Monica is responsible for the extinction of the dinosaurs.*

Both these statements mean the exact same thing, even though the premise and conclusion indicators are different!

Use the premise and conclusion indicators to guide yourself through arguments. When indicators are present, they are a reliable way to identify argument parts. However, the aim of this book is to change the way you think. I don't want you to *just* perform a little seek-and-find game to locate the indicators on every stimulus. That would leave you to throw your hands up in frustration when the indicators are absent.

**The indicator words will not always be there to indicate what part of the argument every statement is.** Instead of just looking for indicator words, go deeper. Ask yourself about the personality of the statements. Are they facts or claims? This lets you engage with the argument on an analytical level, which is the key to success in Logical Reasoning.

# Valid Conclusions & Invalid Conclusions

Now that we have the basics of premises and conclusions, let's enter into the realm of good and bad. **Not all conclusions are created equal.**

## VALID CONCLUSIONS = PROVEN

Some conclusions are sturdily supported. We call these beautiful starships valid conclusions. A valid conclusion must be true, if its premises are true. Since we always assume our premises to be true, **a valid conclusion is one that must be true.** That's right; valid conclusions *have to be* true. They're provable. 100%. No question. No wiggle room.

Let's look at a few simple valid conclusions:

| | |
|---|---|
| **PREMISE 1** | Avocados and gingerbread both contain **nitrogen**. |
| **PREMISE 2** | **Nitrogen** is an element. |
| **VALID CONCLUSION** | Avocados and gingerbread have an element in common. |

**Notice the bolded overlapping term, nitrogen, in the two premises. This point of similarity is an interlocking point.** The interlocking point lets us create something new by combining both things we know about nitrogen into one sentence. That's what our valid conclusion did — it combined. This is a great introductory way to come up with valid conclusions: **Look for a common term between two premises and figure out what that repetition allows you to conclude.** In this case, I basically just replaced the word "nitrogen" in the first premise with the definition of nitrogen supplied in the second premise.

| | |
|---|---|
| **PREMISE 1** | Rishad is **10 inches tall**. |
| **PREMISE 2** | Prejudice toward those **under 12 inches tall** is never justified. |
| **VALID CONCLUSION** | Prejudice toward Rishad is never justified. |

This is a slightly more complex example of a valid conclusion. We don't see any exact phrases repeated between the premises, but we can see that the state of affairs from the first premise, being 10 inches tall, fits into the category outlined in the second premise. That's our bolded interlocking point. Since Rishad is 10 inches tall, he fits into the under 12 inches tall category and the judgment associated with that category applies to him. The conclusion just applies the "prejudice never justified" standard to Rishad.

| | |
|---|---|
| **PREMISE 1** | Maya won't **eat grapefruit**. |
| **PREMISE 2** | Only those who always **eat grapefruit** will be committed to the mental institution. |
| **VALID CONCLUSION** | Maya will not be committed to the mental institution. |

This is our most advanced example of a valid conclusion for now. The interlocking point here is more stealthy than in our previous two examples. Maya won't eat grapefruit and only those who always eat grapefruit go to the mental institution. By refusing to eat grapefruit, Maya doesn't let herself fall into the category of people who always eat it, right? So, Maya is not in the always-eat category outlined in the second premise. Now, *only* the people in the always-eat category go to the mental institution. If Maya isn't in the category, she can't go.

Check out a simpler example for a second: Imagine that only people wearing red were allowed into a party. You show up wearing teal. Obviously, you aren't allowed into the party (unless you know someone on the inside... because life isn't nearly as fair as the LSAT). This Maya situation is exactly the same as the party example; it's just dressed in slightly fancier language. Our job as LSAT masters is to see through the language to the simple construct lying underneath.

Awesome! Now that we've walked through a few valid conclusions, let's zoom out a little bit. **On the LSAT, most conclusions are invalid**, meaning most arguments you'll encounter are invalid arguments. We'll get to invalid conclusions in a minute, but the valid conclusions we've been talking about are going to be a big part of our LSAT experience in another context. That's because **valid conclusions have a twin called an Inference,** which is not part of an argument and is much more frequently encountered on the LSAT. The same sentence can be called an Inference or a valid conclusion based solely on context.

### INFERENCES VS. VALID CONCLUSIONS

**Valid conclusions** are always presented as **part of an argument**, like so:

> *Avocados and gingerbread both contain nitrogen. Since nitrogen is an element, avocados and gingerbread have an element in common.*

**Inferences**, on the other hand, are **not part of an argument**. Inferences are something we come up with ourselves from a Premise Set. This is what the same information would look like as an Inference:

> *Avocados and gingerbread both contain nitrogen. Nitrogen is an element.*

> **INFERENCE**        Avocados and gingerbread have an element in common.

**An Inference is a valid conclusion you design yourself, not a conclusion inside an argument.** Isn't it amazing how the exact same information can be two different things based only on context? The LSAT will often ask you to design an Inference from a Premise Set in the exact same way we just did. That Inference will be the correct answer to many questions.

### INVALID CONCLUSIONS = NOT PROVEN

**Invalid conclusions are the LSAT's bread and butter.** Seriously, the vast majority of our time in Logical Reasoning is spent handling invalid conclusions. There are approximately infinity ways to go wrong when making an argument, and they are all super funny and awesome. Let's start exploring invalid conclusions with the premises we used to create valid conclusions.

*[handwritten margin note: Inferences & valid conclusions are the same, simply presented differently]*

| | |
|---|---|
| **PREMISE 1** | Avocados and gingerbread both contain nitrogen. |
| **PREMISE 2** | Nitrogen is an element. |
| | Avocados and gingerbread are the same food. |
| | Avocados and gingerbread taste the same. |
| **INVALID CONCLUSIONS** | Avocados and gingerbread have most things in common. |
| | Avocados and gingerbread are similar. |
| | Avocados and gingerbread are both natural. |

Notice how I came up with a ton of invalid conclusions. To come up with an invalid conclusion, you just say whatever you feel. Don't worry about whether it's reasonable. The more unreasonable, the better! This is exactly what the test writers do with most stimuli containing arguments. They're just saying whatever they feel in the conclusion. In designing these invalid conclusions, I tried to not go too out there. I chose conclusions that someone could hypothetically come up with and believe.

Let's look at why each invalid conclusion is not ironclad proven. We'll do this by objecting to each conclusion. Our objections are designed to be super powerful; they call attention to a specific situation where the conclusion falls apart. These super-powered objections are called **Loopholes**.

Remember, pay special attention to every mention of Loopholes and Inferences. You're going to design plenty of these yourself soon.

| INVALID CONCLUSION | LOOPHOLE |
|---|---|
| **Avocados and gingerbread are the same food.** | What if just because you have an element in common doesn't mean you're the same food? Avocados and gingerbread could be different in every other way. |
| **Avocados and gingerbread taste the same.** | What if having nitrogen in common doesn't necessarily affect taste at all? |
| **Avocados and gingerbread have most things in common.** | What if we only know they have one thing in common? Let's not generalize that out to a bunch more things. |
| **Avocados and gingerbread are similar.** | What if nitrogen is one of many elements in avocados and gingerbread? Having one element in common isn't enough to justify calling the two things similar. Everything else about them could be different. |
| **Avocados and gingerbread are both natural.** | What if the nitrogen in avocados and gingerbread isn't even naturally derived? And even if the nitrogen is natural, everything else in avocados and gingerbread could be artificial. |

Take a second to notice the critical instinct present in these Loopholes. **We're questioning authority.** We're putting every conclusion to the "What if?" test. This is the attitude you'll have toward every argument in Logical Reasoning. **Valid conclusions aren't vulnerable to reasonable Loopholes. Invalid conclusions are.**

Now, let's look at our next example:

| | |
|---|---|
| **PREMISE 1** | Rishad is 10 inches tall. |
| **PREMISE 2** | Prejudice toward those under 12 inches tall is never justified. |
| | Rishad is short. |
| | We can be prejudiced toward people over 12 inches tall. |
| **INVALID CONCLUSIONS** | Rishad would be hurt by prejudice. |
| | Prejudice is a bad thing. |
| | We should be nice to Rishad. |

OK, let's explore why each of these conclusions is invalid:

| INVALID CONCLUSION | LOOPHOLE |
|---|---|
| **Rishad is short.** | What if I'm talking about my cat named Rishad? In that case, Rishad is a perfectly normal height. **Always assume there is something being left out of what the author chooses to present to you.** What the stimulus doesn't say is almost more important than what it does say. |
| **We can be prejudiced toward people over 12 inches tall.** | What if we don't know anything about people over 12 inches tall? The second premise only gives us information about what to do with those under 12 inches tall. We have no clue what the rules are for people over 12 inches tall. Never assume the opposite judgment holds for the opposite of the group being discussed. |
| **Rishad would be hurt by prejudice.** | What if we can't predict Rishad's feelings? We know that prejudice toward Rishad wouldn't be justified, but we don't know what his reaction would be to that prejudice. We're not allowed to fill in these gaps for the author. |
| **Prejudice is a bad thing.** | What if prejudice is good in this fantasy world? Rishad could live in a sci-fi dystopia for all we know. From our two premises, we have no information on how good or bad prejudice is. We only know about one case when prejudice is not justified. The *premises* have to prove the conclusion; outside knowledge about prejudice can't lend a helping hand. |
| **We should be nice to Rishad.** | What if lack of prejudice doesn't mean we have to be nice to Rishad? We know that we shouldn't be prejudiced against Rishad, but we could just ignore Rishad's height and choose to like or dislike him based on his merits as a human/cat. |

OK, last example:

| | |
|---|---|
| **PREMISE 1** | Maya won't eat grapefruit. |
| **PREMISE 2** | Only those who always eat grapefruit will be committed to the mental institution. |
| | Maya will be committed to the mental institution. |
| | Maya has no mental health issues. |
| **INVALID CONCLUSIONS** | The number of people committed to mental institutions is small. |
| | Only those who love grapefruit will be committed to the mental institution. |
| | Maya has great taste in food. |

Now, let's see why these aren't valid.

| INVALID CONCLUSION | LOOPHOLE |
|---|---|
| **Maya will be committed to the mental institution.** | What if Maya has disqualified herself from being committed? We only commit people who always eat grapefruit. Maya doesn't do that, so she doesn't fit into the category of people who get committed. |
| **Maya has no mental health issues.** | What if having mental health issues is separate from being committed to a mental institution? Confusing two ideas like this is exactly the kind of trick the LSAT often plays. |
| **The number of people committed to mental institutions is small.** | What if we don't know how many people always eat grapefruit? It could, sadly, be a large group of people. And even if we knew how many people always eat grapefruit, we still wouldn't know the number committed: Eating grapefruit is only a minimum qualification. It doesn't guarantee admission. |
| **Only those who love grapefruit will be committed to the mental institution.** | What if loving grapefruit and always eating grapefruit are not necessarily the same thing? Maybe the people always eating it are just starving to death and actually hate grapefruit. |
| **Maya has great taste in food.** | What if not liking grapefruit doesn't necessarily mean you have great taste? This conclusion, while undoubtedly true in real life, is not provable. We don't have any premises about what's great. |

**Notice how all of the invalid conclusions took something for granted**, whether it was that being 10 inches tall is short or that refusing grapefruit means you have great taste in food. In real life, you could make the argument that these things are true, but when you bring these kinds of **assumptions** into LSAT arguments, you are walking on shaky ground. We call out this shaky ground by creating objections called **Loopholes**. We have a whole chapter on assumptions and Loopholes coming up soon, so bookmark this concept for now. It is one of the most important topics in Logical Reasoning.

Valid conclusions are proven by their premises. Invalid conclusions aren't proven by their premises. Loopholes are how we attack invalid conclusions.

## Conclusions Drill

### INSTRUCTIONS

*Design one valid and one invalid conclusion for each pair of premises. The premises' wordiness level (reading difficulty level) increases every four questions. The first question is the simplest and the last question is the wordiest.*

---

This drill contains purposely counterfactual premises for you to add up. These whimsical premises keep you from bringing too much outside knowledge into the drill, which would cause you to make possibly unwarranted assumptions without realizing it. We want to train you to stay within the world of the premises, whatever those premises happen to be.

You have to assume that the premises are true on the LSAT, no matter how outlandish they are. **In Logical Reasoning, the world of the premises is your whole world.** In this drill, you will look past the content into the pattern of how the premises interlock.

---

**1.**

**PREMISE 1**  Fish are made of pure green light.

**PREMISE 2**  Pure green light probably contains ultraviolet gas.

**VALID CONCLUSION**  Fish are probably made of ultraviolet gas

**INVALID CONCLUSION**  Fish are also very bright

**2.**

**PREMISE 1**  Monica and Frida hate fine-tooth combs.

**PREMISE 2**  Monica and Frida enjoy a good pizza.

**VALID CONCLUSION**  Monica and Frida have hate/enjoy one thing in common

**INVALID CONCLUSION**  Monica and Frida are bestfriends

**3.**

**PREMISE 1**  There is no one good enough for my Julian.

**PREMISE 2**  Christina is interested in my Julian.

**VALID CONCLUSION**  Christina is not good enough for Julian

**INVALID CONCLUSION**  Christina likes Julian

**4.** **PREMISE 1** — Microphones drink coffee at 8:36 AM every morning.

**PREMISE 2** — Coffee drinkers are more likely to have perfect pitch than non-coffee drinkers.

**VALID CONCLUSION** — Microphones are more likely to had perfect pitch than non-coffee drinkers

**INVALID CONCLUSION** — Microphones have perfect pitch

**5.** **PREMISE 1** — Titanium ink injuries may be one of the main contributors to the recent rise in the incidence of tardiness at Tea University.

**PREMISE 2** — Chapped lips and chapped toes are the only titanium ink injuries.

**VALID CONCLUSION** — Chapped lips and chapped toes may be the reason incidence of tardiness has risen

**INVALID CONCLUSION** — Chapped lips cause tardiness

**6.** **PREMISE 1** — In order to maintain her perfect GPA, Liara will assert that "it's like not even music if it's not on vinyl" and eat a heaping plate of chicken tikka masala.

**PREMISE 2** — Chicken tikka masala cannot be made less than 20 spice points above lamb saag.

**VALID CONCLUSION** — In order to maintain her perfect GPA Liara will not eat food that is less than 20 spice points above lamb saag

**INVALID CONCLUSION** — In order to maintain her perfect GPA Liara will not eat spicy food

**7.** **PREMISE 1** — Ancient Mesopotamian artifacts indicate that our forefathers preferred the taste of saffron to that of sassafras.

**PREMISE 2** — Anything indicated by an ancient Mesopotamian artifact must be a bald-faced lie.

**VALID CONCLUSION** — The claim that our forefathers preferred the taste of saffron to sassafras is a lie

**INVALID CONCLUSION** — our forefathers loved sassafras

**8.**

**PREMISE 1**

The postulation maximization theory presented in Theodore's text does not even once make mention of recent innovation in Halcyon Science.

**PREMISE 2**

Halcyon Science has recently supplied us with the quagmire hypothesis, the jewelry box paradox, and most importantly, the antiquarian ice principle.

**VALID CONCLUSION**

The postulaton maximizaton theory presentd by Theodore does not menton antiquarian ice prin.

**INVALID CONCLUSION**

Theodore ignores the existence of Halcyan Science

**9.**

**PREMISE 1**

Morality has a conversely inverse proportional relationship with garlic aioli's less-recognized, and well-regarded in condiment circles, cousin chipotle mayonnaise.

**PREMISE 2**

All cousins of garlic aioli, including mild marinara, a blend of tomato, cumin, and barbecue sauce, are on the recently internationally recognized endangered condiments list.

**VALID CONCLUSION**

Chipotle mayo is on the endangered condiments list

**INVALID CONCLUSION**

Morality is conversy more pearparent to avid mariara

**10.**

**PREMISE 1**

Judging on the basis of his recent performance on the competition circuit, Huey outranks all his fellow gentlemen when one calculates only his winks in his success per unit of machinations effort score (SPUMES), but when one includes nods along with winks in his success per unit of machinations effort score (SPUMES), Huey is swiftly bested by his buddy Guillermo, who also outranks all other gentlemen.

**PREMISE 2**

The gentleman who outranks all other gentlemen in his success per unit of machinations effort score (SPUMES) will be thrown into the void.

**VALID CONCLUSION**

Guillermo will be thrown into the void when one includes nods in SPUMES score

**INVALID CONCLUSION**

~~If Forty Renkes event count~~
Huey Huey will be thrown into the void after Guillermo

**11.**

**PREMISE 1**    The mayor of New Brunswick often wonders about a recently broadcasted news program, which may have been disseminated with extreme prejudice, that offered a harsh critique of the evolution and dissemination of the standard QWERTY keyboard.

**PREMISE 2**    Anyone who wonders about anything possibly, in the present, past, future, and otherwise (including parallel realities), impugning the sterile and stellar reputation of our beloved QWERTY keyboard should be thrown in prison, if not for the duration of their entire natural life, then at least until they have had enough time in the box to read Marcel Proust's seminal classic, *Time, Memory, and Transcendent Madeleines*.

**VALID CONCLUSION**    The Mayor of New Brunswick Should be thrown In prison

**INVALID CONCLUSION**    The mayor will die in prison

**12.**

**PREMISE 1**    One study performed by the Atomic Research Health Institute (ARHI), based in Milltown, indicated that there will be a 73% increase in the rate of cholesterol in Sophie Spradlin, star of the hit original series *Legacy House*, which could increase her risk of typographical errors by 21% over the course of the next three years, if her moon continues to stay in Virgo, which, by all accounts, is highly unlikely.

**PREMISE 2**    Stars of a hit original series, a designation under which *Legacy House* certainly qualifies, who undergo cholesterol increases are some of, literally, the best people in the world to know if you are an up-and-coming star on the brink of success, even if you've been on audition after audition and are starting to think that, literally, nothing ever will be coming your way.

**VALID CONCLUSION**    Sophie Spradlin is one of the best people know if you are an upcoming star on the brink of success

**INVALID CONCLUSION**    Its is wrong Sophie's typing skills will deteriorate.

Where's the answer key?

You'll find the answer key at the end of the chapter on page 58.

## Reflections on the Conclusions Drill

If you got through the last few questions and didn't gnaw straight through your own arm, congratulate yourself immediately. If you did indeed gnaw through your own arm just now, pay special attention to the Basic Translation Drill on page 92. That is where we tackle the LSAT's confusing language.

In this exercise, you found the interlocking point between premises. When **a word or concept is used in two premises, we can usually connect them to come up with a new idea.** Think of this new idea as what the two premises were *trying* to say without actually doing the work of saying it. The same interlocking points exist in both simple and complex language. The complex language is just noise to disguise that connective thread.

Remember, you didn't just practice valid and invalid conclusions in this drill. You also practiced designing Inferences. **All those valid conclusions you came up with are Inferences! You'll design an Inference, as part of the CLIR, every time you see a Premise Set in Logical Reasoning. Plus, several question types ask you to choose an Inference in the correct answer.** Designing Inferences is an essential skill that will greatly increase your Logical Reasoning score.

> The expert test taker runs the LSAT through a filter. You're filtering to find the signal (reasoning) in the noise (wordiness). There is much more noise than signal on this test. The LSAT wants to distract you with fancy words. Don't let them.

Now that you have an idea of how to work with premises and conclusions, let's complicate this picture a little bit.

# Complex Arguments

Sometimes, arguments are a little more complicated than:

Premise 1 + Premise 2 = Conclusion :)

*[handwritten: → Sub - conclusion - supporting main conclusion]*

Every so often, you'll encounter intermediate conclusions. <u>An intermediate conclusion fulfills the argumentative</u> <u>role of both a premise and a conclusion.</u> It both supports the argument's main conclusion and is supported by its premises. Remember your blocks and cake and interesting life? They're back.

Can your blocks hold up anything besides cake? Yes! They can. Blocks are useful and can hold up all kinds of things. Things like other blocks! An intermediate conclusion is like a marzipan block. It's pretty sturdy and useful, but it's also delicious and needs to be held up off the ground just like cake does. Don't put your marzipan on the ground, folks.

## HARK, A COMPLEX ARGUMENT

{CAKE}  ⟵ Conclusion (squishy claims)

{Marzipan Block}  ⟵ Intermediate Conclusion (claim supporting another claim)

[BLOCK] [BLOCK]  ⟵ Premises (solid facts)

*[handwritten: → not a solid end]*

<u>The intermediate conclusion needs support because it's a squishy claim just like the main conclusion.</u> The only difference between the intermediate conclusion and the main conclusion is that the intermediate conclusion supports the main conclusion. <u>The main conclusion is proven with the help of the intermediate conclusion.</u>

Here's an example of a complex argument:

> *Fish are made of pure green light. Pure green light contains ultraviolet gas.* **Therefore,** *fish contain ultraviolet gas. Anything containing ultraviolet gas will nourish us.* **So,** *fish are likely to nourish us.*

Notice that there are two conclusion indicators in this example! That's a huge giveaway that the argument contains an intermediate conclusion. Now, let me take the argument apart for you:

| | |
|---|---|
| **PREMISE 1** | Fish are made of pure green light. |
| **PREMISE 2** | Pure green light contains ultraviolet gas. |
| **INTERMEDIATE CONCLUSION** | Fish contain ultraviolet gas. |
| **PREMISE 3** | Anything containing ultraviolet gas will nourish us. |
| **MAIN CONCLUSION** | Fish are likely to nourish us. |

**So how do you tell the difference between an intermediate conclusion and a main conclusion? You look for which statement relies on the other one.** The statement that relies is the main conclusion; it's at the top of our

Intermediate conclusions are also known as subsidiary conclusions or sub-conclusions.

conclusion tower. It's the squishiest, so it needs all the support it can get. The statement that's getting leaned on is the intermediate conclusion. It's sturdier.

Let's see which statements each of our fish conclusions lean on. We can do this by asking how we know each conclusion.

| | |
|---|---|
| **How do we know that "fish contain ultraviolet gas"?** | Because fish are made of green light and that stuff has ultraviolet gas. We're relying on two premises for this one. Since we're leaning on premises, we know this is some type of conclusion. |
| **How do we know that "fish are likely to nourish us"?** | Because fish contain ultraviolet gas and that nourishes us. Notice that **I'm citing the intermediate conclusion as a reason for the main conclusion**. That's how I know I've found the main conclusion: The intermediate conclusion supports it and it doesn't support anything else. |

### FIGURING OUT ARGUMENT PARTS WITHOUT INDICATOR WORDS

You can interrogate your statements, like we just did above, whenever you're confused about whether something is a premise or a conclusion. Let's test it out by interrogating the following example.

*The stegosaurus likes eucalyptus leaves. Eucalyptus leaves have a pleasant aroma. The stegosaurus likes something with a pleasant aroma.*

| | |
|---|---|
| **How do I know that the stegosaurus likes eucalyptus leaves?** | Because... reasons? |
| **How do I know that eucalyptus leaves have a pleasant aroma?** | Because... reasons? |
| **How do I know that the stegosaurus likes something with a pleasant aroma?** | Because he likes eucalyptus leaves and they have a pleasant aroma! |

**If you have no better answer than "reasons" for why something is true, it's a premise.** If you have evidence for why it's true, it's some kind of conclusion. If something both has evidence for why it's true and is evidence itself, it's an intermediate conclusion.

*Handwritten margin note: When doing very confusing (informal) for main, how do I ask yourself, how do I know this?*

# Nested Claims & Hybrid Arguments

But what about if someone other than the author hops into the stimulus and starts concluding things? **When someone besides the author makes a claim, we call it a nested claim.**

*[handwritten: → when Someone other than the author makes a claim]*

Here are a couple examples of nested claims:

> ***Dr. Hamilton's study found that*** Red Bull actually does give you wings.

> ***Felipe believes that*** we're all nothing but atoms bumping together.

Nested claims always look like this; they're a description of how someone believes something. If the author concludes anything themselves, they will use the nested claim as a premise for their conclusion. In this case, treat the nested claim as a premise and critique the author's conclusion.

Check out how a nested claim looks when the author concludes something and uses the nested claim as a premise:

> *Dr. Hamilton's study found that Red Bull actually does give you wings. But Dr. Hamilton is wrong. I have never once grown wings after drinking Red Bull.*

No worries, right? But, **when the stimulus is only premises and a nested claim (no author's conclusion), we call the stimulus a hybrid argument and critique the nested claim.** When the author doesn't supply their own conclusion, the nested claim acts as the conclusion of the hybrid argument. In this case, we question the validity of the nested claim just like a normal conclusion.

Let's check out a hybrid argument example. The author will not conclude anything themselves:

> *Dr. Hamilton's study found that Red Bull actually does give you wings. Dr. Hamilton separated 20 volunteers into two groups. Group 1 drank one Red Bull per day over the course of a two-year period. Group 2 drank a Red Bull placebo once a day over the same two-year period. After two years, 80% of the group that drank Red Bull had grown wings, as compared to only 30% of the control group.*

Since there is no conclusion from the author, our critical side eye leans toward Dr. Hamilton's study, the nested claim. Notice how the premises "support" the study's findings. We can critically investigate just how well the premises are proving these findings.

*Why do hybrid arguments matter?*

It's important to recognize hybrid arguments because you always want to pay attention to the highest-ranking claim in the stimulus. This will help you predict the correct answer to many Logical Reasoning questions before you even know the question type.

A hybrid argument is just a nested claim with a few premises attached.

We'll learn more about how to attack studies like this in Chapter 7, The Classic Flaws.

# Intermediate Conclusions & Nested Claims Drill

## INSTRUCTIONS

*In this drill, we will identify nested claims and intermediate conclusions in a few arguments.* **You will mark the argument parts in the following way:**

- *If there is a nested claim, bracket the beginning and end of the nested claim.*
- *If there is an intermediate conclusion, underline the intermediate conclusion.*

*After marking the nested claim or intermediate conclusion (if they are present), determine whether the example qualifies as a hybrid argument. If the example is a hybrid argument, circle* **TRUE**. *If the example is not a hybrid argument, circle* **FALSE**.

If you get stuck during this drill, look back at the premise and conclusion indicators at the beginning of this chapter. Use the indicators to start identifying the argument parts.

**1.** When fashion industries avoid complete financial ruin, there's always a chance, based on changing trends, that the industry in question may regain its former prominence. Since fedoras are still popular in some parts of our nation, the fedora industry has likely avoided total bankruptcy. So the fedora will probably soon regain the cultural prominence it enjoyed during the 1920s.

 TRUE OR FALSE    This example is a hybrid argument.

Remember, if the author concludes something on their own, the nested claim does not create a hybrid argument.

**2.** A recent study suggested that [the fez may be a causal factor in crime prevention efforts.] But the study relied on faulty data to reach its conclusion. Therefore, the fez is not a factor in crime prevention.

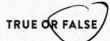 TRUE OR FALSE    This example is a hybrid argument.

**3.** Aaron suggests that [trucker hats are contributing to the rising rate of jaywalking in our community.] Talia had never jaywalked before, but as soon as she tried on a trucker hat, she felt compelled.

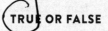 TRUE OR FALSE    This example is a hybrid argument.

**4.** Because beanies are the warmest of hats, we know that their fabric must insulate the most heat. But temperature experts suggest that [the beanie's weave may instead be responsible for its superior performance.] However, there are many competing hat formats with similar weaves and inferior heat-insulating performance. Therefore, it must be the 60-40 wool-rayon blend that keeps heat in, since all beanies are characterized by this exact blend.

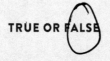 TRUE OR FALSE    This example is a hybrid argument.

*Where's the answer key?*

You'll find the answer key at the end of the chapter on page 60.

**5.** Berets don't qualify as legitimate headwear because they only cover at most 40% of the skull. Berets should not be carried at RealHeadWearOnly.com since they only stock legitimate headwear.

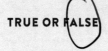 TRUE OR FALSE    This example is a hybrid argument.

# How to Attack an Argument

Learning to attack an argument is a game changer for your Logical Reasoning score. Loopholes are how you're going to get the questions right quickly, intuitively, and easily.

Throughout your LR training, you will try to destroy all the conclusions you encounter by designing Loopholes. To build this skill set, always ask yourself *why* the conclusion is supposed to be true. Think through the possibilities that cast doubt on the way the premises (supposedly) add up to lead to the conclusion. Do this every single time you read a conclusion on the LSAT and hear someone make a questionable claim in real life. Most of the next few chapters are devoted to how to attack an argument, but let's start off with a few quick intro tips.

We'll return to our delicious conclusion tower:

{CAKE}               ⟵ Conclusion (squishy claims)

[BLOCK] [BLOCK]      ⟵ Premises (solid facts)

You're going to try to throw the cake on the ground by knocking the blocks out from under the cake. To do this, you will apply force to expose the gaps between the blocks. **Attack the premises' relationships to one another and to the conclusion, but never question the truth of the premises.** The premises are factually true, no matter how outlandish they sound or how much you may disagree with them.

Attacking the relationship between the premises makes sense. When we were critiquing the conclusion about Rishad, we didn't say, "Well, what if Rishad actually isn't 10 inches tall?" We worked with the premises we were given to find a gap. Questioning whether Rishad is actually 10 inches tall is akin to setting your premise blocks on fire.

But who would set blocks on fire just to knock a piece of cake on the ground? It's way less effort (and less psycho) to just knock the blocks over — blowing up those gaps *between* the blocks. The blocks themselves stay intact; the blocks' relationships to one another, and to the conclusion, change. They don't stack up so neatly and your cake is no longer supported. And when the cake hits the ground... Logical Reasoning starts to get way more fun.

※ You are always knocking the cake on the ground. What a waste of cake.

**REMEMBER!**   *Always assume there is something being left out of what the author chooses to present to you. Never attack the truth of the premises; attack what the premises purposefully aren't telling you.*

---

### ARGUMENTS & INFERENCES GAME PLAN

- Memorize the premise and conclusion indicators now. Always identify conclusions.

- Most LSAT conclusions are invalid. Expect the premises to not add up.

- Look for the gaps between the premises. Knock that cake on the ground.

- Inferences are just valid conclusions you draw from Premise Sets yourself. Remember this when you start seeing Premise Sets in real LSAT sections.

## Quiz 2 ARGUMENTS & INFERENCES

### INSTRUCTIONS

*Answer these questions based on your knowledge of the chapter. Attempt to answer without looking back at the chapter first. If you don't know the answer, circle the question number and go find the answer in the chapter. Study the sections of the chapter that you couldn't remember at first.*

### Word Bank

| | | |
|---|---|---|
| ~~premise(s)~~ | valid | specifier(s) |
| ~~claim(s)~~ | ~~conclusion(s)~~ | invalid |
| must | ~~evidence~~ | Loophole(s) |

*Use the word bank to answer the fill-in-the-blank questions. Some words will not be used and others may be used more than once.*

**1.** The two things that always make up an argument are __premise(s)__ and __Conclusion(s)__.

**2.** A premise serves as __evidence__.

**3.** A conclusion is a(n) __claims__.

**4.** Premises support the __Conclusn__.
Conclusions rely on the __premises(s)__.

**5.** An intermediate conclusion supports the main __Conclusn__ and is supported by the __premise(s)__.

**6.** Inferences are __valid__ conclusions we design ourselves.

56

Circle the correct answer to the following questions.

**7.**  **TRUE OR ~~FALSE~~**   There will always be indicator words to show us what part of the argument every statement is.

**8.**  **TRUE OR ~~FALSE~~**   You can question the truth of a premise.

**9.**  **TRUE OR ~~FALSE~~**   A conclusion can be valid without premises to support it.

**10.**  **TRUE OR ~~FALSE~~**   You shouldn't assume there is something being left out of what the author chooses to present to you.

**11.**  **~~TRUE~~ OR FALSE**   You can tell the difference between an intermediate conclusion and a main conclusion by asking which statement relies on the other one.

**12.**  **~~TRUE~~ OR FALSE**   You should question how the premises stack up.

**13.**  Seek and find!   Circle only the premise indicators in the word cloud.

| only | ~~since~~ | hence | therefore |
|------|-----------|-------|-----------|
| every | ~~because~~ | ~~for~~ | accordingly |
| so | ~~given that~~ | ~~as~~ | if |

**14.**  Seek and find!   Circle only the conclusion indicators in the word cloud.

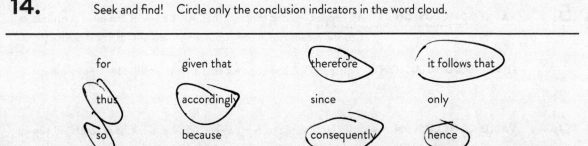

| for | given that | ~~therefore~~ | ~~it follows that~~ |
|-----|------------|---------------|---------------------|
| ~~thus~~ | ~~accordingly~~ | since | only |
| ~~so~~ | because | ~~consequently~~ | ~~hence~~ |

Where's the answer key?

You'll find the answer key at the end of the chapter on page 61.

## Conclusions Drill   ANSWER KEY

There is more than one possible right answer, especially for invalid conclusions. Don't assume that what you did is wrong just because it isn't exactly what I came up with. Use this answer key to analyze the differences and similarities between our answers. If they're similar, awesome. If not, puzzle out how I got to my answer.

**1.**   **VALID CONCLUSION**   Fish probably contain ultraviolet gas.

 **INVALID CONCLUSION**   Fish are likely to nourish us.

**2.**   **VALID CONCLUSION (OPTION 1)**   Some people who hate fine-tooth combs also enjoy a good pizza.

 **VALID CONCLUSION (OPTION 2)**   Monica and Frida have some likes and dislikes in common.

 **INVALID CONCLUSION**   Monica and Frida have good taste.

**3.**   **VALID CONCLUSION**   Christina is not good enough for my Julian.

 **INVALID CONCLUSION**   Julian will never find love.

**4.**   **VALID CONCLUSION**   Microphones are more likely to have perfect pitch than non-coffee drinkers.

 **INVALID CONCLUSION**   Microphones are the best singers.

**5.**   **VALID CONCLUSION**   Chapped lips and chapped toes may be one of the main contributors to the recent rise in the incidence of tardiness at Tea University.

 **INVALID CONCLUSION**   Chapped lips and chapped toes are extremely dangerous injuries.

**6.**   **VALID CONCLUSION**   If Liara maintains her perfect GPA, she will have to eat a heaping plate of something at least 20 spice points above lamb saag.

 **INVALID CONCLUSION**   Liara's perfect GPA requires her to like spicy food.

**7.**  **VALID CONCLUSION**   The statement that "our forefathers preferred the taste of saffron to that of sassafras" is a bald-faced lie.

   **INVALID CONCLUSION**   The ancient Mesopotamian artifact indicates that our forefathers were misfits.

**8.**  **VALID CONCLUSION**   The postulation maximization theory presented in Theodore's text does not mention the quagmire hypothesis, the jewelry box paradox, or the antiquarian ice principle.

   **INVALID CONCLUSION**   The postulation maximization theory presented in Theodore's text is contradictory.

**9.**  **VALID CONCLUSION**   Morality has a conversely inverse proportional relationship with a condiment on the endangered condiments list.

   **INVALID CONCLUSION**   Garlic aioli is on the endangered condiments list.

**10.**  **VALID CONCLUSION**   If one includes only winks in one's SPUMES calculation, Huey will be thrown into the void, but if one includes both winks and nods in one's SPUMES calculation, Guillermo will be thrown into the void.

   **INVALID CONCLUSION**   Huey and Guillermo are both great guys.

**11.**  **VALID CONCLUSION**   The mayor of New Brunswick should be thrown in prison for either the duration of his natural life or however long it takes him to read *Time, Memory, and Transcendent Madeleines*.

   **INVALID CONCLUSION**   The mayor of New Brunswick has harsh opinions about the evolution and dissemination of the QWERTY keyboard.

**12.**  **VALID CONCLUSION**   Sophie Spradlin is one of the best people to know if you are a star on the brink of success, if the ARHI study is correct.

   **INVALID CONCLUSION**   If Sophie Spradlin's moon does not continue to stay in Virgo, she will not be of any use to a star on the brink of success.

## Intermediate Conclusions & Nested Claims Drill    ANSWER KEY

If present below, the nested claim is bracketed and the intermediate conclusion is underlined.

**1.** When fashion industries avoid complete financial ruin, there's always a chance, based on changing trends, that the industry in question may regain its former prominence. Since fedoras are still popular in some parts of our nation, <u>the fedora industry has likely avoided total bankruptcy.</u> So the fedora will probably soon regain the cultural prominence it enjoyed during the 1920s.

**FALSE**                    This example is a hybrid argument.

**2.** [A recent study suggested that the fez may be a causal factor in crime prevention efforts.] But the study relied on faulty data to reach its conclusion. Therefore, the fez is not a factor in crime prevention.

**FALSE**                    This example is a hybrid argument.

**3.** [Aaron suggests that trucker hats are contributing to the rising rate of jaywalking in our community.] Talia had never jaywalked before, but as soon as she tried on a trucker hat, she felt compelled.

**TRUE**                    This example is a hybrid argument.

**4.** Because beanies are the warmest of hats, <u>we know that their fabric must insulate the most heat.</u> [But temperature experts suggest that the beanie's weave may instead be responsible for its superior performance.] However, there are many competing hat formats with similar weaves and inferior heat-insulating performance. Therefore, it must be the 60-40 wool-rayon blend that keeps heat in, since all beanies are characterized by this exact blend.

**FALSE**                    This example is a hybrid argument.

**5.** <u>Berets don't qualify as legitimate headwear</u> because they only cover at most 40% of the skull. Berets should not be carried at RealHeadWearOnly.com since they only stock legitimate headwear.

**FALSE**                    This example is a hybrid argument.

**1.**    The two things that always make up an argument are **premises** and **conclusions**.

**2.**    A premise serves as **evidence**.

**3.**    A conclusion is a **claim**.

**4.**    Premises support the **conclusion**. Conclusions rely on the **premises**.

**5.**    An intermediate conclusion supports the main **conclusion** and is supported by the **premises**.

**6.**    Inferences are **valid** conclusions we design ourselves.

**7.**    False. There will *not* always be indicator words to show us what part of the argument every statement is.

**8.**    False. You *cannot* question the truth of a premise.

**9.**    False. A conclusion *needs* premises to be valid.

**10.**    False. You *should* assume there is something being left out of what the author chooses to present to you.

**11.**    True.

**12.**    True.

**13.**    You should have circled the following premise indicators and no other words: because, for, since, as, given that.

**14.**    You should have circled the following conclusion indicators and no other words: therefore, so, accordingly, thus, consequently, hence, it follows that.

# OMMMM.

chapter two. now you're through.

These are quotations from real LSAT students! These former students were in your shoes not too long ago, and they wanted to share a few key takeaways from their prep experiences.

### KELLY

1. Don't let nerves get in the way of your performance — have the right mindset and approach to the whole process.

2. Take the June or July test! I'm not a morning person so I would've felt most comfortable during the June exam.

3. Don't assume you will be stronger in some sections than others. I thought my strongest section would be RC, weakest in LG. The first time I took the LSAT, I had a perfect LG section and missed 6 RC questions. You can't assume the same things you would assume in other standardized tests.

4. LG is by far the easiest to learn/improve section in the LSAT. I'm not math-oriented at all and I cannot emphasize how possible it is to get into the groove of LG. So many people leave so many points on the table by giving up on LG. You can break through, and when you do, it's the best feeling — doing the games feels like a break from the rest of the test!

5. Don't listen to the "you can't improve more than 3 or so points on the LSAT" nonsense. You totally can. It is not ridiculous to aim high.

### NIRA

1. Go into each Logical Reasoning stimulus with judge goggles on. The LSAT is funny and doesn't have its business together. The mindset, going into each question, should always be: How does this argument suck? How can this argument be stronger? What is wrong with the picture here? I wish I had known that I am better than the stimulus. Knowing that you are not a victim improves your approach. The LSAT is not something that is happening to you — it's you doing something!

2. I wish the Basic Translation Drill existed when I started studying. Instead, Ellen developed it for me. This had the single greatest impact on my score. It taught me to be disciplined in how I approach the reading on the test.

3. The concepts need time to marinate. I wish I was more patient with myself and wasn't always trying to move on to learning the next thing before mastering what I was focusing on.

4. Don't obsess over large goals (I need a 167 on the exam!). Focus on smaller, incremental, more achievable goals that will eventually lead to that 167. For example, I want to do two LR sections of the Basic Translation Drill for the next 4 days, so that I can understand the stimulus on my first read soon.

5. Hyper-Skipping is crucial to finishing in time. Camo Review is crucial to getting as much out of your sections as possible. These little things make a *huge* difference.

Get ready, this is the one time I'll ever OK skipping ahead! **Go learn what Hyper-Skipping is on page 415 right now.** While you're there, read the whole Answer Choice Strategy Section!

THE
POWER
PLAYERS

## Must, Cannot, Could, Not Necessarily

The most important words in an argument are the Power Players: **MUST**, **CANNOT**, **COULD**, **NOT NECESSARILY**, and their synonyms.

**THE POWER PLAYERS**

| POWER PLAYERS | | EXAMPLES |
|---|---|---|
| **Certainty** | MUST | *always, every single time, no exceptions ever, you can't get out of doing this no matter what* |
| | CANNOT | *never, impossible in any circumstance, no way* |
| **Possibility** | COULD | *possible, can, there's a chance, maybe, might, encompasses both something unlikely and something likely, may or may not* |
| | NOT NECESSARILY | *doesn't have to be the case, literally "not must," could be an exception, not guaranteed* |

The Power Players are likely not words you've ever been taught to focus on. Why are they so important? Because of the difference in how hard it is to prove each of the following conclusions:

1. We **MUST** get Chinese food.

2. We **CANNOT** get Chinese food.

3. We **COULD** get Chinese food.

4. We are **NOT NECESSARILY** getting Chinese food.

*[handwritten: } diff'r levels of proof required]*

Imagine you encountered each of these conclusions on the LSAT. Which ones would be easy to prove and which ones would be harder? Which ones would be easy to attack and which ones would be more resilient? The Power Players are solely responsible for the differences in each of these conclusions. Just one or two words have changed, and yet each of these conclusions puts forth very different ideas. Let's look at them one by one:

1. We **MUST** get Chinese food.

This is pretty tough to prove and easy to attack. To prove **MUST**, you need some powerful premises to back you up. Premises like: We can't get any food besides Chinese food and we have to eat. Without premises like that, any Loophole that offers an alternative to Chinese food would invalidate this conclusion. On the LSAT, **MUST** has a huge burden of proof.

2.   *We* **CANNOT** *get Chinese food.*

This is also difficult to prove and easy to attack. To prove **CANNOT**, you need powerful premises. You need something like: We're all allergic to Chinese food and we never get food we're allergic to. Without premises like that, any Loophole that shows Chinese food to be a remote possibility unravels this claim. On the LSAT, **CANNOT** has a massive burden of proof as well.

3.   *We* **COULD** *get Chinese food.*

This is much easier to prove and harder to attack. To prove **COULD**, we just need premises that allow Chinese food to be a possibility. Premises like this would work: There is Chinese food available to us and we have the means to obtain it. Loopholes are going to have to be *much* stronger to invalidate every possibility of Chinese food. On the LSAT, **COULD** doesn't have to work that hard to enter valid territory. **COULD** is easily provable.

4.   *We are* **NOT NECESSARILY** *getting Chinese food.*

This is also easier to prove and harder to attack. To prove **NOT NECESSARILY**, we just need a premise saying we don't have to get Chinese food. We could use premises like: We might go hungry or get pasta. Loopholes are going to have to be very strong to invalidate this conclusion; a Loophole would have to prove that we will get Chinese food. On the LSAT, **NOT NECESSARILY** easily enters valid territory. **NOT NECESSARILY** is easily provable.

What's a Loophole?

As we saw in Chapter 2, a Loophole is a statement that, if true, would destroy the conclusion.

> Arguments are made or broken by how certain you are that the conclusion has to be true. When you can change one word and the ease of proving the claim radically changes, you know you're handling loaded language. That's why we call these words Power Players. Because they're so damn powerful.

## CONTENT VS. POWER PLAYERS

Content is the replaceable stuff in the argument. The specifics. The story of the stimulus is all content. The content in our examples above, getting Chinese food, remained the same in every example, even as the provability of our claim changed.

Arguments are mostly content in raw word count. They're filled with things like lobsters and the Great Depression. The problem with focusing on the content to the exclusion of the Power Players is that you end up missing the major errors that authors make. Content is interchangeable. You can analyze arguments about monkeys, heart disease, and Sylvia Plath exactly the same way. The reason you can do this is because arguments differ in meaningful ways according to their Power Players.

Power Players are what make the argument strong or weak.

Imagine your argument is like your house. It's got beams and insulation in the walls, but you don't really think about that in your day-to-day interactions with the house. You think about the couch, the desk, the bed. That's what you interact with. How solid your house is doesn't depend on what kind of couch you have though. The solidity of your house depends on whether the beams are joined the right way. The beams are your Power Players.

Imagine you're trying to destroy a house with a wrecking ball. You want to focus on the beams that are holding the house up, not the sofa that happens to be sitting inside. It's the same thing with argumentation. **Destroying an argument requires focusing on its infrastructure, the Power Players.**

# Certainty Power Players THE 100% & THE 0%

Now, we're going to go in depth with our two Certainty Power Players, **MUST** and **CANNOT**. These two are the heavy-lifting, straightforward Power Players.

As a language, English defaults to certainty. **In English, if you don't specify that you're not sure about something, you imply that you are sure.** For instance, "I will not go to the park" implies that there is a 0% chance I will go to the park, even though I didn't *exactly* say that it's impossible. "I am going to the park" works the same way. I didn't specifically state that I have to go, but it's implied because I said it was happening with no caveats.

**When you don't see any indicators of certainty or uncertainty, you are handling a sentence that is claiming certainty.**

## MUST: THE 100%
## ABSOLUTELY POSITIVELY SURE.

When I look over at a wall and say to a friend, "There's a cool tree shadow on that wall," I'm stating that there is 100% a cool tree shadow on the wall. I didn't use **MUST** in that sentence, but it was implied. This assumption of certainty in everyday language translates to the LSAT.

When you see a sentence on the LSAT that either uses **MUST** (or a **MUST** synonym) or does nothing to indicate its certainty level, **the author is saying that there are no exceptions**. Say a conclusion states, "Therefore, inflation is a cause of the zombie war." This means they're claiming there *must* be a causal relationship between inflation and the zombie war. Inflation has to have the exact causal relationship indicated. If we find any evidence that it doesn't necessarily have the causal relationship indicated, the argument instantly unravels.

When the stimulus authors make these **MUST** statements, they're taking on a huge burden of proof that we don't typically recognize when we're just talking in everyday life.

## CANNOT: THE 0%
## NEVER NEVER NEVER.

When you say, "I can't go to your party," you are claiming there is no way you will be at the party. It is absolutely impossible. Likewise, when the LSAT says **CANNOT**, it doesn't mean very unlikely. If there's even a remote chance that something may occur, the stimulus will use **COULD**, not **CANNOT**.

## Possibility Power Players   THE 1-100% & THE 0-99%

Possibility Power Players are more nuanced than Certainty Power Players. They are not confined to one specific percentage of likelihood. Instead, both **COULD** and **NOT NECESSARILY** encompass a wide range of possibility.

**COULD** and **NOT NECESSARILY** overlap, which can cause some confusion. If there's a 57% chance of rain, then rain both might happen and might not happen. It *could* rain, and it will rain 57% of the time. But it is doesn't *have to* rain. 43% of the time it won't rain, so rain is not necessary. **Take a second to think about what this paragraph meant before you move on.**

What's the difference between **COULD** and **NOT NECESSARILY** then? They differ in their extremes:

|  | COULD | NOT NECESSARILY |
|---|---|---|
| Includes | 100% / **MUST** | 0% / **CANNOT** |
| Doesn't Include | 0% / **CANNOT** | 100% / **MUST** |

### COULD: THE 1% TO 100%
### EVERYTHING BUT 0% LIKELY.

**COULD** is much easier to prove than **MUST**.

When someone claims, "Black and white photography could be causing writer's block," they are saying that there is at least a small chance that black and white photography is the cause. Seriously, all they're claiming is that it's not impossible for black and white photography to cause writer's block. That sounds a lot easier to prove than if this were a **MUST** claim, right?

You can always replace **COULD** with "not impossible" and retain the same meaning. Check out how a few statements sound after replacing **COULD** with "not impossible" in the chart below. Your instinctual reaction to the statement will probably change after the switch from **COULD** to "not impossible."

| COULD | NOT IMPOSSIBLE |
|---|---|
| *I could win the lottery next week.* | *It is not impossible for me to win the lottery next week.* |
| *I could blow all my lottery winnings on candy and exotic beverages.* | *It is not impossible for me to blow all my lottery winnings on candy and exotic beverages.* |
| *I could end up back in Philadelphia with nothing but a large box of lychee drinking vinegar to my name.* | *It is not impossible for me to end up back in Philadelphia with nothing but a large box of lychee drinking vinegar to my name.* |

Your reaction to the "not impossible" version of the statement is much closer to the logical meaning of **COULD**. Not impossible sounds super basic, right? Like a lot of things aren't impossible. That's what **COULD** means on the LSAT.

**COULD** also has many synonyms. Keep in mind that any language denoting possibility is a **COULD** statement.

Could = Not impossible
within the realm of
possibility

## NOT NECESSARILY: THE 0% TO 99%
## EVERYTHING BUT 100% LIKELY.

NOT NECESSARILY instills fear into the hearts of many, including the barista I've repeatedly explained this chapter to. She just starts shaking her head every time I say the words "NOT NECESSARILY." Unlike the rest of the Power Players, NOT NECESSARILY wasn't ingrained into our young hearts in grade school.

Let's start by taking this two-word phrase apart. I'm pretty sure you know what "not" means. It's just a negative to apply to something. It's that "necessarily" part that confuses people, so let me clear this up right now. **"Necessarily" is a synonym for MUST. So, NOT NECESSARILY literally means "not MUST."** NOT NECESSARILY allows for every single possibility except MUST.

NOT NECESSARILY is an easy claim to prove. It is commonly used when trying to smack down somebody else's argument; in that case, you are critiquing someone else's MUST. You are claiming that whatever someone else says has to be true isn't actually proven. We will take down other people's arguments often throughout the course of our training, which is why NOT NECESSARILY is so important.

Imagine the following debate:

> Tasha: We must enter the cave. The cave contains treasure, and I want the treasure.

> Spencer: Well... the cave also contains ancient death traps. We could build a robot to go into the cave and get the treasure for us. So, it's not necessarily true that we must enter the cave.

Notice Spencer's conclusion. He went after the MUST in Tasha's conclusion, but he did it carefully. He offered another way to get the treasure, and so he was able to say that it wasn't 100% necessary for them to enter the cave.

Here is how NOT NECESSARILY works in real life. Think about the last time a random person said something to you on the street. Imagine the random said, "Politician Archie is a war criminal." You don't actually know if Politician Archie is a war criminal or not, but you're also pretty sure that this random person on the street doesn't know either. If you are the type to engage random people on the street, your response should be, "Sir, that's not necessarily true." You shouldn't claim definitively that Politician Archie is *not* a war criminal because you don't actually know that. This is the glory of NOT NECESSARILY at work.

> NOT NECESSARILY often appears when stimuli begin with "some scientists/ critics/people believe..." and the author smacks "some people" down. When she's smacking them down, if she's staying within her bounds, she'll say that their argument is not necessarily true. Failing to use NOT NECESSARILY in this situation leads to a Possibility ≠ Certainty classic flaw, which we will examine in detail in Chapter 7, The Classic Flaws.

Once you've gotten NOT NECESSARILY under your belt, you can annoy your friends and significant others by responding to their every questionable thought and feeling with the words "NOT NECESSARILY," just like I do. It's a great way to win friends and influence people.

# Power Players & Argument Parts

The Power Players pair with argument parts! We have the following combinations:

| **POWER PLAYER PREMISES** | | **STRENGTH AS EVIDENCE** |
|---|---|---|
| **Certainty Premises** | *Must Premise* | *Strong evidence* |
| | *Cannot Premise* | *Strong evidence* |
| **Possibility Premises** | *Could Premise* | *Weak evidence* |
| | *Not Necessarily Premise* | *Weak evidence* |

| **POWER PLAYER CONCLUSIONS** | | **PROVABILITY** |
|---|---|---|
| **Certainty Conclusions** | *Must Conclusion* | *Difficult to prove* |
| | *Cannot Conclusion* | *Difficult to prove* |
| **Possibility Conclusions** | *Could Conclusion* | *Easy to prove* |
| | *Not Necessarily Conclusion* | *Easy to prove* |

You can identify these combinations by putting together your knowledge of argument parts and what you just learned about the Power Players. For instance, if you see **COULD** (or a synonym) in a conclusion, you know it's a Could Conclusion.

**When the author makes an argument, their job is to prove their conclusion necessarily true, 100%.** This goal does not change, regardless of what kind of conclusion you're trying to prove. In the case of a Could Conclusion, you are trying to 100% prove that something is possible.

Now, we're going to explore how arguments are built using the combinations of Power Players and argument parts. We'll progress through each of the following with specific examples:

- Certainty Premises and Certainty Conclusions
- Possibility Premises and Certainty Conclusions
- Certainty Premises and Possibility Conclusions
- Possibility Premises and Possibility Conclusions

> Don't worry. You're not going to consciously categorize all these things when you sit for your real LSAT. We're doing all the work of deconstructing what goes on in argumentation in order to familiarize you with the core concepts and build up a solid framework. This way, on test day, you'll be a natural.

## Certainty Conclusions

---

> **CERTAINTY PREMISES – CERTAINTY CONCLUSIONS**
>
> Certainty Conclusions almost always require Certainty Premises in order to be valid.

### MUST CONCLUSIONS

Take the following argument:

> *School funding <u>has been</u> on the decline for years. This <u>has led</u> to widespread unemployment amongst koala bears. Senator Henley <u>promised</u> the koala lobby that she would introduce a bill to increase education funding. So, the koalas <u>will</u> soon be back to work.*

Certainty Premises are awesome in terms of what they *can* do. However, just like we see in this example, Certainty Premises are rarely arranged well enough to build a valid Certainty Conclusion on the LSAT.

Let's look for gaps between the premises. Even though Certainty Premises are strong evidence, there will likely still be gaps in how these premises are arranged. And remember, it doesn't matter how powerful the premises are if there are still gaps between them. Gaps mean Loopholes, and when the argument is vulnerable to reasonable Loopholes, we can't call it valid.

> The Power Players are underlined in every koala example in this section. This will help you notice how the Power Players appear in context. In Certainty Premises/Conclusions, the words indicating Certainty are underlined, since the absence of a Power Player indicates Certainty as well.

The biggest gaps surround this premise: "Senator Henley promised the koala lobby that she would introduce a bill to increase education funding." The argument would prefer we fill in the gaps for them. They want us to assume that a promise to introduce a bill will always lead directly to the koalas getting their jobs back soon. But a promise isn't reality – politicians break promises all the time. And even if the bill does get introduced, who says it necessarily passes? And even if it passes, why assume that the increased education funding will go to rehiring koalas soon? **Notice that we didn't negate any of the premises in investigating these gaps. The premises stayed true, but we blew up the gaps between them.**

Now that I've outlined a few gaps between the premises, let's design some Loopholes that exploit these gaps:

> Always assume that the stimulus isn't giving you the full story. They're only telling you the parts that benefit them. They're not going to directly lie to you, but they will definitely lie by omission. The thing they "forget" to tell you is your Loophole.

*What if Senator Henley never keeps her promises?*

*What if the education budget will be raised, but not high enough to rehire the koalas?*

*What if bills introduced by Senator Henley never pass?*

*What if the increased funding for education is used for something besides hiring back workers?*

*What if the schools want to use the money to rehire workers, but suddenly realize they've been letting koalas teach children, so they decline to rehire them?*

*[handwritten: pretend they are hiding something from you]*

*What if the bill passes, but it fails to be implemented until many years down the road?*

Loopholes are the exceptions that let us get around what the argument is trying to prove, all while honoring the argument's premises. **When you're designing Loopholes, any reasonable thing is possible unless it conflicts with the premises.** You can come up with any scenario that a reasonable person would think is reasonable. Each of these Loopholes could be a correct answer to a Weaken question (if we want to get ahead of ourselves). But focusing on the gap the Loophole exposes will lead you directly to the correct answer on most argument-based LR questions, regardless of the question type.

*What's reasonable mean?*

Something reasonable is compatible with common sense.

Has the author proven that the koalas will definitely get their jobs back soon? No, a valid conclusion would not be vulnerable to as many Loopholes as the koala argument is. There are way too many gaps between the premises to prove this conclusion. Let's bridge those gaps now and take a look at a valid version of this Must Conclusion:

> *School funding has been on the decline for years. This has led to widespread unemployment amongst koala bears. Senator Henley promised the koala lobby that she would introduce a bill to increase education funding, **with a specific provision necessitating rehiring the koalas. Every bill that Senator Henley promises to introduce will always be enacted quickly.** So, the koalas will soon be back to work.*

Check out the new bolded premises in the valid version of the argument for a second. They bridge the gaps we attacked with our Loopholes. These new premises are doing a ton for the argument: They ensure that Senator Henley keeps her promise, that raising the budget will actually get the koalas rehired, and that the plan will be enacted soon. Each of our Loopholes was perfectly covered. Now the argument is golden.

**REMEMBER!** *Any gap between the premises is an opportunity for a Loophole.*

## CANNOT CONCLUSIONS

Let's see how a Cannot Conclusion looks:

> *School funding has been on the decline for years. This has led to widespread unemployment amongst koala bears. Senator Henley promised the koala lobby that she would introduce a bill to increase education funding. So, the koalas will not be out of work for long.*

This is basically the same claim as the invalid Must Conclusion above, but I've switched up the wording to phrase it as a Cannot Conclusion. The same Loopholes apply for the same reasons.

The lesson behind this similarity is that **Certainty Conclusions can vary between MUST and CANNOT based on random wording decisions, so they should be handled similarly.** Certainty Conclusions are vulnerable to Loopholes because of how bold their claims are. It doesn't matter if they are phrased in a negative or positive way.

Let's look at the valid version of this Cannot Conclusion:

> *School funding has been on the decline for years. This has led to widespread unemployment amongst koala bears. Senator Henley promised the koala lobby that she would introduce a bill to increase education funding, **with a specific provision necessitating rehiring the koalas. Every bill that Senator Henley promises to introduce will always be enacted quickly.** So, the koalas will not be out of work for long.*

This is valid for the same reasons the Must Conclusion was valid. **Wording will always vary, but the core principles of argumentation do not.**

---

### POSSIBILITY – CERTAINTY

You can't prove a Certainty Conclusion from all Possibility Premises, except under the most irregular circumstances.

---

Now, let's make our koala example even less valid:

> School funding <u>could</u> have been on the decline for years. This <u>could</u> have led to widespread unemployment amongst koala bears. Senator Henley <u>may</u> have promised the koala lobby that she <u>could</u> introduce a bill to increase education funding. So, the koalas <u>will</u> soon be back to work.

That was absurd. I changed every Certainty Premise into a Possibility Premise. Look how the argument crumbles into something so bad that it's unrealistic even for the LSAT. Typically, if Possibility Premises are present, you will see them mixed with Certainty Premises. This dilutes the power of the Certainty Premises, but it is definitely better than being limited to something like what we have above.

Possibility Premises only lead to a valid Certainty Conclusion when arguments are very (very, very, ad infinitum) simple. Arguments are essentially never simple enough on the LSAT for this exception to take hold, but here is an example of one Possibility Premise leading to a valid Certainty Conclusion:

> Senator Henley <u>could</u> introduce a bill to increase education funding. Therefore, it <u>cannot</u> be true that there is no chance Senator Henley will introduce such a bill.

This conclusion is commenting on something inherent to possibility. We're assuming, "When something is possible, something that precludes that possibility can't be true." This assumption is brimming with Certainty and will lead us to a Certainty Conclusion.

You won't see something like this on the LSAT more than once in a blue moon.

# Possibility Conclusions

---

> **CERTAINTY – POSSIBILITY**
>
> It is easy to prove a Possibility Conclusion from Certainty Premises.

## COULD CONCLUSIONS

Let's look at our koala example with a Could Conclusion:

> School funding <u>has been</u> on the decline for years. This <u>has led</u> to widespread unemployment amongst koala bears. Senator Henley <u>promised</u> the koala lobby that she would introduce a bill to increase education funding. So, the koalas <u>could</u> soon be back to work.

Let's talk about the magic of **COULD**. By only concluding that the koalas *could* get their jobs back soon, the author is defending against all the Loopholes we had in the Must Conclusion. Let's examine each of our Must Loopholes one by one and decide how they apply to this argument. Remember, any Loophole worth its salt has to make it *impossible* for the koalas to be hired back soon.

| MUST CONCLUSION LOOPHOLE | WAY AROUND THE LOOPHOLE |
|---|---|
| *What if Senator Henley never keeps her promises?* | *Some other Senator could still get the bill passed.* |
| *What if the education budget will be raised, but not high enough to rehire the koalas?* | *There could still be some special grant just for rehiring the koalas.* |
| *What if bills introduced by Senator Henley never pass?* | *Same problem as the first Loophole. Some other Senator could still get the koalas their jobs back.* |
| *What if the increased funding for education is used for something besides hiring back workers?* | *Same problem we saw with the second Loophole. The funding could still come from another source.* |
| *What if the schools want to use the money to rehire workers, but suddenly realize they've been letting koalas teach children, so they decline to rehire them?* | *This is the best Loophole of the bunch so far, but it still doesn't preclude someone else from rehiring the koalas. Maybe there's a government mandate.* |
| *What if the bill passes, but it fails to be implemented until many years down the road?* | *This bill may fail to be implemented soon, but that doesn't mean some other bill can't help the koalas out sooner.* |

That was brutal for our Loopholes, right? Possibility Conclusions are super difficult (annoying actually, really annoying) to disprove. The Loophole that'll knock out this Could Conclusion is going to have to be badass. It has to prove that it's *impossible* for the koalas to get their jobs back soon. Let's give it a try:

> What if there's a complete rehiring freeze in education that lasts for a long time?

This Loophole is intense. It proves that it is literally impossible for the koalas to get their jobs back soon. Can you really figure out a way for the koalas to be rehired as teachers when there's a complete education rehiring freeze? Nope. No one is getting rehired. If it's impossible for everyone, it's impossible for the koalas too.

The question becomes... Is this Loophole reasonable? Remember, the argument only has to worry about reasonable, commonsense Loopholes. As always, the definition of the word "reasonable" is pretty murky, but I'd make the case that this Loophole is reasonable. The premises did state that school funding has been declining for a while; it's reasonable to believe that rehiring could be frozen.

Let's look at a valid version of this argument:

> *School funding <u>has been</u> on the decline for years. This <u>has led</u> to widespread unemployment amongst koala bears. Senator Henley <u>promised</u> the koala lobby that she would introduce a bill to increase education funding,* **with a specific provision <u>necessitating</u> rehiring the koalas. Every bill that Senator Henley promises to introduce <u>has a chance</u> of being enacted quickly.** *So, the koalas <u>could</u> soon be back to work.*

Notice how we only had to say that there's "a chance" the bill will be enacted quickly. Once that premise is in place, all our potential Loopholes are neutralized. The premises supporting this valid Could Conclusion are similar to the premises supporting the valid Must Conclusion. The only thing that changed is the exact wording of the last premise, which morphed from "will be enacted" to "has a chance of being enacted." This change was optional. The stronger Certainty Premise was needed to prove the Must Conclusion, but it could have proven this Could Conclusion as well.

## NOT NECESSARILY CONCLUSIONS

Let's look at how our koala argument shapes up with a Not Necessarily Conclusion:

> *School funding <u>has been</u> on the decline for years. This <u>has led</u> to widespread unemployment amongst koala bears. Senator Henley <u>promised</u> the koala lobby that she would introduce a bill to increase education funding. Some critics claim that koalas <u>will</u> soon be back to work. The critics' claim, however, is <u>unfounded</u>.*

Notice how the argument had to change to accommodate the Not Necessarily Conclusion. I had to put forth another claim for the author to characterize as not necessarily true.

Just like Could Conclusions, Not Necessarily Conclusions are easy to prove. All you need to do is prove that the author didn't do her job. Unfortunately, in the case of our koala argument, the Not Necessarily Conclusion isn't really proven. The author hasn't provided any reasons to believe that the critics' claim is unfounded. All the ammunition against the critics' claim (specifically the Loopholes from the Must Conclusion section) is left unsaid. Even if you are working with an easy-to-prove conclusion, there still needs to be *some* evidence for the conclusion.

Let's tweak our koala example and see what it looks like as a valid conclusion:

> *School funding <u>has been</u> on the decline for years. This <u>has led</u> to widespread unemployment amongst koala bears. Senator Henley <u>promised</u> the koala lobby that she would introduce a bill to increase education funding. Some critics claim that koalas <u>will</u> soon be back to work. The critics' claim, however, is <u>unfounded</u>* **because Senator Henley <u>never</u> keeps her promises.**

The author actually supplied a premise to support her conclusion! I just added in one of our Loopholes from the Must Conclusion section, and we're a lot closer to proving that the koalas don't have to head back to work. Notice that I added a Certainty Premise; it's strong enough to prove the author's conclusion.

---

**POSSIBILITY – POSSIBILITY**

Possibility Premises can hypothetically prove a Possibility Conclusion, but these arguments are almost always invalid.

---

Let's see how our koala argument looks with all Possibility Premises and a Possibility Conclusion:

> School funding _could_ have been on the decline for years. This _could_ have led to widespread unemployment amongst koala bears. Senator Henley _may_ have promised the koala lobby that she _could_ introduce a bill to increase education funding. So, the koalas _could_ soon be back to work.

It is really tempting to take this Could Conclusion as seriously as we took the last one. The koalas might still be back to work, right? There are a lot of possibilities outside the premises that may lead to that outcome. But remember, in order for this Could Conclusion to be valid, we have to _prove_ that there is definitely not a 0% chance of the koalas getting rehired. In the stimulus above, we don't even know if school funding has been on the decline. We don't know whether the decline, if it occurred, put the koalas out of work. How can we make any claims with such puny premises? We don't even know if the koalas are out of work for sure.

Since **COULD** stands for anything between a 1% and 100% chance, let's look at one way to interpret the **COULDS** mentioned in this example, just to clarify how bad this argument is:

> _There is a 1% chance_ that school funding has been on the decline for years. _There is a 1% chance_ that this decline led to widespread unemployment amongst koala bears. _There is a 1% chance_ that Senator Henley promised the koala lobby that _there is a 1% chance_ she will introduce a bill to increase education funding. So, _there is anywhere from a 1% to a 100% chance_ that the koalas will soon be back to work.

I just took each premise for its most pessimistic possibility in this example. Each of those **COULDS** from the original argument might mean 1% possibility. **When you're evaluating whether an argument is valid, you want to examine it in its most unflattering interpretation.** In this case, taking that uncharitable look makes it a lot easier to see that these premises really add up to nothing. All those 1% premises are very unlikely to connect in the way we would need to build a valid conclusion. **Certainty is our lifeboat and it will either need to be stated or implied to build a valid conclusion. The very idea of validity implies a high level of Certainty** that a bunch of Possibility Premises can't get on their own.

To show you a valid Possibility Conclusion derived from Possibility Premises, we're going to have to simplify again:

> Senator Henley _could_ introduce a bill to get the koalas back to work. So, _there is a chance_ that Senator Henley will have some effect on legislative efforts regarding koala employment prospects.

I had to rely on a reasonable Certainty Assumption to make this conclusion valid. That assumption was that introducing a bill is equivalent to having "some effect on legislative efforts." But, notice how we had to _really_ strip this argument to its bare bones to make this conclusion valid.

All our Must Conclusion Loopholes still apply to this example. Weaker premises make for even greater Loophole vulnerability.

Valid conclusions are hard to come by, especially when you only have Possibility Premises to work with.

## Power Players & Argument Parts Drill

### INSTRUCTIONS

*Identify the Power Player and argument part combinations using the word bank.*

### Word Bank

| | | |
|---|---|---|
| Could Premise | Must Premise | Not Necessarily Premise |
| Cannot Premise | Could Conclusion | Not Necessarily Conclusion |
| Must Conclusion | Cannot Conclusion | |

**1.** Therefore, there is the possibility of electric combat.

*Could conclusion*

**2.** Because we must enter the fray.

*Must premise*

**3.** Since Aubry cannot walk all the way to England.

*Cannot premise*

**4.** For Tony is simply not good enough to save us.

*Cannot premise*

**5.** Consequently, Smitten's claim does not necessarily follow.

*Not necessary conclusion*

**6.** Hence, the inevitable ostrich rise will soon come to pass.

*Must conclusion*

**7.** It is a given that humans are natural enemies of the bird.

*Must premise*

**8.** It follows that Australia may be the first to fall.

*Could conclusion*

**9.** Chris, therefore, cannot be sacrificed to their will.

*Cannot conclusion*

**10.** For it is not guaranteed that the greater hand will prevail.

*Not necessarily premise*

*Where's the answer key?*

You'll find the answer key at the end of the chapter on page 88.

# Power Players & Truthiness

Truth and falsity are the other half of how we encounter the Power Players on the LSAT.

**TRUE and FALSE are truthiness indicators.** The LSAT is all about gradations of things being **TRUE** and **FALSE**. Those two words should always catch your attention. You will get questions right and wrong simply depending on how closely you pay attention to **TRUE** and **FALSE**.

In order to succeed on the LSAT, you will have to know what all of the following mean:

- **MUST BE TRUE**
- **COULD BE TRUE**
- **CANNOT BE TRUE**
- **NOT NECESSARILY TRUE**

- **MUST BE FALSE**
- **COULD BE FALSE**
- **CANNOT BE FALSE**
- **NOT NECESSARILY FALSE**

And beyond strict definitions, you will have to be able to see the relationships between each of these statements. This section will prepare you to tackle that challenge.

## WHY DO I NEED TO KNOW THIS STUFF?

Because the questions on the LSAT are phrased using this language. This is especially true of the Logic Games section. **If you can't handle puzzling out what COULD BE FALSE means quickly, you will not do well.** If you don't know what the questions mean, you can't answer them.

## Equivalence

> Equivalence tells us which pairs of Power Players mean the same thing.

### WHY SHOULD I CARE ABOUT EQUIVALENCE?

We care about Equivalence because some of the Power Player + **TRUE/FALSE** pairings are more difficult to understand than others. For example, if a question asked you, "Which one of the following is **NOT NECESSARILY FALSE**?" you would probably be a little more confused than if that same question asked you, "Which one of the following **COULD BE TRUE**?" The interesting thing is that **NOT NECESSARILY FALSE** and **COULD BE TRUE** mean the exact same thing. I created the following chart to help you translate more confusing wordings into something you can internalize in the heat of a question.

**EQUIVALENCE**

MUST                    COULD

— — — — — — — — — — — — — — — — — — — — *flip line*

CANNOT              NOT NECESSARILY

### HOW TO READ THIS DIAGRAM

When I'm doing an LSAT, sometimes I have to remind myself what a question actually wants me to do. Saying the Equivalent to myself really helps me focus back on the test in these moments.

Notice the **Flip Line** on the diagram above. This line tells you to change your truthiness indicator every time you cross it, meaning if you start with **TRUE**, switch to **FALSE** at the Flip Line. If you start with **FALSE**, switch to **TRUE** at the Flip Line.

All of the combinations of the Power Players and **TRUE/FALSE** can be translated like this. We will go through each of the combinations one by one, but the same theory will hold for all of them. For brevity's sake, I'm only going to demo the combinations starting with **TRUE** and translate them to **FALSE**. The process works the same way for translating **FALSE** to **TRUE**. The key here is that you start to internalize the Equivalent relationships between the pairs of Power Players.

Let's take this diagram for a spin.

## MUST BE TRUE ⟷ CANNOT BE FALSE

1. Put your finger on **MUST** in the diagram. You always start on whichever Power Player is present in the statement you want to translate.

2. Follow the arrow.

3. The arrow crosses the Flip Line, so you switch the **TRUE** in your **MUST BE TRUE** to a **FALSE** and continue where the arrow leads you.

4. The arrow lands on **CANNOT**. You also have a **FALSE** left after crossing the Flip Line. Put **CANNOT** and **FALSE** together, and you arrive at your Equivalent. The Equivalent of **MUST BE TRUE** is **CANNOT BE FALSE**.

## COULD BE TRUE ⟷ NOT NECESSARILY FALSE

1. Put your finger on **COULD** in the diagram. You always start on whichever Power Player is present in the statement you want to translate.

2. Follow the arrow.

3. The arrow crosses the Flip Line, so you switch the **TRUE** in your **COULD BE TRUE** to a **FALSE** and continue where the arrow leads you.

4. The arrow lands on **NOT NECESSARILY**. You also have a **FALSE** left after crossing the Flip Line. Put **NOT NECESSARILY** and **FALSE** together, and you arrive at your Equivalent. The Equivalent of **COULD BE TRUE** is **NOT NECESSARILY FALSE**.

## CANNOT BE TRUE ⟷ MUST BE FALSE

1. Put your finger on **CANNOT** in the diagram. You always start on whichever Power Player is present in the statement you want to translate.

2. Follow the arrow.

3. The arrow crosses the Flip Line, so you switch the **TRUE** in your **CANNOT BE TRUE** to a **FALSE** and continue where the arrow leads you.

4. The arrow lands on **MUST**. You also have a **FALSE** left after crossing the Flip Line. Put **MUST** and **FALSE** together, and you arrive at your Equivalent. The Equivalent of **CANNOT BE TRUE** is **MUST BE FALSE**.

## NOT NECESSARILY TRUE ⟷ COULD BE FALSE

1. Put your finger on **NOT NECESSARILY** in the diagram. You always start on whichever Power Player is present in the statement you want to translate.

2. Follow the arrow.

3. The arrow crosses the Flip Line, so you switch the **TRUE** in your **NOT NECESSARILY TRUE** to a **FALSE** and continue where the arrow leads you.

4. The arrow lands on **COULD**. You also have a **FALSE** left after crossing the Flip Line. Put **COULD** and **FALSE** together, and you arrive at your Equivalent. The Equivalent of **NOT NECESSARILY TRUE** is **COULD BE FALSE**.

You will use this Equivalence Chart in order to understand exactly what you're being asked to do in Logical Reasoning and Logic Games. For most students, it helps to translate **FALSE** to **TRUE**. But just knowing that these Equivalent pairs mean the same thing helps you understand them both.

# Negation

Negation is the art of adding and subtracting a "not" from our Power Players.

## WHY SHOULD YOU CARE ABOUT NEGATION?

So many reasons. **EXCEPT** questions. Loophole construction. Figuring out what wrong answers are supposed to look like so you can do questions by process of elimination. **You should care about Negation because you care about getting questions right.** Honestly, this entire chapter was initially written just to provide the foundation to understand Negation. It's a big deal.

When I say Negation, you may be tempted to think, "Oh, so we're just figuring out the opposites." But hold up a sec. These are negated pairs, not opposites. I'm stressing the annoying jargon because thinking of it like an opposite will really mess you up. Opposite implies polar opposite, meaning as far apart as possible. This would lead you to think that the Negation of **MUST** is **CANNOT**. But that's totally wrong!

> The correct answer to an **EXCEPT** question is the Negation of the Power Player in the question stem. You'll learn much more about **EXCEPT** questions in the Answer Choice Strategy section.

All four of our Power Players have a Negation partner. These partnerships are formed simply by adding or subtracting a "not" from each Power Player, and, in some cases, decoding a bit.

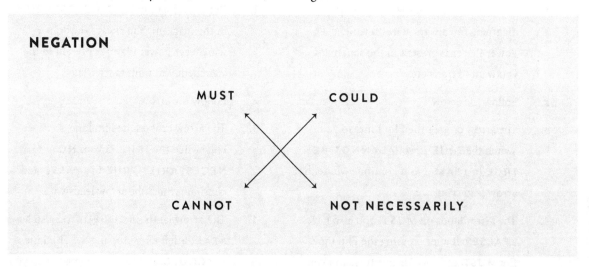

**NEGATION**

MUST        COULD

CANNOT        NOT NECESSARILY

You may have noticed that the Flip Line is missing from our Negation Chart. In the Equivalence Chart, every time you crossed from the positive side of the spectrum to the negative side (or vice versa) you had to flip your truthiness indicator to keep your statement's meaning consistent. You didn't want the meaning to be negated so you had to take that extra step. Now that we actually want to negate our statement, we don't need the Flip Line anymore. **When we're negating, our truthiness indicator always stays the same.**

Just like before, I'll demo each of these pairs using **TRUE** as my starting point, but the process works exactly the same way when using **FALSE**.

**MUST BE TRUE ←—/—→ NOT NECESSARILY TRUE**

1. Put your finger on **MUST** in the diagram. You always start on whichever Power Player is present in the statement you want to negate.

2. Follow the arrow.

3. The arrow lands on **NOT NECESSARILY**. You still have a **TRUE**. Put **NOT NECESSARILY** and **TRUE** together, and you arrive at your Negation. The Negation of **MUST BE TRUE** is **NOT NECESSARILY TRUE**.

**Q.** *Why is* **NOT NECESSARILY TRUE** *the Negation of* **MUST BE TRUE**?

**A.** Add a "not" in front of **MUST**. This leaves you with "not **MUST**," which we know is just a clunky way of saying **NOT NECESSARILY**. So, **NOT NECESSARILY TRUE** is the negated half of **MUST BE TRUE**.

**NOT NECESSARILY TRUE ←—/—→ MUST BE TRUE**

1. Put your finger on **NOT NECESSARILY** in the diagram. You always start on whichever Power Player is present in the statement you want to negate.

2. Follow the arrow.

3. The arrow lands on **MUST**. You still have a **TRUE**. Put **MUST** and **TRUE** together, and you arrive at your Negation. The Negation of **NOT NECESSARILY TRUE** is **MUST BE TRUE**.

**Q.** *Why is* **MUST BE TRUE** *the Negation of* **NOT NECESSARILY TRUE**?

**A.** Subtract the "not" from **NOT NECESSARILY**. This leaves you with "necessarily," which we know is just a fancy way of saying **MUST**. So, **MUST BE TRUE** is the negated half of **NOT NECESSARILY TRUE**.

**CANNOT BE TRUE ←—/—→ COULD BE TRUE**

1.  Put your finger on **CANNOT** in the diagram. You always start on whichever Power Player is present in the statement you want to negate.

2.  Follow the arrow.

3.  The arrow lands on **COULD**. You still have a **TRUE**. Put **COULD** and **TRUE** together, and you arrive at your Negation. The Negation of **CANNOT BE TRUE** is **COULD BE TRUE**.

**Q.** *Why is* **COULD BE TRUE** *the Negation of* **CANNOT BE TRUE?**

**A.** Subtract the "not" from **CANNOT** and you are left with "can." This is a synonym for **COULD**, which leads us to see that **COULD BE TRUE** is the negated half of **CANNOT BE TRUE**.

**COULD BE TRUE ←—/—→ CANNOT BE TRUE**

1.  Put your finger on **COULD** in the diagram. You always start on whichever Power Player is present in the statement you want to negate.

2.  Follow the arrow.

3.  The arrow lands on **CANNOT**. You still have a **TRUE**. Put **CANNOT** and **TRUE** together, and you arrive at your Negation. The Negation of **COULD BE TRUE** is **CANNOT BE TRUE**.

**Q.** *Why is* **CANNOT BE TRUE** *the Negation of* **COULD BE TRUE?**

**A.** Add a "not" to **COULD** and you are left with "not **COULD**." That's super weird and hard to understand, so let's translate it. "Not **COULD**" basically means "not possible," which leads us to **CANNOT**. Therefore, **CANNOT BE TRUE** is the negated half of **COULD BE TRUE**.

---

**POWER PLAYERS GAME PLAN**

- Notice the Power Players when you see them in arguments.

- Remember how hard **MUST/CANNOT** are to prove.

- Remember how easy it is to prove **COULD/NOT NECESSARILY**.

- When you see a confounding wording combination like "**NOT NECESSARILY FALSE EXCEPT**," use the Power Players Charts to translate the statement.

DRILL

## Power Player Truthiness Drill

Now that you have the tools to manipulate the Power Players, let's put your skills to the test.

**INSTRUCTIONS**

*Answer each of the following questions using the charts provided in this chapter.*

**1.** What is the Negation of **NOT NECESSARILY TRUE**?

Must be True

**2.** What is the Equivalent of **COULD BE TRUE**?

Not Necessarily False

**3.** What is the Negation of **CANNOT BE FALSE**?

could be false

**4.** What is the Equivalent of **CANNOT BE TRUE**?

Must be false

**5.** What is the Negation of **MUST BE TRUE**?

could be false / Not necessary true

**6.** What is the Equivalent of **NOT NECESSARILY FALSE**?

could be true

*

*Where's the answer key?*

You'll find the answer key at the end of the chapter on page 89.

## Quiz 3  THE POWER PLAYERS

### INSTRUCTIONS

*Answer these questions based on your knowledge of the chapter. Attempt to answer without looking back at the chapter first. If you don't know the answer, circle the question number and go find the answer in the chapter. Study the sections of the chapter that you couldn't remember at first.*

### Word Bank

| | | |
|---|---|---|
| could | not | 100 |
| argument(s) | 0 | 99 |
| 1 | certainty | possibility |
| must | cannot | not necessarily |
| 95 | Loophole(s) | Inference(s) |

*Use the word bank to answer the fill-in-the-blank questions. Some words will not be used and others may be used more than once.*

**1.** Power Players are what make the _____ Argument _____ strong or weak.

**2.** When you don't see any indicators of certainty or uncertainty, you are handling a sentence that is claiming _____ Certainty _____.

**3.** Our job in argumentation is to prove that our conclusion is _____ 100 _____ % true.

**4.** Any gap between your premises is an opportunity for a(n) _____ Loophole _____.

**5.** Negation is the art of adding and subtracting a(n) "_____ Not _____."

**6.** Complete the table using the word bank.

| POWER PLAYER | CERTAINTY OR POSSIBILITY? | PERCENTAGE OF CERTAINTY/ POSSIBILITY INDICATED |
|---|---|---|
| Must | Certainty | 100% |
| CANNOT | Certainty | 100% |
| could | possibility | 1-100% |
| NOT NECESSARILY | possibility | 0 - 99% |

*Circle the correct answer to the following questions.*

**7.** TRUE OR ~~FALSE~~    Negation means the opposite.

**8.** TRUE OR ~~FALSE~~    A Certainty Premise is weak evidence.

**9.** ~~TRUE~~ OR FALSE    A Possibility Conclusion is easy to prove.

**10.** ~~TRUE~~ OR FALSE    In Logical Reasoning, valid conclusions are hard to come by.

**11.** TRUE OR ~~FALSE~~    When you're evaluating whether an argument is valid, you want to examine the argument in its most flattering interpretation.

*Where's the answer key?*

You'll find the answer key at the end of the chapter on page 90.

## Power Players & Argument Parts Drill   ANSWER KEY

**1.**     Therefore, there is the possibility of electric combat.
Could Conclusion

**2.**     Because we must enter the fray.
Must Premise

**3.**     Since Aubry cannot walk all the way to England.
Cannot Premise

**4.**     For Tony is simply not good enough to save us.
Must Premise or Cannot Premise

**5.**     Consequently, Smitten's claim does not necessarily follow.
Not Necessarily Conclusion

**6.**     Hence, the inevitable ostrich rise will soon come to pass.
Must Conclusion

**7.**     It is a given that humans are natural enemies of the bird.
Must Premise

**8.**     It follows that Australia may be the first to fall.
Could Conclusion

**9.**     Chris, therefore, cannot be sacrificed to their will.
Cannot Conclusion

**10.**    For it is not guaranteed that the greater hand will prevail.
Not Necessarily Premise

## Power Player Truthiness Drill    ANSWER KEY

**1.** What is the Negation of **NOT NECESSARILY TRUE**?

**MUST BE TRUE**

**2.** What is the Equivalent of **COULD BE TRUE**?

**NOT NECESSARILY FALSE**

**3.** What is the Negation of **CANNOT BE FALSE**?

**COULD BE FALSE**

**4.** What is the Equivalent of **CANNOT BE TRUE**?

**MUST BE FALSE**

**5.** What is the Negation of **MUST BE TRUE**?

**NOT NECESSARILY TRUE**

**6.** What is the Equivalent of **NOT NECESSARILY FALSE**?

**COULD BE TRUE**

## Quiz 3 ANSWER KEY

**1.** Power Players are what make the **argument** strong or weak.

**2.** When you don't see any indicators of certainty or uncertainty, you are handling a sentence that is claiming **certainty**.

**3.** Our job in argumentation is to prove that our conclusion is **100%** true.

**4.** Any gap between your premises is an opportunity for a **Loophole**.

**5.** Negation is the art of adding and subtracting a **"not."**

**6.**

| POWER PLAYER | CERTAINTY OR POSSIBILITY? | PERCENTAGE OF CERTAINTY/ POSSIBILITY INDICATED |
|---|---|---|
| **MUST** | Certainty | **100%** |
| **CANNOT** | **Certainty** | **0%** |
| **COULD** | **Possibility** | 1-100% |
| **NOT NECESSARILY** | **Possibility** | **0-99%** |

**7.** False. Negation is *not* the opposite.

**8.** False. A Certainty Premise is *strong* evidence.

**9.** True.

**10.** True.

**11.** False. When you're evaluating whether an argument is valid, you want to examine the argument in its most *unflattering* interpretation.

# OMMMM.

chapter three. see, you're free.

## Chapter Breather BASIC TRANSLATION DRILL

> The Basic Translation Drill is one of the most important things you can do to increase your LSAT score. Your work will pay off. Even if it may feel tedious at times, do not skip any part of this drill. For many students, this is the single biggest source of improvement for their LSAT score.

Now, we're going to put what you've learned into action! The Basic Translation Drill hones two important skills: reading and memory. Both of these competencies are crucial to your success in LR and the LSAT in general.

The goal of translation is to make the stimulus your own. The task is to understand what the stimulus says, process that understanding in your own words, and remember your translation.

### INSTRUCTIONS

*If you haven't actually read the first three chapters of this text, I highly recommend you do so before completing this drill. If you're a rebel, at least read the first chapter for an explanation of what translation is.*

**1.** Grab a clean LR section and start at question #1.

**2.** Read the stimulus well once. You can go back and re-read sentences as you go, as much as you want. Once you hit the last period at the end of the stimulus, you're done.

**3.** Cover up the stimulus with your hand.

**4.** In your head, say, "OK, so..." and tell yourself what happened in the stimulus. Do it casually, like you're explaining a story to a friend.

**5.** This explanation is your translation of the stimulus. Write your translation as a bulleted list in your notebook. Your goal is to reduce the stimulus to things that actually matter. By transforming the stimulus into your own words, you forget about the distracting jargon and focus more clearly.

Timing on the Basic Translation Drill varies widely per student based on previous reading experience and ability. One student, Margot, initially took two hours to complete one Basic Translation Drill. Only three drills later, she could complete the drill with significantly better accuracy in half the time. Another student, Katie, started out taking about 35 minutes to complete one drill and now takes 15 minutes with better accuracy. Your personal balance between reading speed and accuracy is the single greatest determinant of your Logical Reasoning speed; **this drill is how you can increase your reading speed while also increasing your accuracy.**

**6.** Read the stimulus again to see how close you were. Record where you were off base and why.

**7.** Proceed to the next question and repeat these steps until you reach the end of the section. Do not read the question stem or answer choices on any of your Basic Translation Drills.

Understanding what you read is the first step towards excelling in LR, but if you can't retain that understanding, it's worthless. That's where memory training comes in, and it's why covering up the stimulus with your hand is important, even if it's difficult at first.

**PRO TIPS**

- Do not attempt to rewrite the stimulus verbatim. Record what it means, not necessarily what it says.

- **Don't do the questions on Basic Translation Drills.** You are wasting irreplaceable resources by doing the questions before you know what they are. You can (and should) do the questions associated with your Basic Translation Drills later in your prep.

- Use bullet points. Don't write full sentences.

- Use symbols (=, ≠, etc.) and personal shorthand (abbreviations for names).

- If you get confused on a complicated stimulus, read it again with the premises first and the conclusion last. That way, it will seem like a more logical progression.

- Don't try to remember every single literal word. Translation is about meaning, not word sounds.

- Don't regurgitate the stimulus without processing it; get rid of the formalities.

- Handwrite your translation. Don't type it.

✳

Feel free to switch up the order of the argument parts when you translate! Some students find it helpful to recount the premises first and the conclusion last in their translations.

**The expert test taker holds a sieve to the test and filters out the signal from the noise.** This is the task of translation. There is a lot of noise on the LSAT, which is why this skill is so important.

Getting the stimulus down to a bulleted list makes your analytical task a lot easier. Are some things lost? Sure, but **you're creating bookmarks for your thought process**, not trying to remember every single word. If your translations are significantly more complicated than the ones in the answer key in the upcoming drill, you're not going far enough to get rid of the noise.

You may be wondering what you'll do if the question asks about the exact wording of the stimulus. In that case, it's awesome that you still have the stimulus sitting there waiting for you to look up exact words. No one is going to be able to remember every single word verbatim; few people actively try to remember the stimulus at all. You have a huge leg up retaining as much as you do when you translate.

You can (and should!) do the Basic Translation Drill on any LR section. I'm supplying you with two LR sections to translate right here in this text, so you can compare your translations to mine. After you translate these sections, look at the Basic Translation Drill Answer Key online and identify the differences between our translations. Make notes for improvement and complete the Basic Translation Drill Debrief.

There are only two Basic Translation Drills inside this book because it can only be so long, but this does not imply that you should be done with Basic Translation Drills after completing these two. **Most students, especially those who miss more than five per LR section on their blind diagnostic, require far more than two Basic Translation Drills to maximize their LR speed and accuracy.**

> If the Basic Translation Drill is not easy, you need to do it until it becomes easy, even if that means doing a week (or more!) of nothing but Basic Translation Drills.

I know you probably don't want to keep doing Basic Translation Drills until they're easy. You want to get to the questions because that's when it feels like you're "doing the LSAT." But I can tell you that if the Basic Translation Drill is not easy, the questions will be exponentially harder and you will not understand why you are getting them wrong. In order to find success with the questions, you need to minimize your misreads. This is what the Basic Translation Drill is for, so it's not a step you should rush. **Just doing this drill for a week straight has taken previously-plateaued students from missing 10-12 per section to missing 1-3 per section.**

Let's start with an example:

*June 2007.2.1*

Economist:   Every business strives to increase its productivity, for this increases profits for the owners and the likelihood that the business will survive. But not all efforts to increase productivity are beneficial to the business as a whole. Often, attempts to increase productivity decrease the number of employees, which clearly harms the dismissed employees as well as the sense of security of the retained employees.

**TRANSLATION**

- Every business wants more productivity, leads to more owner profits and business survival

- But not every productivity effort is good for the whole business

- Productivity efforts decrease employees = harms fired people, makes other employees less secure

You may notice that we are using all the LR from the June 2007 test for the Basic Translation Drill, CLIR Drill, and full section practice. Using this particular test is a purposeful choice. Since June 2007 is the free test, it's the most likely test to be used for a blind diagnostic score. Usually, we never examine our first diagnostic again, but this is a wasted opportunity. If you've seen these questions before, that's totally fine. You've never used them the way you're going to use them in these drills. By reusing June 2007, you get to employ the questions for a different pedagogical purpose; plus I don't take away a recent test from your practice test arsenal.

Notice that this translation wasn't formal. In fact, you'll never see me be more grammatically sloppy than in the Basic Translation Drill Answer Keys. The translations in the answer keys are more verbose than they would be if I wrote them out for my personal use. This is because you have to be able to understand what the answer key means. I would typically use more abbreviations, symbols, and disjointed language. But *your translation doesn't have to make sense to anyone but you*, and if it does, you're probably doing too much work.

**YOU CAN DO THIS EVEN IF IT'S DIFFICULT RIGHT NOW**

It's normal to not remember the stimulus at first. It's normal to not understand the stimulus in the beginning. This is especially true if you aren't a big reader or if English is not your first language. There is nothing wrong with it being difficult in the beginning. But you can't give up. You will get better by doing this drill. You must do it until it becomes effortless.

Do the first Basic Translation Drill now and check it online before doing the second Basic Translation Drill. You want to learn from the first one to more finely hone your skills in the second one.

**WHERE'S THE ANSWER KEY?**

Online! Go to **elementalprep.com/bonus** to check your answers.

# Basic Translation Drill   JUNE 2007, SECTION 2

**TRANSLATION**

**1.**  Economist:   Every business strives to increase its productivity, for this increases profits for the owners and the likelihood that the business will survive. But not all efforts to increase productivity are beneficial to the business as a whole. Often, attempts to increase productivity decrease the number of employees, which clearly harms the dismissed employees as well as the sense of security of the retained employees.

- Every business wants more productivity, leads to more owner profits and business survival

- But not every productivity effort is good for the whole business

- Productivity efforts decrease employees = harms fired people, makes other employees less secure

**2.**  All Labrador retrievers bark a great deal. All Saint Bernards bark infrequently. Each of Rosa's dogs is a cross between a Labrador retriever and a Saint Bernard. Therefore, Rosa's dogs are moderate barkers.

L → a lot

SB → J.A.P.refrequent

her dogs are a mix

↳ so moderate

**3.**  A century in certain ways is like a life, and as the end of a century approaches, people behave toward that century much as someone who is nearing the end of life does toward that life. So just as people in their last years spend much time looking back on the events of their life, people at a century's end _____.

Centurys = life

at the end of life people look back

Similarly at the end of centuries ___

**4.**  Consumer:   The latest *Connorly Report* suggests that Ocksenfrey prepackaged meals are virtually devoid of nutritional value. But the Connorly Report is commissioned by Danto Foods, Ocksenfrey's largest corporate rival, and early drafts of the report are submitted for approval to Danto Foods' public relations department. Because of the obvious bias of this report, it is clear that Ocksenfrey's prepackaged meals really are nutritious.

O ≠ Nutritious says report

but report by rival

clear bias

so O meals must have

nutritional value

**5.**  Scientist:   Earth's average annual temperature has increased by about 0.5 degrees Celsius over the last century. This warming is primarily the result of the buildup of minor gases in the atmosphere, blocking the outward flow of heat from the planet.

.5° ↑ due to minor

gases preventing gas from escaping

✳

Really. Seriously. This is my solemn plea.

**Never answer the questions on your Basic Translation Drills.**

Answering the questions during a Basic Translation Drill distracts from the immediate goal: improving your reading and memory. This distraction delays your translation improvement, which will keep you on this step longer.

Plus, you don't want to burn irreplaceable materials when you're not in a position to do your absolute best at answering questions *yet*. You can come back to the Basic Translation Drill questions after you've read the Powerful-Provable Primer and Chapters 9-12! The info contained there will help a ton in answering the questions, so focus your time where it should be for now: translation, translation, translation.

**6.** An undergraduate degree is necessary for appointment to the executive board. Further, no one with a felony conviction can be appointed to the board. Thus, Murray, an accountant with both a bachelor's and a master's degree, cannot be accepted for the position of Executive Administrator, since he has a felony conviction.

*AB → GD*
*CF → A̸B̸*
*GD*
*CF → A̸B̸*

**7.** Ethicist: The most advanced kind of moral motivation is based solely on abstract principles. This form of motivation is in contrast with calculated self-interest or the desire to adhere to societal norms and conventions.

*Moral motivation → abstract*
*vs.*
*Self interest → social norms*

**8.** Proponents of the electric car maintain that when the technical problems associated with its battery design are solved, such cars will be widely used and, because they are emission-free, will result in an abatement of the environmental degradation caused by auto emissions. But unless we dam more rivers, the electricity to charge these batteries will come from nuclear or coal-fired power plants. Each of these three power sources produces considerable environmental damage. Thus, the electric car _____ .

*when battery = solved*
*EV widely used and will*
*solve E. problems*
*if more dammed*
*then the electricity source*
*will harm environment*

**9.** Although video game sales have increased steadily over the past 3 years, we can expect a reversal of this trend in the very near future. Historically, over three quarters of video games sold have been purchased by people from 13 to 16 years of age, and the number of people in this age group is expected to decline steadily over the next 10 years.

*- 3yr VG ↑*
*- expected to ↓*
*- # in 13-16 ↓ , primary consumers*

**10.** Double-blind techniques should be used whenever possible in scientific experiments. They help prevent the misinterpretations that often arise due to expectations and opinions that scientists already hold, and clearly scientists should be extremely diligent in trying to avoid such misinterpretations.

*- double blind ✓*
*prevent personal bias*
*should not misinterpret*

**11.** It is now a common complaint that the electronic media have corroded the intellectual skills required and fostered by the literary media. But several centuries ago the complaint was that certain intellectual skills, such as the powerful memory and extemporaneous eloquence that were intrinsic to oral culture, were being destroyed by the spread of literacy. So, what awaits us is probably a mere alteration of the human mind rather than its devolution.

- Intellect destroyed E. media
- Centuries ago Intellect destroyed by literacy
- ~ alteration difference to now we view Internet

**12.** Suppose I have promised to keep a confidence and someone asks me a question that I cannot answer truthfully without thereby breaking the promise. Obviously, I cannot both keep and break the same promise. Therefore, one cannot be obliged both to answer all questions truthfully and to keep all promises.

- Keep a promise
- asks a question that break promise
- Cannot be truthful & keep all promise

**13.** Standard aluminum soft-drink cans do not vary in the amount of aluminum that they contain. Fifty percent of the aluminum contained in a certain group (M) of standard aluminum soft-drink cans was recycled from another group (L) of used, standard aluminum soft-drink cans. Since all the cans in L were recycled into cans in M and since the amount of material other than aluminum in an aluminum can is negligible, it follows that M contains twice as many cans as L.

Aluminum amount same → cans
All L was recycled to M

cans
M has 2x that than L

**14.** A cup of raw milk, after being heated in a microwave oven to 50 degrees Celsius, contains half its initial concentration of a particular enzyme, lysozyme. If, however, the milk reaches that temperature through exposure to a conventional heat source of 50 degrees Celsius, it will contain nearly all of its initial concentration of the enzyme. Therefore, what destroys the enzyme is not heat but microwaves, which generate heat.

or 50
Milk in Microwave at half enzyme
Milk in Clt at 50 full enzyme
nt the heat but microwave that destroys enzyme

**15.** A new government policy has been developed to avoid many serious cases of influenza. This goal will be accomplished by the annual vaccination of high-risk individuals: everyone 65 and older as well as anyone with a chronic disease that might cause them to experience complications from the influenza virus. Each year's vaccination will protect only against the strain of the influenza virus deemed most likely to be prevalent that year, so every year it will be necessary for all high-risk individuals to receive a vaccine for a different strain of the virus.

New policy preventing flu
vaccinate old & high risk
vacc. for most likely to be prevalent strain
each year, preventers will get a different shot for a different strain

**16.** Taylor:   Researchers at a local university claim that 61 percent of the information transferred during a conversation is communicated through nonverbal signals. But this claim, like all such mathematically precise claims, is suspect, because claims of such exactitude could never be established by science.

Sandra:   While precision is unobtainable in many areas of life, it is commonplace in others. Many scientific disciplines obtain extremely precise results, which should not be doubted merely because of their precision.

**17.** Hospital executive:   At a recent conference on nonprofit management, several computer experts maintained that the most significant threat faced by large institutions such as universities and hospitals is unauthorized access to confidential data. In light of this testimony, we should make the protection of our clients' confidentiality our highest priority.

**18.** Modern science is built on the process of posing hypotheses and testing them against observations—in essence, attempting to show that the hypotheses are incorrect. Nothing brings more recognition than overthrowing conventional wisdom. It is accordingly unsurprising that some scientists are skeptical of the widely accepted predictions of global warming. What is instead remarkable is that with hundreds of researchers striving to make breakthroughs in climatology, very few find evidence that global warming is unlikely.

**19.** Historian:   The Land Party achieved its only national victory in Banestria in 1935. It received most of its support that year in rural and semirural areas, where the bulk of Banestria's population lived at the time. The economic woes of the years surrounding that election hit agricultural and small business interests the hardest, and the Land Party specifically targeted those groups in 1935. I conclude that the success of the Land Party that year was due to the combination of the Land Party's specifically addressing the concerns of these groups and the depth of the economic problems people in these groups were facing.

**20.** Gamba: Muñoz claims that the Southwest Hopeville Neighbors Association overwhelmingly opposes the new water system, citing this as evidence of citywide opposition. The association did pass a resolution opposing the new water system, but only 25 of 350 members voted, with 10 in favor of the system. Furthermore, the 15 opposing votes represent far less than 1 percent of Hopeville's population. One should not assume that so few votes represent the view of the majority of Hopeville's residents.

- City against water bill b/c opposed by Assoc.
- Assoc. 15/350 voted for
- less than 1% of popuan
- cannot be used to show city wide disapproval

**21.** Driver: My friends say I will one day have an accident because I drive my sports car recklessly. But I have done some research, and apparently minivans and larger sedans have very low accident rates compared to sports cars. So trading my sports car in for a minivan would lower my risk of having an accident.

- minivans & larger sedans than SC
- true in SC for minivan
- less likely to have accident

**22.** Editorialist: News media rarely cover local politics thoroughly, and local political business is usually conducted secretively. These factors each tend to isolate local politicians from their electorates. This has the effect of reducing the chance that any particular act of resident participation will elicit a positive official response, which in turn discourages resident participation in local politics.

- local politics secret & rarely covered
- isolates politicians from locals
- less likely that one act will get a positive to respond
- discourages political participation

**23.** Philosopher: An action is morally right if it would be reasonably expected to increase the aggregate well-being of the people affected by it. An action is morally wrong if and only if it would be reasonably expected to reduce the aggregate well-being of the people affected by it. Thus, actions that would be reasonably expected to leave unchanged the aggregate well-being of the people affected by them are also right.

- Right → ↑ well being
- wrong → reduce well being
- unchange → Right

**24.** Car companies solicit consumer information on such human factors as whether a seat is comfortable or whether a set of controls is easy to use. However, designer interaction with consumers is superior to survey data; the data may tell the designer why a feature on last year's model was given a low rating, but data will not explain how that feature needs to be changed in order to receive a higher rating.

- ask people about car features
- designer superior to surveys
- designer interactions allow consumer to explain why

**25.** During the nineteenth century, the French academy of art was a major financial sponsor of painting and sculpture in France; sponsorship by private individuals had decreased dramatically by this time. Because the academy discouraged innovation in the arts, there was little innovation in nineteenth century French sculpture. Yet nineteenth century French painting showed a remarkable degree of innovation.

- Academy - most of Art
- private ownership ↓
- Academy - innovation
- innovation in Sculpture ↓
- " in painting ↑

We're looking out for your heavy backpack and putting the Basic Translation Drill Answer Key and Study Planner online: elementalprep.com/bonus

## Basic Translation Drill   JUNE 2007, SECTION 3

**TRANSLATION**

**1.**

Situation:   Someone living in a cold climate buys a winter coat that is stylish but not warm in order to appear sophisticated.

Analysis:   People are sometimes willing to sacrifice sensual comfort or pleasure for the sake of appearances.

*S - buy winter coat for style not appearing*

*A - Some sacrifice comfort for style*

**2.**

After replacing his old gas water heater with a new, pilotless, gas water heater that is rated as highly efficient, Jimmy's gas bills increased.

*replaced old w/ more efficient gas bill increased after*

**3.**

Carolyn:   The artist Marc Quinn has displayed, behind a glass plate, biologically replicated fragments of Sir John Sulston's DNA, calling it a "conceptual portrait" of Sulston. But to be a portrait, something must bear a recognizable resemblance to its subject.

Arnold:   I disagree. Quinn's conceptual portrait is a maximally realistic portrait, for it holds actual instructions according to which Sulston was created.

*C - portrait using DNA but to be a P needs to be recognized*

*A - disagree, is highly realistic*
*- holds real instructions of Arnold*

**4.**

Many corporations have begun decorating their halls with motivational posters in hopes of boosting their employees' motivation to work productively. However, almost all employees at these corporations are already motivated to work productively. So these corporations' use of motivational posters is unlikely to achieve its intended purpose.

*- decorated halls w/ Motivate*
*posters to improve productivity*
*- employees already motivated*
*- unlikely to improve productivity*

**5.** Atrens: An early entomologist observed ants carrying particles to neighboring ant colonies and inferred that the ants were bringing food to their neighbors. Further research, however, revealed that the ants were emptying their own colony's dumping site. Thus, the early entomologist was wrong.

○: Ants bringing food to other colonies
- actually Ants are emptying
  empty a dump site
- When O is wrong

**6.** Jablonski, who owns a car dealership, has donated cars to driver education programs at area schools for over five years. She found the statistics on car accidents to be disturbing, and she wanted to do something to encourage better driving in young drivers. Some members of the community have shown their support for this action by purchasing cars from Jablonski's dealership.

- J donates cars to Edu. prog.
- disturbed by # of accidents
- ↑ Sales at J's dealership increased

**7.** Antonio: One can live a life of moderation by never deviating from the middle course. But then one loses the joy of spontaneity and misses the opportunities that come to those who are occasionally willing to take great chances, or to go too far.

Marla: But one who, in the interests of moderation, never risks going too far is actually failing to live a life of moderation: one must be moderate even in one's moderation.

A: living in moderation eliminates spontaneity and prevents individuals from fully enjoying life

M: In order to be truly moderate need to be spontaneous,
- moderate in moderation

**8.** Advertisement: Fabric-Soft leaves clothes soft and fluffy, and its fresh scent is a delight. We conducted a test using over 100 consumers to prove Fabric-Soft is best. Each consumer was given one towel washed with Fabric-Soft and one towel washed without it. Ninety-nine percent of the consumers preferred the Fabric-Soft towel. So Fabric-Soft is the most effective fabric softener available.

- Fabric Soft softens clothes makes nice
- wants to prove it the best
- test with towel in FS + one w/o
- 99% preferred one w/ FS
- FS is the best FS out there.

**9.** Naturalist:   The recent claims that the Tasmanian tiger is not extinct are false. The Tasmanian tiger's natural habitat was taken over by sheep farming decades ago, resulting in the animal's systematic elimination from the area. Since then naturalists working in the region have discovered no hard evidence of its survival, such as carcasses or tracks. In spite of alleged sightings of the animal, the Tasmanian tiger no longer exists.

- Claims TT exists are false
- were systematically eliminated by sheep farmer
- no trace of existence (tracks ex)
- is extinct despite alleged sightings

**10.** Advertisers have learned that people are more easily encouraged to develop positive attitudes about things toward which they originally have neutral or even negative attitudes if those things are linked, with pictorial help rather than exclusively through prose, to things about which they already have positive attitudes. Therefore, advertisers are likely to _____.

More likely to be positive about something they feel neutral or negative about if that thing is visually linked to a positive association

**11.** Feathers recently taken from seabirds stuffed and preserved in the 1880s have been found to contain only half as much mercury as feathers recently taken from living birds of the same species. Since mercury that accumulates in a seabird's feathers as the feathers grow is derived from fish eaten by the bird, these results indicate that mercury levels in saltwater fish are higher now than they were 100 years ago.

- feathers in 1880s have 1/2 mercury from feathers now
- Mercury comes from fish eaten
- Fish now have more mercury

**12.** Novel X and Novel Y are both semiautobiographical novels and contain many very similar themes and situations, which might lead one to suspect plagiarism on the part of one of the authors. However, it is more likely that the similarity of themes and situations in the two novels is merely coincidental, since both authors are from very similar backgrounds and have led similar lives.

- X & Y similar book
- some suspect saying plagiarism
- not plagiarism b/c both authors came from similar backgrounds

**13.** Therapist:   Cognitive psychotherapy focuses on changing a patient's conscious beliefs. Thus, cognitive psychotherapy is likely to be more effective at helping patients overcome psychological problems than are forms of psychotherapy that focus on changing unconscious beliefs and desires, since only conscious beliefs are under the patient's direct conscious control.

- CP changes conscious beliefs
- more effective than changing a patients unconscious beliefs because conscious beliefs are under patients direct control

**14.** Commentator:    In academic scholarship, sources are always cited, and methodology and theoretical assumptions are set out, so as to allow critical study, replication, and expansion of scholarship. In open-source software, the code in which the program is written can be viewed and modified by individual users for their purposes without getting permission from the producer or paying a fee. In contrast, the code of proprietary software is kept secret, and modifications can be made only by the producer, for a fee. This shows that open-source software better matches the values embodied in academic scholarship, and since scholarship is central to the mission of universities, universities should use only open-source software.

**15.** A consumer magazine surveyed people who had sought a psychologist's help with a personal problem. Of those responding who had received treatment for 6 months or less, 20 percent claimed that treatment "made things a lot better." Of those responding who had received longer treatment, 36 percent claimed that treatment "made things a lot better." Therefore, psychological treatment lasting more than 6 months is more effective than shorter-term treatment.

**16.** Philosopher:    Nations are not literally persons; they have no thoughts or feelings, and, literally speaking, they perform no actions. Thus they have no moral rights or responsibilities. But no nation can survive unless many of its citizens attribute such rights and responsibilities to it, for nothing else could prompt people to make the sacrifices national citizenship demands. Obviously, then, a nation _____.

**17.** When exercising the muscles in one's back, it is important, in order to maintain a healthy back, to exercise the muscles on opposite sides of the spine equally. After all, balanced muscle development is needed to maintain a healthy back, since the muscles on opposite sides of the spine must pull equally in opposing directions to keep the back in proper alignment and protect the spine.

**18.** Editorialist:   In all cultures, it is almost universally accepted that one has a moral duty to prevent members of one's family from being harmed. Thus, few would deny that if a person is known by the person's parents to be falsely accused of a crime, it would be morally right for the parents to hide the accused from the police. Hence, it is also likely to be widely accepted that it is sometimes morally right to obstruct the police in their work.

- Morally right to protect family from harm
- Morally right to hide a falsely accused family member
- Therefore it is sometimes morally right to obstruct police

**19.** Editor:   Many candidates say that if elected they will reduce governmental intrusion into voters' lives. But voters actually elect politicians who instead promise that the government will provide assistance to solve their most pressing problems. Governmental assistance, however, costs money, and money can come only from taxes, which can be considered a form of governmental intrusion. Thus, governmental intrusion into the lives of voters will rarely be substantially reduced over time in a democracy.

- candidates claim that if elected, will be less intrusive
- however people wish for govt assistance
- govt assistance requires taxes which = intrusion
- unlikely that govt intrusion will be reduced in democracy

**20.** We should accept the proposal to demolish the old train station, because the local historical society, which vehemently opposes this, is dominated by people who have no commitment to long-term economic well-being. Preserving old buildings creates an impediment to new development, which is critical to economic health.

- Should demolish building
- people opposing do not have long term interest
- And the old building prevents construction of new buildings

**21.** Ethicist:   On average, animals raised on grain must be fed sixteen pounds of grain to produce one pound of meat. A pound of meat is more nutritious for humans than a pound of grain, but sixteen pounds of grain could feed many more people than could a pound of meat. With grain yields leveling off, large areas of farmland going out of production each year, and the population rapidly expanding, we must accept the fact that consumption of meat will soon be morally unacceptable.

- 16 lbs grain = 1 lb meat
- 1 lb meat > 1 lb grain
- 16 lb grain > 16 lbs meat
- only grain leveling in products
- soon morally unacceptable to eat meat

**22.** If the price it pays for coffee beans continues to increase, the Coffee Shoppe will have to increase its prices. In that case, either the Coffee Shoppe will begin selling noncoffee products or its coffee sales will decrease. But selling noncoffee products will decrease the Coffee Shoppe's overall profitability. Moreover, the Coffee Shoppe can avoid a decrease in overall profitability only if its coffee sales do not decrease.

**23.** Political candidates' speeches are loaded with promises and with expressions of good intention, but one must not forget that the politicians' purpose in giving these speeches is to get themselves elected. Clearly, then, these speeches are selfishly motivated and the promises made in them are unreliable.

**24.** Sociologist: Romantics who claim that people are not born evil but may be made evil by the imperfect institutions that they form cannot be right, for they misunderstand the causal relationship between people and their institutions. After all, institutions are merely collections of people.

**25.** Some anthropologists argue that the human species could not have survived prehistoric times if the species had not evolved the ability to cope with diverse natural environments. However, there is considerable evidence that *Australopithecus afarensis*, a prehistoric species related to early humans, also thrived in a diverse array of environments, but became extinct. Hence, the anthropologists' claim is false.

Your backpack just got preemptively lighter! We put the Basic Translation Drill Answer Key and Study Planner online: elementalprep.com/bonus

106

# CONDITIONAL
# REASONING

# The Art of the If/Then

Conditional reasoning is the art of the if/then. If one thing happens, then another thing must happen. That's it.

Let's explore our first conditional relationship:

*If I'm breathing, then air is present.*

Because you're a thinking human, you can probably guess what this means at a literal level. If I'm breathing, there's air around. The core of the relationship is that simple. If we have one thing, we *must* have the other thing. Just like with the Power Players, we have to take this **MUST** seriously. There is no way around this relationship. If you have the first thing, you have to have the second thing.

For all the ballyhoo about conditional reasoning, you would think it's a lot more complicated than that. The key to keeping conditional reasoning simple through its many applications, which we will examine in detail throughout this chapter, is understanding the concept behind it. I want you to intuitively understand the relationship at the heart of conditionals. Once you have that, the verbal idiosyncrasies that separate one conditional from another will be nothing more than blips on the radar.

Let's start by taking our conditional example apart piece by piece.

### THE SUFFICIENT CONDITION

> The "if" part of the conditional is called the sufficient condition.

*If I'm breathing, then air is present.*

The sufficient condition is a door opener. It's welcoming. It could occur, but it doesn't have to. Just like an open door, someone may walk in, but they don't have to. In the example, I might be breathing or I might not: I could be holding my breath trying to get rid of hiccups or I could be breathing. We don't know. We just know what will happen if I *am* breathing.

**If the sufficient condition is absent, you can completely ignore the conditional statement.** If I'm not breathing, this conditional doesn't matter at all. There might be air; there might not be air. The conditional wasn't activated, so who cares? I'm not breathing, so it doesn't matter.

**But if the sufficient condition is present, the conditional statement must be followed.** If I am breathing, there absolutely 100% has to be air. The conditional statement gets activated and everything goes according to plan.

*What does it mean to activate a conditional?*

It means the sufficient condition is present! So the conditional must be followed.

The sufficient condition extends beyond just the word "if." There is a whole family of words that work just like "if"; they let you know you have a sufficient condition on your hands.

Here are the members of the sufficient family:

| SUFFICIENT INDICATORS | EXAMPLE |
|---|---|
| if | *If I'm breathing, then air is present.* |
| when(ever) | *When I'm breathing, air is present.* |
| | *Whenever I'm breathing, air is present.* |
| any(time) | *Any breathing requires that air is present.* |
| | *Anytime I'm breathing, air is present.* |
| all | *All instances of breathing have air present.* |
| every(time) | *Every instance of breathing has air present.* |
| | *Everytime I'm breathing, air is present.* |
| in order to | *In order to breathe, I must have air.* |
| people who | *People who breathe need air.* |
| each | *Each instance of breathing has air.* |

Notice how all of the sufficient family members have similar personalities. They are all inclusive, open words. Think back to the similarities between these words if/when you get lost in complex language.

I had to smooth out some of the linguistic rough edges to translate that conditional into all the different versions, but the core relationship remained the same. **Language is the challenge of conditionals; you have to distill the same conditional relationship from many different wording combinations.** This is why it's so important to understand the relationship on a deeper level than "look for indicator words." The words are the hard part, so relying on indicators exclusively is a ticking time bomb.

*What's with all the parentheses? What does when(ever) mean?*

The parentheses are referring to an optional addition to the original word. Both "when" and "whenever" are members of the sufficient family. Conditionally, all of the examples in the chart above mean exactly the same thing as our initial example.

## THE NECESSARY CONDITION

> The "then" part of the conditional is called the necessary condition.

*If I'm breathing,* **then air is present.**

The necessary condition slams the door that the sufficient condition opens. It is the place of certainty. I mean just look at its name: It's called the *necessary* condition because it is literally necessary. It has to occur at some point if the conditional relationship is activated. You can prove things that live in the necessary condition.

There is a family of words that serves the same purpose as "then." Each of these words lets you know you have a necessary condition in play. Here are the members of the necessary family:

| NECESSARY INDICATORS | EXAMPLE |
|---|---|
| then | If I'm breathing, **then** air is present. |
| must | Air **must** be present for breathing. |
| necessary | Air is **necessary** for breathing. |
| required | Air is **required** for breathing. |
| only (if) | **Only** the presence of air allows for breathing. |
|  | I'm breathing, **only if** air is present. |
| depends | Breathing **depends** on air being present. |
| need (to) | I **need** air to breathe. |
| have to | I **have to** have air, if I'm breathing. |
| essential | Air is **essential** for breathing. |
| precondition | Air is a **precondition** for breathing. |

Notice the similarities in each of these words. They are all ironclad words. They are serious and restrictive. They are obligations.

All of those statements in the example column mean the exact same thing as the sufficient family examples. It is the exact same concept expressed in a bunch of different ways. What's important isn't how the conditional is expressed, but the core relationship hiding underneath the language. This is why we have a symbolic way of representing conditional relationships, to push past the language and focus only on the relationship between the two variables.

Pay special attention to **ONLY IF**. It is a necessary indicator, even though it contains the word **IF**. You can think of it like the **ONLY** is dominant over the recessive **IF**.

We will go over the symbolic way of representing conditionals shortly! It's called diagramming.

# The Contrapositive

So far, we've explored the sufficient condition, the necessary condition, and the relationship between the two. Specifically, we've gone over the core of the conditional relationship:

*If the sufficient condition occurs, then the necessary condition must occur.*

This relationship is ironclad. We'll call it the **Must Relationship**. Remember this as we explore a conditional thought experiment.

Imagine you're a coffee-obsessed individual. If you're walking, you're on your way to get a coffee. Getting a coffee is the only reason you ever walk anywhere. Every single time you walk, you are getting a coffee.

Now, imagine that you are not on your way to get a coffee.

What do you know about yourself?

Put your guess here: _____ you are not walking _____

STOP

Really try to figure this out right now. Don't read the solution until you have a guess. I put this question to every student. The ones that hazard a guess (either voluntarily or under protest) always come away better off.

If you are not on your way to get a coffee, you haven't met your necessary burden, right? So could you have activated your sufficient condition? NO.

**The fact that you are not on your way to get a coffee means you are not walking.**

> **REMEMBER!**    *If the necessary condition is absent, the sufficient condition is absent too. This is the contrapositive.*

As you've seen, the contrapositive can be produced organically. It is not some foreign process that needs to be performed on conditionals. **The contrapositive is sitting there within the original conditional, waiting to be recognized.** If you have not met your necessary burden, you cannot have activated the sufficient condition.

Let's return to our original example to see how its contrapositive looks:

> *If I'm breathing, then air is present.*

OK, so if I'm breathing, air is needed. I have to have air for the breathing to happen. The air is completely necessary. What if I don't have air? That means I don't have the thing I need. That implies that I couldn't have activated my conditional relationship. So, I can't be breathing. No necessary conditions means there's no sufficient condition.

**The original statement and its contrapositive are all you know from your conditional relationship.** The LSAT will try to tempt you into erroneously surmising other things from your conditional. Don't fall for these ploys. For example, they will give you a conditional statement, and then say, "We know the necessary condition is happening!" When they do this, you should be like, "Cool. So I can ignore the conditional." **The presence of the necessary condition doesn't make anything happen.**

Check out this chart showing what does *and does not* activate your conditional relationship:

| SITUATIONS | WHAT HAS TO HAPPEN? | IF I'M BREATHING, THEN AIR IS PRESENT. |
|---|---|---|
| Sufficient Present | *Must have necessary condition* | *I'm breathing, so there must be air.* |
| Necessary Absent | *Can't have sufficient condition* | *There's no air, so I can't breathe.* |
| Sufficient Absent | *Nothing!* | *There's no breathing happening, so we don't know anything else.* |
| Necessary Present | *Nothing!* | *There's air around, so we don't know anything else.* |

The first two rows of this chart represent the only two situations that make anything happen with your conditional relationship. The conditional is just a rule; it takes the right situation to activate it. Literally anything other than those two things can happen and you don't need to do anything with your conditional. **Without the situations in the first two rows of this chart, the conditional might as well not exist.**

# How to Diagram Conditionals

Now that we have a handle on the Must Relationship, let's take a look at how to represent it symbolically.

| IF $\longrightarrow$ | THEN |
|---|---|
| SUFFICIENT CONDITION | NECESSARY CONDITION |
| when(ever) | must |
| any(time) | necessary |
| all | required |
| every(time) | only (if) |
| in order to | depends |
| people who | need (to) |
| each | have to |
| | essential |
| | precondition |

Memorize these conditional indicators now. You *absolutely need* to be able to recognize these in the context of a Logical Reasoning stimulus or Logic Game.

## THE MUST ARROW

The conditional relationship is ideal for symbolic representation because it is always the same underneath the varying language. We symbolize the conditional relationship with one simple sign:

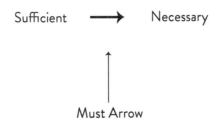

Sufficient $\longrightarrow$ Necessary

Must Arrow

We use the Must Arrow to signify the Must Relationship. It is a reminder of the urgency of conditionals. Every conditional relationship can be written like this. We call it diagramming the conditional.

A standard Must Arrow (the one we see most often) goes from left to right. There are other arrows, but we'll get to them later.

Here are your steps for diagramming a conditional relationship:

1.   See a conditional indicator.

2.   Draw a Must Arrow.

3.   Place an abbreviation of the word or phrase targeted by the conditional indicator on the correct side of the Must Arrow.

  • Sufficient is on the left, before the Must Arrow.

  • Necessary is on the right, after the Must Arrow.

4.   Fill in the other side of the Must Arrow with whatever is left over in the statement.

Let's take diagramming conditionals for a spin together. We'll start with our favorite statement:

*If I'm breathing, then air is present.*

I see a sufficient indicator in front of breathing, so I'll place a **B** in the sufficient condition:

**B ⟶**

Now, I'll fill in the other side of the Must Arrow with **A** for air, since that's what's left in the statement.

**B ⟶ A**

There you go. Your first fully diagrammed conditional! Now let's talk through the contrapositive. If the necessary condition is gone, we know the sufficient is gone as well. We can diagram the contrapositive as:

**~A ⟶ ~B**

Check out a few more contrapositive examples:

Step 3 is undoubtedly the most challenging. How do you know which word the indicator is targeting? What's targeting mean? Ahhhhhhhhhh! Stay strong. We will get to this in a second in the Figuring Out the Language section.

Check out the little squiggle (~) in front of the ~A and ~B. We'll use the squiggle throughout this text to negate variables. Read the squiggle as a "not."

### CONTRAPOSITIVES!

| ORIGINAL STATEMENT | EQUIVALENT CONTRAPOSITIVE |
| --- | --- |
| A ⟶ B | ~B ⟶ ~A |
| Q ⟶ ~R | R ⟶ ~Q |
| ~L ⟶ P | ~P ⟶ L |
| ~Y ⟶ ~X | X ⟶ Y |

Once you have the original statement written down, you can flip and negate both sides to quickly jot down the contrapositive.

I don't recommend diagramming the contrapositive on every conditional you encounter just for the sake of doing so, but sometimes it will be useful to write the conditional in its contrapositive form, either for clarity or to facilitate a chain. **Conditionals can be written either way: as the original statement or as the contrapositive.** Both statements are describing the same relationship.

---

Instead of writing the contrapositive out every time, you can just read the contrapositive when it's relevant. Every conditional can be read two ways:

1. Read it forwards from left to right.

2. Read it backwards from right to left, negating everything as you go (reading the contrapositive without having to write it out).

---

Awesome! Let's talk through some frequent diagramming issues together.

## QUICK CONDITIONAL DIAGRAMMING FAQ

**Q.** *When should I diagram a conditional?*

**A.** **In the *beginning*, you should always diagram conditionals.** This trains you to make sure you're actually thinking conditionally. The language in LR is your biggest obstacle. Diagramming the conditional gets rid of all the linguistic ambiguity. You don't have to look back at the text once you're sure you diagrammed the conditional correctly. (I'll get to how you'll be sure in a second. Hold tight.)

When you are more experienced, you should diagram whenever the stimulus is not easy. I always err on the side of diagramming; I think of it as using the paper to my advantage. If I can take down a note to free myself of the exact words of the stimulus, I'm going to do it. I see far more problems from students declining to diagram than I do from students who diagram too much. If there is more than one conditional in a stimulus, you should diagram them to see if there is chaining potential.

Besides timing concerns, I mostly see people decline to diagram because they aren't confident that their diagram will be correct, and they feel safer sticking to the exact words of the stimulus because then they "can't screw it up." But you need to fail a couple times in order to build the skill. That's how you get better. Don't give up before you start. This leads me to the next question.

**Q.** *How will I ever be sure my conditional is correctly diagrammed?*

**A.** Seeing it work out correctly enough times breeds confidence. In your Wrong Answer Journal, keep track of every time you incorrectly diagram a conditional and make note of exactly how the language tricked you. Study these errors so you don't make the same mistake again. **Your mistakes are your greatest asset.**

The only way to ever be 100% sure that your diagram is right is confidence in your own abilities. There will never be a little green checkmark that spontaneously appears on the page to tell you that you're right.

Everyone messes this up in the beginning. You can't let that kill your confidence. Do the work, build the skill, and you will eventually know that you're right.

**Q.** *But diagramming takes sooooo much time. I need to be fast. Do I really have to?*

**A.** Diagramming does not take nearly as much time as you imagine it does. There is a huge gap between perception and reality when it comes to LR timing. It takes a lot less time to diagram than it does to reread a difficult sentence ad infinitum. Writing things down frees up mental resources for other tasks. You need all the mental power you can get when you're doing LR, so use the paper to your advantage.

Also, you have to walk before you can run. You're not going to be fast at first and that's ok. This book contains strategies designed to help you get faster, but you're not there yet, and attempting to get there now will only delay your progress toward mastering these concepts.

**Q.** *Should I always diagram the contrapositive?*

**A.** No. Many people claim that always diagramming the contrapositive saves time, but it actually ends up costing you much more time than it saves, especially on Logic Games. You should understand conditional reasoning on a deep enough level to look at the original conditional diagram and know that the contrapositive is also true (reading the contrapositive instead of writing it). This works for the same reason you knew the contrapositive was true in our initial contrapositive thought experiment. The contrapositive is not a separate statement. It is contained within the original statement. If you can write it, you can already read it, so don't waste time putting extra noise on the paper.

That said, there are times when diagramming the contrapositive is useful, and you should definitely diagram it if you have a reason to do so. Sometimes you'll need the contrapositive to facilitate a chain. Just don't write the contrapositive out of habit and you'll do great.

**Q.** *What's this abbreviation stuff?*

**A.** When you diagram, you should shorten each condition to a capital letter or two. For example:

*If I'm a chair, then I'm furniture.*

We would shorten the "chair" to **C** and shorten the "furniture" to **F**. Ending up with this diagram:

$$C \longrightarrow F$$

For more complex conditions, just use the minimum number of letters that you will actually understand. Say one of the conditions is "maximum return on investment," you should shorten that to **MRI** or **MR**. Whichever option calls up the condition in your mind will work. **Don't write out the whole word or more than four letters per condition.** The notation becomes cumbersome when you write more than that.

You'll diagram the contrapositive in all the drills in this chapter. Why? I want to verify that you have the ability to identify the contrapositive. Once you see that your contrapositives match the drill answer keys, you'll be more confident simply reading the contrapositive in your head from the original statement.

# Figuring Out The Language

Let's tackle the biggest challenge in conditional reasoning: figuring out the language. We'll start by returning to our first example and pointing out the target of each indicator word.

**The indicator's target is the word or phrase it is referring to.**

In this list, I put the conditional indicator's target in a little bracket cage.

If [I'm breathing], then air is present.

When [I'm breathing], air is present.

Any [breathing] means air is present.

All [instances of breathing] have air present.

Every [instance of breathing] has air present.

In order to [breathe], I must have air.

People who [breathe] need air.

Each [instance of breathing] has air.

I'm breathing, only if [air is present].

Only [the presence of air] allows for breathing.

Breathing depends on [air being present].

I need [air] to breathe.

I have to have [air], if I'm breathing.

Notice that in each of these examples, the indicator is right before its target. This will be the case in the majority of conditional statements you read, but acting on the generalization that the indicator is always immediately before its target will lead you into trouble. This generalization isn't always true:

[Air] must be present for breathing.

[Air] is necessary for breathing.

[Air] is required for breathing.

[Air] is essential for breathing.

[Air] is a precondition for breathing.

In these examples, the target precedes the indicator. Why do they have to make it so difficult, you ask? Because the LSAT wants you to understand what the sentence is really saying. They don't want you to see an indicator word and go on autopilot. You also cannot generalize that these specific necessary indicators will always come after their target. Each of them can switch sides. Look at the variations on a few of these conditionals:

[Air] must be present for breathing. / There must be [air] for us to breathe.

[Air] is necessary for breathing. / Breathing makes it necessary to have [air].

[Air] is required for breathing. / I require [air] to breathe.

Seems hard, right? What can you do to make it easier for yourself? The What Test.

## THE WHAT TEST

**The way you can get around all this ambiguity is by taking the time to actually understand what the sentence is telling you.** When you see an indicator and you have even a little doubt about its target, ask yourself one question:

> What is the indicator referring to?

The What Test is simple. You can perform it by adding a "what" to whichever side of the indicator makes grammatical sense.

Here's how you perform the What Test:

| | | |
|---|---|---|
| *If what?* | *People who what?* | *Depends on what?* |
| *When what?* | *Each what?* | *Need what?* |
| *Any what?* | *Must what?* | *Have to what?* |
| *All what?* | *What's necessary?* | *What's essential?* |
| *Every what?* | *What's required?* | *What's the precondition?* |
| *In order to what?* | *Only (if) what?* | |

The What Test will probably not be necessary for the indicators like "if" and "all" because their target is clear. With some of the more confusing necessary indicators, like "depends" and "required," you may use the What Test more. Here's an example of how the What Test could get you out of a verbal jam.

> *Air is required for breathing. / I require air to breathe.*

We'll start with the first of this pair and see how the What Test works:

> *Air is required for breathing.*

What is required in this sentence? Air is the thing that is required. The sentence literally says, "Air is required," so this is a pretty straightforward example. Because air is required, we know it's in the necessary condition.

> *I require air to breathe.*

What is required in this sentence? Or more specifically, what do I require? I require air. That's the thing I need. So I know that it is in the necessary condition.

The What Test probably seems simple to you, and it is. However, it is only simple because I'm taking the split second to actually understand the sentence and figure out what "require" is referring to. You can do this too! Just be sure to take your time with conditionals in the beginning and you'll be lightning quick in a couple weeks.

# Your Friend, the Personalized If/Then

> Personalized if/thens are translations for conditionals.

Here's another safeguard on conditional diagramming. **Make a habit of translating conditionals into personalized if/thens.**

**Personalized if/thens require you to put yourself in the conditional statement and ask yourself what you know about your situation.** This can get you out of confusion panic and back to the real world.

## HOW TO CREATE A PERSONALIZED IF/THEN

Imagine you're confused on what a conditional means. Instead of panicking:

1. Try to understand the casual, non-conditional meaning of the sentence.

2. Take a guess at which half of the statement is the sufficient condition.

3. Put yourself in your guess' situation and ask what you know about yourself.

4. If your guess is right, you will know that the necessary condition has to pertain.

Let's translate an example into a personalized if/then:

*Orchids depend on frequent conversation.*

Before you proceed, think about what this sentence means for real. You need to understand the casual, non-conditional meaning before you can check your personalized if/then against that meaning. The sentence means orchids need frequent conversation. First we'll guess that orchids is the sufficient condition and see if this fits with our casual meaning of the sentence:

> The key to intuitively understanding conditionals is personalizing them. Always put yourself in the shoes of the conditional, no matter what it's about.

So, if I'm an orchid, what do I know about me? I know that I have to have frequent conversation. I depend on frequent conversation. *If* I'm an orchid, *then* I have frequent conversation. This fits. It is the correct translation of the conditional.

Now, let's imagine that I guessed incorrectly and tried to see if frequent conversation could be the sufficient condition. The personalized if/then would help me catch my error:

So, if I'm a frequent conversation, what do I know about me? If I'm a frequent conversation, what do I need? Do I need an orchid? Ehh… I don't need anything, right? Orchids are the ones who need something in this sentence. If I'm frequent conversation, I don't *need* anything else. This tells me that frequent conversation is not the correct sufficient condition. This is how you can detect that you've made a mistake. It is the incorrect translation of the conditional.

**The personalized if/then is how I *always* do conditionals, unless they are already phrased as if/thens.** It gives me confidence throughout the test that I'm not making a mistake.

## Basic Conditional Drill   MUCH ADO ABOUT NOTHING

The conditional drills in this chapter are each inspired by Shakespeare plays, which you will see identified in the title of each drill. The lines are very lightly edited to highlight their conditionality, but these are more-or-less the real lines from Shakespeare. And yes, Shakespeare is *really* this outlandish; high school didn't do him justice.

### INSTRUCTIONS

*Diagram the following conditional statements. Don't be afraid to look back at the section, if you need any help.*

**1.**   If he were in my books, I'd burn my study.

**ORIGINAL**   IMB → BS

**CONTRAPOSITIVE**   B̸S̸ → I̸M̸B̸

**2.**   Every time I hear my dog bark at a crow, it's like hearing a man swear he loves me.

**ORIGINAL**   DB @ a crow → HMLM

**CONTRAPOSITIVE**   H̸M̸L̸M̸ → D̸B̸ @ a crow

**3.**   If I were a man, I would eat his heart in the marketplace.

**ORIGINAL**   M → EHH

**CONTRAPOSITIVE**   E̸H̸H̸ → M̸

**4.**   I am heart-burned an hour after whenever I see him.

**ORIGINAL**   See him → HB 1 hr

**CONTRAPOSITIVE**   H̸B̸ 1 hr → S̸e̸e̸ him

**5.**   Benedick is always a rare parrot-teacher.

**ORIGINAL**   B → RPT

**CONTRAPOSITIVE**   R̸P̸T̸ → B̸

*Where's the answer key?*

You'll find the answer key at the end of the chapter on page 148.

**6.**   Love requires me to transform into an oyster.

**ORIGINAL**   L → T into O

**CONTRAPOSITIVE**   T̸ into O̸ → L̸

# Conditional Chains

Conditional statements are like Legos. They are more interesting when combined. You can latch them together in predictable ways.

Here's an example:

> *If I buy an espresso machine, I will end up in the highly-caffeinated poor house.*

> *If I end up in the highly-caffeinated poor house, I will finally be cool enough to wear non-ironic plaid.*

Let's think each of these statements through. Let's place ourselves in this situation and see what we know.

Say I go ahead and make the poor decision to buy an espresso machine. What do we know about me? I'm in the poor house. Now what do we know from that? We know enough to activate the second conditional! Since I'm in the poor house, I can finally wear plaid (still not there in real life).

Notice, we only had enough information to activate the first conditional at the beginning, but we ended up at the end of the second conditional. What witchcraft is this? It works because **these statements were set up to chain, meaning they naturally connect.**

## HOW TO KNOW WHEN YOU CAN CHAIN

These two statements chained because the necessary condition of the first statement matched the sufficient condition of the second statement. That's a pretty wordy way of explaining something that is simple when you examine it visually. You'll know you can chain when you can perfectly overlap two conditions and nothing conflicts.

Look at the following two conditionals:

$$L \longrightarrow M$$

$$M \longrightarrow N$$

**I want you to imagine picking up that second conditional and laying it on top of the first one.** You can latch in the second conditional at the **M** on the first one. It fits there. That's your interlocking Lego point. There's room for the **N** to come after the **M** in the first conditional; nothing's there to block it. So you end up with:

$$L \longrightarrow M \longrightarrow N$$

Awesome!

This is how I personally chain conditionals. No jargon about similar sufficient/necessary. That's not intuitive. What is intuitive is looking to see if you have the same variable and an available empty space.

### HOW TO DIAGRAM CHAINS

Instead of writing:

$$A \longrightarrow B$$

$$B \longrightarrow C$$

You should write:

$$A \longrightarrow B \longrightarrow C$$

The combined chain makes the implications of these two statements easier to detect.

From the $A \longrightarrow B \longrightarrow C$ chain, we can see that $A \longrightarrow C$ is true. Wow! We can activate the first term in the chain, skip the middle, and know that the last term is also true.

You can read chains for the contrapositive as well. The same process that applies for individual conditionals also applies here: **You can read the conditional chain backwards, negating everything as you go.** For instance, you can read our example above as $\sim C \longrightarrow \sim B \longrightarrow \sim A$ and detect the $\sim C \longrightarrow \sim A$ implication.

**Do not diagram each conditional individually and then combine them afterward, if you see that a chain is forming as you read.** I see people do this all the time and it's a waste of time. Here is exactly what you should and shouldn't do:

**DO**

1.    Diagram $A \longrightarrow B$.

2.    See that the next sentence indicates $B \longrightarrow C$.

3.    Add $\longrightarrow C$ on to the end of your original $A \longrightarrow B$.

4.    You end up with $A \longrightarrow B \longrightarrow C$.

**DO NOT**

1.    Diagram $A \longrightarrow B$.

2.    Diagram $B \longrightarrow C$ separately

3.    Maybe look back and see that you can chain. Then likely decide you'll "just remember" they can chain because combining the statements on paper is a "waste of time."

The magic of conditional chains lies in how you can read the chain once you have it. Imagine you have the following chain:

$$Q \longrightarrow R \longrightarrow S \longrightarrow T$$

> Want to know why it's not a waste of time to combine the statements? Because you get questions right by combining premises. This is a simple way to do that.

You can read this straight through from beginning to end. Go ahead and skip the middle! For instance, we know $Q \longrightarrow T$ from this chain. This is pretty awesome. This four-part chain implies all of the following:

| INFERENCE | INFERENCE CONTRAPOSITIVE |
|-----------|--------------------------|
| Q ⟶ R | ~R ⟶ ~Q |
| Q ⟶ S | ~S ⟶ ~Q |
| Q ⟶ T | ~T ⟶ ~Q |
| R ⟶ S | ~S ⟶ ~R |
| R ⟶ T | ~T ⟶ ~R |
| S ⟶ T | ~T ⟶ ~S |

That's 12 conditional statements in one! **You can read all of this out of that one chain.** WOAH. You won't be consciously thinking about all of these possibilities every time you look at a chain, but if you have a reason to pay attention to any of them, you'll know it's demonstrated in the chain.

## CONTRAPOSITIVE-FACILITATED CHAINS

**Sometimes you'll have to use the contrapositive of one of your statements to make the chain.** This is fine. The contrapositive is just another way of writing your original statement, so there's no conflict here.

For instance, imagine you encounter the following statements:

V ⟶ ~W

~X ⟶ W

Looking at this, you can see that the second statement can be read as **~W ⟶ X**, if you read it for the contrapositive (read backwards negating as you go). This opens up a chaining opportunity! The two statements can be combined:

V ⟶ ~W ⟶ X

You can take the contrapositive of either statement to facilitate the chain, and it will work equally well. Above, I took the contrapositive of the second statement, but I could have used the first statement instead and come up with this:

~X ⟶ W ⟶ ~V

Either chain is fine. I always try and minimize the number of negated variables in my conditionals, so that's probably why I subconsciously preferred the first option.

This is a more challenging chain to write, so it's totally understandable if you need to write each statement separately in order to see the combination. Once you combine the two statements into a chain, cross out the originals to get rid of the eye pollution. **Always cross out repetitive stuff. The fewer things for your eyes to look at, the better.**

**REMEMBER!** *Always chain your conditionals as soon as you see a chain is possible.*

## And/Or

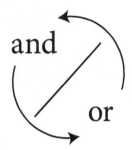

**AND/OR** makes sufficient and necessary conditions more complex. They are mirror images of one another.

Let's explore **AND/OR** with an example:

*If we pursue our music and find success, we will be able to eat.*

There are two conditions we have to meet to activate this conditional. If we have both of them, music and success, we will definitely get to eat. Because the sufficient condition has two parts, you diagram it like so:

$$
\begin{array}{c}
M \\
+ \longrightarrow E \\
S
\end{array}
$$

Notice how the arrow is pointing directly from the **+**. **The arrow points from the + because the conditional is activated by the *combination* of both variables.** That's what the **+** stands for. Keep your notation neat like this. Always draw the arrow directly to/from the **+/OR**.

Now, a contrapositive thought experiment:

What if we know that we don't get to eat? Do you need *both* music and success to not have happened? No, you don't. It would be fine if neither of them happened, but **you only need for at least one of them to be absent**. Just music *or* just success being gone means the sufficient condition was not activated, and so the necessary condition doesn't have to follow. One of them being absent is the minimum. That's what has to be true.

So, the contrapositive of $\begin{array}{c} M \\ + \longrightarrow E \\ S \end{array}$ is $\begin{array}{c} \sim M \\ \sim E \longrightarrow \ \ \text{or} \\ \sim S \end{array}$ .

**REMEMBER!**   *You always switch the* **AND/OR** *when taking the contrapositive of a conditional.*

Let's look at the **OR** side of things:

*If you fall to the ground, you are clumsy or committing insurance fraud.*

$$
\begin{array}{c}
C \\
F \longrightarrow \ \text{or} \\
IF
\end{array}
$$

---

> **Sidebar:**
>
> When you diagram **AND/OR**:
>
> Use **+** for **AND**. Just to shorten it up.
>
> Write out **OR**. It's already pretty short.

Now, to activate the contrapositive of this statement, you are going to need to make sure there's no way the necessary condition can be fulfilled. That means you need both clumsy *and* insurance fraud to be out of the picture. If you just get rid of one of them, the other one could still fulfill the necessary condition and you could still fall to the ground.

This is why  $\begin{matrix} \sim C \\ + \longrightarrow \sim F \\ \sim IF \end{matrix}$  is the contrapositive of  $F \longrightarrow \begin{matrix} C \\ or \\ IF \end{matrix}$ .

When you read a conditional for the contrapositive, you negate terms as you read backwards. You should also switch the AND/OR as you go. **Think of AND as the negated version of OR and vice versa.** **Any time you're negating a conditional and it contains an AND/OR, you must negate the AND/OR.**

### FOLLOW THIS ONE RULE AND BECOME MY FAVORITE HUMAN

Write:

$$\begin{matrix} A \\ or \longrightarrow C \\ B \end{matrix}$$

Do not write:

$$A \ or \ B \longrightarrow C$$

> **NEITHER/NOR** in conditional statements means "not this *and* not that." Whenever you see "neither X nor Y" in a conditional statement, diagram it as $\begin{smallmatrix} \sim X \\ + \\ \sim Y \end{smallmatrix}$. Don't be fooled by this **OR** impostor.

The second variation cripples your chaining potential. It makes it awkward to connect other conditions to the statement. It's also confusing because it looks like the arrow is just coming off of the **B**. This may seem like a small thing, but it will matter a ton on certain Logic Games. Build the habit of always doing it vertically now, and you will be in a good position from the beginning.

**REMEMBER!**    *Always diagram* **AND/OR** *conditionals vertically.*

## If and Only If

IF AND ONLY IF is a double indicator. It is a marriage between the sufficient and necessary families. A *Romeo and Juliet* situation, but with less murder. As soon as you see IF AND ONLY IF, throw down a Double Must Arrow:

$$\longleftrightarrow$$

*Biconditional*

IF AND ONLY IF just means the two variables always go together, hand in hand. You should rejoice when you see it; it vastly simplifies the conditional relationship. IF AND ONLY IF is one conditional indicator, but it is made up of a member of the sufficient family and the necessary family.

Here's an example:

> *We will compromise if and only if I get everything I want.*

Let's take this apart to see why the Double Must Arrow is deployed. Since there are two conditional indicators here, IF and ONLY IF, let's diagram each of them one at a time and combine what we find.

First, let's do the sufficient side:

> *We will compromise if ~~and only if~~ I get everything I want.*

**get everything** $\longrightarrow$ **compromise**

Now, let's diagram the necessary side:

> *We will compromise ~~if and~~ only if I get everything I want.*

**compromise** $\longrightarrow$ **get everything**

Each term is in both the sufficient and necessary condition. We combine the two previous diagrams into one!

**compromise** $\longleftrightarrow$ **get everything**

It doesn't matter who goes on the left or right because each term is both sufficient and necessary. **Whenever you have a double arrow, you can switch who's on the left and right at will.** This is why you don't have to flip the conditional when you negate it in the contrapositive.

The IF AND ONLY IF **relationship is simple: The two terms are always together.** If you have one, you have the other. If one is absent, the other is absent. So, by contrapositive, this statement is also true:

**~get everything** $\longleftrightarrow$ **~compromise**

Every member of the If and Only If Family means the same thing as IF AND ONLY IF. Whenever you see any of these phrases in a conditional context, you should diagram them with the Double Must Arrow.

### IF AND ONLY IF FAMILY

| | | | |
|---|---|---|---|
| *if but only if* | *all and only* | *but not otherwise* | *when and only when* |

# If and Only If & And/Or Drill   THE TAMING OF THE SHREW

## INSTRUCTIONS

*Diagram the following conditional statements. Don't be afraid to look back at the section, if you need any help.*

**1.**   If I am waspish, best beware my sting or try to pluck it out.

ORIGINAL

$$W \rightarrow \begin{matrix} BS \\ or \\ PO \end{matrix}$$

CONTRAPOSITIVE

$$\begin{matrix} \cancel{BS} \\ + \\ \cancel{PO} \end{matrix} \rightarrow \cancel{W}$$

**2.**   You lie if and only if you are called super-dainty Kate.

ORIGINAL

$$L \longleftrightarrow DK$$

CONTRAPOSITIVE

$$\cancel{L} \longleftrightarrow \cancel{DK}$$

**3.**   We will have rings and a fine array if and only if you kiss me, Kate, and marry Sunday.

ORIGINAL

$$\begin{matrix} R \\ + \\ FA \end{matrix} \longleftrightarrow \begin{matrix} Km \\ + \\ KK \\ + \\ MS \end{matrix}$$

CONTRAPOSITIVE

$$\begin{matrix} \cancel{Km} \\ \cancel{KK} \\ \cancel{MS} \end{matrix} \begin{matrix} \cancel{R} \\ or \\ \cancel{FA} \end{matrix} \longleftrightarrow \begin{matrix} \cancel{Km} \\ or \\ \cancel{KK} \\ or \\ \cancel{MS} \end{matrix}$$

**4.**   If and only if you are one half lunatic, would you want me to wed to a mad-cap ruffian and to a swearing Jack.

ORIGINAL

$$HL \longleftrightarrow \begin{matrix} MR \\ + \\ SJ \end{matrix}$$

CONTRAPOSITIVE

$$\cancel{HL} \longleftrightarrow \begin{matrix} \cancel{MR} \\ or \\ \cancel{SJ} \end{matrix}$$

**5.**   I must be armed for some unhappy words, to woo you and be happy.

ORIGINAL

$$\begin{matrix} WY \\ + \\ BH \end{matrix} \rightarrow \cancel{M} \; UW$$

CONTRAPOSITIVE

$$\cancel{UW} \rightarrow \begin{matrix} \cancel{WY} \\ or \\ \cancel{BH} \end{matrix}$$

The conditional drills in this chapter are each inspired by Shakespeare plays. This time, we're using *The Taming of the Shrew*.

*Where's the answer key?*

You'll find the answer key at the end of the chapter on page 149.

## Either/Or   THE INCLUSION INDICATORS

> **EITHER/OR** forces us to include at least one of the two things it targets.

This Must Relationship is a little different, but it has a recognizable pattern that we can learn. Here's an example of how **EITHER/OR** tends to look:

> *Either* I will go with the red pill, *or* I will go with the blue pill.

Let's just think through what **EITHER/OR** means in LSAT terms. It's slightly different from its real world meaning. I call **EITHER/OR** an inclusion indicator because it forces us to include at least one option. It does not imply that you can only have one of the pair. **EITHER/OR implies that you *must* have at least one of the pair.**

Since you have to have at least one of two variables that **EITHER/OR** targets, you need a conditional that will force inclusion. What sufficient condition would yield a Must Relationship that forces inclusion? Well, what if one of the **EITHER/OR** pair was absent? We'd have to have the other half, right? So, the correct personalized if/then is either:

> *If I'm not the red pill, then I'm the blue pill.*

> **OR**

> *If I'm not the blue pill, then I'm the red pill.*

It doesn't matter which option you place in the sufficient condition. Either one will force you to include at least one of the options.

### INCLUSION DIAGRAMMING PROCESS

1.   Negate one half of the statement and put it in the sufficient condition.

2.   Place the other half of the statement in the necessary condition.

Let's use this method on another example:

> *Either I will stare into the distance, or I will make progress.*

1.   I'll negate "stare" and place it in the sufficient condition: **~stare ⟶**

2.   I'll place "progress" in the necessary condition: **~stare ⟶ progress**

So now I know, if I'm not staring, I must be making progress. I've forced one of the options to be included.

Now, let's imagine that I'd chosen the other option for my sufficient condition:

1.   I'll negate "progress" and place it in the sufficient condition: **~progress ⟶**

2.   I'll place "stare" in the necessary condition: **~progress ⟶ stare**

Either of these statements will work. They are equivalent! The two possible diagrams are contrapositives of one another.

# Inclusion Drill   RICHARD II

## INSTRUCTIONS

*Diagram the following conditional statements. Don't be afraid to look back at the section, if you need any help.*

**1.**   Either it is patience or despair.

**ORIGINAL** ~~Despair~~ $\cancel{D} \rightarrow P$

**CONTRAPOSITIVE** $\cancel{P} \rightarrow D$

**2.**   Either time made me his numbering clock or my thoughts are minutes.

**ORIGINAL** $\cancel{NC} \rightarrow TM$

**CONTRAPOSITIVE** $\cancel{TM} \rightarrow NC$

**3.**   Either I waste time, or time wastes me.

**ORIGINAL** $\cancel{WT} \rightarrow TWM$

**CONTRAPOSITIVE** $\cancel{TWM} \rightarrow WT$

The conditional drills in this chapter are each inspired by Shakespeare plays. This time, we're using *Richard II*, the most underrated of Shakespeare's history plays.

*Where's the answer key?*

You'll find the answer key at the end of the chapter on page 150.

## No, None, Nobody, Never   THE EXCLUSION INDICATORS

> The exclusion indicators set up mutually exclusive relationships.

Exclusion sets restrictions. Just like **EITHER/OR**, they're not traditional indicators, but they do result in a predictable Must Relationship.

Exclusion means you're going to have to choose between the two variables introduced in the statement. You can't have both. **If you have one of them, you can't have the other. Rephrasing mutual exclusivity as an if/then is essential.**

Here is the same conditional relationship written with each member of the exclusion family:

*None* of the pocket squares will surrender.         The pocket squares will *never* surrender.

*No* pocket square will surrender.                    *Nobody* who is a pocket square will surrender.

Let's think through what this relationship means in our **NONE** example: None of the pocket squares will surrender. OK, so pocket squares are not allowed to surrender. These two things don't go together. So, if I'm a pocket square, I am not surrendering.

**pocket square ⟶ ~surrender**

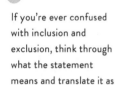

*If you're ever confused with inclusion and exclusion, think through what the statement means and translate it as a personalized if/then.*

All I did here was choose one of the variables in the statement and throw it in the sufficient condition. From there, I knew that I couldn't have the other half. Now, let's imagine I chose the other side of the statement for my sufficient condition. If I just surrendered, what do you know about me? You know that I must not be a pocket square. That's not pocket square-style.

**surrender ⟶ ~pocket square**

Luckily, **pocket square ⟶ ~surrender** and **surrender ⟶ ~pocket square** are equivalent statements! They're contrapositives. So it doesn't matter which side of the statement you put in the sufficient condition, as long as you negate the other side and put it in the necessary. Notice that the exclusion indicator wasn't always applied to the same term in these examples. **NEVER** targeted "surrender," while all the other exclusion indicators targeted "pocket squares." This doesn't matter. The statements are still equivalent; as we saw in **EITHER/OR**, the contrapositive will come to our rescue.

### EXCLUSION DIAGRAMMING PROCESS

1.   Choose one side of the statement and put it in the sufficient condition.

2.   Negate the other side and put it in the necessary condition.

Let's test out this process with our **NEVER** example: The pocket squares will never surrender.

1.   I'll choose "surrender" and put it in the sufficient condition: **surrender ⟶**

2.   I'll negate "pocket squares" and put it in the necessary: **surrender ⟶ ~pocket squares**

If I surrender, you know I'm not a pocket square. Perfect.

# Exclusion Drill  AS YOU LIKE IT

## INSTRUCTIONS

*Diagram the following conditional statements. Don't be afraid to look back at the section, if you need any help.*

**1.** Nobody who lets time stroll would allow it to trot.

**ORIGINAL** $\quad$ S → $\cancel{T}$

**CONTRAPOSITIVE** $\quad$ T → $\cancel{S}$

**2.** No one breaks their shins against their own wit.

**ORIGINAL** $\quad$ S → $\cancel{W}$

**CONTRAPOSITIVE** $\quad$ W → $\cancel{S}$

**3.** Time never travels at the same speed for different people.

**ORIGINAL** $\quad$ ~~TSS → DP~~ $\quad$ TSS → $\cancel{DP}$

**CONTRAPOSITIVE** $\quad$ ~~DP → TSS~~ $\quad$ DP → $\cancel{TSS}$

**4.** Never love men who are falser than vows made in wine.

**ORIGINAL** $\quad$ FTVW → $\cancel{L}$

**CONTRAPOSITIVE** $\quad$ L → $\cancel{FTVW}$

**5.** Those who time gallops for are never those who it stops cold for.

**ORIGINAL** $\quad$ TG → $\cancel{TS}$

**CONTRAPOSITIVE** $\quad$ TS → $\cancel{TG}$

The conditional drills in this chapter are each inspired by Shakespeare plays. This time, we're using *As You Like It*.

*Where's the answer key?*

You'll find the answer key at the end of the chapter on page 151.

## Unless   THE EXCEPTION

---

**UNLESS** is our conditional exception indicator.

---

Exceptions are how we get out of the way things always are. **UNLESS** indicates that we're about to see the *only* way around how things always are. That *only* should give you a hint about which condition **UNLESS** lives in.

Let's start with an example:

> *Purple is hateful, unless it's sleeping.*

"Purple is hateful" doesn't have a conditional indicator attached to it. It is just the way things are. The law of the land. Purple is just hateful. **UNLESS** presents us with the only exception to the tyranny of purple. The only way we can get around the way things are, purple being hateful, is by using our **UNLESS** exception. In this case, the only way to make purple not hateful is for it to be sleeping.

Let's try translating this into a personalized if/then by applying the following rule to the purple case:

  **RULE!**   *If I go against the way things always are, I must have my* **UNLESS** *exception.*

And so following that rule:

> *If purple is not hateful (going against the way things always are), it must be sleeping (our exception).*

**purple not hateful $\longrightarrow$ sleeping**

**~PH $\longrightarrow$ S**

Boom. That's it. This is the way the **UNLESS** diagram will always look:

~[THE WAY THINGS ALWAYS ARE] $\longrightarrow$ EXCEPTION

### UNLESS DIAGRAMMING PROCESS

1.   The target of **UNLESS** is the exception. Throw it in the necessary condition.

2.   The other half of the statement is the way things always are. Go against the grain. Negate the way things always are and put that in the sufficient.

3.   You end up with: **~[THE WAY THINGS ALWAYS ARE] $\longrightarrow$ EXCEPTION**

> **UNLESS** is just a more linguistically complex necessary family member.

Like most conditional terms, **UNLESS** has a family:

---

**THE UNLESS FAMILY**

---

*except*                              *until*                              *without*

---

All of these words mean the same thing as **UNLESS**. **Memorize them.**

Whenever you see any of these words, act as though you saw **UNLESS**. They all target exceptions, so you can do the exact same thing as you do with **UNLESS**.

## THE UNLESS THOUGHT EXPERIMENT

Let's look at another example:

> *Unless you are allergic, kittens bring pure joy.*

In this case, kittens bringing pure joy is the way things always are. It's the way of things. Kittens and joy. What a life. Activating the exception (being allergic) is the one way to avoid this joyful life.

**Think of UNLESS as a last resort. It's what you have to do, not what you want to do.** It doesn't have that open, kind attitude we find in the sufficient family. It's restricted. It's necessary. It's the hero we need, not the hero we want. (Like Batman? Yes, like Batman.)

This is why the exception goes in the necessary condition. It's our only way out. So let's translate our kitten example into an if/then. This time I'm going to make it a little more complicated by giving you a few false starting points in the sufficient condition. **Each of these false starts represents a common error made in diagramming UNLESS. Two of these sufficient conditions don't necessarily lead to anything.**

> *Unless you are allergic, kittens bring pure joy.*

1. You are allergic $\longrightarrow$
2. Kittens bring pure joy $\longrightarrow$
3. Kittens do not bring pure joy $\longrightarrow$

Take a guess right now. Which one of these three sufficient conditions actually leads to something necessary? Circle the number of the option you choose. Something has to be true if one of these three is true. Let's start with option #1.

1. You are allergic $\longrightarrow$

Using this sufficient condition is the most common mistake made when diagramming **UNLESS**. The misunderstanding that leads people here is strong, so let's dispel it piece by piece.

Merely being allergic doesn't make anything happen. Being allergic is the way around things, not the way to make something happen. You can have backups galore in your life, but that doesn't mean you have to use them.

I once knew a guy who kept a 20 dollar bill in his pocket at all times "just in case." "Just in case" of what, you ask? I never found out because he never spent it. This 20 dollar bill was clearly a backup plan for something. It was his exception. But it never made anything happen. Looking back, I always thought this person was absurd, but I was totally wrong. I'm always jealous of him whenever I go to the cash-only taco place nearby and leave empty-handed. When I'm confronted with an atypical situation, I need to activate the backup plan. However, just *having* the backup plan on its own doesn't lead to anything.

**REMEMBER!**    *Do not put the exception in the sufficient condition. It is not sufficient to make anything happen.*

Now we'll tackle option #2.

### 2.    Kittens bring pure joy ⟶

Now you're just saying that things are the way they always are. The status quo doesn't make anything happen.

The common misunderstanding is that the normal way of things means there is no exception active. This is a mistake. Just because the normal way of things is happening doesn't mean you don't have your exception. Remember 20 dollar bill guy? He kept his exception in his pocket every single day even as everything was going according to plan.

Finding kittens to be pure joy does not prove that you are not allergic. There are plenty of allergic people who still find kittens to be pure joy. People are free to throw biological caution to the wind and act against their own immediate health interests.

**REMEMBER!**    *Do not put the way things always are in the sufficient condition. It is not sufficient to make anything happen.*

And now for something that actually works! Onward to option #3!

Still uneasy about **UNLESS**? Check out The Unless Practice Routine at elementalprep.com/bonus for more fun.

### 3.    Kittens do not bring pure joy ⟶ allergic

Aha! We are finally going against the normal way of things now. This is exactly what we have to do to make things happen. If kittens aren't bringing pure joy, the *only* explanation is that the person is allergic. The *only* tells me that my situation is limited enough to throw something in the necessary condition. Remember the conditional arrow is called a Must Arrow. We *must* do the thing on the necessary side if we activate the sufficient. That is why option #3 is the only option that warrants a conditional arrow. This sufficient condition doesn't leave us any choice.

# Unless Drill   AS YOU LIKE IT

## INSTRUCTIONS

*Diagram the following conditional statements. Don't be afraid to look back at the section, if you need any help.*

**1.**   I can suck melancholy out of a song until a weasel sucks eggs.

ORIGINAL         SM → WSE

CONTRAPOSITIVE   WSE → SM

**2.**   They'd call it a compliment without the encounter of the two dog-apes.

ORIGINAL         CC → TDA

CONTRAPOSITIVE   TDA → CC

**3.**   Unless his brain is as dry as the remainder biscuit, he will know.

ORIGINAL         K → BD

CONTRAPOSITIVE   BD → K

**4.**   It is not my suit unless we weed your better judgments.

ORIGINAL         S → WBJ

CONTRAPOSITIVE   WBJ → S

**5.**   Until it meets the squandering glances of a fool, your folly is anatomized.

ORIGINAL         FA → SG

CONTRAPOSITIVE   SG → FA

---

*The conditional drills in this chapter are each inspired by Shakespeare plays. We're using *As You Like It* again here because there were too many amazing lines for just one drill; the dog-apes question alone makes it worth it.*

*Where's the answer key?*

You'll find the answer key at the end of the chapter on page 152.

## Some & Most    ROGUE SUFFICIENTS

**SOME and MOST are rogue members of the sufficient family.** They're less strictly inclusive than their brethren, so they were kicked out of the sufficient household and sent to the end of the chapter. But that doesn't mean you can ignore them, especially if you want a near-perfect LR section. Some of the hardest questions in LR will ask you to diagram **SOME** and **MOST** statements, and then test you on your ability to combine those statements into valid Inferences.

**SOME** means any quantity of one or more. If I have a total of five cookies, and I tell you that *some* of my cookies are salted shortbread, that could mean one, two, three, four, or all five of my cookies are salted shortbread. With **SOME**, anywhere from 1% to 100% of my cookies could be salted shortbread.

**MOST** means any quantity in the majority. If I still have five cookies, but now I say *most* of my cookies contain dark chocolate, that could mean three, four, or all five of my cookies contain dark chocolate. With **MOST**, anywhere from 51% to 100% of my cookies could contain dark chocolate.

Even though **SOME** and **MOST** refer to quantity, we can still diagram them like we do with regular conditionals.

### HOW TO DIAGRAM SOME & MOST

**SOME** and **MOST** are super simple to diagram! **They always go right before their target, and their target goes straight in the sufficient condition.**

For example:

> *"some henchmen"* = henchmen in the sufficient condition = **henchmen $\xleftrightarrow{s}$**

> *"most inkwells"* = inkwells in the sufficient condition = **inkwells $\xrightarrow{m}$**

*Some and Most Arrows have one special quality: They're always activated. The very presence of a Some/Most Arrow implies that the sufficient condition exists.*

But check out those different arrows! Why are the arrows different? Because **SOME** and **MOST** both allow for less than 100% of the group in the sufficient condition to hold the necessary trait, our Must Arrow won't do the job. We need special arrows on the scene.

### THE SOME ARROW

This is your Some Arrow:

$$\xleftrightarrow{s}$$

It's a double arrow! Woah! Let's check out how the Some Arrow works in practice:

> *Some water bottles are hilariously overpriced.*

First step, put the water bottles in the sufficient slot with the Some Arrow. Water bottles are **SOME'S** target.

**water bottles $\xleftrightarrow{s}$**

*Just like with the Double Must Arrow (⟷), you don't have to worry about which side each variable goes on with a Some Arrow ($\xleftrightarrow{s}$). Either variable can be on the left or right.*

Now, take the other half of the statement, hilariously overpriced, and put it in the necessary slot.

**water bottles $\xleftrightarrow{s}$ hilariously overpriced**

This statement can be translated into either of two personalized if/thens:

*If I'm a water bottle, some of me are hilariously overpriced.*

*If I'm hilariously overpriced, some of me are water bottles.*

Since **SOME** is a double arrow, reading **SOME** statements backwards and forwards is totally cool. You can read and diagram every **SOME** statement just like this.

**SOME** has a family too. When you see these indicators, you can draw a Some Arrow:

There is no corollary to a contrapositive with **SOME** statements. Do not try to unlock negated meanings here. If someone is not a water bottle, they may or may not be hilariously overpriced. We don't know, so we can't make claims.

---

### THE SOME FAMILY

| | | | |
|---|---|---|---|
| *few* | *many* | *at least one* | *several* |

## NOT ALL = FANCY SOME

**NOT ALL** is a **SOME** indicator with a twist. **NOT ALL means that some of the target *doesn't* have the quality described.** Just like with the exclusion indicators, the negative is applied to the other side of the statement. Let's look at an example:

*Not all feathers are in caps.*

How can we translate this? Well, if not all feathers are in caps, doesn't that imply that some feathers are *not* in caps? Yeah, there has to be at least one feather that isn't in a cap; *some* feathers are not in caps. Once you have the **SOME** translated in, you can diagram the statement normally:

**feathers $\xleftrightarrow{s}$ not in caps**

I know this takes a second to sink in, but **NOT ALL** is very predictable. Once you diagram it like this a few times, you'll get used to it.

## THE MOST ARROW

And here, my friends, is your Most Arrow:

$$\xrightarrow{m}$$

The Most Arrow goes one way. You can read a Most Arrow a little more like a regular Must Arrow.

Let's practice with our Most Arrow here:

*Most otters are burglars.*

First step, put otters in the sufficient condition with the Most Arrow. Otters are **MOST**'s target.

**otters $\xrightarrow{m}$**

Next, throw the other half of the sentence, burglars, in the necessary slot.

otters $\xrightarrow{m}$ burglars

Now, enjoy the fruits of your labor! Read your **MOST** statement as a personalized if/then:

> *If I'm an otter, most of me are burglars.*

Awesome! There are a few more words that indicate **MOST**. You can draw a Most Arrow when you see these:

| THE MOST FAMILY | | | |
| --- | --- | --- | --- |
| *usually* | *probably* | *mostly* | *more often than not* |

There is also an interesting implication buried inside the **MOST** statement. Let's try to uncover it next.

## THE MOST IMPLICATION

The **MOST** statement above tells us that the majority of otters are burglars, meaning there is at least one otter-burglar out there. We don't know exactly how many because we don't know how many otters or burglars there are total, but at least one otter-burglar exists. **There's a guaranteed overlap between the otters and the burglars.** This overlap is all we need to prove that some burglars are otters. So, **you can read a MOST statement backwards, as long as you switch the MOST to a SOME when you do so.**

For example:

otters $\xrightarrow{m}$ burglars

The implication of this **MOST** statement is:

burglars $\xleftrightarrow{s}$ otters

Some burglars are otters. Perfect.

The implication of **MOST** is **SOME**! How convenient.

# Inferences From Some & Most Chains

Some of the hardest Logical Reasoning stimuli will provide you with premises containing **SOME** and **MOST** and ask you to combine them. You can chain **SOME/MOST** with normal Must Arrows, but you have to handle those chains *very carefully*. **You cannot simply read SOME and MOST chains straight through like with normal conditionals.** But don't fret! There are only three **SOME** and **MOST** chains that lead to any real Inferences.

## THE ONLY VALID SOME/MOST INFERENCES

| PREMISES | VALID INFERENCE | PATTERN |
|---|---|---|
| A $\xleftrightarrow{s}$ B $\longrightarrow$ C | A $\xleftrightarrow{s}$ C | *You can extend the Some Arrow by **pointing away** from it in a chain.* |
| A $\xrightarrow{m}$ B $\longrightarrow$ C | A $\xrightarrow{m}$ C | *You can extend the Most Arrow by **pointing away** from it in a chain.* |
| A $\xrightarrow{m}$ B<br><br>A $\xrightarrow{m}$ C | B $\xleftrightarrow{s}$ C | *Two Most Arrows stacked on the same sufficient condition (A) means there must be a Some Inference overlap between the necessary groups (B & C).* |

These are the only combinations of **SOME** and **MOST** that lead to any valid Inferences. Seriously. This is it. **If the LSAT tries to combine anything other than these three things, they are trying to trick you.** Don't infer anything other than these three things from **SOME/MOST** chains. **Memorize these three Inferences now.**

## A MILLION INVALID SOME/MOST INFERENCES

Do not fall for any of the bad combinations outlined in the chart that follows. It's fine to make these chains as long as you don't try to infer anything new from them. As you will see, inferring from **SOME** and **MOST** doesn't work out more often than it works out. This is to your advantage because you only have to remember the valid combinations.

| PREMISES | MIND THE TRAP | PATTERN |
|---|---|---|
| A $\longrightarrow$ B $\xleftrightarrow{s}$ C | *No valid Inference!* | *Pointing toward the Some Arrow in a chain doesn't let you extend it. Never point to a Some Arrow and infer.* |
| A $\longrightarrow$ B $\xrightarrow{m}$ C | *No valid Inference!* | *Pointing toward the Most Arrow in a chain doesn't let you extend it. Never point to a Most Arrow and infer.* |
| A $\xleftrightarrow{s}$ B $\xleftrightarrow{s}$ C | *No valid Inference!* | **SOME** *chains don't yield any valid Inferences.* |
| A $\xrightarrow{m}$ B $\xrightarrow{m}$ C | *No valid Inference!* | **MOST** *chains don't yield any valid Inferences.* |
| A $\xleftrightarrow{s}$ B $\xrightarrow{m}$ C<br>A $\xrightarrow{m}$ B $\xleftrightarrow{s}$ C | *No valid Inference!* | **SOME** *and* **MOST** *don't yield any Inferences when chained together.* |

Want to guess the page of *The Loophole* I send my tutoring students back to the most in their homework these days? **This one.** By far. (Hi, tutoring students I sent here!) The valid Some/Most Inferences are absolutely crucial to memorize.

Since two overlapping Most Arrows add up to a Some Inference, we can expect the same from two overlapping Must Arrows! Think about it: If two Most Arrows necessitate a Some Inference, two Must Arrows *must* do the same since they're so much more powerful than Most Arrows.

Conditional Reasoning

Remember these three things about chaining **SOME/MOST**:

1. You can point a Must Arrow *away* from a Some/Most Arrow and extend the Some/Most Arrow all the way across the chain from the first to the last term.

2. You can add up two Most Arrows with the same sufficient condition. There's a guaranteed **SOME** overlap between the two necessary conditions.

3. Everything besides these two options is a trap. Mind the traps.

---

**CONDITIONAL REASONING GAME PLAN**

- Translate every difficult conditional into a personalized if/then.

- Diagram every conditional until it's second nature. Always diagram conditional chains.

- Remember that **UNLESS** is the exception. It's *necessary* when we go against the way things always are.

- Diagram **SOME/MOST**. Only infer the three valid **SOME/MOST** inferences.

---

## Some & Most Drill   TWELFTH NIGHT

### INSTRUCTIONS

*Diagram the following conditional statements. Don't be afraid to look back at the section, if you need any help.*

*There are a few regular old conditionals in this drill. They are in here to test your chaining skills. Once you've diagrammed all the statements in this drill,* **combine four of your answers into two chains. One of those chains will give you a valid Inference.** *Write that Inference below.*

**1.**   Some men are born great.

**ORIGINAL**   $M \overset{S}{\longleftrightarrow} BG$

**2.**   Some fellows achieve renown.

**ORIGINAL**   $F \overset{S}{\longleftrightarrow} AR$

**3.**   Most dog-apes have greatness thrust upon them.

**ORIGINAL**   $DA \overset{M}{\longrightarrow} GT$

**4.**   No man should be afraid of greatness.

**ORIGINAL**   $M \rightarrow \cancel{AG}$

**CONTRAPOSITIVE**   $AG \rightarrow \cancel{M}$

**5.**   If the Fates open their hands, you must be a dog-ape.

**ORIGINAL**   $FOH \rightarrow DA$

**CONTRAPOSITIVE**

### THE TWO CORRECT CHAINS

$FOH \rightarrow DA \overset{M}{\longrightarrow} GT$

$M \overset{S}{\longleftrightarrow} BG \ - \ BG \overset{S}{\longleftrightarrow} M \rightarrow AG$

*One of these chains lets you extend the Some/Most Arrow from the first to the last term in the chain. Extend the Some/Most Arrow and write that Inference below.*

### THE CORRECT INFERENCE

Some people who are born great are not afraid of greatness

$BG \overset{S}{\longleftrightarrow} \cancel{AG}$

The conditional drills in this chapter are each inspired by Shakespeare plays. This time, we're using *Twelfth Night*.

If you're having trouble seeing the second chain, remember that you can flip which variable is on each side of the Some Arrow!

*Where's the answer key?*

You'll find the answer key at the end of the chapter on page 153.

# Mega-Conditional Drill   MEGA-SHAKESPEARE MIX

*The Mega-Conditional Drill incorporates all the information presented in the Conditional Reasoning Chapter. It's got your standard if/then indicators, exclusion, inclusion, UNLESS, AND/OR, and SOME/MOST. It's got it all! There are tough questions in this drill. Take your time.*

## INSTRUCTIONS

*Diagram the following conditional statements. Try to not to look back at the chapter for this one. Think of this like your final exam. It's testing your conditional skills as you move forward in your prep.*

On the real LSAT, you'll have to figure out where the conditional phrase stops and starts. In a drill, you can usually assume the entire phrase is there to be diagrammed. I want to prepare you for what you'll face in real LR stimuli, so **this drill will contain a few longer prompts, parts of which may not be conditional. You'll have to isolate just the conditional part of the sentence and diagram that.** Also, some questions will contain two conditionals. You'll have to isolate and diagram each of them.

**1.** All the world's a stage.

ORIGINAL   W → S

CONTRAPOSITIVE   S̸ → W̸

**2.** All the men and women are merely players.

ORIGINAL   M+W → P

CONTRAPOSITIVE   P̸ → M̸ or W̸

**3.** They each have their exits and their entrances.

ORIGINAL   T → exits + entr

CONTRAPOSITIVE   exit or entr̸ → T̸

**4.** One man in his time is required to play many parts.

ORIGINAL   MIT → MP

CONTRAPOSITIVE   MP̸ → MIT̸

**5.** Either men are April when they woo or December when they wed.

ORIGINAL $A\cancel{W} \rightarrow DW$

CONTRAPOSITIVE $D\cancel{W} \rightarrow AW$

**6.** Only beauty provokes thieves sooner than gold.

ORIGINAL $PSG \rightarrow B$

CONTRAPOSITIVE $\cancel{B} \rightarrow P\cancel{S}G$

**7.** Take as much pleasure as you may take upon a knife's point, unless you have the stomach.

ORIGINAL $T\cancel{M}P \rightarrow HS$

CONTRAPOSITIVE $H\cancel{S} \rightarrow TMP$

**8.** Some fools speak wiser than they know.

ORIGINAL $FC \xleftarrow{s} WTK$

**9.** Lunacy is so ordinary that the whippers are always in love too.

ORIGINAL $W \rightarrow L$

CONTRAPOSITIVE $\cancel{L} \rightarrow \cancel{W}$

**10.** Strange capers are a precondition for true lovers.

ORIGINAL $TL \rightarrow SC$

CONTRAPOSITIVE $S\cancel{C} \rightarrow T\cancel{L}$

**11.** The madness, love, depends on a dark house and a whip.

ORIGINAL $ML \rightarrow \begin{array}{c} DH \\ + \\ W \end{array}$

CONTRAPOSITIVE $\begin{array}{c} \cancel{DH} \\ or \\ \cancel{W} \end{array} \rightarrow M\cancel{L}$

**12.** There was no thought of pleasing you when she was christened.

ORIGINAL $C \rightarrow T\cancel{P}$

CONTRAPOSITIVE $TP \rightarrow \cancel{C}$

Remember, there may be parts of the sentence that are not conditional. Your job is to isolate and diagram just the conditional part of the phrase.

**13.**

I'll have no husband, if you be not he.

**ORIGINAL** ~~He~~ ~~~~ → ~~H~~

**CONTRAPOSITIVE** H → He

**14.**

Most men are damned, like an ill-roasted egg, all on one side.

**ORIGINAL** M → D

**15.**

I'll go sleep, if I can; if I cannot, I'll rail against all the first-born of Egypt.

**ORIGINAL** C → S

**CONTRAPOSITIVE** ~~S~~ → ~~C~~

**ORIGINAL** ~~C~~ → AFBE

**CONTRAPOSITIVE** ~~AFBE~~ → C

**CHAIN** ~~S~~ → ~~C~~ → AFBE

**16.**

Only if the compact of jars grows musical will we have discord in the spheres.

**ORIGINAL** DS → JGM

**CONTRAPOSITIVE** ~~JGM~~ → ~~DS~~

**17.**

I thank God and my cold blood, unless I am troubled with a pernicious suitor.

**ORIGINAL** ~~TG~~ → TPS
~~and~~ ar
~~CB~~

**CONTRAPOSITIVE** TPS → ~~TG~~ and ↓ CB

**18.**

Courtesy is never a turncoat.

**ORIGINAL** C → ~~T~~

**CONTRAPOSITIVE** T → ~~C~~

**19.**

I wonder that you will still be talking, Benedick: nobody marks you.

**ORIGINAL** B → ~~MY~~

**CONTRAPOSITIVE** MY → ~~B~~

**20.**

Either I will wash off gross acquaintance or let imagination jade me.

ORIGINAL ___WGA → IJ___

CONTRAPOSITIVE ___~IJ → ~WGA___

**21.**

Cupid kills some with arrows, some with traps.

ORIGINAL ___CK ⟷ₛ A___

ORIGINAL ___CK ⟷ₛ T___

**22.**

Men are deceivers ever if and only if they are constant never.

ORIGINAL ___(N ⟷ M)___

CONTRAPOSITIVE ___~N ⟷ ~M___

**23.**

Silence were the perfectest herald of joy. I were but little happy if I could say how much.

ORIGINAL ___SHM → LH___

CONTRAPOSITIVE ___~LH → ~SHM___

*Where's the answer key?*

You'll find the answer key at the end of the chapter on page 154.

## Quiz 4    CONDITIONAL REASONING

### INSTRUCTIONS

*Answer these questions based on your knowledge of the chapter. Attempt to answer without looking back at the chapter first. If you don't know the answer, circle the question number and go find the answer in the chapter. Study the sections of the chapter that you couldn't remember at first.*

### Word Bank

| | | |
|---|---|---|
| 1 | none | without |
| 100 | some | until |
| present | or | and |
| 51 | absent | nor |

Use the word bank to answer the fill-in-the-blank questions. Some words will not be used and others may be used more than once.

1. If the sufficient condition is ___absent___ , you can completely ignore the conditional statement.

2. If the sufficient condition is ___present___ , the conditional statement must be followed.

3. **NEITHER/NOR** means "not this ___and___ not that."

4. **SOME** means ___1___ - ___100___ % of the sufficient group must hold the necessary trait.

5. **MOST** means ___51___ - ___100___ % of the sufficient group must hold the necessary trait.

**6.** You can read a **MOST** statement backwards, as long as you switch the **MOST** to a(n) _____Same_____ as you do so.

**7.** _____none_____ is an exclusion indicator.

**8.** _____until_____ and _____without_____ are Unless Family members.

*Circle the correct answer to the following questions.*

**9.** (TRUE) OR FALSE   The negated version of **AND** is **OR**.

**10.** TRUE OR (FALSE)   The exception in an **UNLESS** statement is placed in the sufficient condition.

**11.** (TRUE OR FALSE)   There is a contrapositive for **SOME** statements.

**12.** Seek and find!   Circle only the sufficient indicators in the word cloud.

*Where's the answer key?*

You'll find the answer key at the end of the chapter on page 158.

| | | | | |
|---|---|---|---|---|
| then | (if) | (all) | (people who) | necessary |
| precondition | (in order to) | require | (each) | (every) |
| (only) | depends | have to | essential | (when) |
| (any) | only if | need | must | cause |

## Basic Conditional Drill   ANSWER KEY

**1.**   If he were in my books, I'd burn my study.

   **ORIGINAL**          IB $\longrightarrow$ BS (in books $\longrightarrow$ burn study)

   **CONTRAPOSITIVE**    ~BS $\longrightarrow$ ~IB

**2.**   Every time I hear my dog bark at a crow, it's like hearing a man swear he loves me.

   **ORIGINAL**          DB $\longrightarrow$ MSL (dog bark $\longrightarrow$ man swear love)

   **CONTRAPOSITIVE**    ~MSL $\longrightarrow$ ~DB

**3.**   If I were a man, I would eat his heart in the marketplace.

   **ORIGINAL**          M $\longrightarrow$ EHM (man $\longrightarrow$ eat heart marketplace)

   **CONTRAPOSITIVE**    ~EHM $\longrightarrow$ ~M

**4.**   I am heart-burned an hour after whenever I see him.

   **ORIGINAL**          SH $\longrightarrow$ H (see him $\longrightarrow$ heartburn)

   **CONTRAPOSITIVE**    ~H $\longrightarrow$ ~SH

**5.**   Benedick is always a rare parrot-teacher.

   **ORIGINAL**          B $\longrightarrow$ RP (Benedick $\longrightarrow$ rare parrot)

   **CONTRAPOSITIVE**    ~RP $\longrightarrow$ ~B

**6.**   Love requires me to transform into an oyster.

   **ORIGINAL**          L $\longrightarrow$ TO (love $\longrightarrow$ transform oyster)

   **CONTRAPOSITIVE**    ~TO $\longrightarrow$ ~L

## If and Only If & And/Or Drill   ANSWER KEY

**1.**   If I am waspish, best beware my sting or try to pluck it out.

ORIGINAL

$$W \longrightarrow \begin{matrix} BS \\ or \\ PO \end{matrix} \quad \left( waspish \longrightarrow \begin{matrix} beware\ sting \\ or \\ pluck\ out \end{matrix} \right)$$

CONTRAPOSITIVE

$$\begin{matrix} \sim BS \\ + \\ \sim PO \end{matrix} \longrightarrow \sim W$$

**2.**   You lie if and only if you are called super-dainty Kate.

ORIGINAL        $L \longleftrightarrow SDK$

CONTRAPOSITIVE   $\sim SDK \longleftrightarrow \sim L$

**3.**   We will have rings and a fine array if and only if you kiss me, Kate, and marry Sunday.

ORIGINAL

$$\begin{matrix} R \\ + \\ A \end{matrix} \longleftrightarrow \begin{matrix} K \\ + \\ MS \end{matrix} \quad \left( \begin{matrix} rings \\ + \\ array \end{matrix} \longleftrightarrow \begin{matrix} kiss \\ + \\ marry\ Sunday \end{matrix} \right)$$

CONTRAPOSITIVE

$$\begin{matrix} \sim K \\ or \\ \sim MS \end{matrix} \longleftrightarrow \begin{matrix} \sim R \\ or \\ \sim A \end{matrix}$$

**4.**   If and only if you are one half lunatic, would you want me to wed to a mad-cap ruffian and to a swearing Jack.

ORIGINAL

$$HL \longleftrightarrow \begin{matrix} WR \\ + \\ SJ \end{matrix} \quad \left( half\ lunatic \longleftrightarrow \begin{matrix} wed\ ruffian \\ + \\ swearing\ Jack \end{matrix} \right)$$

CONTRAPOSITIVE

$$\begin{matrix} \sim WR \\ or \\ \sim SJ \end{matrix} \longleftrightarrow \sim HL$$

**5.**   I must be armed for some unhappy words, to woo you and be happy.

ORIGINAL

$$\begin{matrix} W \\ + \\ BH \end{matrix} \longrightarrow AUW \quad \left( \begin{matrix} woo \\ + \\ be\ happy \end{matrix} \longrightarrow armed\ unhappy\ words \right)$$

CONTRAPOSITIVE

$$\sim AUW \longrightarrow \begin{matrix} \sim W \\ or \\ \sim BH \end{matrix}$$

## Inclusion Drill   ANSWER KEY

**1.** Either it is patience or despair.

ORIGINAL               ~P ⟶ D (NOT patience ⟶ despair)

CONTRAPOSITIVE         ~D ⟶ P

**2.** Either time made me his numbering clock or my thoughts are minutes.

ORIGINAL               ~TC ⟶ TM (NOT time clock ⟶ thoughts minutes)

CONTRAPOSITIVE         ~TM ⟶ TC

**3.** Either I waste time, or time wastes me.

ORIGINAL               ~WT ⟶ TWM (NOT waste time ⟶ time wastes me)

CONTRAPOSITIVE         ~TWM ⟶ WT

# Exclusion Drill   ANSWER KEY

**1.**   Nobody who lets time stroll would allow it to trot.

   **ORIGINAL**          TS ⟶ ~T (time stroll ⟶ NOT trot)

   **CONTRAPOSITIVE**    T ⟶ ~TS

It's totally cool if you swapped the original statement and the contrapositive in your answers to this drill. Either way is fine.

**2.**   No one breaks their shins against their own wit.

   **ORIGINAL**          BS ⟶ ~AW (break shins⟶ NOT against wits)

   **CONTRAPOSITIVE**    AW ⟶ ~BS

**3.**   Time never travels at the same speed for different people.

   **ORIGINAL**          TSS ⟶ ~DP (time same speed ⟶ NOT different people)

   **CONTRAPOSITIVE**    DP ⟶ ~TSS

**4.**   Never love men who are falser than vows made in wine.

   **ORIGINAL**          LM ⟶ ~FW (love men ⟶ NOT falser wine)

   **CONTRAPOSITIVE**    FW ⟶ ~LM

**5.**   Those who time gallops for are never those who it stops cold for.

   **ORIGINAL**          G ⟶ ~SC (gallop ⟶ NOT stop cold)

   **CONTRAPOSITIVE**    SC ⟶ ~G

## Unless Drill ANSWER KEY

**1.**    I can suck melancholy out of a song until a weasel sucks eggs.

      **ORIGINAL**               ~SMS ⟶ WE (NOT **suck melancholy song** ⟶ **weasel eggs**)

      **CONTRAPOSITIVE**     ~WE ⟶ SMS

**2.**    They'd call it a compliment without the encounter of the two dog-apes.

      **ORIGINAL**               ~C ⟶ DA (NOT **compliment** ⟶ **dog-apes**)

      **CONTRAPOSITIVE**     ~DA ⟶ C

**3.**    Unless his brain is as dry as the remainder biscuit, he will know.

      **ORIGINAL**               ~K ⟶ BB (NOT **know** ⟶ **brain biscuit**)

      **CONTRAPOSITIVE**     ~BB ⟶ K

**4.**    It is not my suit unless we weed your better judgments.

      **ORIGINAL**               S ⟶ WJ (**suit** ⟶ **weed judgments**)

      **CONTRAPOSITIVE**     ~WJ ⟶ ~S

**5.**    Until it meets the squandering glances of a fool, your folly is anatomized.

      **ORIGINAL**               ~FA ⟶ MGF (NOT **folly anatomized** ⟶ **meet glance fool**)

      **CONTRAPOSITIVE**     ~MGF ⟶ FA

## Some & Most Drill   ANSWER KEY

**EXTRA BIG HINT!**   *Read below if you want some extra help with your Inference before checking your answers.*

You can infer something from the **SOME** chain because the Must Arrow pointed *away* from the Some Arrow; this lets you extend the Some Arrow from the first to the last term in the chain. The **SOME** chain yields an Inference.

You can't infer anything from the **MOST** chain because the Must Arrow pointed *toward* the Most Arrow; this precludes you from extending the Most Arrow. The **MOST** chain yields no Inferences.

**1.**   Some men are born great.

   **ORIGINAL**          $M \xleftrightarrow{s} BG$ (men $\xleftrightarrow{s}$ born great)

**2.**   Some fellows achieve renown.

   **ORIGINAL**          $F \xleftrightarrow{s} AR$ (fellows $\xleftrightarrow{s}$ achieve renown)

**3.**   Most dog-apes have greatness thrust upon them.

   **ORIGINAL**          $DA \xrightarrow{m} GTU$ (dog-apes $\xrightarrow{m}$ greatness thrust upon)

**4.**   No man should be afraid of greatness.

   **ORIGINAL**          $M \longrightarrow \sim AOG$ (man $\longrightarrow$ NOT afraid of greatness)

   **CONTRAPOSITIVE**    $AOG \longrightarrow \sim M$

**5.**   If the Fates open their hands, you must be a dog-ape.

   **ORIGINAL**          $FOH \longrightarrow DA$ (fates open hands $\longrightarrow$ dog-ape)

   **CONTRAPOSITIVE**    $\sim DA \longrightarrow \sim FOH$

**THE TWO CORRECT CHAINS**   $FOH \longrightarrow DA \xrightarrow{m} GTU$

   $BG \xleftrightarrow{s} M \longrightarrow \sim AOG$

**THE CORRECT INFERENCE**    $BG \xleftrightarrow{s} \sim AOG$

## Mega-Conditional Drill   ANSWER KEY

**1.**   All the world's a stage.

ORIGINAL            W ⟶ S (world ⟶ stage)

CONTRAPOSITIVE      ~S ⟶ ~W

**2.**   All the men and women are merely players.

ORIGINAL            $\begin{matrix} M \\ + \\ W \end{matrix}$ ⟶ P   $\left( \begin{matrix} \text{men} \\ + \\ \text{women} \end{matrix} \right.$ ⟶ players $\left. \right)$

CONTRAPOSITIVE      ~P ⟶ $\begin{matrix} \text{~M} \\ \text{or} \\ \text{~W} \end{matrix}$

**3.**   They each have their exits and their entrances.

ORIGINAL            T ⟶ $\begin{matrix} \text{EX} \\ + \\ \text{EN} \end{matrix}$   $\left( \text{they} \right.$ ⟶ $\begin{matrix} \text{exit} \\ + \\ \text{entrance} \end{matrix} \left. \right)$

CONTRAPOSITIVE      $\begin{matrix} \text{~EX} \\ \text{or} \\ \text{~EN} \end{matrix}$ ⟶ ~T

> **NOTE ON #3**
>
> I couldn't use two **E**s for #3's abbreviation in this diagram. Since "exit" and "entrance" both start with **E**, I had to abbreviate out to the letter that differentiates the two words. Don't be afraid to do this. It doesn't take a lot of time, and it's more confusing when you don't do it.

**4.**   One man in his time is required to play many parts.

ORIGINAL            M ⟶ PMP (man ⟶ play many parts)

CONTRAPOSITIVE      ~PMP ⟶ ~M

**5.**   Either men are April when they woo or December when they wed.

ORIGINAL            ~AW ⟶ DW (NOT April woo ⟶ December wed)

CONTRAPOSITIVE      ~DW ⟶ AW

**6.** Only beauty provokes thieves sooner than gold.

ORIGINAL              PTS ⟶ B (provoke thieves sooner ⟶ beauty)

CONTRAPOSITIVE        ~B ⟶ ~PTS

**7.** Take as much pleasure as you may take upon a knife's point, unless you have the stomach.

ORIGINAL              ~TPK ⟶ S (NOT take pleasure knife ⟶ stomach)

CONTRAPOSITIVE        ~S ⟶ TPK

**8.** Some fools speak wiser than they know.

ORIGINAL              F ⟷ᔆ SW (fool ⟷ᔆ speak wiser)

**9.** Lunacy is so ordinary that the whippers are always in love too.

ORIGINAL              W ⟶ IL (whipper ⟶ in love)

CONTRAPOSITIVE        ~IL ⟶ ~W

**10.** Strange capers are a precondition for true lovers.

ORIGINAL              TL ⟶ SC (true lovers ⟶ strange capers)

CONTRAPOSITIVE        ~SC ⟶ ~TL

**11.** The madness, love, depends on a dark house and a whip.

ORIGINAL
$$ML \longrightarrow \begin{matrix} DH \\ + \\ W \end{matrix} \left( madness\ love \longrightarrow \begin{matrix} dark\ house \\ + \\ whip \end{matrix} \right)$$

CONTRAPOSITIVE
$$\begin{matrix} \text{~DH} \\ or \\ \text{~W} \end{matrix} \longrightarrow \text{~ML}$$

**12.** There was no thought of pleasing you when she was christened.

ORIGINAL              TP ⟶ ~WC (thought pleasing ⟶ NOT when christened)

CONTRAPOSITIVE        WC ⟶ ~TP

**13.**

I'll have no husband, if you be not he.

| | | |
|---|---|---|
| **ORIGINAL** | ~Y ⟶ ~H | (NOT you ⟶ NOT husband) |
| **CONTRAPOSITIVE** | H ⟶ Y | |

**14.**

Most men are damned, like an ill-roasted egg, all on one side.

| | | |
|---|---|---|
| **ORIGINAL** | M $\overset{m}{\longrightarrow}$ DE | (men $\overset{m}{\longrightarrow}$ damned egg) |

**15.**

I'll go sleep, if I can; if I cannot, I'll rail against all the first-born of Egypt.

| | | |
|---|---|---|
| **ORIGINAL** | C ⟶ S | (can ⟶ sleep) |
| **CONTRAPOSITIVE** | ~S ⟶ ~C | |
| **ORIGINAL** | ~C ⟶ RE | (NOT can ⟶ rail Egypt) |
| **CONTRAPOSITIVE** | ~RE ⟶ C | |
| **CHAIN** | ~RE ⟶ C ⟶ S | |

**NOTE ON #15**

If you got the contrapositive of the chain on this one, that's totally cool too! Remember, the contrapositive and the original statement are equivalent.

**16.**

Only if the compact of jars grows musical will we have discord in the spheres.

| | | |
|---|---|---|
| **ORIGINAL** | DS ⟶ CJM | (discord spheres ⟶ compact jars musical) |
| **CONTRAPOSITIVE** | ~CJM ⟶ ~DS | |

**17.**

I thank God and my cold blood, unless I am troubled with a pernicious suitor.

| | | |
|---|---|---|
| **ORIGINAL** | ~TG<br>or ⟶ TS<br>~CB | ( NOT thank God<br>or ⟶ troubled suitor<br>NOT cold blood ) |
| **CONTRAPOSITIVE** | ~TS ⟶ | TG<br>+<br>CB |

## NOTE ON #17

You may have put an **AND** in the sufficient condition on #17, but it's an **OR**. When I negate "thank God and my cold blood" to place it in the sufficient condition, I have to apply the negative to each part of the phrase. That means applying it to "thank God," "cold blood," and the **AND**! The negated version of **AND** is **OR**.

**18.**    Courtesy is never a turncoat.

     **ORIGINAL**          C $\longrightarrow$ ~T (courtesy $\longrightarrow$ NOT turncoat)

     **CONTRAPOSITIVE**    T $\longrightarrow$ ~C

**19.**    I wonder that you will still be talking, Benedick: nobody marks you.

     **ORIGINAL**          Y $\longrightarrow$ ~M (you $\longrightarrow$ NOT marks)

     **CONTRAPOSITIVE**    M $\longrightarrow$ ~Y

**20.**    Either I will wash off gross acquaintance or let imagination jade me.

     **ORIGINAL**          ~WA $\longrightarrow$ IJ (NOT wash acquaintance $\longrightarrow$ imagination jade)

     **CONTRAPOSITIVE**    ~IJ $\longrightarrow$ WA

**21.**    Cupid kills some with arrows, some with traps.

     **ORIGINAL**          CK $\overset{s}{\longleftrightarrow}$ A (cupid kills $\overset{s}{\longleftrightarrow}$ arrows)

     **ORIGINAL**          CK $\overset{s}{\longleftrightarrow}$ T (cupid kills $\overset{s}{\longleftrightarrow}$ traps)

**22.**    Men are deceivers ever if and only if they are constant never.

     **ORIGINAL**          DE $\longleftrightarrow$ CN (deceivers ever $\longleftrightarrow$ constant never)

     **CONTRAPOSITIVE**    ~CN $\longleftrightarrow$ ~DE

**23.**    Silence were the perfectest herald of joy. I were but little happy if I could say how much.

     **ORIGINAL**          SHM $\longrightarrow$ LH (say how much $\longrightarrow$ little happy)

     **CONTRAPOSITIVE**    ~LH $\longrightarrow$ ~SHM

## Quiz 4    ANSWER KEY

**1.**      If the sufficient condition is **absent**, you can completely ignore the conditional statement.

**2.**      If the sufficient condition is **present**, the conditional statement must be followed.

**3.**      NEITHER/NOR means "not this **and** not that."

**4.**      SOME means **1-100**% of the sufficient group must hold the necessary trait.

**5.**      MOST means **51-100**% of the sufficient group must hold the necessary trait.

**6.**      You can read a MOST statement backwards, as long as you switch the MOST to a SOME as you do so.

**7.**      NONE is an exclusion indicator.

**8.**      WITHOUT and UNTIL are Unless Family members.

**9.**      True.

**10.**      False. The exception in an UNLESS statement is placed in the *necessary* condition.

**11.**      False. SOME statements have no contrapositive.

**12.**      You should have circled the following sufficient indicators and no other words:
if, all, in order to, each, every, when, any, people who.

# OMMMM.

chapter four, ready for more?

These are quotations from real LSAT students! These former students were in your shoes not too long ago, and they wanted to share a few key takeaways from their prep experiences.

## Chapter Breather   WHAT ARE THE BIGGEST MYTHS ABOUT THE LSAT?

### MEHA

The biggest myth is that the LSAT is impossibly hard. It may feel that way in the beginning, but it gets easier and easier when you study consistently.

### KELLY

That you can't improve your score more than 3 or so points. I scored 176 on the final test, but I started *much* lower than that.

### VEENA

That you have to spend 24/7 learning and drilling the material in. That was the biggest mistake I made. Everyone learns differently, but most people need a balanced lifestyle. I think you will achieve better results if you spend six months learning at a slower pace than, say, one month at a very fast pace. The point is to stay consistent.

### LAUREN

That it tests innate skill and ability. Over the years, I have heard from many people that, especially for reading comprehension, your diagnostic score will be similar to your actual LSAT score. While I believe it is helpful to go into LSAT prep with a strong skill base, I also believe that you can hone many of the skills that the LSAT tests. For example, I have struggled with reading comprehension since I was a child and I also struggled with it a lot while studying for the LSAT. However, in studying for the LSAT, my reading comprehension ability improved, and so did my score.

# ASSUMPTIONS
# & THE LOOPHOLE

Pay close attention. This concept is often difficult for students to understand.

## Assumptions THE LINCHPIN OF YOUR LOGICAL REASONING SCORE

Let's start our discussion of assumptions with a simple argument:

| | |
|---|---|
| **PREMISE** | There's banana bread on the table. |
| **PREMISE** | Camille very much enjoys banana bread. |
| **CONCLUSION** | The banana bread will disappear within 20 minutes. |

Let's talk through the gap between the premises and the conclusion. The premises tell us that we've got some banana bread on the table and that Camille enjoys banana bread. That's cool, but there's not much we can infer from those premises besides the fact that Camille enjoys something on the table. Boring Inference, right? But that's good; we love boring. Boring is the valid conclusion signature.

The conclusion above is far from boring, and, hence, far from valid. It brings in disappearing banana bread and 20 minutes, new ideas that don't appear in the premises. Conclusions are supposed to be proven *by the premises*. If disappearing banana bread isn't even mentioned in the premises, chances are the premises aren't proving it 100% true. This is our gap between the premises and the conclusion, the most versatile asset you can detect on the LSAT.

The author is trying to trick you into bridging this gap for them. There's a specific, erroneous path that the untrained thinker will always take to subconsciously connect premises like these to the conclusion. Here's the erroneous thought the LSAT wants you to have: "Oh yeah, that bread is on the table and Camille is super into it. Of course, she'd eat it all. It's fine to say it would disappear." Seems reasonable, right? WRONG.

Most people don't even know they're having the thought described above. They auto-complete the argument without knowing it. Your ability to succeed at Logical Reasoning depends on your ability to notice yourself auto-completing: You can use the content of the auto-complete to your advantage. The auto-complete is *extremely* frequently the correct answer to whatever question follows the stimulus.

**This chapter is about three spins on the auto-complete: the sufficient assumption (SA), the necessary assumption (NA), and the Loophole (my personal favorite).** Let's talk through each of these spins one at a time.

# The Sufficient Assumption   THE ARGUMENT'S SUPERHERO

> A sufficient assumption proves the conclusion 100% true.

**Let's design a sufficient assumption: We'll prove the banana bread will disappear in 20 minutes.**

*Anything* is fair game as long as it **proves** the banana bread will disappear in 20 minutes. We can let our imagination run wild. *If* our idea is true, it will prove that the banana bread will definitely disappear. Here are a few ideas:

Notice the sufficient indicators in the paragraph to the left! Sufficient assumptions are very... sufficient.

| SUFFICIENT ASSUMPTION | WHAT DOES THIS SUFFICIENT ASSUMPTION PROVE? | WHY IS THIS A SUFFICIENT ASSUMPTION? |
|---|---|---|
| *A malevolent stranger will take the banana bread from the table in 10 minutes.* | *The banana bread will disappear within 20 minutes.* | *The malevolent stranger taking the banana bread forces it to disappear.* |
| *Camille always eats everything she enjoys within 20 minutes.* | *The banana bread will disappear within 20 minutes.* | *If Camille eats the banana bread, that forces it to disappear.* |
| *Everything on the table will disappear in 20 minutes.* | *The banana bread will disappear within 20 minutes.* | *Everything on the table includes the banana bread, so it will disappear for sure.* |

Some of these sound crazy, right? Who said anything about a malevolent stranger in the premises? And who says that *everything* on the table has to disappear? These are outlandishly powerful statements; these sufficient assumptions *don't have to be* true. But this is what we want! Sufficient assumptions are supposed to be powerful.

> Notice a few of the commonalities between the sufficient assumptions above. They're each using powerful words (like "will," "always," and "everything") and bridging the gap between the premises and the conclusion.

**The only thing that matters for the sufficient assumption is whether or not it forces the banana bread to disappear in 20 minutes.** *If* it forces the banana bread to disappear, it's golden. Each of these examples makes the banana bread disappear, so they are all sufficient assumptions.

STOP

Pause right here. Pop quiz!

**What does a sufficient assumption do?**

Write your answer here: _Creates a valid conclusion by bridging the premises to the conclusion_

---

\* A sufficient assumption proves the conclusion 100%. That's the only quality a sufficient assumption has to have.

The Loophole in Logical Reasoning | 163

# The Necessary Assumption  THE ARGUMENT'S FOUNDATION

*Necessary assumptions are provable, just like Inferences/valid conclusions.*

> If the conclusion is true, the necessary assumption must also be true.

**Let's see what's proven *if* the banana bread disappears in 20 minutes.** Here's our argument again:

| | |
|---|---|
| PREMISE | There's banana bread on the table. |
| PREMISE | Camille very much enjoys banana bread. |
| CONCLUSION | The banana bread will disappear within 20 minutes. |

**The necessary assumption is proven by the conclusion. It's what the conclusion *needs*,** not what it wants (also like Batman). So what does this conclusion need? Here are a few ideas:

| NECESSARY ASSUMPTION | WHY IS THIS A NECESSARY ASSUMPTION? |
|---|---|
| *The banana bread is movable.* | *If the banana bread disappears, then you have to be able to move it.* |
| *No one is successfully protecting the banana bread all day.* | *If the banana bread disappears, you couldn't have a successful protector on guard.* |
| *Camille isn't saving the banana bread for a party tomorrow.* | *If the banana bread disappears, then Camille isn't saving it for tomorrow.* |

Do these sound super basic to you? Boring, like a valid conclusion? That's awesome. Boring is also the necessary assumption signature.

**A necessary assumption is *proven by the conclusion*, just like a valid conclusion is *proven by the premises*.** Like yeah... of course, no one is protecting the banana bread if it disappears in 20 minutes. Boring. That is *exactly* how you are meant to feel in the presence of a necessary assumption. It is meant to be basic, boring, obvious.

Necessary assumptions are the foundation of your argument's house. You don't have a house without a foundation, just like you don't have an argument without the necessary assumptions that come along with it. But you never think about the foundation in your house until there's a problem with it. You also never think about a necessary assumption until your attention is drawn to it or until you encounter the biggest problem an argument can face, a Loophole.

STOP

Pause right here. Another pop quiz! (I'm cruel.)

*Write in an answer now. Look at the bottom of the page for my answer after you try yourself.*

**What does a necessary assumption do?**

Write your answer here: Acts as the foundation for the argument, it's what needs to be true for the conclusion to be true.

---

** A necessary assumption is what has to be true, if the conclusion is true. It's the necessary foundation for the argument.

# The Assumption Chain

Sufficient and necessary assumptions have different relationships to the conclusion. **The sufficient assumption proves the conclusion, and, in turn, the conclusion proves the necessary assumption.** This relationship is encapsulated in the Assumption Chain:

$$\text{Sufficient Assumption} \longrightarrow \text{Conclusion True} \longrightarrow \text{Necessary Assumption}$$

**The Assumption Chain contains everything you need to know about assumptions.** You can read it just like every other conditional chain you've seen so far. **Memorize it.**

Predictably, the sufficient assumption occupies the sufficient condition of our chain. If the sufficient assumption is true, it activates the chain and the conclusion is forced to be true. Since the conclusion is true, the necessary assumption must also be true.

The necessary assumption occupies the necessary condition in our chain. Since you can't read the conditional chain backwards without negating, you can see that the presence of the necessary assumption doesn't prove anything on its own.

Sufficient and necessary assumptions each have their own question type in Logical Reasoning. Meaning, there is a question that asks you for a sufficient assumption or necessary assumption in the answer choices. We will explore how to tackle those questions in the second half of this book. I'm introducing assumptions now because they are central to argumentation, and a strong grasp of argumentation is what will allow you to dominate the section as a whole, regardless of question type.

Let's look at a simple example of one sufficient and one necessary assumption, and then we'll place them on the Assumption Chain together. This example doesn't include premises, which will help you focus on the relationship between the assumptions and the conclusion.

| | |
|---|---|
| **CONCLUSION** | This egg will break. |
| **SUFFICIENT ASSUMPTION** | The Hammer of Zeus comes down from the sky and crushes this egg. |
| **NECESSARY ASSUMPTION** | The egg is breakable. |

This yields the following Assumption Chain:

$$\text{Hammer of Zeus} \longrightarrow \text{Break this egg} \longrightarrow \text{Egg is breakable}$$

First, let's talk through the sufficient assumption. The Hammer of Zeus is super powerful! It's like the Hand of God, the Trident of Poseidon, a recommendation from the dean of the law school of your dreams. We don't *need* the Hammer of Zeus, but it makes our lives a lot easier when we're trying to prove the egg will break.

Now for the necessary assumption. The egg being breakable is almost redundantly stupid. It's foundational, like how having a college degree is foundational for law school. A degree doesn't guarantee you admission, but you've got no shot without it. The egg being breakable doesn't *prove* that it will break, but we can't get far on breaking the egg without it being breakable.

Here are a few of the key differences between the two types of assumptions:

If you aren't completely secure handling conditional chains, re-read the Conditional Reasoning Chapter now.

| | SUFFICIENT ASSUMPTIONS | NECESSARY ASSUMPTIONS |
|---|---|---|
| **Powerful or provable?** | *Powerful* | *Provable* |
| **Boring or not boring?** | *Not boring* | *Boring* |
| **Does this always prove the conclusion 100% true?** | *Yes* | *No* |
| **If the conclusion is true, does this have to be true?** | *No* | *Yes* |

Let's examine a few examples of sufficient and necessary assumptions together. I will supply you with two example assumptions at a time, one sufficient and one necessary. We will talk through the differences between them.

---

**THE ASSUMPTION TESTS**

As I evaluate the assumption candidates, I will ask the following two questions to determine whether an assumption is sufficient or necessary, a **YES** response means we've correctly identified our assumption:

> **Sufficient Test**: Does [assumption candidate] prove the conclusion?

> **Necessary Test**: If the conclusion is true, must [assumption candidate] be true?

If you're ever confused about whether an assumption is sufficient or necessary, fill in the blanks with the specifics of the argument and ask yourself these two questions.

---

Check out this argument:

> *Coffee is a delicious beverage, and I love anything delicious. Besides coffee, I only find candy canes and Reese's Pieces delicious. Therefore, I will drink coffee tomorrow.*

The conclusion is "I will drink coffee tomorrow"; this is what our assumptions will interact with. **The sufficient assumption will prove that I will drink coffee tomorrow. The necessary assumption will have to be true, if I drink coffee tomorrow.** We'll fill in our Assumption Chain with specifics as we go.

**Sufficient**   $\longrightarrow$   I will drink coffee tomorrow.   $\longrightarrow$   **Necessary**
**Assumption**                                             **Assumption**

Here are our first two assumption candidates:

1. I will drink everything I love tomorrow.

2. I will be able to drink tomorrow.

*Practice differentiating these assumptions now. There's a pretty tough drill in a few pages.*

One of these is sufficient and the other is necessary. Take a guess at which assumption is which now. The sufficient assumption is powerful; it proves the conclusion all on its own. The necessary assumption is more cautious; the conclusion proves the necessary assumption.

Alright, let's try and figure out which one is sufficient first.

**SUFFICIENT TEST**     Does "I will drink everything I love tomorrow" prove that I will drink coffee tomorrow?

Yes! The premises say I love anything delicious and coffee is delicious. So, we know I love coffee. If I drink everything I love tomorrow, we know I'll at least be drinking coffee. Notice how this sufficient assumption used the premises to its advantage. **It picked one point in the premises and built a bridge to the conclusion**, straight from "delicious" to "drink tomorrow." This is a classic sufficient assumption move.

**SUFFICIENT TEST**     Does "I will be able to drink tomorrow" prove that I will drink coffee tomorrow?

No. Being able to do something doesn't equate to actually doing that thing. Just because I have the ability to drink doesn't mean that I will actually use that ability. **The real sufficient assumption has to *make me* drink coffee tomorrow** and this one doesn't deliver.

Let's plug our sufficient assumption into the chain:

I will drink everything I love tomorrow. ⟶ I will drink coffee tomorrow. ⟶ Necessary Assumption

Now that the suspense is gone, let's see why one of these assumptions is necessary.

**NECESSARY TEST**     If I'm drinking coffee tomorrow, must "I will drink everything I love tomorrow" be true?

No, it's not required. It's way too powerful! I'm not required to drink *everything* I love just because I'm drinking coffee.

**NECESSARY TEST**     If I'm drinking coffee tomorrow, must "I will be able to drink tomorrow" be true?

Yes! If I'm going to drink coffee tomorrow, I *have to* be able to drink. **This necessary assumption probably seems super obvious and basic.** Like, yeah, if you're drinking you have to have the ability to drink; why would you even bother pointing that out? Dude, **that is the name of the necessary assumption game.** Remember, boring is our signature.

So our full Assumption Chain looks like this:

I will drink everything I love tomorrow. ⟶ I will drink coffee tomorrow. ⟶ I will be able to drink.

Alright, let's try to differentiate another pair of assumption candidates together.

1.   No one will stop me from drinking everything I find delicious tomorrow. N

2.   Everyone will drink coffee tomorrow. S

Use the principles you saw in action in the previous example to identify these assumption candidates. Write an S next to the assumption you believe is sufficient and an N next to the assumption you believe is necessary.

OK, now that your guesses are in, we'll identify the sufficient assumption together:

*Notice how each condition proves the next one in the chain (like conditional magic).*

**SUFFICIENT TEST**   Does "No one will stop me from drinking everything I find delicious tomorrow" prove that I will drink coffee tomorrow?

No. Just because no one's stopping me doesn't mean I'm actually going to *do* something. For instance, no one's stopping me from getting up right now and running 20 miles. But am I going to do that? NO. You want your sufficient assumption to force the conclusion to be true; this one doesn't do the job.

**SUFFICIENT TEST**   Does "Everyone will drink coffee tomorrow" prove that I will drink coffee tomorrow?

Yes! I'm a part of everyone; this sufficient assumption gives me no choice but to drink coffee. This is exactly how the sufficient assumption should feel.

Let's plug it into our chain:

**Everyone will drink coffee tomorrow.** → I will drink coffee tomorrow. → **Necessary Assumption**

Now, let's look at the necessary assumption:

**NECESSARY TEST**   If I'm drinking coffee tomorrow, must "No one will stop me from drinking everything I find delicious tomorrow" be true?

Yes! Someone stopping me from drinking coffee would be bad news for the conclusion. **This necessary assumption is keeping catastrophe at bay.** It's anticipating the worst-case scenario for the conclusion and saying, "Oh yeah, that? That won't happen." **Guarding against devastating Loopholes is the necessary assumption's job.**

**NECESSARY TEST**   If I'm drinking coffee tomorrow, must "Everyone will drink coffee tomorrow" be true?

No, I could be a rebel. Just because I'm drinking coffee doesn't mean everyone else is. It's super hard to prove that everyone is necessarily doing anything. Language like "everyone" is exceedingly rare in necessary assumptions; it's way too powerful.

Here's our second Assumption Chain:

**Everyone will drink coffee tomorrow.** → I will drink coffee tomorrow. → **No one will stop me from drinking everything I find delicious tomorrow.**

The pieces of all our Assumption Chains are interchangeable. For instance, we could swap the sufficient assumption in our second chain with the sufficient assumption from our first chain, like so:

**I will drink everything I love tomorrow.** → I will drink coffee tomorrow. → **No one will stop me from drinking everything I find delicious tomorrow.**

*This works because any sufficient assumption will do the job. You can perform the same switch on the necessary assumptions and it will still work.*

Pretty cool, right? Let's examine one more pair of assumptions together:

1. Not all of the coffee will be too hot to drink tomorrow. N

2. If I only find coffee, candy canes, and Reese's Pieces delicious, I will drink coffee tomorrow. S

168

Identify which of these two assumptions is sufficient and which is necessary now. Write an S next to the sufficient assumption and an N next to the necessary assumption.

First, we'll talk through the sufficient:

**SUFFICIENT TEST**     Does "Not all of the coffee will be too hot to drink tomorrow" prove that I will drink coffee tomorrow?

No. The sufficient assumption has to *force me* to drink the coffee. All this does is remove a potential barrier, but it doesn't push the conclusion over the validity line.

**SUFFICIENT TEST**     Does "If I only find coffee, candy canes, and Reese's Pieces delicious, I will drink coffee tomorrow" prove that I will drink coffee tomorrow?

Yes! This sufficient assumption is a little more complicated, so let's take our time with it. Notice that the sufficient condition ("if I only find coffee, candy canes, and Reese's Pieces delicious") matches our second premise, and the necessary condition matches our conclusion. This is an IF OUR PREMISES, THEN OUR CONCLUSION construction — it's **the ultimate cheat for the argument.** This construction seriously lets you say, "If the first thing I said, then the second thing I said." Remember that the premises are always true, so you're cool to activate the sufficient condition here. IF OUR PREMISES, THEN OUR CONCLUSION perfectly bridges the gap between the premises and the conclusion.

Let's fill it into our chain:

If I only find coffee, candy canes,
and Reese's Pieces delicious, I will  →  I will drink coffee tomorrow.  →      Necessary
drink coffee tomorrow.                                                        Assumption

Now let's examine the necessary assumption:

**NECESSARY TEST**     If I'm drinking coffee tomorrow, must "Not all of the coffee will be too hot to drink tomorrow" be true?

Yes! Coffee being too hot to drink would preclude me from drinking it; that obstacle has to be taken out for me to have a shot at drinking coffee. This necessary assumption shields the argument against a Loophole.

**NECESSARY TEST**     If I'm drinking coffee tomorrow, must "If I only find coffee, candy canes, and Reese's Pieces delicious, I will drink coffee tomorrow" be true?

SURPRISE YES. Bear with me on this. If the argument is to have any hope, the premises have to prove the conclusion. This is the only way the conclusion is valid within the argument. It's necessary. All IF OUR PREMISES, THEN OUR CONCLUSION does is say that the premises did their job. You need the premises to work for the reasoning in the argument to be valid, and so IF OUR PREMISES, THEN OUR CONCLUSION constructions always have to be true. This makes them necessary assumptions.

IF OUR PREMISES, THEN OUR CONCLUSION **constructions are both sufficient and necessary assumptions.** They can occupy both slots in our chain, but we'll use the other necessary assumption in our last Assumption Chain:

If I only find coffee,                              Not all of the
candy canes, and Reese's                           coffee will be
Pieces delicious, I will  →  I will drink coffee tomorrow.  →  too hot to drink
drink coffee tomorrow.                             tomorrow.

## Sufficient & Necessary Assumption Drill

### INSTRUCTIONS

*Fill in the Assumption Chain with each assumption's letter from the Assumption Candidates Bank. Place sufficient assumptions before the conclusion in the Assumption Chain. Place necessary assumptions after the conclusion in the Assumption Chain.*

✻

If you're having trouble, look back at the previous section for help. Don't proceed to the next section until you have completed this drill. You can do it, reader!

**1.** Justin trimmed at least three inches off for his latest flat top haircut. That kind of drastic change always leads to increased professional success. Therefore, Justin made a great decision with his latest haircut.

### Assumption Candidates Bank

a.   Every decision Justin makes is great.

b.   Trimming off more than two inches of hair is not necessarily a terrible decision.

c.   Justin has the ability to make great decisions.

d.   The decision to get a flat top haircut has the possibility of being great.

e.   Any haircut that trims off two inches or more is a great decision.

f.   All decisions that lead to increased professional success are great.

A
E
F

⟶ **Justin made a great decision with his latest haircut.** ⟶

B
C
D

**2.** The crews of commercial fishing vessels often bond over their shared love of aquatic literature, especially *Moby Dick*. After a few months at sea, reading groups consistently form and increased camaraderie results. Therefore, commercial fishermen are natural bookworms.

**Assumption Candidates Bank**

a. Any person who steps onto a commercial fishing vessel immediately transforms into a natural bookworm.

b. A reading group forming at sea guarantees that all commercial fishermen are natural bookworms.

c. Natural bookworms do not universally dislike aquatic literature.

d. Commercial fishermen are not all illiterate.

e. If any member of a fishing crew loves Moby Dick, all commercial fishermen are natural bookworms.

f. Natural bookworms can experience increased camaraderie.

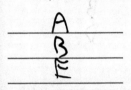 $\longrightarrow$ **Commercial fishermen are natural bookworms.** $\longrightarrow$

**3.** Leslie likes poodles, but detests toy poodles. Unlike most people, Leslie dislikes miniature versions of full-sized entities. This upsets those around her. Therefore, Leslie will not be allowed back in the house.

**Assumption Candidates Bank**

a. Leslie does not hold sole control over entry to the house.

b. When people are upset, they don't let the target of their feelings back in the house.

c. Disliking miniature versions of full-sized entities does not guarantee admittance to the house.

d. Disliking miniature things bars one from entering the house.

e. Those who are upset will build a wall around the house to keep Leslie from getting in.

f. Someone is capable of banning Leslie from the house.

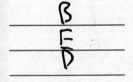 $\longrightarrow$ **Leslie will not be allowed back in the house.** $\longrightarrow$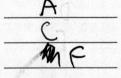

**4.** We can conclude that friendship is equivalent to laundry. We know this because if you don't attend to both friendship and laundry, they both come back to bite you. Regular contact is encouraged in both arenas by the enjoyable nature of warm clothes, a result of laundry, and a warm embrace, a result of friendship.

**Assumption Candidates Bank**

a. Human relationships are capable of being equivalent to household chores.

b. Laundry is capable of equivalency.

c. If two things both have warm results, they are equivalent.

d. Friendship and laundry don't have other differences that would preclude equivalence.

e. One similarity always makes two things equivalent.

f. Any two things that both come back to bite you when you don't attend to them are equivalent.

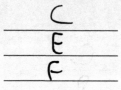

→ **Friendship is equivalent to laundry.** →

*Where's the answer key?*

You'll find the answer key at the end of the chapter on page 183.

**5.** Denim requires little labor to produce and can be sold for wildly varying prices with no difference in quality. These price differences correspond to the reputation of the brands that sell the denim, and any fabric that sells at such variable prices is desirable. Therefore, denim is the uber-fabric.

**Assumption Candidates Bank**

a. Every desirable fabric is the uber-fabric.

b. Wildly varying prices don't preclude a fabric from being deemed an uber-fabric.

c. Desirable fabrics have the possibility of being the uber-fabric.

d. Any fabric that sells at wildly varying price points is the uber-fabric.

e. Any fabric that requires little labor to produce is the uber-fabric.

f. The uber-fabric does not require intensive labor to produce.

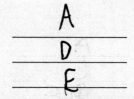

→ **Denim is the uber-fabric.** →

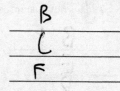

# The Loophole   WHAT IF... CATASTROPHE?

Loopholes are powerful, just like sufficient assumptions.

And finally, we arrive. The Loophole is the cornerstone of our work in Logical Reasoning. Remember the catastrophe we were ruling out in some of our necessary assumptions? This is a section all about that catastrophe.

**The Loophole is the flipside of the necessary assumption.** It's like an evil twin, which let's be honest, is always more fun than the original. Necessary assumptions are about safety. The Loophole is about danger.

The Loophole's mission reminds me of my favorite Omar moment from *The Wire*. Omar is seeking revenge against Marlo, and steals a bunch of his money, shooting a few of his lieutenants. Then Omar sets the money on fire and tells Marlo's man, "Now you make sure you tell old Marlo I burned the money. Cause it ain't about that paper. **It's about me hurtin' his people and messin' with his world."** That's you vs. the author of the stimulus. All you want to do is hurt his people and mess with his world. But hurting the author is easier said than done. You're helping the author without even knowing it.

You know how sometimes you'll accidentally omit words when you're writing? Like you'll forget to put in a really obvious "the" somewhere. For example, "I went to store" sounds dumb, but sometimes our brains auto-correct it. We fill in the gap unconsciously. You can read over a paper with an omitted word a couple times and never see what's missing. You are doing the exact same thing with arguments. **You are filling in the author's missing links for them without even knowing it.**

**Whenever you meet an argument, think of its worst-case scenario.** What is the author trying to hide from you? What are they hoping you won't notice? **There's almost always a big problem the stimulus author wants you to overlook.** They lay the breadcrumbs for you to unconsciously connect their dots for them.

Don't give the author more credit than they have earned with their exact words on the page. Don't give the author the benefit of the doubt. Don't respect them because it's the LSAT and it's intimidating. You are Omar. They are Marlo.

**Your Loophole is how you call the author out on their nonsense.** It's also the single most versatile thought you can have on the LSAT, and our training regimen for the rest of this book is built upon the Loophole.

## QUICK LOOPHOLE FAQ

**Q.**   *How do you design a Loophole?*

**A.**   Loopholes ask, "What if... really bad thing for the argument?" **Always start your Loophole thought process with "What if..."** This will free your mind to **get creative and use your common sense** against the argument. Loopholes don't have to be true, but they could be, and their mere possibility is a problem for the argument. Complete your "What if..." statement with a situation that destroys the argument's validity. That's your Loophole.

**Q.**   *How will I know that my Loophole works?*

**A.**   Your own wits! Ask yourself if the conclusion is still proven in the face of your Loophole. If the Loophole works, the conclusion should no longer be ironclad.

**Q.**  *Why am I doing this?*

**A.**  Because it will give you the answer to most of the questions in Logical Reasoning.

Let's return to our coffee argument one last time:

> *Coffee is a delicious beverage, and I love anything delicious. Besides coffee, I only find candy canes and Reese's Pieces delicious. Therefore, I will drink coffee tomorrow.*

Here are some worst-case scenarios for this argument:

> *What if I won't be able to drink delicious things tomorrow?*
>
> *What if someone stops me from drinking everything I find delicious tomorrow?*
>
> *What if all the coffee is too hot to drink tomorrow?*

**The answer to each of these what ifs is that the conclusion is no longer valid. That's how you know the Loophole works.** If the Loophole is true, the conclusion is screwed.

Notice anything about all these Loopholes? They are the negated necessary assumptions! BOOM.

| LOOPHOLE | NECESSARY ASSUMPTION |
|---|---|
| What if I won't be able to drink delicious things tomorrow? | I will be able to drink something I find delicious tomorrow. |
| What if someone stops me from drinking everything I find delicious tomorrow? | No one will stop me from drinking everything I find delicious tomorrow. |
| What if all the coffee is too hot to drink tomorrow? | Not all of the coffee will be too hot to drink tomorrow. |

**The Loophole and the necessary assumption are two sides of the same coin.** You can use either of them to find the other one as your needs require. Why does this work out so perfectly? Because of the contrapositive of our Assumption Chain!

Here is the Assumption Chain you've seen several times:

$$\text{Sufficient Assumption} \longrightarrow \text{Conclusion True} \longrightarrow \text{Necessary Assumption}$$

The contrapositive of that statement is:

$$\sim \text{Necessary Assumption} \longrightarrow \sim \text{Conclusion True} \longrightarrow \sim \text{Sufficient Assumption}$$

This contrapositive tells us that a negated necessary assumption will destroy the conclusion. What does the Loophole do? It destroys the conclusion. Sounds similar, right? **The Loophole and the negated necessary assumption are the same thing.** Meaning, we can rewrite the contrapositive like so:

$$\text{Loophole} \longrightarrow \text{~Conclusion True} \longrightarrow \text{~}\frac{\text{Sufficient}}{\text{Assumption}}$$

The Loophole (also known as the negated necessary assumption) disproves the conclusion. How cool is that? **The absolute coolest.**

## THREE COMMANDMENTS OF THE LOOPHOLE

1. **The Loophole shalt not negate the premises.**

Remember how I told you not to burn down your blocks in the Arguments & Inferences Chapter? Negating the premises is burning down your blocks.

The premises are true. The sooner you accept that, the better. The biggest mistake rookie Loophole designers make is saying, "What if that premise isn't true?" You have to attack the *relationship* between the premises, the space in between them. Focus on how they (don't) add up.

2. **The Loophole shalt not negate the conclusion.**

Saying, "What if the conclusion doesn't have to be true?" is like driving to the end of a footrace and declaring yourself the gold medal winner. You didn't run the race to earn the medal; you just kind of showed up pretending you had.

Obviously, the conclusion doesn't have to be true, unless it's proven to be true, which isn't the case on most LSAT stimuli. You can't just declare the endpoint true. The Loophole shows *why* the conclusion doesn't have to be true.

3. **The Loophole is there. Thou shalt figure it out.**

Countless students have said, "But I just can't figure out the Loophole." I always respond, "I don't believe you."

In the beginning, it can be difficult to find the right balance that enables you to quickly design a validity-destroying Loophole. But you can do this. Have the patience with yourself to build this skill. The students who tell me this are eventually able to quickly and intuitively design Loopholes. But this only happens once they stop letting themselves give up.

Let's start by talking through a few common Loopholes that you will *definitely* encounter on the LSAT. This is far from an exhaustive list of the Loopholes you'll see on the test, but they are a great place to start.

Be prepared to deploy what you learn in the next few pages on real Logical Reasoning questions. These are the LSAT shortcuts you've been waiting for.

Memorize these
Loopholes so you can use
them during LR sections.

## The Dangling Variable   A DECIDEDLY COMMON LOOPHOLE

**Dangling variables are the most common error in Logical Reasoning.** Many other reasoning errors we'll examine together are just types of dangling variables.

**Dangling variables are new words that appear in the conclusion and not in the premises.** The author pretends that these new words are "basically" the same as different words from the premises.

Dangling variables are traps set for the test taker who lets herself think two things are "basically the same." Nothing is basically the same on the LSAT. **If the author does not do the work to connect the premises and the conclusion *exactly* right, you cannot automatically do it for them.** The author's job is to *prove* something to us, and dangling variables are cheating.

A few phrases that are not necessarily the same:

- "electronics" and "inventions"

- "candy" and "something that is killing you slowly"

- "the European Union" and "a cabal"

Pretty easy to see these pairs aren't the same word, right? But dangling variables work on the same principle magicians use to make us think they're really sawing their assistants in half. **The LSAT uses fancy words to distract us. They put our attention elsewhere (or make us not pay attention at all), so that they can switch something up without us noticing.**

Here are a few examples of phrases that LSAT stimuli have assumed are functionally equivalent in meaning (paraphrased for clarity). You can see that they up the ante on the wording to camouflage that the two objects they're equating are not the same:

- "accurate" and "consistent"

- "interest of shareholders" and "profits high"

- "better developed neural connections" and "greater influence on the brain"

- "detract from social development" and "reduction in time interacting with other people"

- "diets higher in cholesterol" and "Western diets"

In context, many test takers get tricked into taking the assumed connection between these two phrases for granted. One of these phrases *may* imply the other, sure, but they are not necessarily the same. Remember, there is no basically on the LSAT.

**DANGLING**          What if those two things are not necessarily the same?
**VARIABLE LOOPHOLE**

Let's identify the dangling variable in a real LSAT stimulus together:

*June 2007.3.21*

Ethicist: On average, animals raised on grain must be fed sixteen pounds of grain to produce one pound of meat. A pound of meat is more nutritious for humans than a pound of grain, but sixteen pounds of grain could feed many more people than could a pound of meat. With grain yields leveling off, large areas of farmland going out of production each year, and the population rapidly expanding, we must accept the fact that consumption of meat will soon be morally unacceptable.

**CONCLUSION**        Consumption of meat will soon be morally unacceptable.

Check out how the conclusion brought in "morally unacceptable" out of nowhere. That's our dangling variable.

The premises never defined what is and is not morally acceptable. Yeah, we see that you can feed more people with grain than with meat, but that's not inherently connected to morality. And more importantly, the premises never set up the infrastructure for us to talk about morality in the conclusion, so we can't make claims.

**LOOPHOLE**        What if morally unacceptable ≠ not feeding more people?

Your dangling variable Loophole is super simple. Just put a ≠ between the two things the author pretends are the same.

## CONDITIONAL DANGLING VARIABLES

Conditional dangling variables add a new variable to the conclusion's conditional statement.

Check out the following example:

> *Whenever one establishes a dictatorship, one inevitably prefers the water. Preferences for the aquatic must be followed in dictatorship site selection. Therefore, dictatorships always reside in the Bay of Pigs.*

Let's translate this example into a few conditionals:

**PREMISE**        dictatorship ⟶ prefers water (D ⟶ PW)

**PREMISE**        prefers water ⟶ follow preferences (PW ⟶ FP)

This argument's premises chain to **D ⟶ PW ⟶ FP**. But check out the bad behavior in the conclusion:

**CONCLUSION**        dictatorship ⟶ Bay of Pigs (D ⟶ BOP)

Bay of Pigs is the dangling variable, a new term in the necessary condition of the conclusion. We never see anything about the Bay of Pigs in the premises. This is a huge problem for the argument's validity; no way Bay of Pigs is proven when it's not even in the premises. The author assumed that they could stealth glue ⟶ **BOP** on the end of the chain like this: **D ⟶ PW ⟶ FP (⟶ BOP)**. This imaginary chain would indeed yield **D ⟶ BOP** as a valid conclusion, but the author didn't actually include **BOP** in the real chain from the premises. This leads straight to a conditional dangling variable Loophole:

**LOOPHOLE**        What if you can't stealth add ⟶ **BOP** on the end of the chain?

For a few more dangling variable examples, check out the Sufficient & Necessary Assumption Drill from a few pages ago.

Every question has a dangling variable!
#1: "great decision"
#2: "natural bookworm"
#3: "back in the house"
#4: "equivalent"
#5: "uber-fabric"

## Secret Value Judgments    A SUPER COMMON LOOPHOLE

Secret Value Judgments happen when the author gets judgy in the conclusion. **Judgments are a *big deal* on the LSAT.** Authors can't just deem something "moral" or "appropriate" in the conclusion without defining what those words imply in the premises. Your Secret Value Judgments Loophole reminds the author that they can't just assume a convenient definition of these loaded words.

Here are a few keywords to let you know you're handling a Secret Value Judgment:

This is not an exhaustive list of every value judgment out there, but it should give you an idea of the types of words that value judgments tend to use.

### COMMON SECRET VALUE JUDGMENTS

| | | |
|---|---|---|
| *moral/immoral* | *appropriate/inappropriate* | *good/bad* |
| *should/shouldn't* | *prudent/imprudent* | *right/wrong* |

Check out a real LSAT Secret Value Judgment:

*16.2.10*

> A fundamental illusion in robotics is the belief that improvements in robots will liberate humanity from "hazardous and demeaning work." Engineers are designing only those types of robots that can be properly maintained with the least expensive, least skilled human labor possible. Therefore, robots will not eliminate demeaning work—only substitute one type of demeaning work for another.

**CONCLUSION**    Robots will not eliminate demeaning work—only substitute one type of demeaning work for another.

The Secret Value Judgment in the conclusion is "demeaning." The premises describe the work they're substituting as the "least expensive, least skilled human labor." That doesn't say demeaning, and "least expensive, least skilled" doesn't necessarily mean demeaning. Calling something demeaning is a *big* value judgment, and remember, we can't just assume something qualifies as demeaning. That's our opening.

> **PRO TIP** Nobody really knows what "good" means. Philosophers have debated it for millennia, and we still haven't *really* figured it out. If Aristotle can't establish a universally-accepted definition of the good in hundreds of pages, an LSAT stimulus author sure can't assume one in less than 100 words.

**LOOPHOLE**    What if the least expensive and least skilled labor is not demeaning?

Secret Value Judgments are *very* hard for the author to prove and also very common. The author wants you to do them the small favor of just believing that the premises fit into the value judgments they're imagining. Don't fall for it; call Secret Value Judgments on them.

**SECRET VALUE JUDGMENTS**    What if that value judgment doesn't have that definition?

# Secret Downsides   A VERY COMMON LOOPHOLE

Secret Downsides happen when the author compares two things and says one of them is superior without giving you the full story. They'll say their preferred choice has a few upsides, but your Loophole will remind them of the Secret Downsides they're not considering.

Check out a real LSAT Secret Downside:

> 16.2.19
>
> The Volunteers for Literacy Program would benefit if Dolores takes Victor's place as director, since Dolores is far more skillful than Victor is at securing the kind of financial support the program needs and Dolores does not have Victor's propensity for alienating the program's most dedicated volunteers.

| CONCLUSION | The Volunteers for Literacy program would benefit if Dolores takes Victor's place as director. |
|---|---|

Let's find a way around this conclusion. I'm going to find a way Dolores could be even worse than all of Victor's nonsense. Dolores is better than Victor at raising money and not upsetting volunteers, but **we don't know their relative abilities on any other topic**. That's our opening.

So let's make up the most extreme differences we can: What if Dolores assaults the full-time program staff? What if Dolores changes the mission of the organization to suit her personal political views? What if she isn't as hard a worker as Victor and she's only going to put in like an hour a week? We would still honor the truth of the premises, but Dolores would be a worse choice than Victor.

If we distill all of my what ifs into one sentence, we have a great Loophole:

| LOOPHOLE | What if Dolores has some major downside in comparison to Victor that we're not accounting for? |
|---|---|

Secret Downsides is super common. Most Logical Reasoning sections have many stimuli begging for you to call Secret Downsides. They always set up two options and say, "We prefer one of these because it's better in a few ways," but you can't leave it at that. There could always be a Secret Downside to the author's preferred option. The author will always leave out anything inconvenient for them; that's where your Secret Downsides Loophole comes in.

| SECRET DOWNSIDES | What if the argument's preferred option has a big downside? |
|---|---|

## Assumed Universal Goals   A HIGHLY COMMON LOOPHOLE

Assumed universal goals are the things the author assumes *everyone* would want. They're the goals you constantly see commercials about.

---

**COMMON ASSUMED UNIVERSAL GOALS**

| | | |
|---|---|---|
| *losing weight* | *making more money* | *being healthier* |
| *lowering cholesterol* | *being more successful* | |

---

You will see entire arguments built around the assumption that everyone wants to pursue one of these things. This is, of course, nonsense.

**Never assume that it's common knowledge for everyone to want one of these things.** Some people need to gain weight, others should remember more money = more problems. None of these goals are as universal as the author would have you believe.

This is not a complete list of all the assumed universal goals you will ever see in Logical Reasoning. It's a small sample so you can get the gist of the types of things they assume everyone would pursue. Once you see this trick played a few times, it's easy to spot, and you've got a ready-made Loophole on hand for the occasion.

**ASSUMED**
**UNIVERSAL GOAL**     What if they don't want to [assumed universal goal]?

---

**ASSUMPTIONS & THE LOOPHOLE GAME PLAN**

- Try to find the Loophole in everything you hear for the next 24 hours. Welcome to the blessed/ cursed life of the LSAT expert.

- Keep what is left unsaid at the forefront of your mind in every argument. The correct answer to most questions lives in that gap.

- Read every stimulus skeptically. The arguments on the LSAT are mostly terrible.

- Keep studying this chapter until you really know the difference between sufficient and necessary assumptions. Sufficient assumptions are powerful. Necessary assumptions are provable.

---

### INSTRUCTIONS

*Answer these questions based on your knowledge of the chapter. Attempt to answer without looking back at the chapter first. If you don't know the answer, circle the question number and go find the answer in the chapter. Study the sections of the chapter that you couldn't remember at first.*

### Word Bank

| | | |
|---|---|---|
| boring | provable | necessary |
| not boring | sufficient | assumption(s) |
| SA | NA | powerful |
| yes | conclusion(s) | no |

* SA = sufficient assumption

NA = necessary assumption

*Use the word bank to answer the fill-in-the-blank questions. Some words will not be used and others may be used more than once.*

**1.** _Assumptions_ are missing links.

**2.** The Loophole is the negated form of the _necessary assumption_.

**3.** The Assumption Chain: __SA__ → __Conclusion__ True → __NA__

**4.** Circle the correct heading (SA or NA) and then complete the table using the word bank.

| | (SA) or NA | SA or (NA) |
|---|---|---|
| **Powerful or provable?** | Powerful | Provable |
| **Boring or not boring?** | NB | B |
| **Does this always prove the conclusion 100% true?** | Yes | No |
| **If the conclusion is true, does this have to be true?** | No | Yes |

**5.** This is the _____SA_____ Test: Does [assumption candidate] prove the conclusion?

**6.** This is the _____NA_____ Test: If the conclusion is true, must [assumption candidate] be true?

*Circle the correct answer to the following questions.*

**7.** TRUE OR ~~FALSE~~    Loopholes don't have to be true, but they could be.

**8.** TRUE OR (FALSE)    The Loophole helps the conclusion.

**9.** TRUE OR (FALSE)    The Loophole can negate the premises.

**10.** (TRUE) OR ~~FALSE~~    On the LSAT, we can't let the author make assumptions beyond commonsense ones.

**11.** Which one of the following arguments contains a dangling variable?

   a.    I believe I am capable of getting a record deal. Therefore, I will get a record deal.

   (b.)    Australia will be the first to fall. Therefore, the kangaroo will soon be endangered.

*Where's the answer key?*

You'll find the answer key at the end of the chapter on page 184.

**12.** Which one of the following arguments contains an assumed universal goal?

   a.    Maple and bacon were created for one another. Therefore, they are food soulmates.

   (b.)    Maple and bacon cause you to gain weight when you eat them. Therefore, you should stop eating them and become sad.

# Sufficient & Necessary Assumption Drill ANSWER KEY

## 1.

| a |
| e | → Justin made a great decision with his latest haircut. → |
| f |

| b |
| c |
| d |

## 2.

| a |
| b | → Commercial fishermen are natural bookworms. → |
| e |

| c |
| d |
| f |

## 3.

| b |
| d | → Leslie will not be allowed back in the house. → |
| e |

| a |
| c |
| f |

## 4.

| c |
| e | → Friendship is equivalent to laundry. → |
| f |

| a |
| b |
| d |

## 5.

| a |
| d | → Denim is the uber-fabric. → |
| e |

| b |
| c |
| f |

## Quiz 5 ANSWER KEY

**1.** **Assumptions** are missing links.

**2.** The Loophole is the negated form of the **NA**.

**3.** The Assumption Chain: **SA** ⟶ **Conclusion True** ⟶ **NA**

**4.**

|  | SA | NA |
|---|---|---|
| **Powerful or provable?** | Powerful | Provable |
| **Boring or not boring?** | **Not boring** | **Boring** |
| **Does this always prove the conclusion 100% true?** | **Yes** | No |
| **If the conclusion is true, does this have to be true?** | No | **Yes** |

**5.** This is the **Sufficient** Test: Does [assumption candidate] prove [conclusion]?

**6.** This is the **Necessary** Test: If [conclusion], must it be true that [assumption candidate]?

**7.** True.

**8.** False. The Loophole *destroys* the conclusion.

**9.** False. The Loophole *cannot* negate the premises.

**10.** True.

**11.** **B** contains the dangling variable (kangaroo).

**12.** **B** contains the assumed universal goal (not gaining weight).

OMMMM.

chapter five. you survived.

## Chapter Breather    HOW DID YOU MAKE SURE YOU WERE REALLY READING THE STIMULUS?

**KELLY**

I'm always actively assessing/thinking about what I'm reading during the first read. You cannot get away with passive reading on the LSAT. You will waste time if you skim.

**CHRIS**

I made sure I was able to explain the stimulus to someone else without looking at it.

**VEENA**

Remind yourself that if you skim through the stimulus you're probably not picking up key details and are setting yourself up for disaster in the answer choices. You're just going to waste time re-reading it, so do it right the first time.

**NIRA**

My biggest problem was that I wasn't really reading the stimulus, so I have a lot to say on this one. I was stuck for about a year with anywhere between -8 to -12 on every Logical Reasoning section because I wasn't really reading the stimulus. After three sections of the Basic Translation Drill, I got to -3 or -4. A week after starting the Basic Translation Drill, I got a -1 for the first time. I'm at a top 10 law school right now because of the Basic Translation Drill.

Before the drill, I misread almost every stimulus. Although the drill was hard work, I am so thankful for it. It is the reason my stimulus read (and score) improved significantly. Apart from preventing misreads, it helped me improve my memory, and in turn, significantly lessened the time pressure. Before I did the Basic Translation Drill, I wasn't getting to the last 4 questions — but once I did the drill consistently, I always finished the section right on time.

Here's what the Basic Translation Drill gave me (and hence, what enabled me to really read the stimulus):

- What you are reading says *only* what it says – don't go a step further and fabricate/conclude things that aren't actually there.

- My memory improved, which helps so much with timing!

- Because I started giving the stimulus the time it needs, I started noticing patterns in the stimuli that I wasn't noticing before.

- Because the drill forced me to go slow and remember things, I started seeing the gaps in reasoning as I was going. Because I was devoting more time to each sentence, I noticed things that were wrong with the stimulus that I would not have given myself enough time to notice before. Though this took long initially, the time invested was totally worth it because this practice soon became second nature.

- Once I had done the drill enough, my brain was trained to do all of this for every question automatically and much faster.

# CAUSAL
# REASONING

## Cause and Effect

Now that you have Loopholes on the brain, it's the perfect time to introduce you to Loophole-central: causal reasoning.

Causal reasoning is just simple cause and effect. A cause is something that makes something else happen. An effect is the thing that is made to happen by the cause. **A causal argument claims that a cause and effect relationship exists.** That sounds pretty reasonable as a thing for an argument to do, right? WRONG.

Here is a list of words to let you know you're dealing with causal reasoning. Memorize this list.

### CAUSAL INDICATORS

| | | | |
|---|---|---|---|
| *cause* | *produced by* | *leads to* | *effect* |
| *responsible for* | *factor* | *product* | |

**Causal conclusions are extremely Loophole-vulnerable.** The author can essentially never prove their causal conclusion, unless they've stated it as a really weak Possibility Conclusion, which is exceedingly rare. This is great for you as a test taker and burgeoning Loophole detective.

Why are causal conclusions so Loophole-vulnerable? Because every causal conclusion cherry-picks one possible explanation of a phenomenon, and we happen to know some other possible explanations. So, for your Loophole, you just ask, "What if one of those alternate explanations is true?" and you're in business.

Let's explore each of these possible explanations with an example causal argument:

> *Stephanie was screaming as the squirrel ran away. Therefore, Stephanie's scream caused the squirrel to run from her.*

The conclusion claims Stephanie's scream is the cause, and the squirrel running is the effect. On the surface, this looks pretty reasonable, right? Squirrels tend to be easily startled. You probably wouldn't give one of your friends a hard time if they used this sentence in a story about Stephanie. But that surface-level reasonableness is not enough on the LSAT. **Appearances are deceiving in causal reasoning.** Let's go on a Loophole hunt:

1. *What if Stephanie and the squirrel were too far away from one another to see or hear each other?*
2. *What if the squirrel running away is what caused Stephanie to yell?*
3. *What if the squirrel (or Stephanie and the squirrel) was reacting to James' unprovoked squirrel attack?*

Each of these Loopholes proves that the simple cause and effect relationship purported in the conclusion isn't necessarily true. And these Loopholes are so common they have a name: The Omitted Options.

# The Omitted Options

These same three Omitted Option Loopholes pertain to every causal conclusion on the LSAT:

| OMITTED OPTION | SQUIRREL EXAMPLE |
|---|---|
| *What if there's no relationship here at all?* | *Stephanie and squirrel were too far away to interact.* |
| *What if the causation is backwards?* | *Squirrel running caused Stephanie to yell.* |
| *What if a new factor caused one or both these things?* | *James' squirrel attack caused one or both.* |

Let's examine the Omitted Options one by one to understand why they're so devastating:

## NO RELATIONSHIP

> *What if Stephanie and the squirrel were too far away from one another to see or hear each other?*

It's possible that the two things the author claims are causally connected actually have no relationship at all. Remember that **the LSAT lies by omission.** They're leaving out key information. Stephanie could yell all the time. Squirrels definitely run all day. **These things could happen independently of one another.**

How can you know these two things have no relationship? Here are a few Loopholes that show No Relationship:

| WAY TO SHOW NO RELATIONSHIP | SQUIRREL EXAMPLE |
|---|---|
| *What if sometimes the cause happens and the effect doesn't?* | *What if Stephanie yells and the squirrel just chills out?* |
| *What if sometimes the cause doesn't happen and the effect does?* | *What if Stephanie is quiet and the squirrel runs anyway?* |
| *What if the study, survey, experiment, or situation is flawed?* | *What if Stephanie and the squirrel were too far apart to see or hear each other?* |

## BACKWARDS CAUSATION

> *What if the squirrel running away is what caused Stephanie to yell?*

They claimed Stephanie's scream was the cause and the squirrel running was the effect. However, this Loophole suggests that Stephanie's scream is the effect and the squirrel running is the cause. This works. **Reversing the cause and effect like this is almost always a possibility with any causal conclusion on the LSAT.**

## NEW FACTOR CAUSING ONE OR BOTH

> *What if Stephanie and the squirrel were both reacting to James' unprovoked squirrel attack?*

The initial causal conclusion didn't mention James, but that's totally fine. The LSAT is always leaving out crucial bits of information. **There can always be a third factor in the mix that caused one or both things to happen.**

The only time we can't point to Backwards Causation is when the supposed cause occurs *before* the supposed effect. Backwards Causation wouldn't really make sense then, right? You can't cause something if you happen after it. In that case, rely on one of your other Omitted Options.

Correlation vs. causation appears *a lot* every test; the test makers seem to really care that you know how to call them on it.

## Correlation & Causation    THE LR FRENEMIES

The Omitted Options always work as Loopholes because causal stimuli always make the same erroneous assumption: correlation = causation. This is a very bad assumption.

A correlation is when two things occur together. They could have occurred together once or many times — either way, it's a correlation. Like when you make a peanut butter and jelly sandwich, peanut butter is correlated with jelly. They're always occurring together. But is peanut butter *causing* you to put jelly on your sandwich? No, peanut butter doesn't control minds.

Why does the LSAT consistently equate correlation with causation? Well, it's easy to prove that two things are correlated. Things occur together and they're correlated. Open and shut case. It's much more interesting and Loophole-laden to claim that one thing *causes* another. Logical Reasoning is a Loophole test, so it makes sense to throw down a bunch of flawed causal conclusions instead of making ironclad claims about correlation.

If you remember one thing from this whole chapter, let it be this:

CORRELATION ≠ CAUSATION

When two things (**A** and **B**) are correlated with one another, there are four possible explanations for that occurrence:

| | |
|---|---|
| **A causes B.** | Cherry-picked causal explanation |
| **B causes A.** | Backwards causation |
| **C causes B or both A and B.** | New factor causing one or both |
| **Nobody causes anything.** | No relationship |

None of these four explanations are inherently more likely than any other. That's why I said causal conclusions are cherry-pickers. They're choosing their favorite option somewhat randomly. **They choose to believe that A causes B when any of the other three possibilities, the Omitted Options, are equally likely.**

You will see a real LSAT example of causal reasoning at the beginning of the very next chapter!

The Omitted Options are your ready-to-go Loopholes on every causal conclusion you encounter.

---

### CAUSAL REASONING GAME PLAN

- Learn to recognize causal reasoning in the wild. Use your indicator words and knowledge of cause/effect to make this happen.

- Always have your consistent causal reasoning attack ready. It's the same thing every time.

- The Omitted Options are always viable Loopholes in causal reasoning. Use them.

- Repeat this mantra until it's annoyingly obvious: correlation ≠ causation.

---

# Causal Reasoning Drill

## INSTRUCTIONS

*Circle the correct description of the potential Omitted Option in each argument. Some potential Omitted Options may not be real Omitted Options (confounded impostors); in this case, you should circle "Not Omitted Option." You may choose the same Omitted Option more than once per argument.*

**1.** Studies have shown that over time, professional typists, all of whom type for more than six hours per day, have a significantly increased risk of hypertension. Thus, typing for more than six hours per day causes hypertension.

| POTENTIAL OMITTED OPTION | CORRECT DESCRIPTION | |
|---|---|---|
| What if having hypertension causes one to type more than six hours per day? | No relationship | ~~Backwards causation~~ |
| | New factor | Not Omitted Option |
| What if having a type-A personality causes one to both suffer from hypertension and pursue a career as a professional typist? | No relationship | Backwards causation |
| | ~~New factor~~ | Not Omitted Option |
| What if most people who type for more than six hours per day and are not professional typists do not suffer from an increased rate of hypertension? | ~~No relationship~~ | Backwards causation |
| | New factor | Not Omitted Option |

**2.** A study concluded that not receiving adequate Vitamin C through one's diet results in decreased vigor throughout the day. A group of college seniors were found to have a significant Vitamin C deficiency and all suffer from an extreme lack of vigor.

| POTENTIAL OMITTED OPTION | CIRCLE THE CORRECT DESCRIPTION | |
|---|---|---|
| What if college seniors are overworked, which contributes to both vitamin deficiency and a lack of vigor? | No relationship | Backwards causation |
| | ~~New factor~~ | Not Omitted Option |
| What if most of the population doesn't receive adequate Vitamin C and very few experience a lack of vigor? | ~~No relationship~~ | Backwards causation |
| | New factor | Not Omitted Option |
| What if Vitamin C deficiency is a serious health concern? | No relationship | Backwards causation |
| | New factor | ~~Not Omitted Option~~ |

*Where's the answer key?*

You'll find the answer key at the end of the chapter on page 194.

## Quiz 6   CAUSAL REASONING

### INSTRUCTIONS

*Answer these questions based on your knowledge of the chapter. Attempt to answer without looking back at the chapter first. If you don't know the answer, circle the question number and go find the answer in the chapter. Study the sections of the chapter that you couldn't remember at first.*

### Word Bank

| | | |
|---|---|---|
| Loophole(s) | sufficient | causation |
| effect(s) | correlation(s) | cause(s) |
| Inference(s) | certainty | possibility |
| A | B | C |

*Use the word bank to answer the fill-in-the-blank questions. Some words will not be used and others may be used more than once.*

**1.** A causal argument claims that a(n) _____cause_____ and _____effect_____ relationship exists.

**2.** Causal reasoning is extremely _____Loophole_____ -vulnerable.

**3.** The Omitted Options always work as Loopholes because causal stimuli always make the same erroneous assumption: _____Correlation_____ = _____Causation_____ .

**4.** When an author claims that **A** causes **B**, the three other possible explanations are:

a. _____B_____ causes _____A_____ .

b. _____C_____ causes _____B_____ or both _____A_____ and _____B_____ .

c. No relationship between _____A_____ and _____B_____ .

*Circle the correct answer to the following questions.*

**5.** **TRUE OR FALSE** One of the Omitted Options is more likely than the others.

**6.** Seek and find! Circle only the causal indicators in the word cloud.

  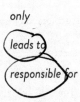

if

for

factor

produced by

effect

so

cause

every

product

only

leads to

responsible for

**7.** Seek and find!   Circle only the Omitted Options in the word cloud.

no relationship

new factor causing one or both

overgeneralized relational

forwards causation

backwards causation

loophole correlation

*Where's the answer key?*

You'll find the answer key
at the end of the chapter
on page 195.

## Causal Reasoning Drill   ANSWER KEY

**1.**   Studies have shown that over time, professional typists, all of whom type for more than six hours per day, have a significantly increased risk of hypertension. Thus, typing for more than six hours per day causes hypertension.

| POTENTIAL OMITTED OPTION | CORRECT DESCRIPTION |
|---|---|
| What if having hypertension causes one to type more than six hours per day? | Backwards causation |
| What if having a type-A personality causes one to both suffer from hypertension and pursue a career as a professional typist? | New factor |
| What if most people who type for more than six hours per day and are not professional typists do not suffer from an increased rate of hypertension? | No relationship |

**2.**   A study concluded that not receiving adequate Vitamin C through one's diet results in decreased vigor throughout the day. A group of college seniors were found to have a significant Vitamin C deficiency and all suffer from an extreme lack of vigor.

| POTENTIAL OMITTED OPTION | CORRECT DESCRIPTION |
|---|---|
| What if college seniors are overworked, which contributes to both vitamin deficiency and a lack of vigor? | New factor |
| What if most of the population doesn't receive adequate Vitamin C and very few experience a lack of vigor? | No relationship |
| What if Vitamin C deficiency is a serious health concern? | Not an Omitted Option |

**1.**      A causal argument claims that a **cause** and **effect** relationship exists.

**2.**      Causal reasoning is extremely **Loophole**-vulnerable.

**3.**      The Omitted Options always work as Loopholes because causal stimuli always make the same erroneous assumption: **correlation** = **causation**.

**4.**
     a.    **B** causes **A**.

     b.    **C** causes **B** or both **A** and **B**.

     c.    No relationship between **A** and **B**.

**5.**      False. *None* of the Omitted Options are more likely than any other.

**6.**      You should have circled the following causal indicators and no other words: cause, effect, produced by, responsible for, leads to, factor, product.

**7.**      You should have circled the following Omitted Options and no other words: "no relationship," "backwards causation," and "new factor causing one or both."

# OMMMM.

chapter six. you're in the mix.

# Chapter Breather    A FEW "COMMON KNOWLEDGE" SCIENCE TERMS YOU NEED TO KNOW

You may be taking the LSAT to run as fast as you can away from science. If so, rest assured that I didn't take one science class in college; I promise not to get too complicated.

The LSAT loves Darwinism and genetics. Let's look at a few oft-used terms:

| SCIENCE! | EXPLANATION |
|---|---|
| Charles Darwin | Charles Darwin pioneered the theory of evolution and natural selection. |
| natural selection | According to natural selection, traits that give an organism a reproductive advantage will be more likely to persist in future generations, gradually changing the species. |
| gene | A gene is made of DNA. Our genes determine traits like height and shoe size. |
| mutation | A mutation is a random genetic change. As genes replicate, sometimes there are errors and these errors create random new traits. |
| nature vs. nurture | Nature vs. nurture is the debate over whether traits are genetic or from our environment. |

You'll also see some stimuli (and passages in Reading Comprehension) about earth and space:

| SCIENCE! | EXPLANATION |
|---|---|
| atmosphere | The atmosphere is the many layers of gases that surround the earth and protect us from radiation and such. The stratosphere and troposphere are layers of the atmosphere. |
| planet | A planet orbits a star. The sun is the star that the earth orbits. |
| asteroid | Asteroids also orbit stars, but they're smaller than planets. They're basically space rocks and have irregular orbits. Asteroids can enter our atmosphere as meteors. |
| ecosystem | An ecosystem is the group of all the living things in a given area. Many questions will talk about potential threats to an ecosystem, like an invasive species. |
| global warming | Global warming is the phenomenon that makes the earth's temperature gradually rise and melt the glaciers, which then causes sea levels to rise. It has been linked to carbon dioxide emissions and the burning of fossil fuels. |
| pesticides | Pesticides are chemicals that farmers spray on plants to kill insects. These chemicals can have negative consequences for the plant and the humans that ingest the plant. |
| carbon dating | Carbon dating is a technique used by scientists to find out how old things are. It measures how much the carbon has decayed in the object the scientists want to date. |

That's it! If you already know these terms, that's awesome. If not, memorize them now.

You would be really surprised how many LR and RC questions my students have answered incorrectly because they don't know these words.

THE
CLASSIC
FLAWS

## Loophole Shortcuts    16 CLASSIC FLAWS FOR FUN AND PROFIT

Classic flaws are automatic Loopholes. Humankind has been making arguments for a very long time, and it has been making mistakes for just as long. We tend to make the same mistakes over and over again, and this is a list of the all-time classics.

Classic Flaw is the most popular question type in Logical Reasoning, so you will often be asked to directly recall what you've read in this chapter. But this section will not only serve as a reference for the Classic Flaw questions you'll encounter in the second half of this book; it will also help you identify Loopholes in every argument, regardless of question type.

> A real LSAT stimulus will accompany each classic flaw explanation. The portions of the stimulus that stand out to the expert are bolded. This is one of the most valuable things I can do for you. Logical Reasoning is all about figuring out which parts of the stimulus matter and which don't. The bolded portions are like neon signs for that classic flaw.

**As you study each of these classic flaws, make flashcards.** Name the classic flaw on one side and write your own argumentative example of the classic flaw on the other side. Creating your own example will help you memorize the classic flaw more quickly and easily. Study with these flashcards until you can instantly recognize the classic flaws.

Most of being awesome at Logical Reasoning is pattern recognition and the classic flaws are a bunch of really popular patterns. When you see a classic flaw, designing your Loophole becomes really easy. You can just say, "What if [classic flaw] is nonsense?"

In the Classic Flaw question type section in Chapter 10, you'll see how each classic flaw is commonly described in the answer choices.

# Bad Conditional Reasoning    THE LSAT MISREADS CONDITIONALS

## THE PLAY-BY-PLAY

**1.** There are conditional premises.

OR

**1.** There are conditional premises.

**2.** Crazy person concludes something by reading the conditional premises backwards without negating.

**2.** Crazy person concludes something by negating the conditional premises and reading it forwards.

The author is just bad at conditional reasoning. It's sad really. Bad Conditional Reasoning occurs when the author **reads the conditionals supplied in the premises incorrectly.**

Take this example:

*If you ride a wild horse, you are an adventurous sort. All adventurous sorts desire the thrill of the new. Therefore, if you desire the thrill of the new, you must have ridden a wild horse.*

The premises yield the following conditional chain: **wild horse ⟶ adventurous sort ⟶ thrill of new**

The conclusion then states: **thrill of new ⟶ wild horse**

Blasphemy! The author read the conditional chain backwards without negating! Never trust that the author will read conditionals correctly. They routinely mess it up.

Now, what if the conclusion said this instead:

*Therefore, if you don't ride a wild horse, you don't desire the thrill of the new.*

**~wild horse ⟶ ~thrill of new**

Double blasphemy! The author negated the premise chain and read straight through. They're asking for you to catch them with your superior grasp of conditional reasoning.

**LOOPHOLE**    What if we actually have to follow the rules of conditional reasoning?

Here is how they deploy Bad Conditional Reasoning in a real LSAT stimulus:

*27.4.10*

> Unplugging a peripheral component such as a "mouse" from a personal computer renders all of the software programs that require that component unusable on that computer. On Fred's personal computer, a software program that requires a mouse has become unusable. So it must be that the mouse for Fred's computer became unplugged.

The premises' conditional is simple: **unplug ⟶ unusable**. But the conclusion reads this statement backwards without negating! The conclusion states that Fred *must* have something unplugged because a program isn't working: **unusable ⟶ unplug**, but there are plenty of other reasons this program might not be working. We don't know anything from the presence of the necessary condition.

## Bad Causal Reasoning   REMEMBER THOSE OMITTED OPTIONS

If you skipped here without reading the Causal Reasoning Chapter, go back and read it now. Seriously, it's really short.

### THE PLAY-BY-PLAY

**1.** Crazy person sees that two things are correlated.

**2.** Crazy person concludes that one of those things is causing the other.

The vast majority of causal conclusions on the LSAT are bad. Looking for Bad Causal Reasoning is really just looking for causal reasoning — as soon as you see it, the Omitted Options should start popping into your head. Here's an example:

*Natalie Portman's lack of chemistry with Hayden Christensen and her outlandish costumes made the Star Wars prequels borderline unwatchable. Therefore, Natalie Portman caused the temporary downfall of the franchise.*

Remind the author of the Omitted Options:

| OMITTED OPTION | LOOPHOLE |
|---|---|
| **New factor causing one or both** | *What if the director is the one responsible for the problems with Natalie Portman's performance and the temporary downfall of the franchise?* |
| **No relationship** | *What if actors are too insignificant to movies as a whole to cause the temporary downfall of a franchise?* |
| **No relationship** | *What if Natalie Portman had outlandish costumes and no chemistry in another movie franchise and that franchise flourished?* |

Overall, causal arguments are really lucky finds. They always have the same Loophole:

**LOOPHOLE**        What if one of the Omitted Options is the case?

Let's see how Bad Causal Reasoning looks in a real LSAT stimulus:

*15.3.9*

> **Chronic fatigue** syndrome, a condition that afflicts thousands of people, is invariably **associated with lower-than-normal** concentrations of **magnesium** in the blood. Further, **malabsorption of magnesium** from the digestive tract to the blood is also often **associated with** some types of **fatigue**. These facts in themselves demonstrate that treatments that **raise** the concentration of **magnesium** in the blood would provide an effective **cure for the fatigue** involved in the syndrome.

The two correlated factors in this example are fatigue and low magnesium, but the author assumes a causal relationship. The author assumes that low magnesium levels are the cause and fatigue is the effect, so raising magnesium would cause fatigue levels to improve. While this is a serviceable mid-party hypothesis, it is not valid reasoning. There are many possible explanations for this correlation; for instance, there could be a new factor (like malnutrition) causing both fatigue and low magnesium.

# Whole-to-Part & Part-to-Whole  PARTS ≠ WHOLES

**THE PLAY-BY-PLAY**

1. Crazy person says a member of a category has a property.

OR

1. Crazy person says a category has a property.

2. Crazy person concludes that the category itself also has that property.

2. Crazy person concludes that a member of that category also has that property.

Imagine that you have the best kind of pie, a pumpkin pie. You cut a normally proportioned piece of pie for yourself. That piece of the pie is vaguely triangular, right? Now you turn to a friend and tell them that since this piece of the pie is triangular, the whole pie is triangular. The friend you say this to is no longer your friend.

Now, imagine you have the same piece of pie in your hand and you look at another friend and say that since the whole pie is circular, this piece of pie you have in your hand is circular. You've now lost two friends.

That's Whole-to-Part, reader. It's a friend-losing proposition.

The examples in this chart may sound more reasonable than the pie example, but they rest on the exact same classic flaw in reasoning. You can never assume from wholes to parts or from parts to wholes.

**LOOPHOLE**  What if wholes don't necessarily equal parts?

Here is an example of Whole-to Part in a real LSAT stimulus:

*17.3.16*

> **Each of the elements** of Girelli's recently completed design for a university library **is copied** from a different one of several historic libraries. The design includes various features from Classical Greek, Islamic, Mogul, and Romanesque structures. Since no one element in the design is original, it follows that the **design of the library cannot be considered original**.

| PART | WHOLE |
|---|---|
| *a Starbucks location* | *Starbucks Corporation* |
| *Mars* | *the solar system* |
| *stop signs* | *government property* |
| *a member of the mock trial team* | *the mock trial team* |
| *bricks in a building* | *the building* |

The bolded portions here look like a big neon Part-to-Whole light to the expert test taker. When you go from premises about all the parts of something having a property to a conclusion about the whole having that property, the Loophole is simple. In this case, all the elements of the design were not original, so the author concluded that the design itself couldn't be original. But what if no one had ever mixed those design elements exactly that way before? The combination of parts could be original. This is why Part-to-Whole doesn't work. Composition of the parts is something in itself.

The Loophole in Logical Reasoning | 203

## Overgeneralization   PART ≠ ALL THE PARTS

### THE PLAY-BY-PLAY

**1.** Crazy person talks about something having a property.

**2.** Crazy person concludes that a bunch of other things also have that property.

Let's return to our pumpkin pie. Imagine you cut yourself a generous piece of pie. It's about the size and shape of your palm. Then you turn to your last remaining friend and tell them their piece is also the size of your palm. They look down at their piece. You then say that all the pieces in the world are the size of your palm. No friends left.

Overgeneralization takes something small and turns it into something big. It occurs when you have premises about something specific — say, a hot temperature. A temperature could be hot, could be cold, could be pleasantly temperate. **To overgeneralize, you take a premise about hot temperatures and conclude about temperatures in general.**

### A COLLECTION OF OVERGENERALIZED PAIRS

These pairs overgeneralize a part of a spectrum to everything on that spectrum:

| SMALL PREMISES | BIG CONCLUSION |
| --- | --- |
| [adjective] + thing | thing |
| cold rooms | rooms |
| moderate caffeine intake | caffeine intake |

These pairs overgeneralize a part of a category to all the parts of a category:

| SMALL PREMISES | BIG CONCLUSION |
| --- | --- |
| one category member | all category members |
| Grover Cleveland | all forgettable presidents |
| Comic Sans | any other font |

Check out a few examples of Overgeneralization:

- Liana was quite **clever in her paper on shark anatomy**. So Liana is a **clever person**.

- We got **better** results at **70° rather than 60°**. So the **hotter** our lab, the **better** our results will be.

- **Pellegrino** tastes like adventure water when chilled. Thus, **all water** tastes like adventure water when chilled.

**LOOPHOLE**   What if we can't generalize from this one thing to a bunch of other things?

This is how Overgeneralization is deployed in a real LSAT stimulus:

*42.2.12*

Politician:   Those economists who claim that **consumer price increases have averaged less than 3 percent** over the last year are **mistaken**. They clearly have not shopped anywhere recently. **Gasoline** is **up 10 percent** over the last year; **my auto insurance,** 12 percent; **newspapers, 15** percent; **propane, 13** percent; **bread, 50** percent.

It's a big Overgeneralization to apply facts about bread and my auto insurance to a claim about *all prices*. A lot more things have prices than just what was listed, so you can't take these tiny premises and make such a big claim.

# Survey Problems    MANY LSAT SURVEYS ARE DONE BY IMBECILES

Surveys on the LSAT are all smoke and mirrors. **You should always assume surveys are done with the greatest possible incompetence.** Imagine every survey you ever see on this test is conducted by Eric, a freshman in an introductory psychology class. Eric's not a bad guy, but he's also 18 and has never conducted a survey before. Here are the mistakes Eric makes:

### BIASED SAMPLE

Eric is conducting a survey to find America's favorite movie and only asks guys on his football team. So the survey only includes respondents from that unrepresentative group. Eric's claims about *America's* favorite movie are problematic because America contains many types of people who are not football players, and those other people likely have different favorite movies.

### BIASED QUESTIONS

Eric knows he'll get a better grade if his survey returns consistent results so he crafts his questions to get certain answers. He is assigned to find out if people prefer red or blue. He asks, "Good people prefer red to blue. Do you prefer red?" Most people probably won't say blue.

### OTHER CONTRADICTORY SURVEYS

Eric forgets to do his survey, so he just makes up that the US Congress has a 100% approval rating. But Eric's TA sees that every survey in the past five years has shown Congress' approval rating to never top 20%. Those contradictory surveys give us ammunition to doubt Eric's conclusion.

Surveys are opportunities for both intentional and unintentional manipulation.

### SURVEY LIARS

Eric conducts a survey asking people if they have ever used illegal drugs. But everyone knows Eric's mom is a DEA agent. No one is going to admit to using illegal drugs in Eric's survey. This question gives the respondent reason to lie, but people can lie on surveys even when they don't have a specific incentive.

### SMALL SAMPLE SIZE

Eric forgot to run his survey for class, so he asks the girl walking into class next to him, "Do you ever have trouble sleeping?" She says, "No." Eric reports that 100% of respondents do not have trouble sleeping. But small samples mean it's really easy to get to that 100% (or alternatively 0%), so the conclusion means very little.

**All of these errors are possible Loopholes in every LSAT stimulus containing a survey, unless the stimulus explicitly accounts for the error.**

**LOOPHOLES**    What if the sample was biased, the questions were biased, there are other contradictory surveys, people lie on surveys, or the sample is too small?

Let's take a look at some Survey Problems in a real LSAT stimulus:

> *5.1.14*
>
> A **survey of alumni** of the class of 1960 at Aurora University yielded puzzling results. When asked to indicate their academic rank, **half of the respondents reported that they were in the top quarter of the graduating class** in 1960.

This stimulus is a Paradox. We'll get to what exactly that means in the next chapter, but this stimulus perfectly illustrates Survey Problems.

How could half the respondents be in the top quarter of the class? What if academically-motivated people are more likely to respond to the survey? What if people lie about their grades? Any of our Survey Problems explain the results.

## False Starts    THE TWO GROUPS ARE ALWAYS INCONVENIENTLY DIFFERENT

False Starts are deployed on almost every LSAT stimulus that contains two groups and a comparison between them.

### THE PLAY-BY-PLAY

**1.** There's a study with two groups.

**2.** Crazy researcher assumes the two groups are the same in all respects except those pointed out as part of the study.

**3.** Crazy researcher concludes that the differences in the study results are due to the one key difference the study is focusing on.

Imagine you're a researcher comparing two groups: one exercises and one doesn't. You get results saying the exercise group is healthier. It's easy to assume they're healthier because of the exercise, right? But therein lies the trap! There could be crucial differences between the two groups besides the exercise.

**False Starts researchers always assume that the two groups are same in all respects except the ones called out as part of the study.** Despite the researcher's assumption, the two groups always have the possibility of being different. Here are a few possible differences that the researchers ignored:

| FALSE START | EXAMPLE |
| --- | --- |
| **Possible differences in diet.** | *Maybe the exercise group only eats kale and chia water and non-exercise group eats only Doritos and Mountain Dew Code Red.* |
| **Possible differences in age.** | *Maybe at the beginning of the study, the exercise group was all 18 years old and the non-exercise group was all 68 years old.* |

Once in a blue moon, the stimulus will guard against these attacks by adding, "We tested two large and diverse groups of active and sedentary participants. The groups were similar in all relevant respects except exercise regimen." **The LSAT knows they're supposed to put that line in every stimulus comparing two groups. They don't do it because they are trying to trick you.**

    **LOOPHOLE**         What if the two groups were different in a key respect?

Here is how False Starts is deployed in a real LSAT stimulus:

*42.4.9*

> In a recent study, each member of two groups of people, **Group A (composed of persons sixty-five to seventy-five years old) and Group B (composed of college students),** was required to make a telephone call to a certain number at a specified time. The time when each call was initiated was recorded electronically. **Group A proved far better** at remembering to make a telephone call precisely at a specified time **than did Group B**. There were fourteen lapses in Group B but only one lapse in Group A. Clearly, **at least one type of memory does not suffer as a person ages.**

They're assuming that the college students and old people are equal in all respects except their age. They've ignored the fact that college students don't have as ready access to phones (this question is from 2003) and that college students might have more time commitments that interfere with their ability to make this random call.

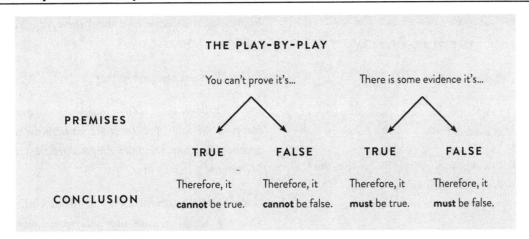

Possibility ≠ Certainty comes down to a lack of comfort with ambiguity. It's fine to say that someone hasn't proven their conclusion, that it's not necessarily true. But stop there. Things go wrong when you say that the other person hasn't proven their conclusion, so their conclusion can't be true. Facts are not affected by the failure of an argument.

There are two Possibility ≠ Certainty patterns to know and they each come with their own catchphrase!

### LACK OF EVIDENCE ≠ EVIDENCE OF LACKING

It's **NOT NECESSARILY TRUE**, so it **CANNOT BE TRUE**.

*It has not been proven that the lack of snacks caused the Model UN tournament to be poorly attended. It could have been poorly attended because of the growing disillusionment with multi-national bureaucratic institutions. Therefore, the lack of snacks **must not** have been the reason.*

### PROOF OF EVIDENCE ≠ EVIDENCE OF PROOF

It **COULD BE TRUE**, so it **MUST BE TRUE**.

*There is some evidence that playing music turns you into a narcissist. For instance, both Kanye West and Justin Bieber are undeniably narcissists. Therefore, playing music **must** turn people into narcissists.*

Just like with the Power Players, I demoed this pattern with **TRUE**, but it works the same way with **FALSE**.

**LOOPHOLES**   What if lack of evidence ≠ evidence of lacking?

What if proof of evidence ≠ evidence of proof?

Here is how Possibility ≠ Certainty looks in a real LSAT stimulus:

*16.3.2*

> Despite the best efforts of astronomers, **no one** has yet **succeeded in exchanging messages with intelligent life** on other planets or in other solar systems. In fact, **no one** has even managed to **prove that** any kind of **extraterrestrial life exists**. Thus, there is clearly **no intelligent life** anywhere but on Earth.

It hasn't been proven that intelligent life exists, but that doesn't mean it necessarily *cannot* exist. This conclusion went too far. Lack of evidence ≠ evidence of lacking, bro. There could still be aliens out there.

## Implication   FACTS ≠ SOMEONE BELIEVING THOSE FACTS

### THE PLAY-BY-PLAY

1. Blair has a belief.

2. Crazy person mentions a factual Implication of that belief.

3. Crazy person claims that Blair believes the Implication of the belief.

Implication tells people what they believe, which is always a dangerous idea.

Let's look at an example together:

*Josefina **believes** there is an omnipotent robot overlord in charge of our daily lives. Robot overlords always wear neckties. Therefore, Josefina **believes** a necktie wearer is in charge of our daily lives.*

Notice how the argument starts with Josefina's belief. It then adds in a factual premise, supplying factual information that relates to something Josefina believes. But **opinions and facts don't play well together**. When the conclusion adds in those facts to Josefina's beliefs, they're assuming too much about Josefina. Why? Josefina may be completely illogical. She could be ignorant of the consequences of her beliefs. Just because you're in the know doesn't mean she is. The author clearly hasn't met enough irrational people.

Josefina may be unaware of the fact that robots always wear neckties. If she's unaware, you can't say that she necessarily believes in it. But let's be generous and say that Josefina is aware of the neckties. She can be aware and yet still hold a counterfactual belief! Josefina does what she feels.

**LOOPHOLE**   What if the person in question isn't aware of what their belief implies?

Here is how Implication looks in a real LSAT stimulus:

*31.2.21*

> **Bank deposits are credited** on the date of the transaction only when they are **made before 3 P.M. Alicia knows** that the bank **deposit was made before 3 P.M**. So, **Alicia knows** that the bank deposit was **credited** on the date of the transaction.

In this example, the author starts with a fact: deposits are credited on the date only when they're done before 3:00. Alicia knows one part of this, so the author infers that she knows the other part. The problem is that we don't know that Alicia is aware of the bank deposit rules. The conclusion is flawed because it's telling Alicia what she believes. Nobody tells Alicia what to believe.

LSAC really did put a malevolent robot overlord in charge of our daily lives. It's called the Digital LSAT.

This stimulus actually contains two classic flaws! Good on you if you spotted the Bad Conditional Reasoning in addition to the Implication flaw!

# False Dichotomy   THERE ARE MORE THAN TWO OPTIONS

A False Dichotomy pretends there are only two options when there really could be more.

There are two ways False Dichotomies go wrong:

1. Limiting a spectrum

2. Limiting options

## LIMITING A SPECTRUM

**On a spectrum, you can go up, go down, or stay the same.** Spectrum-limiting authors pretend there are only two options, when there are really three: up, down, or unchanged. Here are the two tricks to seeing through every limited spectrum:

NOT MORE ≠ LESS                    NOT LESS ≠ MORE

And here's an example of how to limit a spectrum:

> *The quality of the orange zest **didn't deteriorate** overnight, so it must have **improved**.*

## LIMITING OPTIONS

Limiting options is a little more tricky than limiting a spectrum. **Limiting options pretends that there are only two options when there could be more.** We know that things can stay the same in a spectrum, but sometimes the LSAT will play word games with us to make us think that they have legit limited the field to two options when they actually haven't. Check out the following examples of limiting options:

> *My career **options include** becoming an astronaut **and** becoming a personal assistant. I've decided I'm afraid of space, so I'm going to be a personal assistant.*

"Include" is the keyword here. I might have more options than just becoming an astronaut or a personal assistant, so it's invalid to conclude that I *must* become a personal assistant.

**LOOPHOLE**        What if there are more than just two options?

Let's look at how False Dichotomies are deployed in a real LSAT question.

> *39.4.26*
>
> Commentator:   Because of teacher hiring freezes, the quality of education in that country **will not improve**. Thus, it **will surely deteriorate**.

The quality of education isn't going up, so it must go down. This is a prototypical spectrum-limiting False Dichotomy.

> Because Raoul is a vegetarian, he **will not have the pepperoni** pizza for lunch. It follows that he **will have the cheese** pizza.

The author limited options by assuming there are only cheese and pepperoni pizzas in the world (what a sad, *sad* place).

False Dichotomy is also known as a False Dilemma.

Both of these examples are from one Parallel Flaw question.

The first example is the stimulus and the Raoul pizza example is an *incorrect* answer. It was incorrect because there's a difference between limiting a spectrum and limiting options.

## Straw Man    ARGUMENTS FOR COWARDS

### THE PLAY-BY-PLAY

1.    Sane person makes a claim.

2.    Crazy person responds to an entirely different claim, but pretends they responded to the sane person.

Straw Man arguments "respond" to an opponent by "mishearing" what was said to them. They respond to something entirely different, something so outlandish that it's easy to dismiss out of hand.

Check out an example:

*Kasra: We need to create a more reliable schedule for feeding the alligators in the preserve. It's dangerous for us to enter the pen when the alligators are hungry.*

*Thomas: So what you're really saying is that we should let the alligators get their own food whenever they want! That's even more dangerous than leaving them hungry. I should give the alligators your job.*

Notice that Kasra did not say the alligators should feed themselves. **Thomas distorted what Kasra said to make Kasra's point easier to take down. That's the Straw Man move.**

When the Thomas of the moment starts his rebuttal with "so what you're really saying is…" or "so what you mean is…" you might as well have a neon **STRAW MAN ARGUMENT** sign blinking above the stimulus. Straw Man is harder to spot when those key words aren't present, so always look out for a mismatch between the first speaker's real argument and what the second speaker is talking about.

> **LOOPHOLE**    What if what they said has nothing to do with the claim they're pretending to respond to?

Let's take a look at how Straw Man appears in an actual LSAT stimulus:

*7.4.9*

> Student representative:    Our university, in expelling a student who verbally harassed his roommate, has **erred by penalizing** the student for doing what he surely has a right to do: speak his mind!

> Dean of students:    **But what you're saying is that our university should endorse verbal harassment.** Yet surely if we did that, we would threaten the free flow of ideas that is the essence of university life.

The dean of students misdescribes the student representative's position here. The student representative never claims that the university should endorse verbal harassment. That's absurd. By addressing this absurd point instead, the dean gets away from addressing the student representative's actual point.

Excerpt from my daily life:

**Ellen**: Yeah, I turned down Harvard Law School to write an LSAT book. I am so happy.

**Straw man stranger**: So what you're really saying is you want to be poor.

## Ad Hominem   BAD PROPONENT ≠ BAD ARGUMENT

### THE PLAY-BY-PLAY

**1.** Sane person makes a claim.

**2.** Crazy person talks about how the sane person is somehow awful.

**3.** Crazy person concludes that the sane person's claim is false.

Ad Hominem premises insult the proponent of a position, but then the conclusion challenges the truth of the position itself. The problem is that proponents don't affect the truth/falsity of their position.

Let me tell you a true story:

*Isaac Newton destroyed the last known portrait of Robert Hooke, one of his intellectual rivals, so history would never know what Hooke looked like. He lied to Edmund Halley about having to "rework some figures" so he could publish their shared work without having to credit Halley. Isaac Newton was a complete jerk. That's why gravity is wrong.*

Ad Hominem is Latin for "to the person." This encapsulates exactly why this classic flaw is great: It's just about insulting people.

Seriously, the premises in this example are actually true! And I didn't even use half of the dirt out there on Newton — seriously, ask the internet.

This example did a good job proving you shouldn't trust Isaac Newton. But the conclusion isn't about trustworthiness. The conclusion is about the truth or falsity of gravity. Isaac Newton was a major proponent of gravity, but we shouldn't doubt the existence of gravity just because Isaac Newton was a jerk.

Ad Hominem can also attack the proponent's motivations. If the proponent is biased, it's natural to doubt the truth of what they're claiming. However, you can't fall for this one on the LSAT. **A proponent's bias for/against a position does not affect the truth or falsity of that position.** Here's a simple Ad Hominem example:

*John says that the square is **red**, but **John works for the Red Lobby**. So the square is definitely **not red**.*

Complete idiots make correct choices all the time. And great people make bad calls all the time. People with suspicious motivations sometimes happen to advocate for correct positions. Those with pure motives are attached to positions that happen to be wrong. This stuff happens by complete chance. **Premises about character and motivation only prove claims about character and motivation.**

**LOOPHOLE**       What if this person's character/motivation doesn't affect the truth?

Here is an example of an Ad Hominem attack in a real LSAT stimulus:

*19.2.14*

> Herbalist:   Many of my customers find that their physical coordination improves after drinking juice containing certain herbs. A few **doctors assert that the herbs are potentially harmful**, but **doctors are always trying to maintain a monopoly over medical therapies**. So there is **no reason not to try my herb juice**.

Ad Hominem is also referred to as a source argument.

The herbs could still be harmful even though the doctors are biased. The truth or falsity of whether these herbs are harmful is not affected by the potentially biased doctors, especially when doctors are relevant authorities on bodily harm.

## Circular Reasoning    WHY? CAUSE IT'S CIRCULAR REASONING OBVIOUSLY

**THE PLAY-BY-PLAY**

1. Crazy person concludes something.

2. Crazy person supplies premises that assume the conclusion is already true.

**Why is Circular Reasoning circular? Because any attempt to prove it otherwise has failed due to the fact that Circular Reasoning is circular.**

A circular argument assumes the conclusion is true before doing the work of proving it so. Often, circular arguments rule out objections to the conclusion simply because those objections are incompatible with the conclusion. Yeah, you read that right. They say an objection must not be true because the objection disproves the conclusions, assuming there's *no way* this conclusion can be wrong. This is nonsense, of course. It's the stimulus author's job to prove the conclusion without dirty circular tricks like this.

Circular Reasoning derives much of its difficulty from its language. Here's an example of how a circular wording game might play out:

> *Explaining Circular Reasoning is* **futile.** *Explaining complex concepts may seem a worthy aim. After all, it may be the only way to convey information. But since it will* **never work,** *there's* **no point.**

Here's the trick: *futile = never work = no point*

All of those phrases mean the same thing. I was repeating myself just like "Circular Reasoning is circular because Circular Reasoning is circular." The LSAT will likely not be kind enough to simply reuse words to let you know they're repeating themselves. You have to look out for synonyms and similar concepts explained using different words.

**LOOPHOLE**      What if we can't use the conclusion as evidence for itself?

Here's how Circular Reasoning looks in a real LSAT stimulus:

*17.2.2*

> Many people do not understand themselves, nor do they try to gain self-understanding. These people might try to understand others, but these attempts are sure to fail, because **without self-understanding it is impossible to understand others.** It is clear from this that **anyone who lacks self-understanding will be incapable of understanding others.**

It's tough to figure out where the conclusion even is in this stimulus. You have to rely on "it is clear from this that," the conclusion indicator in the last sentence. This is common in Circular Reasoning because circular arguments often repeat their conclusion. Let's see exactly how they repeat themselves:

> *"without self-understanding it is impossible to understand others"*  =  *"anyone who lacks self-understanding will be incapable of understanding others"*

When you see that repetition between the premises and conclusion, you know you're dealing with Circular Reasoning.

# Equivocation  HOMONYMS UNLEASHED

Imagine you're talking to someone you just met at a networking mixer (*blech*) since you don't have any friends left after Overgeneralization. You start telling this person about how great your arms look after this new workout plan. Your arms are just on point, top shape. Then you conclude that your top-notch arms mean you're ready to intervene in a complex foreign political conflict you don't truly understand. The mixer person is never going to become your new friend.

You started off your argument using the word "arms" to discuss the things that are attached to hands, and then you conclude that argument as if you initially introduced "arms" to mean things like tanks and machine guns. Like seriously! This is a thing people actually do in a subtler way on the LSAT and in real life.

**Equivocation happens when the author changes the meaning of a word throughout an argument.** You have to be on your toes to catch Equivocation. At first glance, it may look like nonsense words. Look closer. Put yourself in the author's shoes. Tune in to where the author thought they were going, and you'll learn to love Equivocation.

Equivocation may also seem like a deliberate pun. But fun puns don't get a reasoning pass on the LSAT. Any time a word changes in meaning, it's Equivocation.

> **LOOPHOLE**   What if we shouldn't let words change in meaning?

Check out how Equivocation has been presented in a real LSAT stimulus:

*19.2.1*

> Director of Ace Manufacturing Company:   Our management consultant proposes that we reassign staff so that all employees are doing both what they like to do and what they do well. This, she says, will "increase productivity by **fully exploiting our available resources**." But Ace Manufacturing has a long-standing commitment **not to exploit its workers**. Therefore, implementing her recommendations would cause us to violate our own policy.

The word "exploit" changes in meaning throughout the two bolded premises. The management consultant means "exploit" as in use to its fullest extent. The company uses "exploit" to refer to its more negative definition: to unfairly take advantage of someone. Poor management consultant.

*I used to really dislike Equivocation because I didn't understand it, but now I think it's phenomenal. It's so funny. Equivocation stimuli look strange at first, but once you learn to cut through the confusing wording, they're totally doable.*

*Go to elementalprep.com/bonus for a super fun Equivocation Drill!*

## Appeal Fallacies   OPINION ≠ FACT

### THE PLAY-BY-PLAY

1.  Crazy person says that a person or group believes something.

2.  Crazy person concludes that thing must be true.

Appeal Fallacies are about turning someone's opinion into a fact. This often happens in two ways:

- Invalid appeal to authority

- Invalid appeal to public opinion

**There is a huge difference between opinion and fact.** You can never assume, "Jaison thinks this, therefore it is true," except in one specific case: when Jaison is an expert in the field he's commenting on.

### INVALID APPEAL TO AUTHORITY

An invalid appeal to authority happens when the author uses a non-expert opinion to support their conclusion. For instance, the author can't use a zookeeper's opinion to support a conclusion about baseball. Zookeepers are not recognized baseball experts. The appeal to authority would be valid if the author used Derek Jeter's opinion on baseball because Derek Jeter actually is a baseball expert.

### INVALID APPEAL TO PUBLIC OPINION

Appeals to public opinion are invalid because people are unreliable. **A high percentage of random people believing anything has very little bearing on whether that thing is actually true.** For instance, over 50% of Brits believe in the supernatural according to a recent poll. For real, I looked it up. Does that make ghosts and séances necessarily real? No. They could be real — who knows — but the existence of ghosts isn't proven real based on those beliefs.

**LOOPHOLE**          What if this opinion doesn't equal evidence of fact?

Check out an Appeal Fallacy in a real LSAT stimulus:

*15.2.17*

> **Most people believe that yawning is most powerfully triggered by seeing someone else yawn.** This belief about yawning is widespread not only today, but also has been commonplace in many parts of the world in the past, if we are to believe historians of popular culture. **Thus, seeing someone else yawn must be the most irresistible cause of yawning.**

Notice how almost the exact same phrase is repeated in a premise and in the conclusion. The only difference: The premise stated the phrase as an opinion and the conclusion stated it as a fact. This is always a problem. Never jump from opinion to fact or from fact to opinion unless you have a real expert to back you up.

---

## THE PLAY-BY-PLAY

1. Crazy person supplies a few premises.

2. Crazy person concludes something that is unrelated to those premises.

*Irrelevant!* occurs when the premises are entirely unrelated to the conclusion.

Let's have some fun:

*Current efforts to recapture the grizzly bear on the loose at Sunbird Acres are misguided. While the bear did maul a number of residents, bears have long been appreciated by zoologists and the general public as beautiful creatures. The beauty of the grizzly bear has been documented extensively, as in literalbearsimjealousof.tumblr.com.*

The problem here is that bears being beautiful has nothing to do with whether a particular bear should be recaptured, especially when the issue with the bear is community mauling. You could unconsciously fill some big logical gaps and *make beauty matter*, but you should exploit these gaps, not make them work.

Every flawed argument could technically be labeled *Irrelevant!*, so you need to be careful in the answer choices on Classic Flaw questions. You can't call a Whole-to-Part stimulus *Irrelevant!* just because premises about a whole aren't relevant to a conclusion about parts. *Irrelevant!* is kind of a cop-out, so only choose it when you don't detect a more specific, compelling classic flaw in the stimulus.

LOOPHOLE                What if the premises and the conclusion have nothing to do with one another?

Here's how *Irrelevant!* has been deployed on a real LSAT stimulus:

7.1.17

> Office manager:   **I will not order recycled paper for this office.** Our letters to clients must make a good impression, so we cannot print them on **inferior paper**.

> Stationery supplier:   Recycled paper is not necessarily inferior. In fact, **from the beginning, the finest paper has been made of recycled material**. It was only in **the 1850s** that paper began to be made from wood fiber, and then only because there were no longer enough **rags** to meet the demand for paper.

Notice that the office manager is talking about their pending office supply order. The stationery supplier replies with some nonsense about the history of paper, pretending that this impacts a present-day office supply order and the quality of the recycled paper she could order today. All the stuff about rags doesn't impact the office manager's order and there are no other classic flaws in the stimulus. It's *Irrelevant!*

## Percentages ≠ Numbers  THEY'RE NOT FRIENDS

### THE PLAY-BY-PLAY

1. Crazy person says, "A percentage went up!"

2. Crazy person concludes that the associated real number also went up.

**OR**

1. Crazy person says, "A real number went up!"

2. Crazy person concludes that the associated percentage also went up.

Premises about numbers (#) almost never lead to conclusions about percentages (%) and vice versa.

A rising percentage doesn't necessarily imply a rising number and vice versa. Why? Whenever an argument mentions numbers and percentages, **there's one big thing they're purposefully not mentioning: group size.**

Here's how bad things happen:

- Tariq sold **1,000 more** (#) yo-yos today than he did yesterday. Therefore, his **share of the market (%)** must have **risen** considerably.

- Tariq's **share of the world yo-yo market (%) rose** from 10% yesterday to 20% today. Therefore, he must have **sold many more yo-yos (#)** today than he did yesterday.

Why is this bad? Because these conclusions only work when the overall group size is *just right*. If the total number of yo-yos sold in the world (group size) changes inconveniently, these claims about Tariq don't have to be true.

**Percentages ≠ Numbers arguments always assume group size remains the same.** They do this because if the group size remains the same, their conclusion is valid. Basically, they're trying to cheat. Check out an example with the same group size:

| | TODAY | TOMORROW |
|---|---|---|
| **Same Group Size** | *1000 yo-yos sold in the world* | *1000 yo-yos sold in the world* |
| **Real Numbers Up** | *Tariq sold 50 yo-yos* | *Tariq sold 100 yo-yos* |
| **Percentage Up** | *5% of world yo-yo market* | *10% of world yo-yo market* |

In this case, because I left the group size the same, the increase in the real numbers really did lead to an increase in percentage. But the group size doesn't *have to* remain the same. **The LSAT wants you to call them on their assumption that group size stays the same.** Look what happens when I change the group size:

|  | TODAY | TOMORROW |
|---|---|---|
| **Changing Group Size** | *300 yo-yos sold in the world* | *2000 yo-yos sold in the world* |
| **Real Numbers Up** | *Tariq sold 30 yo-yos* | *Tariq sold 100 yo-yos* |
| **Percentage Down** | *10% of world yo-yo market* | *5% of world yo-yo market* |

Because I changed the group size, the increasing number did not result in an increasing percentage! See how unreliable inferring from numbers to percentages is? This is why Numbers ≠ Percentages is one of our classic flaws.

Here is how Percentages ≠ Numbers plays out in a real LSAT stimulus:

*19.2.7*

> A commonly accepted myth is that **left-handed people are more prone** to cause accidents than are right-handed people. But this is, in fact, **just a myth**, as is indicated by the fact that **more household accidents are caused by right-handed** people than are caused by left-handed people.

Don't be afraid to test example group sizes; this can really help clarify difficult questions.

So there's a myth that lefties are more accident-prone (higher percentage of lefties causing accidents) than righties, but this is not true because a greater number of accidents are caused by righties. The issue here is the comparative group size between righties and lefties. As you might have guessed, there are a lot more righties in the world than there are lefties. Let's say there are a million righties in the world and 10 lefties. It makes sense that the number of accidents caused by righties would be higher, even if the percentage of righties causing accidents is much lower.

---

**CLASSIC FLAWS GAME PLAN**

- Make your classic flaw flashcards now. Write the classic flaw on one side and your own example of the flaw on the other side.

- Memorize the classic flaws.

- Think of the classic flaws as predictable Loopholes. They rely on predictably bad assumptions.

- Ask yourself why the classic flaws are flawed. Gaining insight into what makes an argument invalid will help you formulate Loopholes in all the arguments.

---

## Quiz 7   THE CLASSIC FLAWS

### INSTRUCTIONS

*Answer these questions based on your knowledge of the chapter. Attempt to answer without looking back at the chapter first. If you don't know the answer, circle the question number and go find the answer in the chapter. Study the sections of the chapter that you couldn't remember at first.*

### Word Bank

| | | |
|---|---|---|
| *whole* | *proof* | *cause(s)* |
| *effect(s)* | *correlation(s)* | *overgeneralization* |
| *assumption(s)* | *certainty* | *possibility* |
| *lacking* | *part(s)* | *Loophole(s)* |

*Use the word bank to answer the fill-in-the-blank questions. Some words will not be used and others may be used more than once.*

**1.** Classic flaws are automatic ___Loopholes___.

**2.** Overgeneralization is the ___part___-to-___part___ flaw.

**3.** Lack of evidence ≠ evidence of ___lacking___.

**4.** Proof of evidence ≠ evidence of ___proof___.

*Circle the correct answer to the following questions.*

**5.** TRUE OR ~~FALSE~~   It's totally fine to read a conditional statement backwards without negating!

**6.** ~~TRUE OR FALSE~~   Overgeneralization is the same flaw as Whole-to-Part.

**7.** TRUE OR FALSE   Facts are not affected by the failure of a given argument.

**8.** TRUE OR FALSE   Someone's bias for/against a given position does not affect the truth of that position.

**9.** **TRUE OR FALSE**  Percentages ≠ Numbers stimuli always assume that group size is changing.

**10.** Circle the correct classic flaw in the table below.

| LOOPHOLE | CIRCLE THE CORRECT CLASSIC FLAW | | |
|---|---|---|---|
| What if we can't use the conclusion as evidence for itself? | Bad Causal Reasoning | Irrelevant! | (Circular Reasoning) |
| What if this opinion doesn't equal evidence of fact? | Possibility ≠ Certainty | (Appeal Fallacies) | Survey Problems |
| What if what they said has nothing to do with the claim they're pretending to respond to? | (Straw Man) | False Starts | Ad Hominem |
| What if the premises and the conclusion have nothing to do with one another? | (Irrelevant!) | Possibility ≠ Certainty | Equivocation |
| What if the sample was biased? | Bad Causal Reasoning | Irrelevant! | (Survey Problems) |
| What if this person's character/motivation doesn't affect the truth? | Whole-to-Part | (Ad Hominem) | Bad Causal Reasoning |
| What if the two groups were different in some key respect that's not accounted for? | Implication | False Dichotomy | (False Starts) |
| What if there are more than just two options? | Irrelevant! | Possibility ≠ Certainty | (False Dichotomy) |

*Where's the answer key?*

You'll find the answer key at the end of the chapter on page 220.

## Quiz 7 ANSWER KEY

**1.** Classic Flaws are automatic **Loopholes**.

**2.** Overgeneralization is the **part-to-part(s)** flaw.

**3.** Lack of evidence ≠ evidence of **lacking**.

**4.** Proof of evidence ≠ evidence of **proof**.

**5.** False. It's Bad Conditional Reasoning to read a conditional statement backwards without negating.

**6.** False. Overgeneralization is *not* the same flaw as Whole-to-Part. It generalizes from one part to other parts.

**7.** True.

**8.** True.

**9.** False. Percentages ≠ Numbers stimuli always assume that group size remains the same.

**10.**

| LOOPHOLE | CORRECT CLASSIC FLAW |
|---|---|
| What if we can't use the conclusion as evidence for itself? | **Circular Reasoning** |
| What if this opinion doesn't equal evidence of fact? | **Appeal Fallacies** |
| What if what they said has nothing to do with the claim they're pretending to respond to? | **Straw Man** |
| What if the premises and the conclusion have nothing to do with one another? | **Irrelevant!** |
| What if the sample was biased? | **Survey Problems** |
| What if this person's character/motivation doesn't affect the truth? | **Ad Hominem** |
| What if the two groups were different in some key respect that's not accounted for? | **False Starts** |
| What if there are more than just two options? | **False Dichotomy** |

# OMMMM.

chapter seven. this is heaven.

## Chapter Breather   A FEW BUSINESS TERMS FOR BUSINESS STIMULI

A handful of Logical Reasoning questions require a basic understanding of business and finance. Don't worry. I didn't take any business classes in college, so I'm going to keep this super short and simple.

The easiest way to introduce you to this concept is to define the terms you'll see in these stimuli and then put those terms into action together.

| BUSINESS! | EXPLANATION |
|---|---|
| revenue | Revenue is the total amount of money a business brings in. |
| gross sales | Gross sales is one type of revenue. It's all the sales a business makes. |
| costs | Costs are the money the business spends. |
| profit | Profit is the difference between the business' revenue and costs. |
| market | The market for something is the overall group of everyone selling and buying that thing. |
| free market | The free market is a characteristic of capitalism where people sell things to one another without too much interference. |
| communism | Communism interferes with the free market by redistributing wealth. For the purposes of the LSAT, you can think of communism as the opposite of capitalism. |
| monopoly | A monopoly occurs when one company has sole meaningful control over an industry. This means competition is lacking and pricing/unfair advantages can get out of control. |
| GDP | GDP is all the things produced by a country. People use it to talk about the size of a country's economy. It stands for Gross Domestic Product. |

### BUSINESS WORDS IN ACTION

Imagine you make balloons for a living. Your life is great. In the course of making and selling your balloons, you spend $10,000 a year. These are your costs. But you bring in a total of $25,000 a year in balloon sales. This is your revenue (or gross sales). Since $25,000 (revenue) minus $10,000 (costs) is $15,000, you made $15,000 in profit! Awesome.

Since you're a person who sells balloons, you are participating in the balloon market. That's the overall number of balloons sold by all the balloon sellers to all the balloon buyers. If you have 10% of the balloon market, that means you sell 10% of the balloons in the world. In a capitalist system with a free market, you can buy and sell balloons without much interference from the government. In a communist system, the balloon market is more controlled and forces outside the market redistribute wealth.

THE
CLIR
*(pronounced
"clear")*

## The Answer is in the Stimulus

> Refresh yourself on the Stimulus Framework section before beginning this chapter.

I have the same seemingly magical experience with every student at the beginning of their Logical Reasoning journey. They bring me a question that stumped them from a practice test, some question they're already *seething* about. They're telling me the correct answer isn't fair and the test is stupid. I say, "It's ok. Let me give it a shot."

Since there are over 4,000 LR questions, I don't have them all memorized. I do their unfair question blind, talking out my interior monologue. I let them hear what goes on in my mind when I do a question without knowing the answer. I'll translate the stimulus and work through my intuitive analytical process (what the CLIR is modeled after) without looking at the question type or answer choices. About 30 seconds into talking it through, the student will interrupt me with, "Well, that's the right answer!" They're half mad, half taken aback.

Obviously, there are questions that go sideways. No one is claiming that I can say the answer verbatim on *every* question before I know the question type.

This happens on probably 70% of blind questions I do. I will almost verbatim say the correct answer before I know the question type. This doesn't happen because I'm "just a genius"; that's stupid and a cop-out. It happens because of a replicable system that's been internalized to the point of intuition. The CLIR is the system that leads to that result. And this is the chapter that will train you to use it too.

### SO WHAT IS THIS CLIR THING REALLY?

Remember our four stimulus types? They're the backbone of the CLIR. Here are the stimulus type and CLIR pairings:

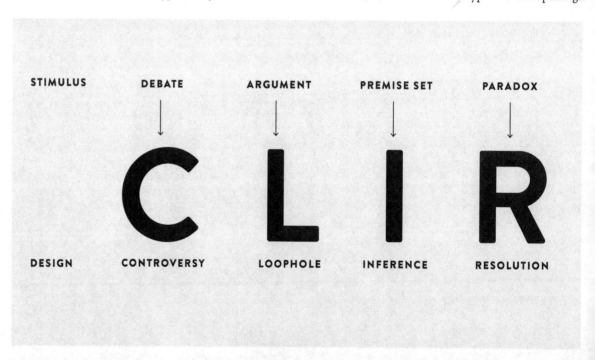

When you approach an LR question, you will detect the stimulus type and design the associated CLIR before looking at the question type or answer choices. Once you have the CLIR, you can answer most questions quickly and easily.

Are you jazzed to get started? I'm jazzed to get started.

**Q.**  *BUT WAIT... Do I really have to do this CLIR thing? I just want to answer the question.*

**A.**  Our brains operate on the law of conservation of energy. If we feel like we don't *have to* do something to get an acceptable result, we won't do it. This isn't an inherently evil thing. Why would I take a longer route home when I can just go straight there and get cozy faster? I wouldn't because that's dumb and inefficient. But imagine that instead of being able to walk straight home, bopping along to my podcast, I have to choose between two options of equal length:

1. Start running home immediately. There are traps in the sidewalk. I will also be blindfolded.

2. Take a second to survey the path first. Figure out where the traps are. No blindfold.

Would anyone really take the blindfolded option? No! But you are taking the blindfolded "shortcut" right now in how you approach LR. Designing the CLIR means surveying the path before you rush headlong toward your destination. Commit to it. You underestimate how much time you spend in answer choice traps.

## THE CLIR TRAINING REGIMEN

When you encounter a stimulus during training, you will perform each of these steps in order:

**1.  Outline**

   Bracket and label the stimulus' argument parts.

**2.  Categorize**

   Is the stimulus a Debate, Argument, Premise Set, or Paradox?

   Tag the stimulus with a D, A, PS, or PX accordingly.

**3.  Design**

   Design the CLIR associated with the stimulus type:

   **Debate ⟶ Controversy**

   **Argument ⟶ Loophole**

   **Premise Set ⟶ Inference**

   **Paradox ⟶ Resolution**

 Notice how the training steps abbreviate to OCD? Not an accident.

 If you train well, you won't even consciously try to do these steps once you begin timed practice tests; they will just happen subconsciously. Muscle memory will take over.

The point of this chapter is to train you to effortlessly design a CLIR the way I described at the start of this chapter. Obviously, this training regimen differs from how you will complete timed LR sections. Don't worry; I'm not asking you to label argument parts on test day.

## Outline

In the first step of the CLIR training regimen, you outline the argument parts. This solidifies your understanding of the role each statement plays in the stimulus.

> Students who get 10 or more wrong per Logical Reasoning section often struggle with this step. Once they master outlining the argument parts, they see an immediate, substantial improvement. Your goal is to recognize the conclusion instantly.

The CLIR training regimen progresses sequentially from basic to advanced. Depending on where you're starting with your skills on LR, outlining the argument parts may seem like busy work. However, **knowing your argument parts is essential** and most students mess it up at the beginning of their training.

You have to be able to identify a conclusion in your sleep before you can effortlessly answer LR questions. Seriously, if you have *any trouble* identifying conclusions in the upcoming CLIR Drill, re-read Chapter 2 immediately. You will only delay your progress by delaying that re-read.

To Outline:

1. Read the stimulus.

2. Bracket the beginning and end of each argument part.

3. Label each argument part to the side of the stimulus.

Here's an example of a real LSAT stimulus with outlined argument parts:

*16.2.19*

> C [The Volunteers for Literacy Program would benefit if Dolores takes Victor's place as director], P1 [since Dolores is far more skillful than Victor is at securing the kind of financial support the program needs] P2 [and Dolores does not have Victor's propensity for alienating the program's most dedicated volunteers.]

Here are the abbreviations to use for your argument parts!

| ARGUMENT PART | ABBREVIATION |
|---|---|
| Conclusion | C |
| Intermediate Conclusion | IC |
| Premise 1 | P1 |
| Premise 2 | P2 |
| Premise 3 | P3 |

The premise numbering continues depending on how many premises are in the stimulus. Where you cut off each premise is up to you, but don't assume that one sentence always equals one argument part. Complex sentences will often contain two argument parts (at least), and the more finely you break down the stimulus, the easier it will be to work with.

> The Digital LSAT doesn't allow us to mark up the stimulus like this, but that's totally cool. Outlining is just a practice step to sharpen your skills while you're still working on paper. You can transition to just underlining the conclusion once you start digital PTs.

*If the stimulus contains two speakers, bracket off the argument parts within each speaker as normal, treating them like two separate Arguments or Premise Sets.*

*Refer back to Chapter 2, Arguments & Inferences, to aid you in outlining the argument parts.*

# Categorize THE FOUR STIMULUS TYPES

You've learned a lot since we first introduced the stimulus types in the Stimulus Framework section between Chapters 1 and 2. I hadn't yet bombarded you with the first half of at least 621 mentions of the word Loophole. (That changes a person.) Now that you know what premises and conclusions are, the stimulus types will be a lot easier to understand.

| STIMULUS TYPE | ABBREVIATION | DESCRIPTION |
|---|---|---|
| Debate | D | *Two people speaking* |
| Argument | A | *Conclusion supported by premises* |
| Premise Set | PS | *No conclusion: Premises do not contradict one another* |
| Paradox | PX | *No conclusion: Premises contradict one another* |

## ARGUMENT

If your stimulus contains a conclusion, it's an Argument. Check out this Argument with pre-labeled argument parts:

*17.2.10*

> Cafeteria patron:  P1 [The apples sold in this cafeteria are greasy.] P2 [The cashier told me that the apples are in that condition when they are delivered to the cafeteria and that the cafeteria does not wash the apples it sells.] P3 [Most fruit is sprayed with dangerous pesticides before it is harvested, and is dangerous until it is washed.] C [Clearly, the cafeteria is selling pesticide-covered fruit, thereby endangering its patrons.]

**STEALTH ARGUMENTS**

If the stimulus looks like this:

**Principle:** Do stuff this way!

**Application:** Eddie did stuff this way.

Bracket off the Principle as premises and Application as the conclusion. These are Stealth Arguments. They seem special because of the weird colons, but the principle is always the evidence given to justify the particular application. You can Loophole them like normal Arguments.

Arguments are the backbone of Logical Reasoning. You've spent the last couple hundred pages learning how to manipulate Arguments (*high five*), so this should be your comfiest stimulus type. As you know, Arguments on the LSAT are rife with Loophole-potential. Loopholes will be at the forefront of your mind every time you encounter an Argument in Logical Reasoning.

## PREMISE SET

If your stimulus does not contain a conclusion, it's either a Premise Set or a Paradox. If the premises do not contradict one another, the stimulus is a Premise Set. Here's a Premise Set with pre-labeled argument parts:

**FILL IN THE BLANK**

If the stimulus contains a blank at the end, categorize the stimulus as a Premise Set. The question will always ask you to fill in the blank.

*12.1.8*

> P1 [At Happywell, Inc., last year the average annual salary for dieticians was $50,000,] P2 [while the average annual salary for physical therapists was $42,000.] P3 [The average annual salary for all Happywell employees last year was $40,000.]

Premise Sets are another very popular stimulus type. Remember, your Premise Sets are always begging to be added up into an Inference. Whenever you read a Premise Set on the LSAT, start looking for the interlocking point between premises, the word or concept that's repeated multiple times.

## PARADOX

Now we're heading into some new territory with our stimulus types! Get ready to enter the wild world of Paradoxes and Debates.

If your stimulus does not contain a conclusion, it's either a Premise Set or a Paradox. If the premises contradict one another, the stimulus is a Paradox. Check out this Paradox with pre-labeled argument parts:

*19.4.20*

> P1 [There is strong evidence that the cause of migraines (severe recurrent headaches) is not psychological but instead is purely physiological.] P2 [Yet several studies have found that people being professionally treated for migraines rate higher on a standard psychological scale of anxiety than do people not being professionally treated for migraines.]

Paradoxes crash your brain. Something appears to be wrong as soon as you encounter them. They play with your expectations. **The first premise leads you in one direction… and the second premise goes in the opposite direction.** The first premise gives you every indication that things are bad, and yet they somehow end up good. Or the first premise gives you evidence that things are great, and everything turns out poorly. **Paradoxes make the world of the stimulus make no sense.**

Here are a few examples of premises that appear to be in conflict with one another:

| CONTRADICTORY PREMISE 1 | CONTRADICTORY PREMISE 2 |
|---|---|
| *Cassandra is an incompetent saleswoman.* | *Cassandra got the highest bonus in her sales group.* |
| *The coffee shop added 10 new tables today.* | *Tables are harder to find now than they were yesterday.* |
| *Demand for sea urchin has increased.* | *The price of sea urchin has decreased.* |
| *Sharksburg Hospital has better doctors and facilities than Whales Hospital.* | *Sharksburg Hospital has a higher fatality rate than Whales Hospital.* |

See how the first premise suggests a likely outcome? If a hospital has better resources, you're likely to predict that the next sentence will be something about how things are going better at that hospital. The author upends your expectations by constructing a Paradox, playing to the opposite of what you think is coming.

A common Paradox construction involves the first premise mentioning that a given object has a value that is going up/down (sea urchin demand is going up) or has a high/low value to begin with (Cassandra is an incompetent saleswoman). We expect this object to have more attributes in line with this initial characterization. We expect the fact that Cassandra is an incompetent saleswoman to lead to other negative values, like getting fired or being paid less than others. It's jarring when the stimulus abruptly switches tracks. This jarring feeling can lead you to quick Paradox identification.

## DEBATE

If your stimulus has two speakers in it, it's a Debate. Debates don't require much theory to identify, since you can literally see that **there are two names listed with colons after each of them**. Check out this Debate with pre-labeled argument parts:

*19.2.6*

> Legislator:   P1 [ Your agency is responsible for regulating an industry shaken by severe scandals.] P2 [ You were given funds to hire 500 investigators to examine the scandals, but you hired no more than 400.] C [ I am forced to conclude that you purposefully limited hiring in an attempt to prevent the full extent of the scandals from being revealed.]

> Regulator:   P1 [ We tried to hire the 500 investigators] P2 [ but the starting salaries for these positions had been frozen so low by the legislature that it was impossible to attract enough qualified applicants.]

Debates are often constructed with a long statement from the first speaker that serves as an introduction to the issue at hand. Then the second speaker follows with a cryptic premise or two. The example above falls into this category; notice how the second speaker doesn't conclude anything on their own.

The second speaker always means to finish their point, but they act a lot like we do in real life. When someone says something you think is dumb, you probably respond with, "Yeah, but… [inconvenient fact for them]." We don't bother adding "therefore" and concluding when we object. We just offer the fact that we think contradicts something they said or assumed. This is natural, and it's exactly what the second speaker is doing in LSAT Debates. Our task as LSAT test takers is to *target* the second speaker's objection back up to the first speaker.

When you read a Debate on the LSAT, the goal is to connect the two speakers to one another. So the lack of information from the second speaker can be vexing. How can you see how the two speakers connect when the second speaker isn't giving you much information? **You have to use your Inference skills to complete the second speaker's thought for them.** This will be the task we practice in the Controversy section.

# Design

The final step is designing your CLIR and jotting it down next to the stimulus.

**The CLIR is what forces you to take an active stance with the stimulus.** It's all well and good to say "be active" or "analyze the stimulus," but the truth is that almost no one does it unless they have a specific goal in mind (years of experience repeating the phrase "be active" taught me that one). Generalities are the enemies of progress. The CLIR is specific. **Designing the CLIR on every stimulus fundamentally changes the way you conceptualize Logical Reasoning for the better.**

The whole point of this book is to make you a more intuitive critical thinker; this has the useful side effect of dramatically improving your Logical Reasoning LSAT score. When you design the CLIR on every stimulus, you eventually can't resist critiquing arguments (both on the LSAT and in everyday life). That's the expert mindset. That's how the CLIR becomes fast and automatic. Along with the CLIR, the correct answer to the majority of questions will appear to you effortlessly.

When you CLIR all the time, you build the instinct. The CLIR becomes just how you do the question. **No conscious steps. Just intuition. When you're in this mindset… Logical Reasoning is fun.** Seriously. It's a puzzle. You're Omar and the questions are Marlo. You're in control, kicking ass and taking names on 90% of questions. That's my experience with Logical Reasoning. That's the experience I want for you.

Writing a short version of the CLIR to the side of the stimulus will force you to build the CLIR habit. Keep writing the CLIR on the side of the stimulus throughout your untimed practice. Once you have thoroughly ingrained the habit, you can stop writing it and move toward doing it in your head. When you make this move, it's critical that you remain honest with yourself about whether you're actually continuing to design the CLIR. **Your accuracy and speed will both suffer if you cut out the CLIR once timing starts.** You won't write the CLIR down once you start timed practice, so it's crucial that you ingrain the habit while you're still working untimed.

Return to writing down the CLIR if you find yourself skipping it.

# Designing Loopholes

Whenever you detect an Argument, design a Loophole.

To design your Loophole:

1.   Identify your conclusion.

2.   Say, "This conclusion is not necessarily true. **What if...**" Finish this sentence with a possibility that destroys the conclusion.

Let's design the Loophole in a real LSAT stimulus together:

> *17.2.10*
>
> Cafeteria patron:   P1 [The apples sold in this cafeteria are greasy.] P2 [The cashier told me that the apples are in that condition when they are delivered to the cafeteria and that the cafeteria does not wash the apples it sells.] P3 [Most fruit is sprayed with dangerous pesticides before it is harvested, and is dangerous until it is washed.] C [Clearly, the cafeteria is selling pesticide-covered fruit, thereby endangering its patrons.]

Alright, first let's translate:

> *The cafeteria is selling greasy apples. The apples come that way and the cafeteria doesn't wash them. Most fruit has pesticides and is dangerous until you wash it. So the cafeteria is selling pesticide fruit and putting us in danger.*

But what if...

1.   The apples are washed by someone else before they get to the cafeteria?

2.   These apples aren't part of the "most fruit" that gets the pesticides? Grease ≠ pesticides

Both of these are valid Loopholes, but I would personally go with the first one. That is the most glaringly omitted possibility. The Argument really should have addressed it.

Don't worry too much about coming up with the "perfect" Loophole. I invented this whole system – essentially rigging the game so I could be the best player – and you can see that I have options for which Loophole I may choose. Not all of them are going to be the correct answer. That's ok!

**It's more important to think freely and creatively than it is to get the Loophole "right."** If I don't find my Loophole in the answer choices, I just look at the stimulus from a different angle to see where else I can dig in. It's not a big deal; it's not a failure. Even if you never come up with the "correct" Loophole, you're still engaging with the stimulus analytically, and that's way better than the alternative. Every stimulus improves your skills a little more.

**REMEMBER!**   *To design your Loophole, ask yourself, "What if..." and complete your thought with the most powerful worst-case scenario for the conclusion.*

---

If you're stuck for the Loophole, ask yourself, "Why do they think their conclusion is true?" Answer yourself specifically and then **attack that justification**.

The Designing Loopholes section is intentionally kept brief because Loophole design is extensively covered in Chapters 2-3 and 5-7. Pretty much all the pages up until this point have been preparing you for this exact task. Look back and you'll be surprised just how much of Chapter 2 is about Loopholes.

If you over-critique yourself and obsess over the "right" Loophole, you'll likely end up with no Loophole at all, which defeats the purpose of building this skill through practice.

## Designing Inferences

Whenever you detect a Premise Set, design an Inference.

Want to hear the best news ever? You've already practiced this step extensively! Remember how the Conclusions Drill had you add up two premises to create a valid conclusion back in the Arguments & Inferences Chapter? You had to find something that the two premises added up to when taken together. You designed 12 Inferences in that drill! Designing Inferences with real LSAT stimuli is the same mental process you used back then.

Let's see how this works with a real LSAT stimulus:

*12.1.8*

> P1 [At Happywell, Inc., last year the average annual salary for dieticians was $50,000,] P2 [while the average annual salary for physical therapists was $42,000.] P3 [The average annual salary for all Happywell employees last year was $40,000.]

We'll start off with a translation of this stimulus and then add up these premises to design an Inference.

> *At Happywell, dieticians make $50K, physical therapists make $42K, and the average salary is $40K.*

Pretty simple, right? Now we have to connect these premises to come up with something new. The dieticians and physical therapists are both making more than the average salary. How is the average getting dragged down?

**INFERENCE**     Therefore... someone at Happywell makes less than the dieticians and physical therapists.

This Inference has to be true because there have to be lower numbers to get to that $40K average. Notice that there's a hidden common knowledge premise here: how averages work. If you know there are numbers higher than an average, you have to have something to balance them out. The dieticians and physical therapists are the high points, and you need low points to weigh down the average.

This Inference may sound super boring. It's super safe and uninteresting, right? But remember, that's what Inferences (and valid conclusions and necessary assumptions) are. They're provable. All you have to do is connect the different parts of the stimulus to one another and you'll be creating provable Inferences in no time. **Find that interlocking point** and run with it.

**Stick to the exact words of the stimulus** when you design Inferences. They're laying out the pieces; just put them together. The answer choices are temptresses; they're going to try and lead you away from the stimulus. Your Inference will safeguard you against wrong answers if it sticks close to the stimulus.

---

*Remember, Inferences and valid conclusions are the same thing.*

*The Designing Inferences section is intentionally kept brief because Inference design is covered in Chapters 2-3. All previous insights about building valid conclusions are applicable to Inferences.*

*When Premise Sets are conditional, chain the conditional statements together. You can read from the first to the last term in the chain for a quick, automatic Inference!*

# Designing Controversies    ADVANCED INFERENCES

Whenever you detect a Debate, design a Controversy.

**The <u>Controversy is what the two speakers are disagreeing over.</u>** It's the point they're debating. One of them agrees with it and the other disagrees. Controversies are most easily phrased as "whether" statements. The two speakers are disagreeing over *whether* something is true. Phrasing it this way will pinpoint exactly what the two speakers disagree about.

Here's how a simple Controversy could appear in real life:

> *Someone points at an animal and says, "That's a meerkat." A friend replies, "No, that's a rat. We're in the New York City Subway."*

They're disagreeing about whether the animal is a meerket. That's their Controversy. Simple, right? Now, let's see how you're going to design these yourself on real LSAT stimuli.

## HOW TO DESIGN THE CONTROVERSY

---

### LINK THE TWO SPEAKERS

1.  Take an Inference from the second speaker's statements.

    *   Add up the second speaker's premises (and conclusion, if there is one) to connect them to the first speaker. This is your Second Speaker Inference.

2.  Stick a "whether" in front of your Second Speaker Inference and smooth out the language.

---

*[handwritten margin note: ← Create Inference from Second Speaker]*

**The tide of the Debate rises and falls on the second speaker. <u>This is where the money is in Debates.</u>** Controversies are about disagreements, and in order to disagree, you must have something on the table to disagree with. The first speaker puts this information on the table, and **the second speaker is the one doing the disagreeing.** That's why we take a Second Speaker Inference. It's only natural to focus on the person who is actively disagreeing when designing a Controversy.

The problem with the second speaker is that they aren't always clear with how their statements relate to the first speaker. In designing the Controversy, **we need to make the second speaker's point more explicit. We need to link them back up to the first speaker** to figure out what the two speakers are disagreeing about.

Let's explore the Controversy with an example first:

> **Margot:** *You shouldn't pretend to be a robot when we text. It makes me uncomfortable.*
>
> **Lara:** *I disagree! I don't pretend to be a robot to make you comfortable. I do it to amuse you, which I undoubtedly do.*

Let's practice our Second Speaker Inference skills to link Lara up to Margot. Margot concluded that Lara shouldn't pretend to be a robot. Margot's premise is that Lara pretending to be a robot makes her uncomfortable. Lara replies that comfort isn't her goal, taking Margot's premise out of contention. Lara says she pretends to be a robot to amuse

Let your internal monologue keep talking at the end of Lara's statements and the Inference will come naturally.

Margot and she's pretty sure she's succeeding at that. So where is Lara going with this? She's achieving her goal and she doesn't care about the downside for Margot. Therefore… **Lara doesn't think she should stop pretending to be a robot.** Margot thinks Lara should stop. That's their Controversy.

**CONTROVERSY**        whether Lara should stop pretending to be a robot when she texts Margot

**REMEMBER!**        *The Second Speaker Inference bridges the unspoken gap between the two speakers.*

Let's take a real LSAT Debate apart and design the Controversy together!

*19.2.6*

Legislator:    P1 [Your agency is responsible for regulating an industry shaken by severe scandals.] P2 [You were given funds to hire 500 investigators to examine the scandals, but you hired no more than 400.] C [I am forced to conclude that you purposefully limited hiring in an attempt to prevent the full extent of the scandals from being revealed.]

Regulator:    P1 [We tried to hire the 500 investigators] P2 [but the starting salaries for these positions had been frozen so low by the legislature that it was impossible to attract enough qualified applicants.]

First, we'll do a quick translation:

*The first speaker says the 500 investigator hiring goal was not met and he believes the regulator's agency failed purposefully. The second speaker says they tried to hire 500 investigators, but they couldn't because starting salaries were frozen too low.*

We're definitely going to have to rely on the background information supplied by the first speaker to design our Second Speaker Inference. The second speaker is responding to an accusation, that they purposefully limited hiring, and that accusation is crucial to their point. **We have to place the second speaker's statements in the context of that accusation.** Let's add up what the second speaker said to link them back up to the first speaker:

1.    We tried to hire 500 investigators.

2.    We couldn't because salaries were frozen too low.

What is the second speaker getting at here? They're being accused of impropriety by the first speaker, but, because they attempted to hire the 500 investigators, we know that they didn't fail to meet their hiring goal on purpose. The second speaker is trying to prove that they are not guilty of purposefully limiting hiring, the accusation hurled by the first speaker.

**SECOND SPEAKER INFERENCE**        Therefore… we did not purposefully limit hiring.

Notice that purposefully limiting hiring came directly from the first speaker. That's the interlocking point. I'm addressing the first speaker in my Second Speaker Inference, which is exactly how you want to frame your Controversy.

The Second Speaker Inference process is very similar to what we did in the Conclusions Drill in the Arguments & Inferences Chapter. The only difference is connecting the Second Speaker Inference to the first speaker.

<br>

**CONTROVERSY PRO TIPS**

- **Always make your Controversy specific.**

   You can't just say they disagree about whether the first speaker is right or wrong. While that may be true, it's not helpful as an analytical tool.

- **Don't assume the second speaker is always disagreeing with the first speaker's conclusion.**

   This is not even close to true all the time. Think about if you were in a Debate. Would you always straight up disagree with your opponent's conclusion, or would you focus on taking out one of your opponent's key premises? Taking out those premises leaves your opponent with no leg to stand on.

- **Always use background information from the first speaker for your Second Speaker Inference.**

Let's try out our process on another real LSAT Debate:

*14.2.17*

   Consumer activist:    P1 [By allowing major airlines to abandon, as they promptly did, all but their most profitable routes,] C [the government's decision to cease regulation of the airline industry has worked to the disadvantage of everyone who lacks access to a large metropolitan airport.]

   Industry representative:    P1 [On the contrary, where major airlines moved out, regional airlines have moved in] P2 [and, as a consequence, there are more flights into and out of most small airports now than before the change in regulatory policy.]

First, translate:

*The first speaker says that the government screwed over small town people by allowing the airlines to abandon their less lucrative routes. The second speaker says that regional airlines stepped in once the big guys left, so there are more flights at small airports now than there were before.*

The second speaker is targeting something the first speaker said. It's our job to find out what it is. Let's add up the second speaker's statements for our Second Speaker Inference:

1.   When the big airlines left, regional airlines moved into the small airports.

2.   There are more flights in and out of small airports now because of the regulation change.

According to the second speaker, there have been benefits, not disadvantages, since the big airlines left. This means the airlines leaving was actually good for small town people, which connects to the last statement from the first speaker (that the airlines moving out is bad for small town people).

| SECOND SPEAKER INFERENCE | Therefore... the government didn't screw over small town people by deregulating the airlines. |
|---|---|

They're disagreeing over the deregulation's effect on small town people.

| CONTROVERSY | whether the government screwed over small town people by deregulating the airlines |
|---|---|

## HOW TO SHORTHAND YOUR CONTROVERSY

Here's a shorthand for marking the Controversy in training. This will let you write less for most Debates.

1. Make the Second Speaker Inference. A fair amount of time, this Inference will just be NOT [something first speaker said].

2. Bracket the offending statement from the first speaker.

3. Draw a line straight to it from the second speaker.

4. X out that line to note the disagreement.

Check out an example:

Legislator:   Your agency is responsible for regulating an industry shaken by severe scandals. You were given funds to hire 500 investigators to examine the scandals, but you hired no more than 400. I am forced to conclude that [you purposefully limited hiring] in an attempt to prevent the full extent of the scandals from being revealed.

Regulator:   We tried to hire the 500 investigators but the starting salaries for these positions had been frozen so low by the legislature that it was impossible to attract enough qualified applicants.

This notation process will speed up your training time and lead you to become more disciplined in inferring from the second speaker to disagree with the first speaker.

# Designing Resolutions   ADVANCED LOOPHOLES

Whenever you detect a Paradox, design a Resolution.

Resolutions return a sense of order to Paradoxes. If the Resolution had been provided initially, the stimulus would not be a Paradox at all. In designing your Resolution, ask yourself one question:

WHAT WOULD MAKE THIS ALL MAKE SENSE?

Sense is your mission. When you're designing Resolutions, don't be afraid to go for broke. Imagine something as powerful as possible. All the Resolution has to accomplish is sense.

> *Focus on designing powerful Resolutions. Don't be cautious about bringing new information into the stimulus.*

## HOW TO DESIGN A RESOLUTION

---

### THE RESOLUTION BRIDGE

1.  Split up the two contradictory premises and put a Resolution in the middle.

    *   **PREMISE 1**, but **RESOLUTION**, so **PREMISE 2**.

2.  Fill in the Resolution with something that makes **PREMISE 1** naturally lead to **PREMISE 2**.

---

The Resolution Bridge transforms the Paradox into an Argument, which should be much more familiar to you. These transformed Paradoxes don't have to yield 100% valid arguments, but they do have to make sense. You don't have to prove that Premise 1 necessarily leads to Premise 2, just that it's not totally outside the realm of possibility.

> *Usually the first premise in the stimulus will have more introductory information, which makes it easier to list it first in the Resolution Bridge. If you ever feel like it's easier to switch the order of the premises for the Resolution Bridge, feel free to do so.*

Let's try out our process on one of our Paradox examples:

> *Cassandra is an incompetent saleswoman.*        *Cassandra got the highest bonus in her sales group.*

Remember that Resolutions return us to the world of reasonable satisfaction of expectation. So let's try filling in some blanks to see if we can get ourselves to expect Premise 2.

> *Cassandra is an incompetent saleswoman, but* **RESOLUTION**, *so Cassandra got the highest bonus in her sales group.*

What can we put in this blank to take us straight from incompetent saleswoman to expecting her to get the highest bonus in her group? Let's tap into our Loophole creativity. How could this be possible?

| RESOLUTION | RESOLUTION BRIDGE |
|---|---|
| What if all the other salespeople in Cassandra's group are even worse than she is? | *Cassandra is an incompetent saleswoman, but [**all the other salespeople in Cassandra's group are even worse than she is**], so Cassandra got the highest bonus in her sales group.* |
| What if Cassandra's company is super corrupt and awards bonuses for non-performance-based reasons? | *Cassandra is an incompetent saleswoman, but [**Cassandra's company is super corrupt and awards bonuses for non-performance-based reasons**], so Cassandra got the highest bonus in her sales group.* |
| What if all the other people in Cassandra's group haven't been at the company long enough to qualify for any kind of bonus at all? | *Cassandra is an incompetent saleswoman, but [**all the other people in Cassandra's group haven't been at the company long enough to qualify for any kind of bonus at all**], so Cassandra got the highest bonus in her sales group.* |

Awesome! These all effectively bridge the gap. I would personally go with the first one for my CLIR because the quality of the rest of Cassandra's group is a pretty big hole to leave open.

Now, let's design a Resolution in a real LSAT stimulus:

*16.3.10*

> P1 [Michelangelo's sixteenth-century Sistine Chapel paintings are currently being restored.] P2 [A goal of the restorers is to uncover Michelangelo's original work, and so additions made to Michelangelo's paintings by later artists are being removed.] P3 [However, the restorers have decided to make one exception: to leave intact additions that were painted by da Volterra.]

First, let's do a quick translation of the contradictory premises:

1. *The restorers want to uncover Michelangelo's original work so they're removing additions by later artists.*
2. *The restorers are leaving in the additions by da Volterra.*

Awesome, now let's set up our Resolution Bridge:

> *The restorers want to uncover Michelangelo's original work so they're removing additions by later artists,* but **RESOLUTION**, *so they're leaving da Volterra's additions in.*

We need to find a way that leaving da Volterra's stuff alone could still be compatible with the restorers' goal of uncovering Michelangelo's original work. Unlock your creativity here. Try to come up with something.

The first things that come to mind for me are:

| RESOLUTION | RESOLUTION BRIDGE | EFFECT |
|---|---|---|
| What if da Volterra was painting Michelangelo's original work for Michelangelo (like he's an apprentice or something)? | *The restorers want to uncover Michelangelo's original work so they're removing additions by later artists, but [da Volterra was painting Michelangelo's original work for Michelangelo], so they're leaving da Volterra's additions in.* | *Leaving da Volterra in is good for the original work.* |
| What if removing da Volterra's stuff would damage the original work? | *The restorers want to uncover Michelangelo's original work so they're removing additions by later artists, but [removing da Volterra's stuff would damage the original work], so they're leaving da Volterra's additions in.* | *Taking da Volterra out is bad for the original work.* |

Notice how "original work" was all over my Resolutions. That's because I bought into the restorers' goal in order to make their actions make sense. The restorers are the ones who left da Volterra in, so we have to get into their heads to make their actions add up.

Don't be alarmed that there's more than one possible Resolution to each Paradox. Even if your Resolution doesn't appear in the answer choices, taking the stimulus apart this way allows you to see what the right answer needs to accomplish. It shows you the gears spinning within each stimulus. This allows you to get the question right more often and more quickly.

Onward to another real LSAT example:

> 19.4.20
>
> P1 [There is strong evidence that the cause of migraines (severe recurrent headaches) is not psychological but instead is purely physiological.] P2 [Yet several studies have found that people being professionally treated for migraines rate higher on a standard psychological scale of anxiety than do people not being professionally treated for migraines.]

First, let's translate the contradictory premises:

1. *Migraines are not caused by psychological stuff.*
2. *People being professionally treated for migraines rate higher on the anxiety scale than those not being treated for migraines.*

We need to find a way for migraines to not be psychologically caused and to still have professional migraine treatment correlated with anxiety. This Paradox is about causation, so let's use our Omitted Options.

> *But wait, why are these premises contradictory?*
>
> The first premise leads us to believe that migraines do not have a psychological cause. Our brains expect the next sentence to talk more about that, providing more evidence about how migraines and psychological things are separate. Instead, the next premise links migraines and psychological stuff more closely. How rebellious.

Let's set up our Resolution Bridge:

*Migraines are not caused by psychological stuff, but* **RESOLUTION**, *so people being professionally treated for migraines rate higher on the anxiety scale than those not being treated for migraines.*

The Resolution Bridge makes this one a little clearer. Basically, you're being asked to explain a correlation (professionally treated for migraines and anxiety) while you've already been told that one of the causal possibilities is not the case. They're asking you to propose alternative causal explanations. Here are a few possibilities:

| **RESOLUTION** | **RESOLUTION BRIDGE** | **OMITTED OPTION** |
| --- | --- | --- |
| *What if migraines cause anxiety?* | *Migraines are not caused by psychological stuff, but [**migraines cause anxiety**], so people being professionally treated for migraines rate higher on the anxiety scale than those not being treated for migraines.* | *Backwards Causation* |
| *What if high-performing people tend to have both anxiety and muscle tension, which causes migraines?* | *Migraines are not caused by psychological stuff, but [**high-performing people tend to have both anxiety and muscle tension, which causes migraines**], so people being professionally treated for migraines rate higher on the anxiety scale than those not being treated for migraines.* | *New Factor Causing One or Both* |
| *What if those who seek professional treatment for anything are more likely to have psychological problems?* | *Migraines are not caused by psychological stuff, but [**those who seek professional treatment for anything are more likely to have psychological problems**], so people being professionally treated for migraines rate higher on the anxiety scale than those not being treated for migraines.* | *New Factor Causing One or Both* |

Causal reasoning is everywhere! Any of these Omitted Options would be a valid Resolution.

 REMEMBER! *It's just as important to notice what the stimulus leaves out as it is to notice what the stimulus includes.*

# Training Goals

The CLIR trains your instincts. When you start timed practice, you should no longer be consciously completing the CLIR in steps. Instead, you should read the stimulus, have the analytical instinct to critique it, and move forward with the fruit of that intuition. It should be automatic – not steps.

Once you've practiced to the point of intuition, the CLIR analytical instinct usually manifests as something like "they're assuming the groups are the same" or "dangling variable" (or, if you're me, something much more expletive-laden). It does not manifest as "OK, this is an Argument, so I need a Loophole... umm... what if... wait I think this is causal reasoning so I should talk about one of the Omitted Options... What were those? Backwards something?" That interior monologue is a sign you are not yet practiced enough with the CLIR (and LR in general) to make it intuitive. You can get there and you will get there, but you have to do the work to make it happen. Games are won on the practice field.

## TRAINING GAME PLAN

**Do *at least* six untimed CLIR Drills on six full LR sections. Start with the two sections supplied in the forthcoming CLIR Drill.** This is a minimum, not a maximum. If you are not comfortable after six practice sections, review Chapters 2-3 and 5-7 and continue doing CLIR Drills until you are comfortable.

For the love of all that is good and beautiful in this world, do not do the questions on your CLIR Drills.

**Do not read the question stem and answer choices on any of your CLIR Drills.** You have to focus on ingraining the CLIR intuition. We'll add the question types and answer choices to your process next. You can re-approach the questions from your CLIR Drills at that point.

If you don't practice the CLIR, you're wasting any time you've put into reading this chapter. It is not enough to just read my explanations of how to design the CLIR. It's easy to read this book and think my explanations make sense, but CLIRing yourself is a different animal. You'll only improve through practice.

I know training can be challenging. LSAT stimuli are *hard*, even for naturals. Struggling is how you get better. Have you ever heard that "Pain is weakness leaving the body" cliché in sports movies? Well, I'm going to steal it here:

Try to do practice sections and drills in one sitting. If you take breaks after only a few questions, you're not preparing yourself for test day conditions.

PAIN IS WEAKNESS LEAVING THE BODY

Nice, now you've been properly clichéd. Keep pushing when you feel like you "can't" figure it out. You actually can; you just don't know it yet. Now, go rock this CLIR Drill.

---

**THE CLIR GAME PLAN**

- Complete the CLIR Drill now.

- **Relentlessly practice** the CLIR mindset. Make the critiquing impulse automatic, not conscious steps.

- Re-read Arguments & Inferences, if you have conclusion identification errors in the CLIR Drill. It is crucial that you can identify conclusions before you move to the question types.

- Consult Chapters 1-8 as a reference moving forward. They are the foundation you need to excel in Chapters 9-12.

## CLIR Drill   JUNE 2007, SECTION 2

### INSTRUCTIONS

*Outline the argument parts, categorize the stimulus, and circle the correct CLIR from the two options provided.*

By using the June 2007 LR in both the Basic Translation Drill and the CLIR Drill, we're layering the skills required to master LR on top of one another one by one. This is best accomplished by showing you the same question again with a new task. Now that you've translated June 2007, you've got the wording difficulty out of the way and you're ready to conquer the analytical difficulty. If you took this test already, you're in an even better spot because you'll be able to see how your perspective on LR has changed from the skills you've internalized so far.

\* Continue to translate these stimuli in your head before doing the CLIR. You don't need to cover the stimuli up when you translate.

**1.** Economist: Every business strives to increase its productivity, for this increases profits for the owners and the likelihood that the business will survive. But not all efforts to increase productivity are beneficial to the business as a whole. Often attempts to increase productivity decrease the number of employees, which clearly harms the dismissed employees as well as the sense of security of the retained employees.

STIMULUS TYPE ___Argument___

A) What if the retained employees hold a longstanding grudge that damages company productivity?

B) *(circled)* What if the efforts' upsides outweigh the downsides enough to be beneficial to the business as a whole?

**2.** All Labrador retrievers bark a great deal. All Saint Bernards bark infrequently. Each of Rosa's dogs is a cross between a Labrador retriever and a Saint Bernard. Therefore, Rosa's dogs are moderate barkers.

STIMULUS TYPE ___Argument___

A) What if Rosa's dogs also have another breed of dog in their pedigree?

B) *(circled)* What if traits don't mix to produce 50/50 results?

**3.** A century in certain ways is like a life, and as the end of a century approaches, people behave toward that century much as someone who is nearing the end of life does toward that life. So just as people in their last years spend much time looking back on the events of their life, people at a century's end _____.

STIMULUS TYPE ___Premise SC___

A) Look back over their lives.

B) *(circled)* Look back over the last century.

**4.** Consumer:   The latest *Connorly Report* suggests that Ocksenfrey prepackaged meals are virtually devoid of nutritional value. But the Connorly Report is commissioned by Danto Foods, Ocksenfrey's largest corporate rival, and early drafts of the report are submitted for approval to Danto Foods' public relations department. Because of the obvious bias of this report, it is clear that Ocksenfrey's prepackaged meals really are nutritious.

STIMULUS TYPE ___Argument___

A) *(circled)* What if Danto's bias doesn't affect the truth?

B) What if Ocksenfrey's meals aren't nutritious?

**5.** Scientist: Earth's average annual temperature has increased by about 0.5 degrees Celsius over the last century. This warming is primarily the result of the buildup of minor gases in the atmosphere, blocking the outward flow of heat from the planet.

STIMULUS TYPE _Argument_

**A)** What if the warming isn't serious?

**B)** What if something else is causing the warming?

**6.** An undergraduate degree is necessary for appointment to the executive board. Further, no one with a felony conviction can be appointed to the board. Thus, Murray, an accountant with both a bachelor's and a master's degree, cannot be accepted for the position of Executive Administrator since he has a felony conviction.

STIMULUS TYPE _Argument_

**A)** What if the Executive Administrator isn't subject to the same qualifications as the executive board?

**B)** What if Murray's felony conviction would keep him from doing his job?

**7.** Ethicist: The most advanced kind of moral motivation is based solely on abstract principles. This form of motivation is in contrast with calculated self-interest or the desire to adhere to societal norms and conventions.

STIMULUS TYPE _Premise set_

**A)** Something based on abstract principles contrasts with self-interest and adherence to societal norms.  → be boring

**B)** Someone who follows societal norms can never be moral.

**8.** Proponents of the electric car maintain that when the technical problems associated with its battery design are solved, such cars will be widely used and, because they are emission-free, will result in an abatement of the environmental degradation caused by auto emissions. But unless we dam more rivers, the electricity to charge these batteries will come from nuclear or coal-fired power plants. Each of these three power sources produces considerable environmental damage. Thus, the electric car _____ .

STIMULUS TYPE _Premise set_

**A)** Will spur further innovation in green technology.

**B)** Will also produce environmental damage, unless we dam more rivers.

**9.** Although video game sales have increased steadily over the past 3 years, we can expect a reversal of this trend in the very near future. Historically, over three quarters of video games sold have been purchased by people from 13 to 16 years of age, and the number of people in this age group is expected to decline steadily over the next 10 years.

STIMULUS TYPE _Argument_

**A)** What if the video game industry shifts focus in an attempt to attract older customers?

**B)** What if the way it's been historically has changed recently so people outside 13-16 are buying?

**10.** Double-blind techniques should be used whenever possible in scientific experiments. They help prevent the misinterpretations that often arise due to expectations and opinions that scientists already hold, and clearly scientists should be extremely diligent in trying to avoid such misinterpretations.

STIMULUS TYPE _Argument_

**A)** What if there's another way of preventing misinterpretations?

**B)** What if double-blind techniques are expensive?

**11.**
It is now a common complaint that the electronic media have corroded the intellectual skills required and fostered by the literary media. But several centuries ago the complaint was that certain intellectual skills, such as the powerful memory and extemporaneous eloquence that were intrinsic to oral culture, were being destroyed by the spread of literacy. So, what awaits us is probably a mere alteration of the human mind rather than its devolution.

STIMULUS TYPE _Argument_

(A) What if there's a difference between the oral-literary shift and the literary-electronic shift?

B) What if a powerful memory isn't as useful as extemporaneous eloquence?

**12.**
Suppose I have promised to keep a confidence and someone asks me a question that I cannot answer truthfully without thereby breaking the promise. Obviously, I cannot both keep and break the same promise. Therefore, one cannot be obliged both to answer all questions truthfully and to keep all promises.

STIMULUS TYPE _Argument_

A) What if you could both keep and break the same promise?

B) What if that hypothetical question that requires promise breaking is never actually asked?

**13.**
Standard aluminum soft-drink cans do not vary in the amount of aluminum that they contain. Fifty percent of the aluminum contained in a certain group (M) of standard aluminum soft-drink cans was recycled from another group (L) of used, standard aluminum soft-drink cans. Since all the cans in L were recycled into cans in M and since the amount of material other than aluminum in an aluminum can is negligible, it follows that M contains twice as many cans as L.

STIMULUS TYPE _Argument_

(A) What if some of the aluminum is lost in the recycling process?

B) What if the other 50% of the aluminum contained in M (not the aluminum from L) was of very poor quality?

**14.**
A cup of raw milk, after being heated in a microwave oven to 50 degrees Celsius, contains half its initial concentration of a particular enzyme, lysozyme. If, however, the milk reaches that temperature through exposure to a conventional heat source of 50 degrees Celsius, it will contain nearly all of its initial concentration of the enzyme. Therefore, what destroys the enzyme is not heat but microwaves, which generate heat.

STIMULUS TYPE _Argument_

(A) What if microwave heat is different from conventional heat in a way that kills lysozyme?

B) What if the destruction of lysozyme has been linked to radiation that also causes cancer?

**15.**
A new government policy has been developed to avoid many serious cases of influenza. This goal will be accomplished by the annual vaccination of high-risk individuals: everyone 65 and older as well as anyone with a chronic disease that might cause them to experience complications from the influenza virus. Each year's vaccination will protect only against the strain of the influenza virus deemed most likely to be prevalent that year, so every year it will be necessary for all high-risk individuals to receive a vaccine for a different strain of the virus.

STIMULUS TYPE _Argument_

(A) What if the same strain is prevalent for more than one year?

B) What if a particular strain is so virulent that it is fatal to any high-risk individual who's exposed to it?

**16.** Taylor: Researchers at a local university claim that 61 percent of the information transferred during a conversation is communicated through nonverbal signals. But this claim, like all such mathematically precise claims, is suspect, because claims of such exactitude could never be established by science.

*[handwritten: P]*

*[handwritten: prima facie]*

Sandra: While precision is unobtainable in many areas of life, it is commonplace in others. Many scientific disciplines obtain extremely precise results, which should not be doubted merely because of their precision.

STIMULUS TYPE ___Debate___

**A)** whether 61% of information is necessarily transferred nonverbally

**B)** whether simply being precise necessarily makes a claim suspect

**17.** Hospital executive: At a recent conference on nonprofit management, several computer experts maintained that the most significant threat faced by large institutions such as universities and hospitals is unauthorized access to confidential data. In light of this testimony, we should make the protection of our clients' confidentiality our highest priority.

STIMULUS TYPE ___Argument___

**A)** What if we shouldn't listen to computer experts about hospital management (invalid appeal to authority)?

**B)** What if the computer experts were biased toward creating business for themselves (ad hominem)?

**18.** Modern science is built on the process of posing hypotheses and testing them against observations—in essence, attempting to show that the hypotheses are incorrect. Nothing brings more recognition than overthrowing conventional wisdom. It is accordingly unsurprising that some scientists are skeptical of the widely accepted predictions of global warming. What is instead remarkable is that with hundreds of researchers striving to make breakthroughs in climatology, very few find evidence that global warming is unlikely.

STIMULUS TYPE ___Argument___

**A)** What if scientists are very close to a breakthrough on global warming?

**B)** What if global warming is correct and can't be disproven?

*[handwritten right margin: whether or not they are close, a breakthrough or not, it doesn't matter, the conclusion is about whether it is more likely or not]*

**19.** Historian: The Land Party achieved its only national victory in Banestria in 1935. It received most of its support that year in rural and semirural areas, where the bulk of Banestria's population lived at the time. The economic woes of the years surrounding that election hit agricultural and small business interests the hardest, and the Land Party specifically targeted those groups in 1935. I conclude that the success of the Land Party that year was due to the combination of the Land Party's specifically addressing the concerns of these groups and the depth of the economic problems people in these groups were facing.

STIMULUS TYPE ___Argument___

**A)** What if people don't vote based on the issues?

**B)** What if the Land Party was unpopular with urban voters?

**20.** Gamba: Muñoz claims that the Southwest Hopeville Neighbors Association overwhelmingly opposes the new water system, citing this as evidence of citywide opposition. The association did pass a resolution opposing the new water system, but only 25 of 350 members voted, with 10 in favor of the system. Furthermore, the 15 opposing votes represent far less than 1 percent of Hopeville's population. One should not assume that so few votes represent the view of the majority of Hopeville's residents.

STIMULUS TYPE ___Argument___

**A)** What if some members of the Neighbors Association were in favor of the measure?

**B)** What if it's a representative sample?

**21.** Driver: My friends say I will one day have an accident because I drive my sports car recklessly. But I have done some research, and apparently minivans and larger sedans have very low accident rates compared to sports cars. So trading my sports car in for a minivan would lower my risk of having an accident.

STIMULUS TYPE _Argument_

**A)** What if it's the type of driver who purchases a minivan that causes minivans to be safer?

**B)** What if some minivans perform worse than sports cars in certified crash tests?

**22.** Editorialist: News media rarely cover local politics thoroughly, and local political business is usually conducted secretively. These factors each tend to isolate local politicians from their electorates. This has the effect of reducing the chance that any particular act of resident participation will elicit a positive official response, which in turn discourages resident participation in local politics.

STIMULUS TYPE _Premise Set_

**A)** If the news media covered local politics more, our democracy would be enlivened.

**B)** The news media's lack of coverage of local politics influences resident participation in local politics.

Whenever you encounter a conditional argument, make sure to diagram the premises and conclusion separately! This helps you more clearly see the gap between the premises and the conclusion.

For extra flair, write ∴ in front of the conclusion to set it apart. ∴ means "therefore" in logic talk.

**23.** Philosopher: An action is morally right if it would be reasonably expected to increase the aggregate well-being of the people affected by it. An action is morally wrong if and only if it would be reasonably expected to reduce the aggregate well-being of the people affected by it. Thus, actions that would be reasonably expected to leave unchanged the aggregate well-being of the people affected by them are also right.

STIMULUS TYPE _Argument_

**A)** What if an action can be morally neutral, neither morally right nor morally wrong?

**B)** What if morally wrong actions don't always reduce well-being?

**24.** Car companies solicit consumer information on such human factors as whether a seat is comfortable or whether a set of controls is easy to use. However, designer interaction with consumers is superior to survey data. The data may tell the designer why a feature on last year's model was given a low rating, but data will not explain how that feature needs to be changed in order to receive a higher rating.

STIMULUS TYPE _Argument_

**A)** What if designer interaction with consumers also wouldn't explain how the feature needs to be changed?

**B)** What if almost no seats are rated comfortable?

We've put the CLIR Drill Answer Key online! elementalprep.com/bonus

**25.** During the nineteenth century, the French academy of art was a major financial sponsor of painting and sculpture in France; sponsorship by private individuals had decreased dramatically by this time. Because the academy discouraged innovation in the arts, there was little innovation in nineteenth century French sculpture. Yet nineteenth century French painting showed a remarkable degree of innovation.

STIMULUS TYPE _Paradox / Argument_

**A)** What if innovation in sculpture requires more experience than innovation in painting does?

**B)** What if painters are less reliant on sponsors because their materials cost less?

Brilliant! Now that you've completed your first CLIR Drill, check your answers online at elementalprep.com/bonus.
**Take note of your mistakes in your Wrong Answer Journal before proceeding to the next CLIR Drill.**

# CLIR Drill  JUNE 2007, SECTION 3

*Now that you've learned to differentiate between two CLIRs, it's time to start CLIRing on your own. Use the space below to outline the argument parts, categorize the stimulus, and design your own CLIR.*

**1.** Situation: [Someone living in a cold climate buys a winter coat that is stylish but not warm in order to appear sophisticated.] P

Analysis: [People are sometimes willing to sacrifice sensual comfort or pleasure for the sake of appearances.] C

STIMULUS TYPE _Argument_

CLIR _what if staying warm is uncomfortable for this person? what if they don't a winter coat to stay warm? "what if they're not sacrificing comfort b/c they're lazy"_

**2.** After replacing his old gas water heater with a new, pilotless, gas water heater that is rated as highly efficient, Jimmy's gas bills increased.

STIMULUS TYPE _Paradox_

CLIR _what if Jimmy started using his new heater more often than he did his old one?_

**3.** Carolyn: [The artist Marc Quinn has displayed, behind a glass plate, biologically replicated fragments of Sir John Sulston's DNA, calling it a "conceptual portrait" of Sulston.] But to be a portrait, something must bear a recognizable resemblance to its subject.] C

Arnold: I disagree. [Quinn's conceptual portrait is a maximally realistic portrait,] for [it holds actual instructions according to which Sulston was created.]

STIMULUS TYPE _ddoto Debate_

CLIR _whether or not the portrait bears a resemblance to Sir John Sulston. "whether somthy has to bear a resemb to it's subject to be called a portrait"_

**4.** [Many corporations have begun decorating their halls with motivational posters in hopes of boosting their employees' motivation to work productively.] However, [almost all employees at these corporations are already motivated to work productively,] so [these corporations' use of motivational posters is unlikely to achieve its intended purpose.] C

STIMULUS TYPE _Argument_

CLIR _what if already motivated workers can be motivated further?_

**5.** Atrens: [An early entomologist observed ants carrying particles to neighboring ant colonies and inferred that the ants were bringing food to their neighbors.] Further research, however, [revealed that the ants were emptying their own colony's dumping site.] Thus, [the early entomologist was wrong.] C

STIMULUS TYPE _Argument_

CLIR _what if the "dumpings" can be consumed as food? "what if there was food in the dumping site?-"_

**6.** Jablonski, who owns a car dealership, has donated cars to driver education programs at area schools for over five years. She found the statistics on car accidents to be disturbing, and she wanted to do something to encourage better driving in young drivers. Some members of the community have shown their support for this action by purchasing cars from Jablonski's dealership.

STIMULUS TYPE _Premise Set_

CLIR _Premise, Jablonski's_ _program donating have led_ _to new sales_ _"Jablonski has benefited..."_

**7.** Antonio: One can live a life of moderation by never deviating from the middle course. But then one loses the joy of spontaneity and misses the opportunities that come to those who are occasionally willing to take great chances, or to go too far.

Marla: But one who, in the interests of moderation, never risks going too far is actually failing to live a life of moderation. One must be moderate even in one's moderation.

STIMULUS TYPE _Debate_

CLIR _what it means_ _to live moderately_ _"whether never deviating from_ _the middle counts as a_ _life in moderation"_

**8.** Advertisement: Fabric-Soft leaves clothes soft and fluffy, and its fresh scent is a delight. We conducted a test using over 100 consumers to prove Fabric-Soft is best. Each consumer was given one towel washed with Fabric-Soft and one towel washed without it. Ninety-nine percent of the consumers preferred the Fabric-Soft towel. So Fabric-Soft is the most effective fabric softener available.

STIMULUS TYPE _Argument_

CLIR _What if Fabric-soft_ _was tested against other_ _softeners?_ _What if 100 people is_ _not a representative sample?_ _"what if any would use both_ _preferable to none"_

**9.** Naturalist: The recent claims that the Tasmanian tiger is not extinct are false. The Tasmanian tiger's natural habitat was taken over by sheep farming decades ago, resulting in the animal's systematic elimination from the area. Since then naturalists working in the region have discovered no hard evidence of its survival, such as carcasses or tracks. In spite of alleged sightings of the animal, the Tasmanian tiger no longer exists.

IC

STIMULUS TYPE _Argument_

CLIR _what if lack of_ _evidence doesn't mean_ _lacking?_

**10.** Advertisers have learned that people are more easily encouraged to develop positive attitudes about things toward which they originally have neutral or even negative attitudes if those things are linked, with pictorial help rather than exclusively through prose, to things about which they already have positive attitudes. Therefore, advertisers are likely to _____.

STIMULUS TYPE _Premise set_

CLIR _use more positively_ _associated pictures in_ _advertising_

_"more likely to prominently link_ _their products to known positives"_

**11.** [Feathers recently taken from seabirds stuffed and preserved in the 1880s have been found to contain only half as much mercury as feathers recently taken from living birds of the same species.] Since mercury that accumulates in a seabird's feathers as the feathers grow is derived from fish eaten by the bird, these results indicate that mercury levels in saltwater fish are higher now than they were 100 years ago.]

*P₁* (margin)

STIMULUS TYPE _Argument_

CLIR _What if Mercury levels don't stay constant over time?_

**12.** [Novel X and Novel Y are both semiautobiographical novels and contain many very similar themes and situations, which might lead one to suspect plagiarism on the part of one of the authors.] However, it is more likely that the similarity of themes and situations in the two novels is merely coincidental, since both authors are from very similar backgrounds and have led similar lives.]

*P₁* (margin)

STIMULUS TYPE _Argument_      "no necessary men"

CLIR _What if having a similar life and background doesn't translate into many similarity, c/o plagiarism?_

**13.** Therapist: [Cognitive psychotherapy focuses on changing a patient's conscious beliefs.] Thus, cognitive psychotherapy is likely to be more effective at helping patients overcome psychological problems than are forms of psychotherapy that focus on changing unconscious beliefs and desires, since only conscious beliefs are under the patient's direct conscious control.]

*P₁* (margin)

STIMULUS TYPE _Argument_

CLIR ~~what if the beliefs to overcome~~ What if a patient's level of control is irrelevant in overcoming psychological problems?

"what if focus won't under person's control doesn't make patients more effectively overcome psychological problems"

**14.** Commentator: [In academic scholarship, sources are always cited, and methodology and theoretical assumptions are set out, so as to allow critical study, replication, and expansion of scholarship.] [In open-source software, the code in which the program is written can be viewed and modified by individual users for their purposes without getting permission from the producer or paying a fee.] In contrast, the code of proprietary software is kept secret, and modifications can be made only by the producer, for a fee.] This shows that open-source software better matches the values embodied in academic scholarship,] and since scholarship is central to the mission of universities,] universities should use only open-source software.]

STIMULUS TYPE _Argument_

CLIR _what if Academic Scholarship is different than programming Software?_

_What if the university has Software that they want even Staff to access?_

_What if the university has uses for proprietary Software_

"what if the university has other priorities w/its special programming that overrides scholarship"

**15.** [A consumer magazine surveyed people who had sought a psychologist's help with a personal problem.] [Of those responding who had received treatment for 6 months or less, 20 percent claimed that treatment "made things a lot better."] Of those responding who had received longer treatment, 36 percent claimed that treatment "made things a lot better."] Therefore, psychological treatment lasting more than 6 months is more effective than shorter-term treatment.]

STIMULUS TYPE _Argument_

CLIR _What IF those who stayed felt it worked better prior to 6 months and decided to stay?_

_what if the 36 min were groggy me?_

"what if people aren't capable of evaluating the effectiveness of their own psychological treatment?"

*[handwritten top:] [A Nation] must have it citizens hold a belief about it that is literally false, if it is to survive.*

**16.** Philosopher: Nations are not literally persons; they have no thoughts or feelings, and, literally speaking, they perform no actions. Thus they have no moral rights or responsibilities. But no nation can survive unless many of its citizens attribute such rights and responsibilities to it, for nothing else could prompt people to make the sacrifices national citizenship demands. Obviously, then, a nation _____

STIMULUS TYPE *Premise Set*
CLIR *can only survive if citizens attribute moral rights or responsibilities to it*

**17.** When exercising the muscles in one's back, it is important, in order to maintain a healthy back, to exercise the muscles on opposite sides of the spine equally. After all, balanced muscle development is needed to maintain a healthy back, since the muscles on opposite sides of the spine must pull equally in opposing directions to keep the back in proper alignment and protect the spine.

STIMULUS TYPE *Argument*
CLIR *what if someone already has a muscle imbalance?*

*"what if exercising muscles equally doesn't lead to balanced muscle development?"*

**18.** Editorialist: In all cultures, it is almost universally accepted that one has a moral duty to prevent members of one's family from being harmed. Thus, few would deny that if a person is known by the person's parents to be falsely accused of a crime, it would be morally right for the parents to hide the accused from the police. Hence, it is also likely to be widely accepted that it is sometimes morally right to obstruct the police in their work.

STIMULUS TYPE *Argument*
CLIR *what if by hiding the accused from the police real harm is done to the accused?*

*"what if hiding the accused does not obstruct the police?"*

**19.** Editor: Many candidates say that if elected they will reduce governmental intrusion into voters' lives. But voters actually elect politicians who instead promise that the government will provide assistance to solve their most pressing problems. Governmental assistance, however, costs money, and money can come only from taxes, which can be considered a form of governmental intrusion. Thus, governmental intrusion into the lives of voters will rarely be substantially reduced over time in a democracy.

STIMULUS TYPE *Argument*
CLIR *what if the current state of government is not indicative of how it will act in the future?*

*"what if politicians don't keep their promises"*

**20.** We should accept the proposal to demolish the old train station, because the local historical society, which vehemently opposes this, is dominated by people who have no commitment to long-term economic well-being. Preserving old buildings creates an impediment to new development, which is critical to economic health.

STIMULUS TYPE *Argument*
CLIR *what if having no commitment to society doesn't mean that your goals about it?*

*what if we don't care about economic health?*

*what if we should all adhere...?*

**21.** Ethicist: On average, animals raised on grain must be fed sixteen pounds of grain to produce one pound of meat. A pound of meat is more nutritious for humans than a pound of grain, but sixteen pounds of grain could feed many more people than could a pound of meat. With grain yields leveling off, large areas of farmland going out of production each year, and the population rapidly expanding, we must accept the fact that consumption of meat will soon be <u>morally unacceptable</u>.

*P₁* *P₂* *P₃* *C*

STIMULUS TYPE _Argument_

CLIR _what if nutrition ≠ feeding?_
_what if being morally acceptable_
_does not necessarily mean_
_feeding more people?_

---

**22.** If the price it pays for coffee beans continues to increase, the Coffee Shoppe will have to increase its prices. In that case, either the Coffee Shoppe will begin selling noncoffee products or its coffee sales will decrease. But selling noncoffee products will decrease the Coffee Shoppe's overall profitability. Moreover, the Coffee Shoppe can avoid a decrease in overall profitability only if its coffee sales do not decrease.

P↑ ⊃C↑    ADP → CS↓

STIMULUS TYPE _Argument Provide Set_

CLIR _If the price it pays for_
_coffee beans increases then_
_the overall profitability decreases_

---

**23.** Political candidates' speeches are loaded with promises and with expressions of good intention, but one must not forget that the politicians' purpose in giving these speeches is to get themselves elected. Clearly, then, these speeches are selfishly motivated and the promises made in them are unreliable.

*P₁* *C*

STIMULUS TYPE _Argument_

CLIR _what if something can be_
_both selfishly motivated and reliable?_
_" what if you can keep a promise made for_
_the purpose of getting elected?"_

---

**24.** Sociologist: Romantics who claim that people are not born evil but may be made evil by the imperfect institutions that they form cannot be right for they misunderstand the causal relationship between people and their institutions. After all, institutions are merely collections of people.

*C* *P₁* *P₂*

STIMULUS TYPE _Argument_

CLIR _what if the collections of_
_people act and influence each other_
_differently than individuals?_
_what if part ≠ whole and/or whole ≠ part?_

---

**25.** Some anthropologists argue that the human species could not have survived prehistoric times if the species had not evolved the ability to cope with diverse natural environments. However, there is considerable evidence that *Australopithecus afarensis*, a prehistoric species related to early humans, also thrived in a diverse array of environments, but became extinct. Hence, the anthropologists' claim is false.

*P₁* *P₂*

STIMULUS TYPE _Argument_

CLIR _what if something_
_necessary is not sufficient_
_for survival?_

*Your study bag has been lightened! We put the CLIR Drill Answer Key online: elementalprep.com/bonus*

## Quiz 8  THE CLIR

### INSTRUCTIONS

*Answer these questions based on your knowledge of the chapter. Attempt to answer without looking back at the chapter first. If you don't know the answer, circle the question number and go find the answer in the chapter. Study the sections of the chapter that you couldn't remember at first.*

### Word Bank

| | | |
|---|---|---|
| *Debate(s)* | *Controversy* | *categorize* |
| *Resolution* | *analysis* | *Inference(s)* |
| *Paradox* | *design* | *Loophole(s)* |
| *second* | *outline* | *Argument(s)* |
| *Premise Set* | *sufficient* | *first* |

*Use the word bank to answer the fill-in-the-blank questions. Some words will not be used and others may be used more than once.*

**1.** Draw a line from each stimulus type to its correct CLIR pairing.

| | |
|---|---|
| Premise Set | Loophole |
| Argument | Controversy |
| Paradox | Inference |
| Debate | Resolution |

**2.** The three steps in the CLIR Training Regimen are _____, _____, and _____.

**3.** The two stimuli categories that do not contain a conclusion are _____ and _____.

**4.** If a stimulus contains a blank at the end, categorize the stimulus as a(n) _____.

**5.** The Debate rises and falls upon the _____ speaker.

*Circle the correct answer to the following questions.*

**6.**     **TRUE OR FALSE**     To create a provable Inference, you should connect the different parts of the stimulus to one another.

**7.**     **TRUE OR FALSE**     Both speakers should have the same the opinion on the Controversy.

**8.**     **TRUE OR FALSE**     You should always assume the second speaker is disagreeing with the first speaker's conclusion.

**9.**     **TRUE OR FALSE**     You should place your Resolution Bridge in between the two contradictory premises.

**10.**     **TRUE OR FALSE**     The Resolution Bridge must turn the Paradox into a 100% valid argument.

*Where's the answer key?*

You'll find the answer key at the end of the chapter on page 254.

## Quiz 8 ANSWER KEY

**1.**

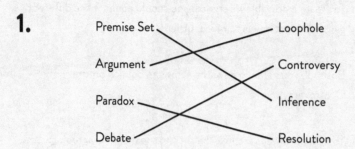

Premise Set — Inference
Argument — Loophole
Paradox — Resolution
Debate — Controversy

**2.** The three steps in the CLIR Training Regimen are **outline**, **categorize**, and **design**.

**3.** The two stimuli categories that do not contain a conclusion are **Premise Set** and **Paradox**.

**4.** If a stimulus contains a blank at the end, categorize the stimulus as a **Premise Set**.

**5.** The Debate rises and falls upon the **second** speaker.

**6.** True.

**7.** False. The two speakers should have *opposing* opinions on the Controversy.

**8.** False. You should *not* assume the second speaker is disagreeing with the first speaker's conclusion.

**9.** True.

**10.** False. The Resolution Bridge does *not* need to turn the Paradox into a 100% valid argument.

# OMMMM.

chapter eight. you're outta the gate.

## Chapter Breather   A BIAS, E BIAS, AND THE ANSWER CHOICE RESET

You'll find more answer choice pro tips like this one in the Answer Choice Strategy Section.

I've noticed two patterns in students' wrong answers over the years:

> **A** gets erroneously crossed out more often than other answer choices.
>
> **E** gets erroneously chosen more often than other answer choices.

I call this tendency **A** Bias and **E** Bias.

### WHY A BIAS HAPPENS

If you've CLIR-ed the stimulus and flipped your CLIR according to the question type, you have a freshly-minted, dream correct answer ready when you read **A**. It's a perfect and beautiful starship. Any deviation from that starship can lead the unpracticed student to erroneously cross **A** out, even if it's conceptually promising. Impulsivity kicks **A** in the shins. Once **A** is crossed out, it's never looked at again. A worse answer is chosen because the cross out on **A** blinds us to its potential. This can then lead to **E** Bias.

> **SOLUTION**   Only cross out **A** if you *know* it's wrong. If you're unsure about **A**, leave it open, and evaluate it again once you've read the other answer choices.

### WHY E BIAS HAPPENS

You've crossed **A**, **B**, **C**, and **D** out, and now you're starting to read **E**. There is a natural inclination to not scrutinize **E** as harshly as you did **A**, **B**, **C**, and **D**. This happens because you want two things: You want to believe you were correct in your judgment of **A**, **B**, **C**, and **D**, and you want to move on from this question. Nobody wants to admit they were wrong and read the answer choices again.

This leads to lots of choosing **E**, even when you know it's not an awesome answer choice. All the other ones are crossed off so you feel backed into a corner. Don't fall for this. **E** is no more likely to be correct than any other answer choice; it doesn't deserve special favors just because no other answer choice was obviously correct.

I personally say, "I hope it's **E**" every time, and I know it inoculates me against choosing **E** just because it's convenient.

> **SOLUTION**   If you've crossed off **A**, **B**, **C**, and **D**, say "Well, I hope it's **E**..." to yourself in your head. When you do this, you acknowledge your potential **E** Bias.

### NEXT LEVEL REMEDY FOR A BIAS AND E BIAS: THE ANSWER CHOICE RESET

Making a Mission and the Back-Up Plans will be explored in detail in the coming pages.

**If you've read E and none of the answers seem worth choosing, erase all the marks you've made on the answer choices.** Start completely fresh. Look back at the stimulus for what you've missed. They've obviously taken an angle you weren't expecting. Make a Mission. Use the Back-Up Plans. Do not just choose an answer you know sucks because you can't see why the right answer is right at that moment. I guarantee that the correct answer definitively does not suck.

THE POWERFUL-PROVABLE PRIMER
The Question Type Framework

## The Questions, Simplified

Onwards to the question stem! We've spent the first half of this book exploring the stimulus in depth. Now we're ready to apply the skill set we've built to choosing correct answers.

But the question types can get complicated. There are a ton of them! When students rush to doing full timed LR sections without a strong foundation, the questions can get *really* frustrating. Students don't understand why certain answers are right because they don't understand argumentation, what the question wants them to do, and what the metrics of success for answer choices are. It's a mess. But even when students *do* have a strong foundation, they will sometimes still fall prey to the answer choices. The LSAT is hard, man. Here's the struggle, distilled into a frequent dialogue from my life a few years ago:

| | |
|---|---|
| *student:* | Why is this answer wrong? |
| *me:* | It's too strong… [long explanation about why that's bad in this instance] |
| *student:* | OK, so just never choose strong answers. |
| *me:* | *gasp* WOAH! Hold on… It's not like never. Sometimes you want strong answers, just not now. |
| *student:* | OK, so, uh… sometimes don't choose strong answers? |
| *me:* | *single tear streams down face* |

This exchange benefits no one. The student understandably feels like they can't win. They're damned if they do and damned if they don't. For every question where they get in trouble for choosing an answer that's too strong, there's another question where they get in trouble for choosing an answer that's not strong enough. **But there's a solution. It's called Powerful-Provable, and it's the easiest way to find the correct answer:**

EVERY CORRECT ANSWER ON THE LSAT IS EITHER POWERFUL OR PROVABLE

The word "provable" is an adjective that's pronounced "prove-uh-ble." It means "able to be proven"!

**Every Logical Reasoning question type wants either a powerful correct answer or a provable correct answer.** Each question type wants the same thing every time, so we can split the question types into two categories, those looking for powerful correct answers and those looking for provable correct answers.

| **A Powerful Question will have a powerful correct answer.** | **A Provable Question will have a provable correct answer.** |
|---|---|
| *The more powerful the answer choice, the more likely it is to be correct.* | *The more provable the answer choice, the more likely it is to be correct.* |

Now, we're going to place the question types (and soon the answer choice types!) along the Powerful-Provable Spectrum. The Powerful-Provable Spectrum is simple. Powerful types are on the left, and Provable types are on the right.

| POWERFUL | PROVABLE |
|---|---|
| STRENGTHEN | CONCLUSION |
| WEAKEN | INFERENCE |
| SUFFICIENT ASSUMPTION | MOST STRONGLY SUPPORTED |
| COUNTER | FILL IN |
| CONTRADICTION | CONTROVERSY |
| EVALUATE | AGREEMENT |
| RESOLUTION | NECESSARY ASSUMPTION |
| | METHOD |
| | ARGUMENT PART |
| | CLASSIC FLAW |
| | LOOPHOLE FLAW |
| | PRINCIPLE CONFORM |
| | PARALLEL REASONING |
| | PARALLEL FLAW |

QUESTION TYPES

The question types are classified as Powerful or Provable based only on the characteristics of their correct answer. That's why we have Contradiction chilling with Sufficient Assumption. Those two question types have nothing to do with one another outside of how their correct answers tend to sound.

Use the Powerful-Provable Spectrum to help you select the correct answer. It's a great way to sort the answers on both your first read through and when you're stuck between choices. When you're confused, use the question type's location on the Powerful-Provable Spectrum to remember whether you want a powerful or a provable answer.

## POWERFUL

**Powerful Questions desire strongly worded correct answers.** You can evaluate the success of an answer choice in these question types based on how powerful it is.

| POWERFUL QUESTIONS | | POWERFUL ANSWER KEYWORDS | | POWERFUL CLIR |
|---|---|---|---|---|
| Strengthen | Contradiction | all | every | |
| | | | | Loophole |
| Weaken | Evaluate | none | never | |
| Sufficient Assumption (SA) | Resolution | only | required | |
| | | | | Resolution |
| Counter | | every time | always | |

Powerful answer choices make big pronouncements. They're fearless. They contain specific, concrete details that link new information directly to the stimulus. Powerful answer choices are strongly worded. They usually make the stimulus more valid or less valid. They mount an attack or stage a defense.

There are two ways an answer choice can be powerful: linguistically and conceptually. The best answer choices combine both of these types of power.

You'll get more information on linguistic power in the Strong Answers section (page 404) of The Answer Choices Chapter.

Linguistic power is expressed with the powerful answer choice keywords, words like "always" and "never." This type of power is easy to spot – it's basically a keyword matching game. Conceptually powerful answer choices matter to the stimulus. They link to the stimulus where it's vulnerable. Conceptual power tops linguistic power in terms of importance. **You should always prefer a conceptually powerful answer choice over a misdirected, but powerfully-worded answer choice.**

## PROVABLE

**Provable Questions desire conservatively worded correct answers.** You can evaluate the success of an answer choice in these question types based on how provable it is.

On Provable Questions, **the stimulus has to prove the correct answer.** This is why the strength of the stimulus' language is the theoretical maximum for the strength of the correct answer's language. Don't outkick the stimulus' coverage here.

| PROVABLE QUESTIONS | | PROVABLE ANSWER KEYWORDS | | PROVABLE CLIR |
|---|---|---|---|---|
| Conclusion | Method | could | usually | |
| Inference | Argument Part | can | possible | Inference |
| Most Strongly Supported (MSS) | Necessary Assumption (NA) | (at least) some | not necessarily | |
| Fill In | Classic Flaw | (at least) one | possibly | |
| Controversy | Loophole Flaw | tend to | sometimes | |
| Agreement | Principle Conform | not all | may | Controversy |
| Parallel Reasoning | Parallel Flaw | varies | does not depend on | |

Provable answer choices are safe havens. They're straightforward. They're easily proven. They are sometimes viewed as "too easy" or "too simple." That critique is nonsense. Provable answer choices stay within themselves and the stimulus. They don't go out on limbs. They're a comfort in the crazy storm of the answer choices. Your Inferences and Controversies are eminently provable.

There are two ways an answer choice can be provable: linguistically and conceptually. The best answer choices combine both of these types of provability.

There's more information on linguistic provability in the Weak Answers section (page 408) of The Answer Choices Chapter.

Linguistic provability is expressed with the provable answer choice keywords, words like "tends to" and "could." This type of provability is apparent on the surface – you just have to look for provable keywords. Conceptually provable answer choices are boring; they're just replaying what you saw in the stimulus. Conceptual provability tops linguistic provability in terms of importance. **You should always prefer a conceptually provable answer choice over a misdirected, but provably-worded answer choice.**

*Can you do me just one personal favor?*

**Never eliminate an answer choice because it's "too simple" or "too easy."** Provable answers are too simple *and* too easy! Eliminating answers for those reasons ensures that you get Provable Questions wrong.

# The Powerful-Provable Spectrum

**Power and provability are inverses of one another. The more provable an answer choice is, the less powerful it is. The more powerful an answer choice is, the less provable it is.** It makes sense; powerful answer choices do big things. That's the exact opposite of what a provable answer choice does. This inverse relationship is awesome. It allows us to see answer choice attractiveness as a spectrum:

**POWERFUL**                                                      **PROVABLE**

---

Great answer choices lie at the extremes of the Powerful-Provable Spectrum. Powerful answer choices are great for Powerful Questions. Provable answer choices are great for Provable Questions.

Bad answer choices lie in the middle of the Powerful-Provable Spectrum. If an answer choice is neither powerful nor provable, it's always wrong, no matter the question type.

---

You've actually been handling power and provability for your entire journey through Logical Reasoning! It started as early as the Arguments & Inferences Chapter when we first started talking about Loopholes (powerful) and Inferences (provable). Even in the CLIR Chapter, we sought only power or provability. Your Loophole and Resolution have to be powerful. Your Inference and Controversy have to be provable.

> **THROWBACK.** Remember the Power Players? They're powerful and provable too! In fact, I've got one more Power Players Chart for you:
>
> | POWERFUL | PROVABLE |
> |---|---|
> | MUST | COULD |
> | CANNOT | NOT NECESSARILY |

Always choose the answer choice that is closest to the end of the Powerful-Provable Spectrum you're aiming for. But beware of becoming exclusively reliant on keywords. The correct answer to a Powerful Question *could* include the word "some"! This is possible! Despite the possible presence of a provable keyword, the correct answer to a Powerful Question will still be the most conceptually powerful answer choice available. And concepts always beat keywords.

## THE PARTY TRICK

**The Powerful-Provable Spectrum is how I can sometimes choose the correct answer without reading the stimulus or the question type.** Yes, you read that right. This is a real thing. And I'm going to show you how.

I call this a party trick because I choose answers without the stimulus as a trick at literal LSAT parties/test reviews. My students think I'm a witch for a minute, but the trick is simple. I evaluate the language of the answer choices for power and provability. When there's only one powerful or provable answer choice, I guess it. When both powerful and provable answer choices are present, I guess between them based on the question type. **Obviously, guessing without reading the stimulus is not a real test-taking strategy (except in a *serious* timing emergency).** However, the secret behind the trick can point you in the right direction when you're doing questions for real. If Powerful-Provable can get you the answer without the stimulus, imagine how well it can work when you actually read the stimulus like a responsible test taker.

Let's party trick a real set of LSAT answer choices together. For this one, we'll make it a challenge round and not even look at the question stem. This means we'll just look for *any* answer that's either powerful or provable.

This answer choice set is from June 2007, Section 2, #24. Feel free to look over the entire question once you're done with this section.

**A)** Getting consumer input for design modifications can contribute to successful product design.

*So getting input can contribute to successful design. This looks like a prototypical provable answer choice. It's got that nice "can" in the middle. And conceptually, it's saying that one thing "can contribute" to something else; that's so easy to prove! Any type of contribution will work – small, large, positive, or negative. Any of these situations would make* **A** *correct. There are so many possible stimuli that could prove* **A***. It's a good bet if I'm going in blind.*

**B)** Car companies traditionally conduct extensive postmarket surveys.

*So car companies traditionally do extensive surveys after sale. Alright, this answer is way less provable. To prove this one, I would need to back up "traditionally" and "extensive," which is way harder to do. Proving that something "traditionally" occurs requires data across a long time period, and "extensive" just makes the answer more extreme. This answer isn't very powerful either. Speaking to tradition isn't powerful; they usually use this language to try and sucker you into generalizing from past to future. And "extensive," while more powerful than provable, is one of those adjectives that usually functions as a synonym for "important." You'll see Important answer choices are Red Flags in The Answer Choices Chapter.* **B** *is out of the running.*

**C)** Designers aim to create features that will appeal to specific market niches.

*So designers aim to make features that specific niches will like. Eh, this one isn't especially powerful or provable either.* **Talking about intentions ("designers aim") is dangerous in LSAT answer choices, unless the stimulus talks about intentions specifically.** *The chances that this mystery stimulus talks about intentions are low (those stimuli are relatively rare), so if I'm playing the odds, I'd say* **C** *is neither powerful nor provable.*

You'll find out more about conditional answer choices like this one in The Answer Choices Chapter!

**D)** A car will have unappealing features if consumers are not consulted during its design stage.

*So if they don't consult the consumer, the car will be unappealing. Alright, now we have a conditional answer choice. It could be powerful or provable if it was activated in the stimulus, but there's no way to know for sure without looking. Chances are it wasn't activated in the stimulus though. Unlike* **A***, there's only a narrow range of stimuli that could make* **D** *the correct answer. So if I'm playing the odds, I don't choose* **D***.*

Comparative answers are only potentially powerful/provable when paired with a stimulus containing a comparative relationship (major Answer Choices Chapter preview here). Beware of choosing a comparative when you're playing the odds.

**E)** Consumer input affects external rather than internal design components of cars.

*So input affects external instead of internal components of the car. This is almost a comparative answer choice, a dangerous option if you don't have specific ammunition from the stimulus.* **E** *would only be powerful or provable if the stimulus gave us reason to believe that external matters in relation to internal. Chances are there was not a comparative relationship outlined in the stimulus, especially if there's only one comparative answer choice in the set. It's probably not* **E***.*

So if I'm just party tricking based on Powerful-Provable, I would choose **A**. **A** is the easiest to prove; it has the widest variety of possible stimuli that could substantiate it as a correct answer. There weren't any especially powerful answer choices in this bunch, so I'm not tempted on that side. **A** is the only answer choice that is particularly powerful or provable.

You can probably guess that **A** is, indeed, the correct answer. Cause I wouldn't include an example that didn't confirm my theory, right? And you're right, I wouldn't do an example that didn't work when explaining a concept; that would be *really* bad writing. **But guess how many questions I had to skim to find one that worked… three. And that's to get one to work without the question stem — which is *way* harder.** And you've already seen the stimulus that led to this correct answer. It's from the June 2007 exam you just used for your CLIR Drill. Not that cherry-picked, eh?

Let's do another party trick. This time we'll use the question stem to our advantage:

> Which one of the following is most strongly supported by
> the editorialist's statements?

This is a Most Strongly Supported (MSS) question. MSS is a Provable Question, so we want to find an answer choice with conservative, minimal, provable language.

**A)** Particular acts of resident participation would be likely to elicit a positive response from local politicians if those politicians were less isolated from their electorate.

*So if politicians were less isolated, some resident participation would likely get a good response. We've got another conditional answer choice, a second string answer choice when we're playing the Powerful-Provable odds. This could be a provable conditional, but we would need some really specific ammunition in the stimulus for that to be the case. If all the other answers are super powerful, I'll look at **A** again, but we probably don't have the specific ammunition that **A** needs to be proven. I'll move on and leave **A** in reserve in case I need it.*

Notice how I put the "if" part of the conditional first in my answer choice translation. This helps clarify conditional answer choices.

**B)** Local political business should be conducted less secretively because this would avoid discouraging resident participation in local politics.

*So local politics should be less secretive to stop discouraging resident participation. Notice the "should" in this answer choice; "should" is recommendation language. **Recommendation answer choices are not provable unless there was recommendation language ("should") in the stimulus.** And **B** isn't just making us prove "should"; it's making us prove "should" for one specific reason, which is even harder. This is a very common answer choice trick. **B** is probably wrong.*

This answer choice set is from June 2007, Section 2, #22. Feel free to look over the entire question once you're done with this section.

**C)** The most important factor influencing a resident's decision as to whether to participate in local politics is the chance that the participation will elicit a positive official response.

*So the most important factor for resident participation is whether they'll likely get a good response from politicians. This answer choice has two major answer choice Red Flags in it (which will be outlined in detail in The Answer Choices Chapter): Best Way and Important. That "most important factor" line is a tough blow to this answer choice's chances of being either powerful or provable. It's really tough to prove that anything is "the most important factor" and that squishy value judgment language isn't particularly powerful either. **C** is done for.*

**D)** More-frequent thorough coverage of local politics would reduce at least one source of discouragement from resident participation in local politics.

*So more frequent coverage of politics would reduce at least one source of resident discouragement. Alright, now we've got something provable to work with. That "at least one source" language is money. To prove this answer we just need to affect one source of a phenomenon – we don't even have to necessarily have an effect on the phenomenon itself, just its source. And we just have to "reduce" that one source; we could reduce that one thing a little or a lot, either way our answer is cool.* **D** *has a low burden of proof. Looks like an answer choice we should keep around.*

**E)** If resident participation in local politics were not discouraged, this would cause local politicians to be less isolated from their electorate.

*So if we didn't discourage resident participation, politicians would be less isolated. Now we've got another conditional answer choice that would take a very particular stimulus to be provable. Judging by the fact that only two of the answer choices were conditional, this probably isn't a heavily conditional stimulus that would definitely prove a conditional answer choice. I already have something way easier to prove on the table, so I'm not going to stress over* **E**.

You can probably guess again that **D** is indeed the correct answer. And you can probably guess that it is from the same section. But it's actually only two questions earlier in the section. I purposefully started looking for examples in the most typically challenging part of the first June 2007 LR section to defeat any objection that Powerful-Provable only works on "easy" questions. These two examples were numbers 24 and 22, respectively.

And yes, this was the first section I looked in.

I ask all my students to party trick a section on their own, just to get the hang of using Powerful-Provable in the answer choices. **In my experience, a typical student achieves approximately 50% accuracy just using the question stem and Powerful-Provable to select answer choices.** Students who know The Answer Choices Chapter well can do better than that. This makes party tricking a great escape hatch in dire timing emergencies (two minutes left and more than four questions unanswered). Party tricking gives you

*Want to be able to replicate the magic I performed in these two examples?*

Really read and retain Chapter 12, The Answer Choices. Students often overlook The Answer Choices Chapter because it comes late in this monster. Read The Answer Choices Chapter multiple times, until you can identify the answer choice types immediately in the wild. This chapter is the fruit of *a lot* of LSAT research and experience.

There is no guessing penalty on the LSAT! Always select an answer before moving on.

about a 50% chance of choosing the correct answer; that's a lot better than the 20% chance you get choosing a random letter or (heavens forbid) the 0% chance you get if you don't select an answer at all.

Obviously, I want you to achieve greater than 50% accuracy in LR overall, so I would not recommend party tricking whole sections on test day. However, Powerful-Provable is a potent tool in your arsenal, and should *always* be used in combination with the stimulus when you are doing sections for real. If Powerful-Provable can get you the answer 50% of the time without the stimulus, imagine how useful it is when you've actually read the stimulus.

How can you remember which questions are Powerful and which are Provable? With a handy mnemonic device!

**The Powerful Questions spell out SW SCCER**, which sounds like Southwest Soccer. The SW stands for **S**trengthen and **W**eaken, which is easy to remember because they naturally pair together. The SCCER stands for **S**A, **C**ounter, **C**ontradiction, **E**valuate, and **R**esolution.

Just remember this one mnemonic: Southwest Soccer. **If you see a question type that starts with any letter not represented in SW SCCER, you know you need a provable answer choice.** For instance, say you get stuck on a Method question. You're really floundering and you start to wonder what you want in an answer choice. There's no M in SW SCCER, so... you must need something provable.

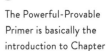

There are five question types starting with C (Counter, Contradiction, Controversy, Classic Flaw, and Conclusion). So yeah, sorry about that. You'll have to straight up memorize their placement on the spectrum.

## THE REST OF THIS BOOK

The next section will explore our question type Back-Up Plans and Making a Mission, then we'll head into each question type by category. We'll start with Powerful Questions, then Provable Questions, and finally Principle & Parallel Questions. While Principle & Parallel Questions are Provable Questions, they are unique enough that they get their own chapter. You're still looking for provable correct answers in Principle & Parallel Questions; I'm just separating the text into more manageable chunks.

After we tackle the question types, we'll dive into the Powerful-Provable strategy for the answer choices. We'll classify answer choices into Powerful Answers, Provable Answers, and Red Flags, which fall into the mediocre middle of our Powerful-Provable Spectrum. This will complete your journey through Logical Reasoning strategy. Excite!

The Powerful-Provable Primer is basically the introduction to Chapter 12, The Answer Choices. Come back here to review when you get to Chapter 12!

---

**POWERFUL-PROVABLE PRIMER GAME PLAN**

- Tattoo SW SCCER on your brain.

- Notice the powerful and provable language in answer choices. Categorize the answer choices ("This one is super powerful") as you read them.

- When you're doing questions, filter the answer choices by whether they're powerful or provable, depending on the question type.

- When you go over your wrong answers, look at whether the correct answer was more powerful/provable than the one you chose.

---

## Quiz 8.5    THE POWERFUL-PROVABLE PRIMER

### INSTRUCTIONS

Answer these questions based on your knowledge of The Powerful-Provable Primer. Attempt to answer without looking back first. If you don't know the answer, circle the question number and go find the answer in The Powerful-Provable Primer. Study the sections that you couldn't remember at first.

Circle the correct answer to the following questions.

**1.**    Seek and find!   Circle only the Powerful Questions in the word cloud.

| | | |
|---|---|---|
| Resolution | Parallel Reasoning | Argument Part |
| Method | Contradiction | Fill In |
| Loophole Flaw | Counter | Most Strongly Supported |
| Agreement | Inference | Evaluate |
| Conclusion | Weaken | Controversy |
| Classic Flaw | Principle Conform | Sufficient Assumption |
| Parallel Flaw | Strengthen | Necessary Assumption |

**2.**  **TRUE OR FALSE**    The more provable an answer choice is, the less powerful it is.

**3.**  **TRUE OR FALSE**    Great answer choices lie in the middle of the Powerful-Provable Spectrum.

**4.**  **TRUE OR FALSE**    A question type is powerful or provable based on the characteristics of its correct answer.

*Where's the answer key?*

You'll find the answer key on page 273, right after the Making a Mission section.

# MAKING A MISSION
## The Question Type Back-Up Plan

# You Need Back-Up

You mean I still can't "just figure it out in the answer choices"? Come on, devil woman...

Hold tight. Each question type's Back-Up Plan is provided in the forthcoming question type sections.

A lot of LSAT questions are easy, but some of them are decidedly not easy. That's ok; you can do the difficult questions! You just need to use the tools in your arsenal to adapt. One of these tools is each question type's Back-Up Plan. **A Back-Up Plan is a question you can ask each answer choice to determine if it is correct.**

But the Back-Up Plans are versatile! You can also apply them to the stimulus to make a Mission. The difference between a Mission and a Back-Up Plan is one thing: specificity. **A Mission is a specific iteration of your Back-Up Plan.** When you apply your Back-Up Plan to the stimulus, you get a Mission, the specific task you want each answer to accomplish in the context of the stimulus. If an answer choice accomplishes your Mission, it is correct.

Here's how it works. The Back-Up Plan for a Method question is: "Did this happen?" To make a Mission, you ask the stimulus, "What happened?" The answer to that question is your Mission.

---

A Mission is what you want the correct answer to do.

---

### HOW TO MAKE A MISSION

You'll find all of the Back-Up Plans for each chapter's question types on pages 274, 312, and 362.

1.  Apply the Back-Up Plan to the stimulus.

2.  Say what the correct answer will specifically have to do. This is your Mission.

3.  Find an answer choice that meets your Mission.

Let's talk through how a Mission works and then we'll do a couple examples together.

---

### MISSION PRO TIPS

- **Simple specificity is key.**

  You need your Mission to be specific enough to be helpful in the answer choices (not "I need to weaken this."), but it must cast a wide enough net to catch a variety of answer choices ("Dust is cause" instead of "The dust was emitted from neighboring factory Q at 12:34 PM.").

- **Jot down a couple words summarizing your Mission right below the question stem.**

  Keep it short. If your Mission is long, it will be difficult to check the answer choices against it. I always write my Mission in all caps to force myself to keep it short.

- **Check each answer choice against your Mission instead of rereading the stimulus and the answer choices a million times.**

  Does the answer choice accomplish your Mission? Yes? Keep it. No? Cross it out. Not sure? Leave it alone and return later. It's not necessary to double check your chosen answer against the stimulus. You did the heavy lifting to create the Mission and you don't need to repeat your work.

---

You may be hesitant to attempt to make a Mission because you have the following thoughts running through your head. Let's tackle your objections with a quick Mission FAQ.

## QUICK MISSION FAQ

**Q.** *But what if my Mission is wrong?*

**A.** Yeah, you could be wrong. Any of us could be wrong. But that's not an attitude you can tolerate if you plan on succeeding on the LSAT. **Stop worrying about being wrong and start assuming you're probably right.** It's a powerful change of mindset when it comes to this test.

**Q.** *Do I have to write the Mission down? Can't I just keep it in my head?*

**A.** It's a personal choice that depends on how good your memory is and how difficult the question is. If you can easily keep the Mission in your head as you run down the answer choices, there's no pressing need to write it down. However, you should write the Mission down when you have trouble keeping track of it in the answer choices, which tends to happen on difficult questions.

Now let's make a Mission on a real LSAT question together!

*16.3.10*

Michelangelo's sixteenth-century Sistine Chapel paintings are currently being restored. A goal of the restorers is to uncover Michelangelo's original work, and so additions made to Michelangelo's paintings by later artists are being removed. However, the restorers have decided to make one exception: to leave intact additions that were painted by da Volterra.

Which one of the following, if true, most helps to reconcile the restorers' decision with the goal stated in the passage?

(A)     The restorers believe that da Volterra stripped away all previous layers of paint before he painted his own additions to the Sistine Chapel.

(B)     Because da Volterra used a type of pigment that is especially sensitive to light, the additions to the Sistine Chapel that da Volterra painted have relatively muted colors.

(C)     Da Volterra's additions were painted in a style that was similar to the style used by Michelangelo.

(D)     Michelangelo is famous primarily for his sculptures and only secondarily for his paintings, whereas da Volterra is known exclusively for his paintings.

(E)     Da Volterra's work is considered by certain art historians to be just as valuable as the work of some of the other artists who painted additions to Michelangelo's work.

We just CLIR-ed this Paradox a few pages ago, so it's perfect for our first Mission. You're already familiar with the translation and structure, which eliminates possible confusion from those steps.

Let's look at how the answer choices respond to a Mission. We'll start off with a translation:

> *People are restoring Michelangelo's 16th century Sistine Chapel paintings. The restorers want to uncover Michelangelo's original work so they're removing additions by later artists. But the restorers are leaving in the additions by da Volterra.*

The question type is Resolution. That means that we just need to go find our Resolution from the CLIR in the answer choices. Now, for the sake of this exercise, let's pretend that for some reason, the CLIR did not get you the answer to this question. Maybe you misread something or found this question particularly difficult. You return to the stimulus frustrated. We'll make a Mission together.

Let's use our Resolution Back-Up Plan: Does this make the Paradox make sense? To apply the Back-Up Plan to the stimulus, we'll ask, "What would make the restorers' decision make sense?" The restorers want to uncover Michelangelo's original work, so why would they leave da Volterra in? The restorers would only leave da Volterra in if taking him out hurts their goal. The answer choices might come up with lots of innovative ways to imply that taking da Volterra out is bad, but underneath all the spins on that idea, any correct answer will reduce to some downside in taking da Volterra out. This downside could even include losing a benefit that keeping da Volterra would provide.

*Notice how I filled in the specifics of the Paradox (changed "Paradox" to "the restorers' decision") when I applied the Back-Up Plan to the stimulus. This helps a ton.*

*Notice how I shortened up the Mission when I jotted it down. I want something quick and simple that I can run past all the answers.*

**MISSION**     DV OUT = BAD

Now let's check our answer choices against our Mission.

A) The restorers believe that da Volterra stripped away all previous layers of paint before he painted his own additions to the Sistine Chapel.

*So the restorers think da Volterra destroyed all the paint under his additions. Could this be a reason taking da Volterra out would be bad? Yes, if you take da Volterra out, you won't uncover Michelangelo. It'll just be plain wall underneath, not Michelangelo's original work.* **A** *meets our Mission.*

B) Because da Volterra used a type of pigment that is especially sensitive to light, the additions to the Sistine Chapel that da Volterra painted have relatively muted colors.

*So da Volterra's pigments were light sensitive and his additions are muted colors. Could this be a reason taking da Volterra out would be bad? No. We don't know if muted colors are good or bad, and assuming one way or the other is bad news. This answer choice does not impact what would happen if we remove da Volterra.* **B** *doesn't meet our Mission.*

C) Da Volterra's additions were painted in a style that was similar to the style used by Michelangelo.

*So da Volterra's additions were a similar style to Michelangelo's. Could this be a reason taking da Volterra out would be bad? No. Michelangelo is still the goal. Da Volterra might be in the same style, but that doesn't mean we should leave him in when what we want is Michelangelo's original work.* **C** *doesn't meet our Mission.*

D) Michelangelo is famous primarily for his sculptures and only secondarily for his paintings, whereas da Volterra is known exclusively for his paintings.

*So Michelangelo is mostly famous for sculptures and less so for paintings, and da Volterra is only famous for paintings. Could this be a reason taking da Volterra out would be bad? No, they're trying to trick us into thinking da Volterra is preferable to Michelangelo here, but that's not the goal of the restorers.* **D** *doesn't meet our Mission.*

| E) | Da Volterra's work is considered by certain art historians to be just as valuable as the work of some of the other artists who painted additions to Michelangelo's work. | *So some art critics think da Volterra is just as good as other people adding to Michelangelo. Could this be a reason taking da Volterra out would be bad? No. The other people are getting taken out and that wasn't bad, so why not da Volterra too? This is the opposite of why da Volterra should get an exception; it makes him equal to the artists getting no exception. **E** doesn't meet our Mission.* |
|---|---|---|

**A** is our correct answer. It's the only one that meets our Mission.

Let's make another Mission together:

> *16.2.21*
>
> Several years ago, as a measure to reduce the population of gypsy moths, which depend on oak leaves for food, entomologists introduced into many oak forests a species of fungus that is poisonous to gypsy moth caterpillars. Since then, the population of both caterpillars and adult moths has significantly declined in those areas. Entomologists have concluded that the decline is attributable to the presence of the poisonous fungus.
>
> Which one of the following, if true, most strongly supports the conclusion drawn by the entomologists?
>
> (A) A strain of gypsy moth whose caterpillars are unaffected by the fungus has increased its share of the total gypsy moth population.
>
> (B) The fungus that was introduced to control the gypsy moth population is poisonous to few insect species other than the gypsy moth.
>
> (C) An increase in numbers of both gypsy moth caterpillars and gypsy moth adults followed a drop in the number of some of the species that prey on the moths.
>
> (D) In the past several years, air pollution and acid rain have been responsible for a substantial decline in oak tree populations.
>
> (E) The current decline in the gypsy moth population in forests where the fungus was introduced is no greater than a decline that occurred concurrently in other forests.

✳ This stimulus is a perfect example of a nested claim from Chapter 2, Arguments and Inferences! If you forgot what a nested claim is, go back to Chapter 2 and do a quick refresher now.

Let's start off with a translation:

> *Years ago, the entomologists wanted to get rid of the gypsy moths and so they poisoned the oak leaves, their food source. Since the poisoning, gypsy caterpillar and moth populations have gone down. Entomologists say the fungus caused the population decline.*

Awesome. We'll pretend this question was chaos and recover by making a Mission. The question type is Strengthen. So we'll use our Strengthen Back-Up Plan: Does this make the conclusion more likely to be true? To apply the Back-Up Plan to the stimulus, we'll ask, "What would make the fungus more likely to cause the gypsy moth population decline?" That's what the correct answer has to do — it must make the fungus more likely to cause the decline.

✳ Notice how we filled the stimulus' conclusion into our Back-Up Plan to make a Mission.

**MISSION**   FUNGUS KILLS MOTHS

This is a simplified version of the conclusion; it's what the correct answer has to suggest. We can now evaluate every answer for whether it is making this specific idea more likely to be true. That's our Mission.

| | | |
|---|---|---|
| **A)** | A strain of gypsy moth whose caterpillars are unaffected by the fungus has increased its share of the total gypsy moth population. | *So the immune moths are increasing their share of the population. This means that the non-immune moths are decreasing their share. Why? Probably because they're dying of fungus. Does this make it more likely that the fungus is killing the moths? Yes. If fungus immunity is the differentiating factor, it holds a ton of power over gypsy moth life expectancy. **A** meets our Mission.* |
| **B)** | The fungus that was introduced to control the gypsy moth population is poisonous to few insect species other than the gypsy moth. | *So the fungus is poisonous to few insects besides the moths. Does this make it more likely that the fungus is killing the moths? No, the fungus not bothering other insects does nothing for its relationship to the moth. **B** doesn't meet our Mission.* |
| **C)** | An increase in numbers of both gypsy moth caterpillars and gypsy moth adults followed a drop in the number of some of the species that prey on the moths. | *So there were more moths after a drop in some predators. Does this make it more likely that the fungus is killing the moths? No, **C** strengthens the casual connection between moth population and a new factor, predator populations. This is the opposite of what we want. **C** doesn't meet our Mission.* |
| **D)** | In the past several years, air pollution and acid rain have been responsible for a substantial decline in oak tree populations. | *So pollution and acid rain have been killing a bunch of oak trees for the past few years. Does this make it more likely that the fungus is killing the moths? No! It's giving another reason why the gypsy moth populations could decline besides the fungus; that's the opposite of what we want. **D** doesn't meet our Mission.* |
| **E)** | The current decline in the gypsy moth population in forests where the fungus was introduced is no greater than a decline that occurred concurrently in other forests. | *So the population decline isn't worse than a decline that happened in similar forests. Does this make it more likely that the fungus is killing the moths? No! This answer is comparing our decline with other declines, but it doesn't give us any information on what's causing either decline. **E** doesn't meet our Mission* |

**A** is our correct answer. It's the only one that meets our Mission.

We will return to the Mission and the Back-Up Plans throughout Chapters 9-11. The Mission is your productive ticket out of panic and toward the correct answer. It's simple and effective – there's no reason not to make a Mission when the correct answer eludes you.

**1.** You should have circled the following Powerful Questions and no other question types: Strengthen, Weaken, Sufficient Assumption, Counter, Contradiction, Evaluate, and Resolution.

**2.** True.

**3.** False. Great answer choices lie at the *extremes* of the Powerful-Provable Spectrum.

**4.** True.

## Powerful Questions Road Map

The correct answer to all of the following question types will prefer powerful language. Use this chart as a centralized study aid after you've read the chapter to help yourself commit these key points to memory.

Notice the Back-Up Plans for each question type! These are the questions we used in the Making a Mission section. But Back-Up Plans are doubly useful. When you ask the answer choices the Back-Up Plan question directly, it will lead you directly to the correct answer.

| QUESTION TYPE | CORRECT ANSWER | BACK-UP PLAN | QUESTION STEM KEYWORDS |
|---|---|---|---|
| Strengthen | The most powerful thing you can find to help the argument's conclusion | Does this make the conclusion more likely to be true? | • strengthen<br>• most helps to + justify / strengthen / support |
| Weaken | The most powerful thing you can find to destroy the argument's conclusion | Does this make the conclusion less likely to be true? | • weaken<br>• most undermines the conclusion |
| Sufficient Assumption (SA) | The most powerful thing you can find to prove the conclusion 100% valid | If this is true, is the argument 100% valid? | • enable the conclusion to be properly drawn / the conclusion follows logically if<br>• justify the conclusion |
| Counter | The most powerful thing the first speaker could say to destroy the second speaker's argument | Is this something the first speaker would say and does it hurt the second speaker's argument? | • counter<br>• in response to |
| Contradiction | The thing that contradicts literal words from the stimulus | Does this contradict the stimulus? | • cannot be true<br>• violate the principle<br>• could be true EXCEPT |
| Evaluate | A powerful pop quiz for the argument's validity | Is this crucial for the argument's validity? | • evaluate the argument<br>• most helpful to know / relevant to evaluating |
| Resolution | The most powerful thing you can find to make the Paradox make sense | Does this make the Paradox make sense? | • most helps to + explain / resolve / account for<br>• discrepancy / paradox / surprising result |

POWERFUL
QUESTIONS

## Weaken

Certain Question Stem Keywords (like "most vulnerable" or "assumes") may indicate a few different question types. Keywords narrow down the question type possibilities, but you'll still have to think through what the question stem means to determine the type.

"TL;DR" is just internet speak for "too long; didn't read."

There is no great mystery to Weaken questions. You are exceedingly prepared for them. If a Weaken question is difficult, it's because the argument or the answer choices associated with it are difficult. **Difficulty occurs independently of question type.**

| QUESTION STEM KEYWORDS | POPULARITY | About 1-2 questions per section |
|---|---|---|
| • which of the following, if true<br>• weaken<br>• most undermines the conclusion<br>• most vulnerable<br>• count as evidence against<br>• calls into question | WHAT YOU'RE LOOKING FOR | The most powerful thing you can find to destroy the argument's conclusion |
| | ROLE OF THE LOOPHOLE | The correct answer to a Weaken question is essentially the Loophole. You want the most powerful answer available that points to the weakness exposed by the Loophole. |
| **QUESTION STEM EXAMPLES**<br><br>Which one of the following, if true, most seriously weakens the argument above?<br><br>Which one of the following, if true, most tends to undermine the argument? | TL;DR STRATEGY | You already have a Loophole.<br><br>The Loophole zeroes in on the argument's weakness.<br><br>Go find the Loophole actualized in the answer choices. |
| | BACK-UP PLAN | Does this make the conclusion less likely to be true?<br>• If yes, choose it.<br>• If no, cross it off.<br>• If you're not sure, leave it for later. |

**WEAKEN GAME PLAN**

Weaken questions ask you to attack the argument, putting your Loophole into action. In designing your Loophole, you've already found the big hole in the argument, so your work is mostly done. **You just have to find powerful language in the answer choices that mimics your Loophole.**

Pretty simple, right? But there are still difficult Weaken questions out there. Let's tackle the worst-case scenario. What if you aren't seeing how any of the answer choices weaken? There are two possible explanations:

1. The correct answer is super wordy, but it's gesturing toward the same exploit you are.
2. The correct answer is taking a whole different approach in its attack on the argument.

When you aren't seeing the correct answer, go back to the stimulus and look for clues like a bloodhound. The correct answer just picked up on something you haven't yet. You can find the correct answer once you make yourself notice the relevant details. Make a Mission and move forward.

## TINY TIPS

- Weaken is a popular destination for **EXCEPT** questions. Make sure to deploy our Except Mark (more on this in the Answer Choice Strategy Section). The Except Mark is especially crucial if you ever get **EXCEPT** questions wrong because you forget they're **EXCEPT**.

## BIGGEST TRAP

- This thought is a huge problem: "But that seems too big. It doesn't have to be true. I'm going to cross it out." When you do this on Weaken questions (or any Powerful Question), you're essentially eliminating an answer because it's right. We *want* powerful answer choices on Weaken questions. If you ever catch yourself doing this, note the mistake in your Wrong Answer Journal.

## REAL WEAKEN EXAMPLE

*18.4.7*

Advertisement: Over 80 percent of the people who test-drive a Zenith car end up buying one. So be warned: you should not test-drive a Zenith unless you are prepared to buy one, because if you so much as drive a Zenith around the block, there is a better than 80 percent chance you will choose to buy it.

If the advertisement is interpreted as implying that the quality of the car is unusually impressive, which one of the following, if true, most clearly casts doubt on that implication?

(A) Test-drives of Zenith cars are, according to Zenith sales personnel, generally more extensive than a drive around the block and encounter varied driving conditions.

(B) Usually dealers have enough Zenith models in stock that prospective purchasers are able to test-drive the exact model that they are considering for purchase.

(C) Those who take test-drives in cars are, in overwhelming proportions, people who have already decided to buy the model driven unless some fault should become evident.

(D) Almost 90 percent of the people who purchase a car do not do so on the day they take a first test-drive but do so after another test-drive.

(E) In some Zenith cars, a minor part has broken within the first year, and Zenith dealers have issued notices to owners that the dealers will replace the part with a redesigned one at no cost to owners.

> Every question type section will include a real LSAT example walk-through. We will demo the whole process for each question type together before sending you off to the Challenge Questions that follow.

First, translate.

*80% of test-drivers buy a Zenith, so be warned that you should not test-drive a Zenith unless you're ready to buy. Because if you even drive a Zenith around the block you will have an 80% chance of buying it.*

Let's apply some common sense: The premises are about test-drivers, and most people who test-drive a car are pretty serious about buying said car. The conclusion, however, is about *you*, not test-drivers. The reaction that 80% of test-drivers have doesn't necessarily generalize to the reaction *you* would have in a similar situation. Since you're not someone independently pursuing a test-drive, you probably wouldn't have that serious car-buyer predisposition. It could be that predisposition that's making them especially likely to buy, not the test-drive itself. This leads to our Loophole:

The correct answer to a Weaken question can hurt the argument anywhere from 1% to 100%, but try to be closer to 100% in the answer you choose.

The question stem is a little weird on this one, but it's still Weaken. The interpretation it adds was already implied by the stimulus. Our Loophole has already taken the "unusually impressive" implication into account.

**LOOPHOLE**     What if test-drivers are much more likely to buy a car?

Since it's a Weaken question, we're just looking for something powerful that points toward our Loophole. We're ready to move to the answer choices.

Every LSAT example will include powerful/provable styled answer choices. The answer choices are styled this way to help you learn to notice powerful and provable language.

Powerful language is mint and bolded.

*Provable language is mint and italicized.*

**A)** Test-drives of Zenith cars are, according to Zenith sales personnel, *generally more* extensive than a drive around the block and encounter varied driving conditions.

*So test-drives are varied and more than just around the block. Does it matter? Not really. If 80% of people are buying a Zenith after a test-drive, they're experiencing this more extensive driving experience, and the conclusion is about what you would do if you had that same experience. The premises and conclusion match, so nothing really changes.* **A** *doesn't speak to the test-driver bias; it's not powerful.*

**B)** *Usually* dealers have enough Zenith models in stock that prospective purchasers are *able to* test-drive the exact model that they are considering for purchase.

*So the exact model you test-drive is usually in stock to buy. Who cares if people can test-drive the exact model of Zenith they're considering? The stimulus doesn't differentiate between models of Zenith. For all we know, it could allow for test-driving one Zenith model and buying another. Not a powerful choice.*

**C)** Those who take test-drives in cars are, in overwhelming proportions, people who have already decided to buy the model driven unless some fault should become evident.

*So test-drivers are already set on buying. Hey, hey, hey. This is very close to our Loophole. If* **C** *is true, the quality of the test-drive has almost nothing to do with the 80% of test-drivers who end up buying. The test-drivers have already decided, so the test-drive itself isn't compelling people to buy the Zenith. This destroys the conclusion; it's a powerful answer choice.*

**D)** Almost 90 percent of the people who purchase a car do not do so on the day they take a first test-drive but do so after another test-drive.

*So almost 90% of car purchasers buy after a second test-drive, not after the first. This is accounted for in the stimulus. It says 80% of test-drivers "end up buying one." The premise doesn't specify how many times they test-drove the Zenith. They could have test-driven the Zenith a hundred times and the argument would be unaffected. Not a powerful answer choice.*

**E)** In *some* Zenith cars, a minor part has broken within the first year, and Zenith dealers have issued notices to owners that the dealers will replace the part with a redesigned one at no cost to owners.

*So a minor part in some Zeniths broke and the dealers are replacing it for free. By pointing out that a minor part has to be replaced, they think they're proving that the quality of the Zenith is not impressive, but one part being replaced in some Zeniths doesn't necessarily affect the quality of the Zenith overall. Not a powerful answer.*

❋ Notice how every little word in the stimulus can matter for an answer choice's chances. This is why translation is so important.

**C** is the correct answer. It's the only answer that speaks to the Loophole. It hits them where it hurts.

We'll cap off almost every question type section with one or more Challenge Questions. Complete these Challenge Questions methodically. This is your chance to make sure you understand the strategies associated with each question type before you start your section-based practice.

**If you struggle with any of the Challenge Questions, be sure to check out the Challenge Question Explanations online at elementalprep.com/bonus.**

## WEAKEN CHALLENGE

*17.2.13*

Public health will improve more quickly in the wake of new medical discoveries if medical researchers abandon their practice of waiting until their findings are published in peer-reviewed journals before informing the press of important research results. That is because the public release of new medical information allows people to use that information in order to improve their health, but the peer-review process is unavoidably very slow.

Which one of the following, if true, most seriously weakens the argument?

(A) Peer review often prevents the publication of false conclusions drawn on the basis of poorly conducted medical research.
(B) People often alter their lifestyles on the basis of new medical information made available through the press.
(C) Some improvements in public health are due to factors other than the discovery of new medical information.
(D) Some newspapers would be willing to publish the results of medical research before those results have appeared in peer-reviewed journals.
(E) Most peer-reviewed scientific journals would refuse to give up the practice of peer review.

*18.4.23*

Doctors in Britain have long suspected that patients who wear tinted eyeglasses are abnormally prone to depression and hypochondria. Psychological tests given there to hospital patients admitted for physical complaints like heart pain and digestive distress confirmed such a relationship. Perhaps people whose relationship to the world is psychologically painful choose such glasses to reduce visual stimulation, which is perceived as irritating. At any rate, it can be concluded that when such glasses are worn, it is because the wearer has a tendency to be depressed or hypochondriacal.

Each of the following, if true, weakens the argument EXCEPT:

(A) Some people wear tinted glasses not because they choose to do so but because a medical condition of their eyes forces them to do so.

(B) Even a depressed or hypochondriacal person can have valid medical complaints, so a doctor should perform all the usual objective tests in diagnosing such persons.

(C) The confirmatory tests were not done for places such as western North America where the usual quality of light differs from that prevailing in Britain.

(D) Fashions with respect to wearing tinted glasses differ in different parts of the world.
(E) At the hospitals where the tests were given, patients who were admitted for conditions less ambiguous than heart pain or digestive distress did not show the relationship between tinted glasses and depression or hypochondria.

*Where's the answer key?*

You'll find the answer key for all the Challenge Questions at the end of the chapter on page 306.

## Strengthen

| QUESTION STEM KEYWORDS | POPULARITY | About 2-3 questions per section |
|---|---|---|
| • which of the following, if true<br>• strengthen<br>• most helps to + justify/strengthen/ support | WHAT YOU'RE LOOKING FOR | The most powerful thing you can find to help the argument's conclusion |
| | ROLE OF THE LOOPHOLE | The correct answer to a Strengthen question patches up the weakness exposed by the Loophole. One of the easiest ways to strengthen an argument is to cover up its weaknesses. |
| **QUESTION STEM EXAMPLES**<br><br>Which one of the following, if true, most helps to strengthen the argument?<br><br>Which one of the following, if true, most strengthens the argument?<br><br>Which one of the following principles, if valid, most strongly supports the reasoning above?<br><br>Which one of the following principles, if valid, most helps to justify the reasoning in the argument? | TL;DR STRATEGY | You already have a Loophole.<br><br>The Loophole exposed the argument's weakness. Come up with something that plugs the hole exposed by the Loophole.<br><br>Go find that helping hand in the answer choices. |
| | BACK-UP PLAN | Does this make the conclusion more likely to be true?<br><br>• If yes, choose it.<br>• If no, cross it off.<br>• If you're not sure, leave it for later. |

### STRENGTHEN GAME PLAN

Strengthen asks you to defend the argument against the weakness exposed by the Loophole. The correct answer is powerful; it can bring in powerful new information to help the conclusion out.

Your goal is to supply a fact that makes the Loophole's exploit less of a problem. The correct answer can be phrased generally or specifically, so don't hastily eliminate answers without considering them in the context of the premises.

### BIGGEST TRAPS

- Often, the challenge of Strengthen questions comes in the answer choices. Sometimes, the correct Strengthen answer choice is decidedly stealthy, meaning it's not obvious how it applies to the stimulus. You'll have to broaden your approach to catch the answer.

- Stealth Strengthen correct answers often sound a little like necessary assumptions; they're strengthening the argument by covering for a very specific possible weakness. Once you see that possible weakness, these stealth answers are like Magic Eye puzzles. You can't unsee them. But when you first read these answers, they're frustrating because they don't immediately look correct. **To ensure you catch the stealth correct answer on especially difficult questions, do a full Answer Choice Reset (page 256) and return to the stimulus to make a Mission.**

Strengthen is the flipside of Weaken. Just like Weaken, Strengthen is as straightforward as it sounds.

## REAL STRENGTHEN EXAMPLE

*17.2.7*

The fishing industry cannot currently be relied upon to help the government count the seabirds killed by net fishing, since an accurate count might result in restriction of net fishing. The government should therefore institute a program under which tissue samples from the dead birds are examined to determine the amount of toxins in the fish eaten by the birds. The industry would then have a reason to turn in the bird carcasses, since the industry needs to know whether the fish it catches are contaminated with toxins.

Which one of the following, if true, most strengthens the argument?

 (A) The seabirds that are killed by net fishing do not eat all of the species of fish caught by the fishing industry.

 (B) The government has not in the past sought to determine whether fish were contaminated with toxins by examining tissue samples of seabirds.

(C) The government cannot gain an accurate count of the number of seabirds killed by net fishing unless the fishing industry cooperates.

(D) If the government knew that fish caught by the fishing industry were contaminated by toxins, the government would restrict net fishing.

(E) If net fishing were restricted by the government, then the fishing industry would become more inclined to reveal the number of seabirds killed by net fishing.

First, translate.

*The government can't depend on the fishing industry to tell them how many birds they kill with nets because being honest could mean restrictions that hurt the fishing industry. Since the fishing industry has a motive not to help, we should incentivize them by analyzing the toxicity of the fish eaten by the dead birds. This would give the fishing industry a motive to turn in the dead birds because they care about toxicity in their fish.*

Wow, the government is going to crazy lengths to incentivize the fishing industry, right? They want to create this whole test-the-toxicity program just to incentivize the fishing industry to comply with their request. But why go to all this trouble?

It seems like an oddly elaborate plan, given that the government probably has other options at its disposal to figure out how many birds are getting killed by nets. Like why not just threaten the fishermen with sanctions if they don't comply? Or put out regulators to observe directly? The government has options here. That leads us straight to our Loophole:

**LOOPHOLE**      What if there's another way to figure out the number of dead birds without placating the fishing industry?

Since it's a Strengthen question, we want to patch up the problem identified by our Loophole. Here's what we're looking for:

**STRENGTHEN**      There isn't another way to find out the number of dead birds without placating the fishing industry.

Now that we have an idea of what the correct answer will look like, we're ready to head to the answer choices.

**A)** The seabirds that are killed by net fishing *do not eat all* the species of fish caught by the fishing industry.

*So these birds don't eat every single species of fish caught by the fishing industry. Who cares? If anything, this weakens the conclusion since it makes the toxicity bonus less useful for the fishing industry. With less of a reason to comply, it's just not a powerful approach to helping the conclusion.*

**B)** The government has not in the past sought to determine whether fish were contaminated with toxins by examining tissue samples of seabirds.

*So the government never did this toxicity testing before. Who cares? Does it really matter if the government did this awhile ago? The stimulus seems to imply that they're not doing it now (otherwise, why institute a new program?), so the past doesn't affect the benefit the new program might have for the fishing industry.* **Beware of generalizing from past to future. It's not a powerful (or provable) approach.**

**C)** The government cannot gain an accurate count of the number of seabirds killed by net fishing unless the fishing industry cooperates.

*So the government can't do this without the fishing industry. Ding, ding, ding. This addresses our Loophole. It tells us the government needs the fishing industry, meaning any potential solution to this bird problem needs to address the fishing industry hurdle. This makes instituting a new program just to placate the fisherman seem much more reasonable.* **C** *is a conceptually powerful choice — it's patching up the argument where it's most vulnerable.*

**D** is a perfect example of one of our answer choice types: the Dormant Conditional. A Dormant Conditional is a conditional that isn't activated by the stimulus (meaning a valid sufficient condition isn't in the premises). Dormant Conditionals are awesome because they're always wrong! You'll learn more about why in The Answer Choices Chapter.

**D)** If the government knew that fish caught by the fishing industry were contaminated by toxins, the government would restrict net fishing.

*So if the government knew there were toxins in the fish, they'd restrict net fishing. This tells us that the government could do the exact thing the fishing industry wants to avoid, making cooperation less palatable to the fishing industry.* **D** *hurts the conclusion, not great in a Strengthen question.*

**E)** If net fishing were restricted by the government, then the fishing industry would become more inclined to reveal the number of seabirds killed by net fishing.

*So if the government actually did restrict (the thing the fishing industry doesn't want), the fishing industry would give them the dead bird numbers.* **E** *is our Loophole; it's supplying us with another way to get the dead bird numbers. If another option would achieve the government's goal, why are we messing around with this toxicity program? It's way easier to just set a restriction.* **E** *hurts the conclusion, not what we want in a Strengthen question.*

**C** is the correct answer. It's the only answer that patches up our Loophole and helps the conclusion.

*17.3.12*

One year ago a local government initiated an antismoking advertising campaign in local newspapers, which it financed by imposing a tax on cigarettes of 20 cents per pack. One year later, the number of people in the locality who smoke cigarettes had declined by 3 percent. Clearly, what was said in the advertisements had an effect, although a small one, on the number of people in the locality who smoke cigarettes.

Which one of the following, if true, most helps to strengthen the argument?

(A) Residents of the locality have not increased their use of other tobacco products such as snuff and chewing tobacco since the campaign went into effect.

(B) A substantial number of cigarette smokers in the locality who did not quit smoking during the campaign now smoke less than they did before it began.

(C) Admissions to the local hospital for chronic respiratory ailments were down by 15 percent one year after the campaign began.

(D) Merchants in the locality responded to the local tax by reducing the price at which they sold cigarettes by 20 cents per pack.

(E) Smokers in the locality had incomes that on average were 25 percent lower than those of nonsmokers.

*17.3.18*

Although tales of wonder and the fantastic are integral to all world literatures, only recently has the fantasy genre had a commercial resurgence in North America. During the last 20 years, sales of fantasy-fiction books written for adults have gone from 1 to 10 percent of total adult-fiction sales. At the same time, the number of favorable reviews of fantasy books has increased markedly. Some booksellers say that the increased sales of fantasy books written for adults can be traced to the increased favorable attention given the genre by book reviewers.

Which one of the following, if true, most strongly supports the booksellers' explanation of the growth in sales of fantasy-fiction books for adults?

(A) Many experts report that on average the reading level of book buyers has declined over the past 20 years.

(B) Because life during the past 20 years has become complex and difficult, many readers have come to prefer the happy endings that fantasy fiction often provides.

(C) Some fantasy publishers take advantage of the popularity of certain books by commissioning similar books.

(D) Because few readers of mystery novels were buying fantasy fiction, 10 years ago the major publishers of fantasy fiction created an advertising campaign directed specifically at those readers.

(E) After fantasy fiction began to be favorably reviewed by respected critics 20 years ago, book buyers began to regard fantasy books as suitable reading for adults.

*Where's the answer key?*

You'll find the answer key for all the Challenge Questions at the end of the chapter on page 306.

## Sufficient Assumption (SA)

| QUESTION STEM KEYWORDS | POPULARITY | About 1-2 questions per section |
|---|---|---|
| • which of the following if true / assumed <br> • enable the conclusion to be properly drawn / justify the conclusion <br> • the conclusion follows logically if | WHAT YOU'RE LOOKING FOR | The most powerful thing you can find to prove the conclusion 100% valid |
| | ROLE OF THE LOOPHOLE | The correct answer to an SA question plugs the Loophole on overdrive. |

| QUESTION STEM EXAMPLES | | |
|---|---|---|
| The conclusion drawn above follows logically if which one of the following is assumed? <br><br> The argument's conclusion can be properly drawn if which one of the following is assumed? <br><br> Which one of the following is an assumption that would allow the conclusion above to be properly drawn? | TL;DR STRATEGY | You already have a Loophole. <br><br> Go overboard filling the gap exposed by the Loophole until the conclusion is 100% proven. Build that ironclad bridge between the premises and the conclusion. <br><br> Go find that bridge in the answer choices. |
| | BACK-UP PLAN | If this is true, is the argument 100% completely valid? <br> • If yes, choose it. <br> • If no, cross it off. <br> • If you're not sure, leave it for later. |

If you don't remember Chapter 5, Assumptions & The Loophole, and would like help with Sufficient Assumption questions, head back to that chapter now for a detailed explanation of both sufficient and necessary assumptions.

### SUFFICIENT ASSUMPTION GAME PLAN

The correct answer to a Sufficient Assumption question is, you guessed it, a sufficient assumption. This is awesome because you already practiced sufficient assumptions a ton in Chapter 5.

In an SA question, your job is to hyper-plug the leak exposed by the Loophole. **The correct answer will completely remedy the problem the Loophole exposes; it will amplify that remedy until it sends the argument firmly into valid territory**. Remember, SAs let you go as crazy as you want as long as they prove the conclusion.

But how do you know when an answer choice hyper-plugs the Loophole? Check out a few examples of hyper-plugged Loopholes to get an idea of how to flip between the Loophole and an SA:

| LOOPHOLE | SUFFICIENT ASSUMPTION |
|---|---|
| *What if it was something else?* | *This is the **only** possible thing it could be.* |
| *What if Xandu has some downside as a candidate?* | *Xandu is **superior to all** other candidates in **every** respect.* |
| *What if there was an asteroid impact?* | *There has **never** been an impact of **any** object from space in the history of the planet.* |

Notice how the hyper-plugged Loopholes aren't just negations of the Loophole. They go *all out* on the powerful language, bolded here to help you learn to notice it.

## TINY TIPS

- SA is a popular destination for dangling variable stimuli. Be ready to connect some terms.

- **IF OUR PREMISES, THEN OUR CONCLUSION** constructions are common correct answers to SA questions.

## BIGGEST TRAPS

- **The biggest trap in SA is misidentifying the question stem. If you see the word "most," it is NOT an SA question.** SA is not a question type for shades of gray and "most" is super gray.

- SA is one of the question stems that students most frequently misidentify. Some think it's an NA question, others think it's a Strengthen question. Both of those mistakes will result in unnecessary stress and incorrect answers. **Of all the question types, SA requires the highest level of power in the correct answer.** The correct answer always has to be very powerful. So if you misidentify SA, you're unlikely to meet its burden without a lot of luck. Know your questions stems to avoid this problem.

## REAL SUFFICIENT ASSUMPTION EXAMPLE

*17.3.14*

Many artists claim that art critics find it easier to write about art that they dislike than to write about art that they like. Whether or not this hypothesis is correct, most art criticism is devoted to art works that fail to satisfy the critic. Hence it follows that most art criticism is devoted to works other than the greatest works of art.

The conclusion above is properly drawn if which one of the following is assumed?

(A) No art critic enjoys writing about art works that he or she dislikes intensely.
(B) All art critics find it difficult to discover art works that truly satisfy them.
(C) A work of art that receives extensive critical attention can thereby become more widely known than it otherwise would have been.
(D) The greatest works of art are never recognized as such until long after the time of their creation.
(E) The greatest works of art are works that inevitably satisfy all critics.

**LOOPHOLE**     What if the greatest art can be disliked by critics?

First, translate.

*So artists claim that it's easier for critics to write about art they dislike than art they like. Most art criticism is about art the critic doesn't like. Therefore, most art criticism isn't about the greatest art.*

This is a classic dangling variable stimulus. It's perfect for SA. The dangling variable in the conclusion is "the greatest works of art." The premises only demonstrate that most art doesn't satisfy the critics. They're assuming a connection between critics disliking art (the premises) and that art not being the greatest (the conclusion). Common sense tells us that what they're assuming doesn't have to be true. Great works of art can go unrecognized by critics and still remain great. This dangling variable is perfect for our Loophole:

If dangling variables don't sound familiar, head back to Chapter 5 to review them now. Dangling variables are covered in detail on page 176.

Circle the dangling variable in this stimulus before reading the accompanying explanation. What's the new idea in the conclusion?

Carl Jung's review compared James Joyce's *Ulysses* to "how the devil tortures souls in hell." Van Gogh died in more or less complete obscurity. Not all great art is recognized by contemporary critics.

Since it's SA, we're looking for something that hyper-fills the gap exposed by the Loophole. The correct answer will render the conclusion valid. We're building the bridge between the premises and the conclusion; we need to buy that most art criticism really isn't about the greatest art. We want something resembling the following:

**SUFFICIENT ASSUMPTION**

If the critic doesn't like it, it's not the greatest work of art.

This links the dangling variable to the premises. Now we're ready to find our SA in the answer choices!

**A)** No art critic enjoys writing about art works that he or she dislikes intensely.

*So art critics never enjoy writing about art they dislike. What the art critic enjoys doesn't factor into the conclusion. This means **A** doesn't address the dangling variable (the greatest works of art), the most problematic part of the argument. Not a powerful answer choice.*

**B)** All art critics find it difficult to discover art works that truly satisfy them.

*So it's hard for art critics to find art that satisfies them. Who cares about how difficult it is to find satisfying art? Again, this doesn't address the dangling variable. We need our answer choice to build a bridge between the premises and the conclusion; that's not what we're getting here.*

**C)** A work of art that receives extensive critical attention can thereby become more widely known than it otherwise would have been.

*So getting more critical attention can help artwork become more well known than it would have been otherwise. Becoming more widely known is no substitute for addressing the dangling variable, greatest works of art. Receiving critical attention and becoming more well known don't bridge the gap. Not a powerful answer choice.*

**D)** The greatest works of art are never recognized as such until long after the time of their creation.

*So the greatest works of art aren't recognized as such until way later. At last, the dangling variable is included in an answer choice! But it's a fake-out. **D** has "greatest works of art," but it's not connecting greatness to our premises. We want to connect satisfying critics and greatness in our SA. **D** emphasizes the disconnect between greatness and critical recognition, which sounds more like a Loophole. Not what we're looking for.*

**E)** The greatest works of art are works that inevitably satisfy all critics.

*So the greatest artworks always satisfy every critic. Yaaaaaaaaaaaaay. The dangling variable is both mentioned and used correctly! **E** connects greatest works of art to our premises, pleasing the critics. **E** says every great work pleases the critics (**great work ⟶ please**), meaning art that doesn't please the critics isn't the greatest art (**~please ⟶ ~great work**). This is the contrapositive of exactly what we were looking for. It hyper-plugs our Loophole, connecting to the stimulus at its most vulnerable point. Notice how strong **E**'s language is; this is perfect for an SA question. You want language that is strong enough to send the stimulus into the stratosphere of validity.*

Keep in mind that SAs don't have to be true. SA is a Powerful Question, not a Provable Question. **If you're getting rid of an SA answer choice because it doesn't have to be true or it's too big, you're doing something wrong.** SAs are their own bosses. They fly in and grace the argument with their presence at will.

The correct answer to an SA question should give you the following feeling: "Oh? If this is true, yeah, everything is easy." It makes all the validity problems of the argument disintegrate.

**E** is the correct answer. It's the only answer that connects the dangling variable where it's needed.

## SUFFICIENT ASSUMPTION CHALLENGE

*18.4.12*

Although most species of nondomestic mammals in Australia are marsupials, over 100 species—including seals, bats, and mice—are not marsupials but placentals. It is clear, however, that these placentals are not native to this island continent: all nonhuman placentals except the dingo, a dog introduced by the first humans that settled Australia, are animals whose ancestors could swim long distances, fly, or float on driftwood.

The conclusion above is properly drawn if which one of the following is assumed?

 (A) Some marsupials now found in Australia might not be native to that continent, but rather might have been introduced to Australia by some other means.

 (B) Humans who settled Australia probably introduced many of the placental mammal species now present on that continent.

 (C) The only Australian placentals that could be native to Australia would be animals whose ancestors could not have reached Australia from elsewhere.

(D) No marsupials now found in Australia can swim long distances, fly, or float on driftwood.

(E) Seals, bats, and mice are typically found only in areas where there are no native marsupials.

*Where's the answer key?*

You'll find the answer key for all the Challenge Questions at the end of the chapter on page 306.

## Counter

| QUESTION STEM KEYWORDS | POPULARITY | About 0-1 questions per section |
|---|---|---|
| | WHAT YOU'RE LOOKING FOR | The most powerful thing the first speaker could say to destroy the second speaker's argument |
| • which one of the following, if true<br>• counter<br>• in response to | ROLE OF THE CONTROVERSY | The Controversy provides the groundwork for where to start with your comeback. If you don't know what the two speakers are debating, you aren't going to find much success taking sides in the Debate. |
| **QUESTION STEM EXAMPLES** | TL;DR STRATEGY | You already have a Controversy. You know the crux of the issue between the first and second speaker.<br><br>Pretend you're the first speaker and attack the Loophole in the second speaker's argument.<br><br>Go find that attack in the answer choices. |
| Which one of the following, if true, is the strongest counter Laila can make to Timothy's objection?<br><br>Which one of the following, if true, would provide Sina with the strongest counter to Gabriela's response? | BACK-UP PLAN | Is this something the first speaker would say and does it hurt the second speaker's argument?<br><br>• If yes, choose it.<br>• If no, cross it off.<br>• If you're not sure, leave it for later. |

### COUNTER GAME PLAN

When you encounter a Counter question (hehehe, wordplay), you'll already have the Controversy associated with the Debate. This is good because you'll already know the essentials of the Debate, and Counter asks you to take sides. **Your goal in a Counter question is to pretend you're the first speaker and plan your comeback to whatever the second speaker hurled at you.** Identify the Loophole in the second speaker's argument and attack that Loophole as if you're the first speaker.

Counter questions allow you to live out the elusive fantasy of replying with the perfect comeback, the comeback you realize ten minutes after the person you're arguing with has walked away. **Plan your comeback before you go to the answer choices.** It could call the relevance of the second speaker's premises into question, attack their method of reasoning, or bring in new information that makes their conclusion look dumb. It just has to exploit a weakness in the second speaker's argument. Choose the perfect comeback and you have the correct answer.

- Counter questions can zoom by once you are comfortable with getting into the mindset of the first speaker. Believe what they believe. Think what they think. Attack their enemy.

## REAL COUNTER EXAMPLE

*19.4.26*

> Sasha: Handwriting analysis should be banned in court as evidence of a person's character: handwriting analysts called as witnesses habitually exaggerate the reliability of their analyses.
>
> Gregory: You are right that the current use of handwriting analysis as evidence is problematic. But this problem exists only because there is no licensing board to set professional standards and thus deter irresponsible analysts from making exaggerated claims. When such a board is established, however, handwriting analysis by licensed practitioners will be a legitimate courtroom tool for character assessment.

Which one of the following, if true, would provide Sasha with the strongest counter to Gregory's response?

(A) Courts routinely use means other than handwriting analysis to provide evidence of a person's character.

(B) Many people can provide two samples of their handwriting so different that only a highly trained professional could identify them as having been written by the same person.

(C) A licensing board would inevitably refuse to grant licenses to some responsible handwriting analysts for reasons having nothing to do with their reliability.

(D) The only handwriting analysts who claim that handwriting provides reliable evidence of a person's character are irresponsible.

(E) The number of handwriting analysts who could conform to professional standards set by a licensing board is very small.

First, translate.

*Sasha says we should ban handwriting analysis as evidence for someone's character in court because handwriting analysts exaggerate the reliability of their tests.*

*Gregory says yeah, things are bad now, but the problem is that we don't have a licensing board to rein in bad analysts. Once we have this licensing board, handwriting analysis for character assessment will be a legitimate thing to bring up in court.*

Let's take an Inference from Gregory's statements to pinpoint exactly what the Controversy is with Sasha. Gregory thinks everything will be cool once we have this licensing board to keep the bad analysts in check. So, Gregory doesn't think we should necessarily ban handwriting character assessment. We should fix the system instead of abandoning it all together. Obviously, Sasha *does* think it should be banned; that's her conclusion.

This leads to our Controversy:

| **CONTROVERSY** | whether handwriting character assessment should be banned |
|---|---|

Now we see it's a Counter question. We have to act as Sasha and argue that handwriting character assessment should be banned. First, let's look for the Loophole in Gregory's argument. Gregory seems pretty into this licensing board solving everybody's problems, but what if the licensing board can't or won't make handwriting analysis legitimate? The board isn't necessarily a magic cure for what ails us. Maybe there aren't any great analysts out there to provide legitimate handwriting evidence. Maybe the board would be stacked with cronies who take bribes from irresponsible analysts. We can't be sure.

| **GREGORY LOOPHOLE** | What if the licensing board can't or won't make handwriting analysis legitimate? |
|---|---|

Alright, now we're going to pretend we're Sasha and run after this Loophole in Gregory's argument. The correct answer will suggest that the licensing board can't or won't make handwriting analysis a legitimate courtroom tool.

**A)** Courts routinely use means other than handwriting analysis to provide evidence of a person's character.

*So courts have other ways of testifying to character. That's nice, but it has nothing to do with whether handwriting analysis will be legitimate once we have the licensing board. Yeah, we can get around handwriting analysis if there are other ways to testify to someone's character, but that doesn't mean that the board is any more or less likely to solve the problem.* **A** *doesn't go after Gregory's argument; it's not powerful.*

**B)** *Many* people *can* provide two samples of their handwriting so different that *only* a highly trained professional *could* identify them as having been written by the same person.

*So people can give two handwriting samples that are so different only a highly trained expert could tell they're from the same person. It doesn't matter if they can identify the handwriting as being written by the same person. This has nothing to do with whether the licensing board can make handwriting analysis legitimate. Not a powerful answer choice.*

**C)** A licensing board would *inevitably refuse* to grant licenses to *some* responsible handwriting analysts for reasons having nothing to do with their reliability.

*So some good analysts would be rejected by the licensing board. This doesn't affect whether the board will make handwriting analysis legitimate, the aim Gregory has in his conclusion. He needs the board to get rid of the bad analysts; that's the problem that has to be solved.* **C** *wants us to care about rejecting* **some** *good analysts, but denying a few good analysts doesn't imply that the board won't make handwriting analysis more legit. You could let in one out of every ten good analysts and still make handwriting legitimate, as long as you keep out the irresponsible analysts.* **C** *is tempting, but it's just not a powerful answer.*

✳ Notice the "only" in **D**. That powerful language helps **D**'s chances.

**D)** The *only* handwriting analysts who claim that handwriting provides reliable evidence of a person's character are irresponsible.

*So only irresponsible analysts would do this whole handwriting as character evidence thing to begin with. If this is true, it won't matter if we have a licensing board; they would have to reject everyone because everyone applying for a license would be irresponsible. The licensing board can't make handwriting analysis legitimate if there are no responsible analysts to license.* **D** *capitalizes on the Loophole in Gregory's argument. It shows that the licensing board can't do its job. It's a powerful answer.*

**E)** The number of handwriting analysts who *could* conform to professional standards set by a licensing board is very small.

*So there aren't many handwriting analysts who are good enough to meet the licensing board's requirements. This is fine for Gregory's argument. How many handwriting analysts do you really need anyway? Even if there were only a few responsible analysts out there, they would still be regulated and doing responsible work. Not a powerful comeback.*

**D** is the correct answer. It's the only answer that is damaging for Gregory and compatible with Sasha's way of thinking.

*4.1.1*

Rita:   The original purpose of government farm-subsidy programs was to provide income stability for small family farmers, but most farm-subsidy money goes to a few farmers with large holdings. Payments to farmers whose income, before subsidies, is greater than $100,000 a year should be stopped.

Thomas:   It would be impossible to administer such a cutoff point. Subsidies are needed during the planting and growing season, but farmers do not know their income for a given calendar year until tax returns are calculated and submitted the following April.

Which one of the following, if true, is the strongest counter Rita can make to Thomas' objection?

(A)   It has become difficult for small farmers to obtain bank loans to be repaid later by money from subsidies.

(B)   Having such a cutoff point would cause some farmers whose income would otherwise exceed $100,000 to reduce their plantings.

(C)   The income of a farmer varies because weather and market prices are not stable from year to year.

(D)   If subsidy payments to large farmers were eliminated, the financial condition of the government would improve.

(E)   Subsidy cutoffs can be determined on the basis of income for the preceding year.

*Where's the answer key?*

You'll find the answer key for all the Challenge Questions at the end of the chapter on page 306.

## Contradiction

* Contradiction is the anti-Provable Question.

* Rarely, Contradiction questions follow Arguments, so you could have a Loophole leading into the question stem. In this case, you should switch to a Premise Set mindset, assuming *everything* in the stimulus is true.

* Major Answer Choices Chapter preview here! Crazy Nonsense is one of our Answer Choice Red Flags.

| QUESTION STEM KEYWORDS | POPULARITY | About 0-1 questions per section |
|---|---|---|
| • if the statements above are true<br>• cannot be true<br>• violate the principle<br>• could be true EXCEPT | WHAT YOU'RE LOOKING FOR | The thing that contradicts literal words from the stimulus |
| | ROLE OF THE INFERENCE | Contradiction questions *hate* Inferences. The Inference (and anything even remotely resembling an Inference) is incorrect. |
| **QUESTION STEM EXAMPLES** | | You probably have an Inference in your pocket. This Inference is an incorrect answer. Don't choose it. |
| If the statements above are true, then on the basis of them which one of the following cannot be true?<br><br>If the statements above are true, each of the following could be true EXCEPT:<br><br>The information above, if accurate, can best be used as evidence against which one of the following hypotheses? | TL;DR STRATEGY | Find something that can't exist in the world of the stimulus.<br><br>Don't fall for Crazy Nonsense answers. They're incorrect because they don't directly violate the facts of the stimulus. |
| | BACK-UP PLAN | Does this contradict the stimulus?<br><br>• If yes, choose it.<br>• If no, cross it off.<br>• If you're not sure, leave it for later. |

### CONTRADICTION GAME PLAN

Contradiction questions often end up feeling harder than they should. Coming into these, you'll likely have an Inference ready. This is good because you'll know exactly what NOT to choose. If you see anything remotely provable, cross it off right away. **You are looking for an answer that directly contradicts the stimulus**. The correct answer can contradict anywhere in the stimulus, premises or conclusion.

But the answer choices can mislead you on Contradiction questions. They will throw some off-the-wall stuff into the wrong answers. We need to prepare you to resist the Crazy Nonsense temptation. Let's check out an example Premise Set to examine the difference between a true Contradiction and Crazy Nonsense (random words that are unsupported by the stimulus):

> *Rain turns smiles into frowns. Baseball games are sometimes canceled and fans resent the weather's interference in their recreation.*

Now check out the difference between a true Contradiction and Crazy Nonsense:

| CONTRADICTIONS | CRAZY NONSENSE ANSWERS |
|---|---|
| *Baseball games are never canceled.* | *Canceled games are a major inconvenience for* **baseball team owners**. |
| *Fans never resent the weather's interference with their recreation.* | *Rain affects the* **GDP** *of many* **large nations**. |
| *Rain does not affect smiles.* | *Rain only occurs very* **rarely**. |

I've bolded the new words in the Crazy Nonsense. These words are not contradicting; they're dangling variables in the answer choices that are unconnected to the stimulus.

Isn't the Crazy Nonsense kinda tempting? No one wants to give Crazy Nonsense a free pass. People choose it because it's "just so bad" and Contradiction feels like a time to choose "bad" answers. They think they're punishing Crazy Nonsense by choosing it in a "negative" question type, but this is a flawed rationale. **Choose the boring contradictory answer. Study the difference between the examples that contradict facts in the stimulus and those that just toss nonsense words together.**

The correct answer to a Contradiction question is the exact opposite of provable. It has to be so powerful it breaks the stimulus. The stronger the language of an answer choice, the more likely it is to break the rules of the stimulus. Answer choices with weak language are less likely to fully contradict. Since we're trying to break the stimulus, we don't want weaselly weak answers on our side.

## TINY TIPS

- In Contradiction, the stimulus and the correct answer create an ironclad Paradox when considered together. They can't exist together in a world that makes sense.

- Contradiction is pretty rare. You might see one of these on your actual exam, two at the most. Don't ignore them just because they're rare though. If a Contradiction question *does* appear on your actual LSAT, you don't want to be caught unprepared.

## BIGGEST TRAPS

- Do not fall for answers that are totally out of left field. **If an answer choice elicits that "What does that have to do with anything?" feeling, it is WRONG.** The correct answer must call the stimulus a liar.

### REAL CONTRADICTION EXAMPLE

*19.4.13*

Some people think that in every barrel of politicians there are only a few rotten ones. But if deceit is a quality of rottenness, I believe all effective politicians are rotten. They must be deceitful in order to do the job properly. Someone who is scrupulously honest about obeying the rules of society will never be an effective politician.

Assuming that the author's statements are accurate, which one of the following statements CANNOT be true?

(A)    Some people think all politicians are rotten.
(B)    Some politicians are scrupulously honest.
(C)    Some people define a politician's job as obeying the rules of society.
(D)    Some deceitful politicians are ineffective.
(E)    Some scrupulously honest politicians are effective.

*I know it's tempting to diagram the conditionals in this stimulus, but since the conditionals don't chain, it's much easier to tackle this stimulus without diagramming.*

First, imagine a barrel of politicians. Second, translate.

*Some people think few politicians are rotten, but if deceit is rotten, I believe every effective politician is rotten. Politicians have to be deceitful to properly do their jobs. Being honest about obeying rules means you'll never be an effective politician.*

Notice how the author equates "properly do their jobs" (premises) with being an "effective politician" (conclusion). Properly doing their job might not necessarily mean that they're effective. We don't have clear definitions of "effective" and "do the job properly," so there's no reason to assume they are necessarily the same thing. This leads us straight to the Loophole:

**LOOPHOLE**      What if politicians can properly do their jobs and still be ineffective?

Now that we see it's Contradiction, we have to pivot to accepting everything in the stimulus as an ironclad fact. We're looking for something that directly contradicts facts from the stimulus. Let's brainstorm a couple examples. The process is simple; all we have to do is say the opposite of something we read in the stimulus:

**CONTRADICTION**      Politicians can do their jobs properly and not be deceitful.

*or*

**CONTRADICTION**      Scrupulously honest politicians can be effective.

These Contradiction examples took literal words from the stimulus and contradicted them. Those two sentences at the end of the stimulus were the most strongly worded, so I started there since they're the easiest to contradict. Now we're ready for the answer choices.

**A)**  Some people think all politicians are rotten.

*So some think every politician is rotten. We have no clue if this is true or not. There could be some people who believe every politician is rotten, but we don't know. The fact that we don't know means **A** is incorrect.*

**B)**  Some politicians are scrupulously honest.

*So some politicians are honest. Maybe the ineffective ones are honest? It could be true. We don't know. This reasonableness means the answer is incorrect. The correct answer will be entirely unreasonable according to the stimulus.*

**C)**  Some people define a politician's job as obeying the rules of society.

*So some people think it's a politician's job to obey the rules of society. That's nice. That could definitely be something some people think. We have no idea based on what the stimulus tells us. That means **C** is incorrect.*

**D)** *Some* deceitful politicians are ineffective.

*So some deceitful politicians are ineffective. This is the most tempting incorrect answer, but look closely at the stimulus. The stimulus says if you're doing your job properly, then you must be deceitful. We only know deceitful's relationship to doing the job properly, not its relationship to effectiveness. We don't know whether every deceitful politician is necessarily effective or ineffective. That lack of knowledge means **D** is wrong. It's not specifically disallowed by the stimulus, and so it's incorrect.*

**E)** *Some* scrupulously honest politicians are effective.

*So some honest politicians are effective. This directly contradicts the last sentence of the stimulus, which states that someone honest can never be effective. The direct contradiction means **E** is correct.*

**E** is the correct answer. See how refreshing **E** was in comparison to **D**? You have to stretch for **D**, but **E** is right all on its own. That's how the right answer should feel. You don't have to do any favors for the correct answer. **E** is the only answer that says the opposite of something in the stimulus.

## CONTRADICTION CHALLENGE

*17.3.15*

Babies who can hear and have hearing parents who expose them to speech begin to babble at a certain age as a precursor to speaking. In the same way, deaf babies with deaf parents who communicate with them and with each other by signing begin to babble in signs at the same age. That is, they make repetitive hand gestures that constitute, within the language system of signs, the analogue of repeated syllables in speech.

The information above, if accurate, can best be used as evidence against which one of the following hypotheses?

(A)   Names of persons or things are the simplest words in a language, since babies use them before using the names of actions or processes.

(B)   The development of language competency in babies depends primarily on the physical maturation of the vocal tract, a process that requires speech-oriented vocal activity.

(C)   In the absence of adults who communicate with each other in their presence, babies develop idiosyncratic languages.

(D)   In babbling, babies are unaware that the sound or gesture combinations they use can be employed in a purposive way.

(E)   The making of hand gestures by hearing babies who have hearing parents should be interpreted as a part of their developing language.

*Where's the answer key?*

You'll find the answer key for all the Challenge Questions at the end of the chapter on page 306.

## Evaluate

| QUESTION STEM KEYWORDS | POPULARITY | About 0-1 questions per section |
|---|---|---|

<table>
<tr><td>

**QUESTION STEM KEYWORDS**

- the answer to which of the following questions
- which of the following, if true
- evaluate + the argument / the conclusion
- most helpful to know / relevant to evaluating

</td><td>

**POPULARITY** — About 0-1 questions per section

**WHAT YOU'RE LOOKING FOR** — A powerful pop quiz for the argument's validity

**ROLE OF THE LOOPHOLE** — The correct answer to an Evaluate question will ask whether the Loophole is active.

</td></tr>
<tr><td>

**QUESTION STEM EXAMPLES**

Which one of the following would it be most helpful to know in order to judge whether what the scientist subsequently learned calls into question the hypothesis?

The answer to which one of the following would be the most helpful in determining whether William's argument could be logically defended against Marianna's objection?

The answer to which one of the following questions is most relevant to evaluating the conclusion drawn above?

Which one of the following would it be most relevant to investigate in evaluating the conclusion of the argument?

</td><td>

**TL;DR STRATEGY**

You already have a Loophole.

You want to literally evaluate the argument. The Loophole exposed the crux of the argument's validity, so that's where you should focus.

Go find something that asks about whether the Loophole is true in the answer choices.

**BACK-UP PLAN**

Is this crucial for the argument's validity?

- If yes, choose it.
- If no, cross it off.
- If you're not sure, leave it for later.

</td></tr>
</table>

**EVALUATE GAME PLAN**

Evaluate questions are testing whether you know what's important for the argument's validity. They ask, "What does the argument's validity depend on?" Cool story: It depends on your Loophole. **Evaluate questions are asking for the crux of the argument's validity: your Loophole. The correct answer will zero in on this crucial point.**

But say your Loophole doesn't appear in the answer choices. How will you know which answer is crucial to the argument's validity? Look at each answer choice and ask yourself, "Does this matter?" If the dilemma that the answer choice poses actually matters for the conclusion's validity, the answer choice is correct. If it doesn't matter, the answer choice is wrong.

Remember, **a correct Evaluate answer choice is the ultimate pop quiz for the argument's validity**. How you respond to the dilemma it poses determines if the argument passes or fails. Answer one way, the Loophole is activated, and the argument fails. Answer the other way and the argument is cool.

*Many Evaluate answer choices will be worded as questions, while others appear without question marks. You're looking for the same thing regardless of how the answer choices are worded.*

- Evaluate is one of the rarest question types out there. For this reason, students don't have many questions to practice on. Luckily, you have practiced the core skill that Evaluate questions are testing: You know how to zero in on the crux of the argument.

## BIGGEST TRAPS

- It's easy to do too much work to make an answer choice relevant on Evaluate questions. Calm yourself and let these be easy. They basically amount to a relevancy test. They ask, "Do you know which answer choice matters to the argument?"

## REAL EVALUATE EXAMPLE

### 7.1.22

There is a widespread belief that people can predict impending earthquakes from unusual animal behavior. Skeptics claim that this belief is based on selective coincidence: people whose dogs behaved oddly just before an earthquake will be especially likely to remember that fact. At any given time, the skeptics say, some of the world's dogs will be behaving oddly.

Clarification of which one of the following issues would be most important to an evaluation of the skeptics' position?

(A) Which is larger, the number of skeptics or the number of people who believe that animal behavior can foreshadow earthquakes?

(B) Are there means other than the observation of animal behavior that nonscientists can use to predict earthquakes?

(C) Are there animals about whose behavior people know too little to be able to distinguish unusual from everyday behavior?

(D) Are the sorts of behavior supposedly predictive of earthquakes as pronounced in dogs as they are in other animals?

(E) Is the animal behavior supposedly predictive of earthquakes specific to impending earthquakes or can it be any kind of unusual behavior?

First, translate.

*So people believe that you can predict earthquakes from unusual animal behavior, but skeptics say it's just a coincidence. Anybody who has a dog acting weird right before an earthquake will remember that happening, and there are always some dogs acting weird at any given time.*

I'm taking issue with how "unusual animal behavior" and "dogs behaving oddly" were equated in service of the skeptics' claim. Notice that the widespread belief says "unusual animal behavior" and all of the skeptics' premises are exclusively about dogs. For all we know the widespread belief isn't even based on dogs.

While it may be true that there are always some dogs acting weird, what if there's specific unusual behavior that corresponds to earthquakes? They could be referring to penguins walking backwards for all we know. Generally odd dog behavior surely doesn't correlate, but that doesn't mean there isn't some warning sign that's earthquake-specific. This leads me to my Loophole:

This is a hybrid argument. The skeptics' conclusion is promoted to what we'll critique because the author did not state a conclusion themselves.

**LOOPHOLE** What if there's a specific, predictive unusual animal behavior that's separate from general odd dog behavior?

Since it's an Evaluate question, we're going to look for an answer choice that calls attention to the crux of the skeptics' argument: whether there's a specific, predictive animal behavior that's not just weird dogs. Awesome, onward to the answer choices.

**A)** Which is larger, the number of skeptics or the number of people who believe that animal behavior *can* foreshadow earthquakes?

**B)** Are there means other than the observation of animal behavior that nonscientists *can* use to predict earthquakes?

Evaluate questions want to find out if you can tell when something is relevant or irrelevant to the argument's validity. The four incorrect answers on Evaluate questions are irrelevant nonsense.

**C)** Are there animals about whose behavior people know too little to be *able to* distinguish unusual from everyday behavior?

**D)** Are the sorts of behavior supposedly predictive of earthquakes as pronounced in dogs as they are in other animals?

**E)** Is the animal behavior supposedly predictive of earthquakes specific to impending earthquakes or *can* it be *any* kind of unusual behavior?

*So are there more skeptics or more animal believers? Why would we care how many people are on each team?* **A** *is almost a logical flaw in itself. It doesn't matter how many people believe a given thing. Beliefs are true or false independent of whether they're believed. This answer doesn't call attention to the core issue in the argument. Not powerful.*

*So can nonscientists predict earthquakes any other way? This doesn't matter. Nonscientists could predict earthquakes some other way and it could still be possible to predict with animals. This sidesteps the core issue. They could have a bunch of ways to predict or no other ways — either way we're no closer to finding out if animals are reliable.*

*So do mystery animals exist where we don't know enough about them to tell when they're acting weird? Who cares? There could be mystery animals and also understandable animals. The understandable animals are the only ones at issue in the skeptics' conclusion. Mystery animals' existence or non-existence doesn't affect whether we can predict earthquakes with the understandable animals.*

*So is there a difference in how pronounced earthquake behavior is between dogs and other animals? It doesn't really matter. The behavior could be subtle in dogs or in other animals; the important thing is that people notice it. If people notice, it doesn't matter how pronounced it was.* **D** *just isn't crucial for the argument's validity. It doesn't zero in on our Loophole.*

*So is there earthquake-specific behavior or is all odd behavior supposedly predictive of earthquakes? Finally, we get something that's actually talking about our Loophole. If there is no specific earthquake behavior, the skeptics' reasoning is more valid; coincidence is more likely. If there is specific earthquake behavior, the skeptics' position is weakened; coincidence is less likely. This answer calls out the crux of the problem with the skeptics' argument; it's a powerful answer choice.*

**E** is the correct answer. It is the only answer choice that poses a question that affects the skeptics' argument.

*11.2.2*

Sea turtles nest only at their own birthplaces. After
hatching on the beach, the turtles enter the water to
begin their far-ranging migration, only returning to
their birthplaces to nest some 15 to 30 years later. It has
been hypothesized that newborn sea turtles learn the
smell of their birth environment, and it is this smell that
stimulates the turtles to return to nest.

Which one of the following would be most important to
know in evaluating the hypothesis in the passage?

(A)     how long the expected life span of sea turtles is
(B)     what the maximum migratory range of mature sea
          turtles is
(C)     whether many beaches on which sea turtles
          were hatched have since been destroyed by
          development
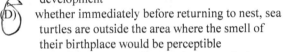
(D)     whether immediately before returning to nest, sea
          turtles are outside the area where the smell of
          their birthplace would be perceptible
(E)     whether both sexes of sea turtles are actively
          involved in the nesting process

❋

*Where's the answer key?*

You'll find the answer
key for all the Challenge
Questions at the end
of the chapter on page
306.

# Resolution

| QUESTION STEM KEYWORDS | | POPULARITY | About 1-3 questions per section |
|---|---|---|---|
| • which one of the following, if true<br>• most helps to + explain / resolve / account for<br>• discrepancy / paradox / conflict / surprising result | | WHAT YOU'RE LOOKING FOR | The most powerful thing you can find to make the Paradox make sense |
| | | ROLE OF THE RESOLUTION | It's the correct answer! YAY! |
| **QUESTION STEM EXAMPLES**<br><br>Which one of the following, if true, does most to explain the surprising result?<br><br>Which one of the following, if true, most helps to resolve the apparent discrepancy in the information above?<br><br>Which one of the following, if true, most helps to resolve the apparent paradox?<br><br>Which one of the following, if true, helps to resolve the apparent conflict described above? | | TL;DR STRATEGY | You already have the Resolution from your CLIR.<br><br>Go choose it. |
| | | BACK-UP PLAN | Does this make the Paradox make sense?<br><br>• If yes, choose it.<br>• If no, cross it off.<br>• If you're not sure, leave it for later. |

If you're having trouble with Resolution Questions, review the Paradox and Resolution sections of the CLIR Chapter.

**RESOLUTION GAME PLAN**

In the CLIR Chapter, we examined how to design the Resolution to a Paradox in detail, so you should be familiar with exactly what Resolution questions want from you. The correct answer to a Resolution question is your Resolution! But you don't want to overlook the correct answer just because it doesn't match your CLIR's exact words. So, let's practice generalizing our Resolutions to catch the most answer choices.

Check out this example Paradox to see how generalized Resolutions work:

> *Yana is a worse singer than Gloria. However, more people bought tickets to Yana's concert than Gloria's.*

So if Yana is worse than Gloria, why are more people buying tickets to her concert? How does that make sense? We need to tip the scales in Yana's favor to explain why people are preferring her concert. A good first thought might be, "The tickets to Yana's concert were less expensive." That is a perfectly serviceable Resolution, but **you have a higher chance of leading yourself directly to the correct answer if you make your Resolution more general**. A generalized version of this Resolution might be:

> *There is something really desirable about Yana's concert in comparison to Gloria's.*

This is a spin on our Secret Downsides Loophole.

This generalized Resolution boils down to Yana = GOOD and Gloria = BAD. It will catch many possible correct answers. Anything specific that gestures at this idea in the answer choices will stand out to us.

- Resolution questions are popular **EXCEPT** destinations. Be ready to find and label four Resolutions. Check out the Answer Choice Strategy Section for advice on how to master **EXCEPT** questions.

## BIGGEST TRAPS

- **Answer choices that affect both sides of the Paradox equally do not resolve anything.** Imagine an answer choice in our Yana-Gloria example that said, "The price of concert tickets is on the rise." This would do nothing for our Paradox because it would affect both Yana and Gloria equally. **It's like adding five pounds to both sides of a scale and expecting the scale to tip in your favored direction.**

## REAL RESOLUTION EXAMPLE

*15.3.20*

Calories consumed in excess of those with which the body needs to be provided to maintain its weight are normally stored as fat and the body gains weight. Alcoholic beverages are laden with calories. However, those people who regularly drink two or three alcoholic beverages a day and thereby exceed the caloric intake necessary to maintain their weight do not in general gain weight.

Which one of the following, if true, most helps to resolve the apparent discrepancy?

(A) Some people who regularly drink two or three alcoholic beverages a day avoid exceeding the caloric intake necessary to maintain their weight by decreasing caloric intake from other sources.

(B) Excess calories consumed by people who regularly drink two or three alcoholic beverages a day tend to be dissipated as heat.

(C) Some people who do not drink alcoholic beverages but who eat high-calorie foods do not gain weight.

(D) Many people who regularly drink more than three alcoholic beverages a day do not gain weight.

(E) Some people who take in fewer calories than are normally necessary to maintain their weight do not lose weight.

First, translate.

*Excess calories normally become fat. Alcohol has a bunch of calories, but people who drink 2-3 drinks a day, and exceed their caloric requirement by doing so, don't gain weight.*

We have to figure out how these 2-3 drinkers are getting away with consuming excess calories and not storing fat. They've found the lifestyle holy grail.

The most obvious Resolution, that they're just decreasing calories in other parts of their diet to make up for the drinking, is accounted for in the stimulus: "And thereby exceed the caloric intake necessary" is crucial to notice. This statement bars that easy Resolution. They are definitely exceeding the calories they need.

So we have to go in a different direction. There has to be some other way that the 2-3 drinkers are magically getting rid of these alcohol calories. So why not just make that our Resolution?

✳

Man, if that first sentence isn't a cluster, I don't know what is. "In excess of those with which the body needs to be provided to maintain" is some of the worst writing I've seen on the LSAT. It is so important to translate this stimulus if you want to handle it with ease.

**RESOLUTION** What if there's some other way the 2-3 drinkers are magically getting rid of these alcohol calories?

Awesome! Now we're ready to look for this Resolution in the answer choices.

**A)** *Some* people who regularly drink two or three alcoholic beverages a day avoid exceeding the caloric intake necessary to maintain their weight by decreasing caloric intake from other sources.

So some 2-3 drinkers decrease calories in the rest of their diet enough to compensate for their drinking. This is the decoy Resolution that the stimulus accounted for, but it's stated with really weak language. The **SOME** that starts the answer could mean one 2-3 drinker out of millions. This doesn't make for a powerful enough Resolution to explain the phenomenon. But beyond that, this base was covered by the stimulus. They precluded us from going this route when they limited their statement with "and thereby exceed the caloric intake necessary to maintain their weight." The stimulus was only talking about the 2-3 drinkers who go over the line. This is a compelling wrong answer, but it just isn't powerful.

Notice how **B**, a conceptually powerful answer, contains provable language. *\*gasp\** But remember, it matters *how* the language is used. In this case, the answer choice as a whole is conceptually powerful despite the provable language in the back half. The context of the provable language matters a lot for its impact; in this case, it's localized.

**B)** Excess calories consumed by people who regularly drink two or three alcoholic beverages a day *tend to* be dissipated as heat.

So the excess calories that 2-3 drinkers consume are dissipated as heat. This sounds like magically getting rid of the calories, right? Notice how the language of this answer choice is powerful enough to encompass all the 2-3 drinkers and speaks exactly to the excess calories, which is what we need to account for. Don't be put off by the fact that "dissipated as heat" wasn't in the stimulus — it's just a specific way of magically getting rid of the calories. You couldn't have predicted this exactly, but that's why we made the Resolution general enough to catch it. **B** is a conceptually powerful answer.

**C)** *Some* people who do not drink alcoholic beverages but who eat high-calorie foods do not gain weight.

So some non-drinkers who eat high-calorie foods don't gain weight. OK, who cares about non-drinkers? This is a stimulus about a specific phenomenon amongst 2-3 drinkers. The high-calorie food eaters not gaining weight doesn't give us any insight into how the 2-3 drinkers aren't gaining weight. Not a powerful answer choice.

**D)** *Many* people who regularly drink more than three alcoholic beverages a day do not gain weight.

So many 3+ drinkers don't gain weight. This is speaking to the wrong group of drinkers. 3+ drinkers don't give us any insight into 2-3 drinkers. We also don't know why these 3+ drinkers aren't gaining weight, so **D** doesn't offer any insight into how magically getting rid of calories could work. Overall, not a powerful answer choice.

**E)** *Some* people who take in fewer calories than are normally necessary to maintain their weight do not lose weight.

So some people who take in fewer calories than they need don't lose weight. This doesn't speak to the specific discrepancy examined in the stimulus. They're trying to trick us into considering it because it decouples calorie intake and weight implications. However, **E** is just telling us that there are more confusing phenomena out there. Cool, but this doesn't help us understand that calorie magic the 2-3 drinkers are performing.

Notice how the correct answer is the only one that doesn't start with **SOME** (or a **SOME** synonym).

**B** is the correct answer. It's the only conceptually powerful answer choice that specifically addresses the 2-3 drinkers.

## RESOLUTION CHALLENGE

*18.4.15*

Goodbody, Inc., is in the process of finding tenants for its newly completed Parrot Quay commercial development, which will make available hundreds of thousands of square feet of new office space on what was formerly derelict property outside the financial center of the city. Surprisingly enough, the coming recession, though it will hurt most of the city's businesses, should help Goodbody to find tenants.

Which one of the following, if true, does most to help resolve the apparent paradox?

(A) Businesses forced to economize by the recession will want to take advantage of the lower rents available outside the financial center.

(B) Public transportation links the financial center with the area around Parrot Quay.

(C) The area in which the Parrot Quay development is located became derelict after the heavy industry that used to be there closed down in a previous recession.

(D) Many of Goodbody's other properties are in the financial center and will become vacant if the recession is severe enough to force Goodbody's tenants out of business.

(E) The recession is likely to have the most severe effect not on service industries, which require a lot of office space, but on manufacturers.

*Where's the answer key?*

You'll find the answer key for all the Challenge Questions at the end of the chapter on page 306.

---

### POWERFUL QUESTIONS GAME PLAN

- Always look for powerful language in the answer choices. **ALL, EVERY, NEVER, MUST,** and **CANNOT** are your friends in Powerful Questions.

- Never get rid of an answer to a Powerful Question because it's too "big," "strong," or unproven by the stimulus. Big, bold answers are the goal in Powerful Questions.

- Use the Powerful Questions Road Map to consolidate the information in this chapter.

- Memorize the question stem keywords for the Powerful Questions now.

## Quiz 9 POWERFUL QUESTIONS

**INSTRUCTIONS**

Answer these questions based on your knowledge of the chapter. Attempt to answer without looking back at the chapter first. If you don't know the answer, circle the question number and go find the answer in the chapter. Study the sections of the chapter that you couldn't remember at first.

**Word Bank**

| | | |
|---|---|---|
| provable | ~~strong~~ (circled) | premise(s) |
| ~~Loophole(s)~~ | dangling variable | Resolution(s) |
| conclusion(s) | Inference(s) | weak |
| Weaken | Strengthen | SA |
| Counter | Contradiction | Evaluate |

Use the word bank to answer the fill-in-the-blank questions. Some words will not be used and others may be used more than once.

**1.** The correct answer to a Powerful Question will prefer ___*Strong*___ language.

**2.** The correct answer to an Evaluate question asks whether your ___*Loophole*___ is active.

**3.** Sufficient Assumption questions are a popular destination for ___*dangling variable*___ stimuli.

**4.** Complete the table using the word bank.

| POWERFUL QUESTION TYPE | CORRECT ANSWER |
|---|---|
| *Contradiction* | The thing that contradicts literal words from the stimulus |
| *Resolution* | The most powerful thing you can find to make the Paradox make sense |
| *SA* | The most powerful thing you can find to prove the conclusion 100% valid |
| *Counter* | The most powerful thing the first speaker could say to destroy the second speaker's argument |

| | |
|---|---|
| _Weakening_ | The most powerful thing you can find to destroy the argument's conclusion |
| _Evaluate_ | A powerful pop quiz for the argument's validity |
| _Strengthen_ | The most powerful thing you can find to help the argument's conclusion |

_Circle the correct answer to the following questions._

**5.** **(TRUE) OR FALSE**    Of all the question types, Sufficient Assumption requires the highest level of power in the correct answer.

**6.** **(TRUE) OR FALSE**    The correct answer to a Powerful Question can bring in new information.

**7.** **TRUE OR (FALSE)**    The correct answer to a Contradiction question is provable.

**8.** **(TRUE) OR FALSE**    In Counter questions, you're attacking the Loophole in the second speaker's argument as though you're the first speaker.

**9.** **(TRUE) OR FALSE**    Correct answers on Strengthen questions don't have to prove the conclusion 100%.

＊

_Where's the answer key?_

You'll find the answer key at the end of the chapter on page 307.

## Powerful Challenge Questions   ANSWER KEY

Looking for a little extra help on these Challenge Questions?

You'll find explanations for each of the Challenge Questions online at elementalprep.com/bonus.

| | | |
|---|---|---|
| Weaken | 17.2.13 | A |
| | 18.4.23 | B |
| Strengthen | 17.3.12 | D |
| | 17.3.18 | E |
| Sufficient Assumption | 18.4.12 | C |
| Counter | 4.1.1 | E |
| Contradiction | 17.3.15 | B |
| Evaluate | 11.2.2 | D |
| Resolution | 18.4.15 | A |

**1.**    The correct answer to a Powerful Question will prefer **strong** language.

**2.**    The correct answer to an Evaluate question asks whether your **Loophole** is active.

**3.**    Sufficient Assumption questions are a popular destination for **dangling variable** stimuli.

**4.**

| POWERFUL QUESTION TYPE | CORRECT ANSWER |
|---|---|
| Contradiction | The thing that contradicts literal words from the stimulus |
| Resolution | The most powerful thing you can find to make the Paradox make sense |
| SA | The most powerful thing you can find to prove the conclusion 100% valid |
| Counter | The most powerful thing the first speaker could say to destroy the second speaker's argument |
| Weaken | The most powerful thing you can find to destroy the argument's conclusion |
| Evaluate | A powerful pop quiz for the argument's validity |
| Strengthen | The most powerful thing you can find to help the argument's conclusion |

**5.**    True.

**6.**    True.

**7.**    False. The correct answer to a Contradiction question is *powerful*.

**8.**    True.

**9.**    True.

# OMMMM.

chapter nine. sounds divine.

# Chapter Breather

There are a handful of LR questions that require a very basic understanding of supply and demand. Don't worry. This isn't Econ 101 redux. I'm going to keep this super short and simple. You only have to know a little bit.

Say you *really* want the red Skittles in your friend's pack of Skittles. Red's the best; it makes sense. You offer your friend a dollar if he'll give you all the red Skittles right now. He's like, "Nah, I want the red ones." But your demand for red Skittles will not be quashed. You say, "OK, two dollars. All the red Skittles now." He gives you the red Skittles. How much you want those red Skittles is the demand. Demand is high, so you're willing to pay more.

This is how the demand half of supply and demand works. The more people want something, the higher the price tends to be. **When demand is high, prices go up.**

Now imagine your friend has yellow Skittles left and you, like any sane person, don't really like yellow Skittles. You basically only eat them because they're chilling there in the pack with the actually good Skittles. You offer your friend only five cents for the yellow Skittles. Your demand for the yellow Skittles is low, so the price you're willing to pay is also low. Nobody else wants the yellow Skittles enough to offer more, so you can get them for only five cents. **When demand is low, prices drop.**

Now, for the supply half, say you're a Skittles dealer. You've got two friends looking greedily at your red Skittles. They each offer you a dollar for five red Skittles. But you only have five red Skittles total; your supply is too low to meet the demand. They can't both get their five red Skittles, so one of them offers $1.50 because they want the red Skittles with an insatiable fervor. The other friend punks out to avoid the potential awkwardness of a Skittle bidding war. You sell the five red Skittles for $1.50; the price went up because the supply was low. **When supply is low, prices go up.**

Now imagine you're in the same situation with your two friends and your red Skittles, but now you have 10 red Skittles total. When your friends each offer you a dollar for five red Skittles, you have a higher supply that you want to get off your hands, so you sell to each of them at this lower price. No one has to offer $1.50 to get what they want. **When supply is high, prices go down.**

> All the trends described on this page assume that a change in supply isn't canceled out by a corresponding, similar change in demand, and vice versa. For instance, if demand drops and supply also drops by a similar amount, the price will stay the same because the demand didn't *really* drop in relation to the supply. The effect of the drop in demand was canceled out. If demand drops and supply stays the same (or goes up), the price will drop just as we described here.

| | | |
|---|---|---|
| **SUPPLY AND DEMAND CHEAT SHEET** | | |
| **High Demand** | usually means | **High Price** |
| **Low Supply** | usually means | **High Price** |
| **Low Demand** | usually means | **Low Price** |
| **High Supply** | usually means | **Low Price** |

# PROVABLE
# QUESTIONS

## Provable Questions Road Map

The correct answer to all of the following question types will prefer provable language. Use this chart as a centralized study aid after you've read the chapter to help yourself commit these key points to memory.

| QUESTION TYPE | CORRECT ANSWER | BACK-UP PLAN | QUESTION STEM KEYWORDS |
|---|---|---|---|
| Conclusion | A provable translation of the conclusion | Is this a translation of the conclusion? | • main point<br>• main conclusion |
| Inference | The thing you can prove definitely must be true | Does this have to be true? | • must be true / follows logically<br>• inference<br>• properly inferred / properly be concluded / properly drawn |
| Most Strongly Supported (MSS) | The thing you can prove is very, very, very likely to be true | Does this pretty much have to be true? | • most strongly supported<br>• most strongly suggests |
| Fill In | The thing you can prove completes the author's thought | Does this have to be true? | • completes / concludes<br>• a blank at the end of the stimulus |
| Controversy | The thing you can prove the two speakers disagree about | Does the first speaker have to believe this is true/false? Does the second speaker have to believe this is true/false? | • point at issue<br>• point of disagreement<br>• disagree<br>• differing opinions |
| Agreement | The thing you can prove the two speakers agree about | Does the first speaker have to believe this? Does the second speaker have to believe this? | • agree on<br>• point of agreement<br>• committed to agreeing |
| Necessary Assumption (NA) | The thing you can prove must be true, if the conclusion is true | If the conclusion is true, does this have to be true? | • necessary / depends / required / relies<br>• assumes / assumption<br>• the conclusion does not follow unless<br>• the argument assumes which one |

| | | | |
|---|---|---|---|
| **Method** | A provable description of what happened in the stimulus | Did this happen? | • argument proceeds by<br>• describes<br>• argumentative technique / method of reasoning / strategy of argumentation<br>• responds by (in Debates) |
| **Argument Part** | A provable description of what the phrase is doing in the argument | Is this what the phrase is doing? | • role in the argument / functions in the argument<br>• argument part<br>• the reference to / the statement that |
| **Classic Flaw** | A provable description of what the argument did wrong | Is this what's wrong with the argument? | • flaw / flawed<br>• most vulnerable to criticism on the grounds that it<br>• questionable technique employed |
| **Loophole Flaw** | A provable description of how the argument overlooked your Loophole | Was it bad that the argument overlooked this? | • most vulnerable to criticism on the grounds that it + [Loophole Flaw Prefix] |

## Conclusion

| QUESTION STEM KEYWORDS | | POPULARITY | About 1-2 questions per section |
|---|---|---|---|
| | | WHAT YOU'RE LOOKING FOR | A provable translation of the conclusion |
| • main point<br>• main conclusion | | ROLE OF THE LOOPHOLE | ~~You will already know what the conclusion is because you designed~~ your Loophole. |
| **QUESTION STEM EXAMPLES** | | | Go back up to the stimulus. |
| | | | Bracket the conclusion (if you haven't already). |
| Which one of the following most accurately expresses the main conclusion of the argument? | | TL;DR STRATEGY | Translate the conclusion. Repeat the translation to yourself. |
| Which one of the following most accurately expresses the overall conclusion drawn in the argument? | | | Find your translation in the answer choices. |
| | | | Is this a translation of the conclusion? |
| | | BACK-UP PLAN | • If yes, choose it.<br>• If no, cross it off.<br>• If you're not sure, leave it for later. |

*Always bracket the conclusion in every argument. It makes life so much easier.*

**CONCLUSION GAME PLAN**

*They are always asking for the main conclusion in Conclusion questions, not an intermediate conclusion.*

The correct answer to a Conclusion question is, you guessed it, the argument's main conclusion. Conclusion questions play to a major strength you've already honed; you should already be identifying the conclusion in every stimulus as part of designing your CLIR.

But the LSAT sometimes uses complex language to make Conclusion questions a little harder. Check out this example:

> *Xena believes that we should reinstate duels as a means of settling our differences. Xena, however, is wrong. Duels bring death and destruction, neither of which are fit for a civilized society.*

**The conclusion is "Xena, however, is wrong," but that might not be the text of the correct answer in a Conclusion question.** Often, the correct answer translates in what Xena was wrong about. Check out all of these possible correct answers:

- Xena is wrong.
- Xena is incorrect in claiming that we should reinstate duels.
- Our society should not reinstate duels.
- Duels should not be reinstated.

Notice how sometimes a correct answer may not even mention Xena! Translation is key. **Always look for a conceptual answer choice match instead of an exact words answer choice match.**

---

### HOW TO ROCK CONCLUSION QUESTIONS

1. **Look back up at the stimulus and bracket the conclusion if you haven't already.**

   Skipping this step to "save time" will result in unnecessary wrong answers.

2. **Translate the conclusion. Repeat that translation to yourself**

   You can't expect the correct answer to always mimic the exact words of the stimulus.

3. **Choose the closest approximation of your translation.**

   Refer back to the exact words of the bracketed conclusion to double check, if needed.

---

## BIGGEST TRAPS

- Sometimes, students just choose something provable on Conclusion questions, instead of looking for a translation of the conclusion. The test makers know about this error. They are likely to insert Inferences and premises into the answer choices and phrase them in simple, inviting language. Don't fall for these answers.

- Students often rush Conclusion questions because they think it's an easy question type and want to "save time." This leads to skimping on the fundamentals and missing completely doable questions.

## REAL CONCLUSION EXAMPLE

*17.2.6*

Engineer:   Some people argue that the world's energy problems could be solved by mining the Moon for helium-3, which could be used for fuel in fusion reactors. But this is nonsense. Even if it were possible to mine the Moon for helium-3, the technology needed to build viable fusion reactors that could use such fuel is at least 50 years away. If the world's energy problems are not solved before then, it will be too late to solve those problems.

The main point of the argument is that

(A)   mining the Moon for helium-3 is currently not feasible

(B)   fusion reactors that are now being planned are not designed to use helium-3 as fuel

(C)   people who advocate mining the Moon for helium-3 do not realize that fusion reactors could be designed to use fuels other than helium-3

(D)   mining the moon for helium-3 is not a possible solution to the world's energy problems

(E)   if the world's energy problems are not solved within the next 50 years, it will be too late to solve those problems

First, translate.

*Some say the world's energy problems could be fixed with helium-3 from the Moon pumped into fusion reactors. But this is nonsense. The helium-3 fusion reactors are 50+ years away and if we don't solve the energy crisis before then, it will be too late.*

The conclusion is "But this is nonsense," but we have to translate a little to figure out exactly what the nonsense is. Let's follow the "this" to find out what it's referring to. "This" typically refers to something that came right before it, so we land on the "some people" assertion in the first sentence, a prime candidate for nonsense. When we apply the nonsense to the first sentence, we see that it's nonsense to think we can solve the world's energy problems with moon rocks:

**CONCLUSION**      The world's energy problems aren't going to be solved with Moon helium-3.

One way around this conclusion is that they only mention the constraints on fusion reactors as limiting the usefulness of mining the Moon. But what if we could use helium-3 for some other energy-producing thing? Then helium-3 could still be useful for the world's energy problems and the "it'll be too late" criticism would be neutralized.

**LOOPHOLE**      What if we could use helium-3 to solve the world's energy problems in some way that doesn't involve fusion reactors?

So we see it's a Conclusion question; all we have to do is find the translation of the conclusion. Awesome! We're looking for something that says helium-3 isn't going to solve the energy problems.

---

> Every LSAT example will include powerful/provable styled answer choices. The answer choices are styled this way to help you learn to notice powerful and provable language.
>
> Powerful language is mint and bolded.
>
> *Provable language is mint and italicized.*

---

**A)**   mining the Moon for helium-3 is currently not feasible

*So we can't currently mine the Moon for helium-3. Is this the conclusion? No, there's nothing about solving the world's energy problems, a key part of the conclusion.* **A**'s *not provable.*

**B)**   fusion reactors that are now being planned are not designed to use helium-3 as fuel

*So the fusion reactors we're planning aren't designed for helium-3. Is this the conclusion? No, this isn't even provable from the stimulus. Definitely not our conclusion.*

**C)**   people who advocate mining the Moon for helium-3 do not realize that fusion reactors could be designed to use fuels other than helium-3

*So Moon advocates don't know that fusion can use other fuels. Is this the conclusion? No,* **C** *isn't provable. Who knows what these people may or may not realize? It's definitely not the conclusion.*

*Notice the powerful language in* **D**. *And it's still the correct answer! This is because* **D** *is conceptually provable. It mimics the stimulus' conclusion almost exactly.*

**D)**   mining the moon for helium-3 is not a possible solution to the world's energy problems

*So mining the moon won't solve the world's energy problems. Is this the conclusion? Yes! This is very close to our translation of the conclusion. Perfect.*

**E)**   if the world's energy problems are not solved within the next 50 years, it will be too late to solve those problems

*So if we don't solve the energy problems in the next 50 years, it'll be too late. Is this the conclusion? No,* **E** *is a premise. Not the correct answer.*

**D** is the correct answer. It's the only answer that resembles our translation of the conclusion.

We'll cap off almost every question type section with one or more Challenge Questions. Complete these Challenge Questions methodically. This is your chance to make sure you understand the strategies associated with each question type before you start your section-based practice.

**If you struggle with any of the Challenge Questions, be sure to check out the Challenge Question Explanations online at elementalprep.com/bonus.**

## CONCLUSION CHALLENGE

*18.4.2*

Zoo director: The city is in a financial crisis and must reduce its spending. Nevertheless, at least one reduction measure in next year's budget, cutting City Zoo's funding in half, is false economy. The zoo's current budget equals less than 1 percent of the city's deficit, so withdrawing support from the zoo does little to help the city's financial situation. Furthermore, the zoo, which must close if its budget is cut, attracts tourists and tax dollars to the city. Finally, the zoo adds immeasurably to the city's cultural climate and thus makes the city an attractive place for business to locate.

Which one of the following is the main conclusion of the zoo director's argument?

(A)   Reducing spending is the only means the city has of responding to the current financial crisis.

(B)   It would be false economy for the city to cut the zoo's budget in half.

(C)   City Zoo's budget is only a very small portion of the city's entire budget.

(D)   The zoo will be forced to close if its budget is cut.

(E)   The city's educational and cultural climate will be irreparably damaged if the zoo is forced to close.

*Where's the answer key?*

You'll find the answer key for all the Challenge Questions at the end of the chapter on page 357.

# Inference

| QUESTION STEM KEYWORDS | | POPULARITY | About 1-2 questions per section |
|---|---|---|---|
| • if the statement above is true / from the statements above <br> • must be true / follows logically <br> • inference <br> • properly inferred / properly be concluded / properly drawn | | WHAT YOU'RE LOOKING FOR | The thing you can prove definitely must be true |
| | | ROLE OF THE INFERENCE | It's the correct answer! YAY! |
| **QUESTION STEM EXAMPLES** | | | |
| If the statement above is true, which one of the following must also be true? <br><br> Which one of the following statements follows logically from the statements above? <br><br> Which one of the following can properly be concluded from the information given above? <br><br> Which one of the following can be properly inferred from the statements above? <br><br> If the statements above are true, which one of the following is an inference that can be properly drawn on the basis of them? | | TL;DR STRATEGY | You already have an Inference. <br><br> Go choose it. |
| | | BACK-UP PLAN | Does this have to be true? <br><br> • If yes, choose it. <br> • If no, cross it off. <br> • If you're not sure, leave it for later. |

### INFERENCE GAME PLAN

The correct answer to an Inference question is the Inference from your CLIR! Yay!

Check out elementalprep.com/bonus for a bonus section on Conditional-Heavy Inference question strategy.

Correct answers to Inference questions are often extremely basic, like "Isn't that too simple?" provable. The correct answer could be a slight rephrase of a premise, or it could underlie a premise, like a spin on a necessary assumption. Remember that **basic, easy, redundant answers are all provable and, hence, desirable on Inference questions**.

### TINY TIPS

- Inference questions are mathematical. The right answer is proven absolutely 100% true.

- When Inference questions follow arguments, the correct answer is often a necessary assumption.

### BIGGEST TRAPS

You can pore over every question explanation in this book and you'll see I never eliminate an answer because it's "too basic." That's because "basic" is a word for PSLs, not LSAT answer choices.

- I often hear students defend their incorrect Inference answers with, "It's not like I actually liked the answer I chose. It's just that the other one was too basic!" This rationale is 100% wrong and will lead you to incorrect answers every time. The "other one" is the correct answer and its basicness is what makes it right.

## REAL INFERENCE EXAMPLE

*20.4.6*

The *Rienzi*, a passenger ship, sank as a result of a hole in its hull, possibly caused by sabotage. Normally, when a holed ship sinks as rapidly as the *Rienzi* did, water does not enter the ship quickly enough for the ship to be fully flooded when it reaches the ocean floor. Full flooding can be achieved, however, by sabotage. Any ship that sinks deep into the ocean when not fully flooded will implode. Deep-sea photographs, taken of the sunken *Rienzi* where it rests on the ocean floor, reveal that the *Rienzi* did not implode.

Which one of the following must be true on the basis of the information above?

 (A)  The *Rienzi* was so constructed as to reduce the risk of sinking by impact.

 (B)  If the *Rienzi* became fully flooded, it did so only after it reached the ocean floor.

 (C)  If the *Rienzi* was not sunk by sabotage, water flooded into it unusually fast.

 (D)  If the *Rienzi* had sunk more slowly, it would have imploded.

 (E)  The *Rienzi* was so strongly constructed as to resist imploding under deep-sea pressure.

First, translate.

*So the Rienzi sank because of a hole in its hull. The hole might have been from sabotage. Usually, a non-sabotage hole doesn't fully flood the ship, but a sabotage hole can fully flood the ship. If a ship isn't fully flooded when it sinks, it implodes. The Rienzi didn't implode.*

For our Inference, we're going to figure out the likely fate of the *Rienzi*. First, we know the *Rienzi* didn't implode, which means it was fully flooded when it sank. We know this from the second to last sentence's conditional: **~fully flood ⟶ implode**. The *Rienzi* didn't implode, so we can activate the contrapositive (**~implode ⟶ fully flood**) and know the *Rienzi* was definitely flooded.

Normally, a non-sabotage hole wouldn't fully flood the ship, but a sabotage hole would. So how did the *Rienzi* get in this predicament? It seems like it was probably sabotaged.

We have to be careful about one thing: How sure are we that the *Rienzi* was sabotaged? We want to stay provable. The premises say the non-sabotage hole "normally" wouldn't fully flood the ship. So it's *possible* that the *Rienzi* sank because of a non-sabotage hole; it just wouldn't be normal. **These are the nitpicky little details you have to be careful about on Provable Questions. The answer choices will prey on you if you gloss over details like "normally."** Abnormal circumstances can happen, so we have to take that into account in our Inference:

> **INFERENCE**  Either the non-sabotage hole is abnormal or the *Rienzi* was sunk by sabotage.

Let's go find our Inference in the answer choices!

**A)**  The *Rienzi* was so constructed as to reduce the risk of sinking by impact.

*So the Rienzi was built to reduce risk of sinking by impact. Do we know this for sure? No, we don't know the intentions behind the Rienzi's design.* **It's always dangerous to speculate about intentions, unless the stimulus is all about intentions.** *The stimulus just doesn't prove* **A**.

**B)**  If the *Rienzi* became fully flooded, it did so only after it reached the ocean floor.

*So if the Rienzi was flooded, it happened after hitting the ocean floor. First off, the Rienzi was fully flooded. We know that because it didn't implode. But according to the stimulus, there's no such thing as flooding once you get to the ocean floor. The Rienzi had to be fully flooded* **before** *it reached the ocean floor to avoid implosion.* **B** *isn't just incorrect; it contradicts the stimulus.*

The margin note reads:

*This stimulus reads like a poorly written spy novel synopsis. The translation really lightens it up.*

❋

Remember Inclusion from Chapter 4? Check back there for help understanding why our Inference's EITHER/OR and C diagram to the same conditional.

**C)** If the *Rienzi* was not sunk by sabotage, water flooded into it unusually fast.

**D)** If the *Rienzi* had sunk more slowly, it would have imploded.

❋

D is another Dormant Conditional like we saw in our Real Strengthen Example. Since Dormant Conditionals aren't activated by the stimulus, they're always wrong. You'll find out more about Dormant Conditionals in Chapter 12, The Answer Choices.

**E)** The *Rienzi* was so strongly constructed as to resist imploding under deep-sea pressure.

*So if it wasn't sabotage, flooding happened abnormally fast. This means the Rienzi is either abnormal or sabotaged, just like our Inference said. C is just a weirdly worded version of our Inference, an if/then version of our Inference's EITHER/OR. Both our Inference and C diagram to ~sabotage ⟶ abnormal. C is provable.*

*So if the Rienzi sank more slowly, it would have imploded. Do we know this for sure? No, we don't know anything about the world where the Rienzi sinks more slowly, so we can't activate this conditional. There is no information from the stimulus to tell us what must be true in that situation. D is not provable.*

*So the Rienzi was just so strong that it was able to not implode. Do we know this for sure? Nah, not according to the stimulus. The stimulus doesn't allow for exceptions to this "if not fully flooded, then implode" conditional rule. There's no way around it for especially strong ships. Also, we have no clue how strong or not strong the Rienzi is. Definitely not provable.*

**C** is the correct answer. It's the only provable option that *has to be* true.

### INFERENCE CHALLENGE

*18.4.6*

People who listen to certain recordings of music are in danger of being unduly influenced by spoken messages that have been recorded backwards on the records or tapes.

A consequence of the view above is that

(A) the spoken messages must be louder than the music on the recordings

(B) backwards messages can be added to a recording while still preserving all of the musical qualities of the recorded performance

(C) the recordings on which such messages appear are chosen for this purpose either because they are especially popular or because they induce a trancelike state

(D) if such messages must be comprehended to exert influence, then people must be able to comprehend spoken messages recorded backwards

(E) when people listen to recorded music, they pay full attention to the music as it plays

*18.4.10*

Almost all of the books published in the past 150 years were printed on acidic paper. Unfortunately, every kind of acidic paper gradually destroys itself due to its very acidity. This process of deterioration can be slowed if the books are stored in a cool, dry environment. Techniques, which are now being developed, to deacidify books will probably be applied only to books with historical significance.

If all of the statements in the passage above are true, which one of the following must also be true?

(A) If a book was published in the past 150 years and is historically insignificant, it will probably deteriorate completely.

(B) Almost all of the books published in the past 150 years will gradually destroy themselves.

(C) Almost all of the books that gradually deteriorate are made of acidic paper.

(D) If a book is of historical significance and was printed before 150 years ago, it will be deacidified.

(E) Books published on acidic paper in 1900 should now all be at about the same state of deterioration.

# Most Strongly Supported (MSS)

## QUESTION STEM KEYWORDS

- the statements above, if true / by the information above
- most strongly supported
- most strongly suggests

## QUESTION STEM EXAMPLES

Which one of the following is most strongly supported by the information above?

The statements above, if true, most strongly support which one of the following?

The information above provides the most support for which one of the following statements?

| | |
|---|---|
| **POPULARITY** | About 1-3 questions per section |
| **WHAT YOU'RE LOOKING FOR** | The thing you can prove is very, very, very likely to be true |
| **ROLE OF THE INFERENCE** | It's more or less the correct answer. Mini-yay. |
| **TL;DR STRATEGY** | You already have an Inference. Go choose it or perhaps a slightly more ambitious approximation of it. |
| **BACK-UP PLAN** | Does this pretty much have to be true? <br>• If yes, choose it. <br>• If no, cross it off. <br>• If you're not sure, leave it for later. |

＊ MSS wants you to choose the most provable option in the answer choice bunch.

## MSS GAME PLAN

**MSS is like a JV Inference question.** It's so similar to Inference that many LSAT prep materials don't even differentiate them. This lack of differentiation mostly works out and things are mostly fine, but there's a crucial difference between Inference and MSS: what you are allowed to accept as the correct answer. **The correct answer to an MSS question does not have to be mathematically proven. It has to be about 95-100% likely to be true.** This means it's very likely to be true, so likely that, if this were not the LSAT, you probably wouldn't question how true it is. You'd just accept it the way reasonable people accept reasonable assertions.

But what's a reasonable assertion? And have any of us ever met a truly reasonable person? Here's an example of a reasonable assertion said by your imaginary friend John, a reasonable person:

> I studied really hard for tomorrow's exam. I did well on all the exams I've studied for in this course, and this exam will be similar to the previous exams. So I infer that I will do well on this exam.

You wouldn't say, "But how can you be sure you won't get test anxiety? How do you know this exam won't be similar in structure to past exams but much more difficult content-wise? How do you know, John?! Hope it's not a logic test. YOUR POINT HASN'T BEEN ADEQUATELY DEMONSTRATED."

This is what the LSAT does to us; it turns us into paranoid crazies. In real life, you'd probably be like, "Yeah, it'll be great." You wouldn't be all caps questioning just how demonstrated John's Inference is, even though all those Loopholes are valid! They do prove John's Inference is not 100%. You'd accept John's Inference because it's reasonable. And that's where MSS questions come in. They let you err on this reasonable person, reasonable position standard.

Don't use this reasonableness standard as an excuse to just do whatever though. You still can't choose Crazy Nonsense. Remember there is only one correct answer in the answer choices. Four of the answer choices do not meet this "very likely to be true" standard.

Here are a few examples of Crazy Nonsense that John could assert:

- I will get the best grade in my class.
- I won't get any questions wrong.
- I will score above the median on this exam.

See the difference between the Crazy Nonsense and John's more provable original Inference ("I will do well on this exam")? "Do well" matched John's premises, so it got more of a pass. The Crazy Nonsense had a bunch of conceptual elements that were absent from John's premises, which made them unprovable. Staying on the provable side of this difference will help you to ace MSS questions.

### TINY TIPS

- **Many correct answers to MSS questions will be 100% properly inferred**, meaning they absolutely must be true. This 95% business is a minimum, not a maximum. If there is a 100% proven answer choice in the bunch, it is correct. Something that's 100% supported by the stimulus will be the most strongly supported answer choice. You'll never see two 100% supported answer choices in MSS or Inference questions.

### BIGGEST TRAPS

Head over to elementalprep.com/bonus for a rollickingly fun deep dive into the differences between the Strengthen and MSS question stems.

- Many test takers chronically confuse MSS and Strengthen questions because both question stems frequently use the word "support." **Don't rush the question stem.** Think about what it means before identifying it. The correct answer to an MSS question is going to be much more provable than the correct answer to a Strengthen question, so this misidentification can be a fatal flaw. But this is a tough mistake to catch on your own. When you're filling in your Wrong Answer Journal, you may still think that it's a Strengthen question, so you aren't going to understand what you did wrong. One piece of advice: If you are very confused about why you're getting a question wrong, check back to see if you really knew the question stem.

## REAL MSS EXAMPLE

### 16.3.5

It is commonly held among marketing experts that in a nonexpanding market a company's best strategy is to go after a bigger share of the market and that the best way to do this is to run comparative advertisements that emphasize weaknesses in the products of rivals. In the stagnant market for food oil, soybean-oil and palm-oil producers did wage a two-year battle with comparative advertisements about the deleterious effect on health of each other's products. These campaigns, however, had little effect on respective market shares; rather, they stopped many people from buying any edible oils at all.

The statements above most strongly support the conclusion that comparative advertisements

(A)   increase a company's market share in all cases in which that company's products are clearly superior to the products of rivals

(B)   should not be used in a market that is expanding or likely to expand

(C)   should under no circumstances be used as a retaliatory measure

(D)   carry the risk of causing a contraction of the market at which they are aimed

(E)   yield no long-term gains unless consumers can easily verify the claims made

First, translate.

*So marketing experts think the best way to increase market share in a non-expanding market is to run comparative negative ads against rivals. Food oil is a non-expanding market. Palm-oil and soybean-oil people did this negative ad strategy against one another. They didn't increase market share; people just stopped buying oils.*

So what can we take away from the food oil war? The marketing experts say comparative ads are the best thing to do in a non-expanding market, but it seems like the oil people did that and all got screwed. There is a clearly demonstrated downside to following the marketing experts' advice. This leads us directly to a provable Inference:

✳ Some test takers are afraid to classify the food oil's "stagnant" market as "non-expanding," but this is 100% OK. The oil market is non-expanding. The word "stagnant" literally means staying the same, not expanding.

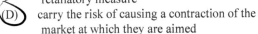

**INFERENCE**      Following the marketing experts' strategy could have a negative consequence.

Now let's look closely at the question stem. It's a normal MSS stem, but it ends in "comparative advertisements" and no punctuation. This means that the answer choices will continue this sentence. Each answer choice has "comparative advertisements" as its implied subject. This stealth fill in the blank plays nicely with our CLIR Inference because the comparative advertisements are the marketing experts' strategy. All we have to do is fill in something like "negative consequence."

**A)**   [Comparative advertisements] increase a company's market share in all cases in which that company's products are clearly superior to the products of rivals

*So comparative ads increase market share when you're superior. Do we know this? No, we don't know that either food oil is clearly superior, so this isn't provable. Since it's not in the stimulus, we don't know what holds in that clearly superior world. **A** isn't a provable answer.*

✳ I'm adding [Comparative advertisements] to the beginning of every answer choice to remind you of the implied subject from the question stem as we evaluate each answer.

**B)**   [Comparative advertisements] should not be used in a market that is expanding or likely to expand

*So don't use comparative ads in expanding/likely to expand markets. Do we know this? No, the marketing experts' advice was only about non-expanding markets. So we don't know anything about what to do in expanding markets. Not provable.*

**C)**  [Comparative advertisements] should under no circumstances be used as a retaliatory measure

So don't use comparative ads as retaliation. Do we know this? No, we don't actually know that anyone was fighting back. For all we know, they started the comparative ads at the same time. We would need a lot more retaliation info in the stimulus to prove **C**.

**D)**  [Comparative advertisements] *carry the risk of causing* a contraction of the market at which they are aimed

So comparative ads could contract the market. Do we know this? Yes! That's exactly the negative consequence that happened in the oil war. The market for food oils ended up contracting because of the comparative ads, and "carry the risk" is super easy to prove. **D** is provable.

**E)**  [Comparative advertisements] *yield no long-term gains unless* consumers can easily verify the claims made

So comparative ads have no long-term gains unless consumers can easily verify them. Do we know this? No, there's nothing about consumers being able to verify stuff in the stimulus, and there's nothing about long-term gains. There's no way to know this for sure. **E** isn't a provable choice.

**D** is the correct answer. It's the only answer the stimulus can prove.

## MSS CHALLENGE

*18.4.24*

The only fossilized bones of large prey found in and around settlements of early humans bear teeth marks of nonhuman predators on areas of the skeleton that had the most meat, and cut marks made by humans on the areas that had the least meat. The predators that hunted large prey invariably ate the meatiest parts of the carcasses, leaving uneaten remains behind.

If the information above is true, it provides the most support for which one of the following?

(A)  Early humans were predators of small prey, not of large prey.

(B)  Early humans ate fruits and edible roots as well as meat.

(C)  Early humans would have been more effective hunters of large prey if they had hunted in large groups rather than individually.

(D)  Early humans were not hunters of large prey but scavenged the uneaten remains of prey killed by other predators.

(E)  Early humans were nomadic, and their settlements followed the migratory patterns of predators of large prey.

*20.1.6*

Besides laying eggs in her own nest, any female wood duck will lay an egg in the nest of another female wood duck if she sees the other duck leaving her nest. Under natural nesting conditions, this parasitic behavior is relatively rare because the ducks' nests are well hidden. However, when people put up nesting boxes to help the ducks breed, they actually undercut the ducks' reproductive efforts. These nesting boxes become so crowded with extra eggs that few, if any, of the eggs in those boxes hatch.

The statements above, if true, most strongly support which one of the following?

(A)  Female wood ducks will establish nests in nest boxes only when natural nesting sites are not available.

(B)  Nesting female wood ducks who often see other female wood ducks are the most successful in their breeding efforts.

(C)  The nesting boxes for wood ducks have less space for eggs than do natural nesting sites.

(D)  The nesting boxes would be more effective in helping wood ducks breed if they were less visible to other wood ducks than they currently are.

(E)  Nesting boxes are needed to supplement the natural nesting sites of wood ducks because of the destruction of much of the ducks' habitat.

# Fill In

| QUESTION STEM KEYWORDS | | POPULARITY | About 0-2 questions per section |
|---|---|---|---|
| • completes | | WHAT YOU'RE LOOKING FOR | The thing you can prove completes the author's thought |
| • concludes | | | |
| • a blank at the end of the stimulus | | ROLE OF THE INFERENCE | It's the correct answer! YAY! |
| **QUESTION STEM EXAMPLES** | | TL;DR STRATEGY | You already have an Inference. Go choose it. |
| Which one of the following most logically completes the argument? | | | Does this have to be true? |
| The conclusion of the argument is strongly supported if which one of the following completes the argument? | | BACK-UP PLAN | • If yes, choose it. <br> • If no, cross it off. <br> • If you're not sure, leave it for later. |

※ Fill In questions always have a blank at the end of the stimulus.

## FILL IN GAME PLAN

**Fill In questions are Inference questions with extra guidance.** You'll design a nice provable Inference, just like you would for any Premise Set, but the stimulus gives you a bit more direction in where to focus your Inference. Your CLIR Inference goes in the blank at the end of the stimulus.

You know that voice in your head as you're reading the stimulus? It's saying the words to you as you read; hopefully it's speaking as you read these words right now. Let that voice keep talking when you hit the blank at the end of the stimulus. **Make sure that voice stays provable**; a provable completion of the last sentence is both your Inference and likely the correct answer. Your Fill In completions must be valid conclusions, just like normal Inferences.

Fill In asks you to put yourself in the author's shoes — whatever the author would say next is what would fill in the blank. That will be the correct answer. But how do you predict what the author would say next? Fill In questions are popular destinations for analogies, which are super predictable. The blank will ask you to continue the analogy and, hence, create an Inference. Let's practice with this simple analogy:

> *Yellow nectarines are much like white peaches. While white peaches get more flavorful with age, their texture suffers. Similarly, a mature yellow nectarine _____.*

So yellow nectarines are similar to white peaches. We get one property of white peaches outlined for us, then a "similarly" to start the next sentence. The "similarly" tells us we can apply this white peach property to yellow nectarines for our Inference. If a mature yellow nectarine is similar to a mature white peach, we know the nectarine will be more flavorful with worse texture. That connection goes in the blank.

※ The stimulus will start a sentence before the blank, so the author gives you the beginning of your Inference! How very neighborly of them.

## TINY TIPS

- **Remember, we always classify stimuli with blanks at the end as Premise Sets, even if there is a conclusion somewhere in the stimulus.** This means that we have to stay provable in our Inference. The boring answer is the correct one.

- Sometimes, Fill Ins will contain a conclusion in another part of the stimulus and the blank will begin with a premise indicator. Follow the same process you would for a normal Inference in this situation. You'll still end up with the correct answer.

## BIGGEST TRAPS

- This thought is a huge problem: "That's too simple. I'm not going to choose it." Students are tempted to overlook correct answers on Fill In questions because they are "too easy" or "too simple." **Correct Fill In answers are supposed to be straightforward. They're supposed to be provable.** Don't overthink yourself out of correct answers.

## REAL FILL IN EXAMPLE

*18.2.18*

The television documentary went beyond the save-the-wildlife pieties of some of those remote from East Africa and showed that in a country pressed for food, the elephant is a pest, and an intelligent pest at that. There appears to be no way to protect East African farms from the voracious foraging of night-raiding elephant herds. Clearly this example illustrates that _____.

Which one of the following most logically completes the paragraph?

- (A) the preservation of wildlife may endanger human welfare
- (B) it is time to remove elephants from the list of endangered species
- (C) television documentaries are incapable of doing more than reiterating accepted pieties
- (D) farmers and agricultural agents should work closely with wildlife conservationists before taking measures to control elephants
- (E) it is unfair that people in any country should have to endure food shortages

First, translate.

*This documentary went beyond the "save the animals" stuff and is showing elephants to be the intelligent East African pests they are. The region is in need of food and there's no way to protect the farms from elephant raids. Therefore...*

The stimulus reveals the dark side of elephants. Apparently, they're stealing food from humans who really need it. This is sad. And even though I wish I could make KILL THE ELEPHANTS the Inference, that wouldn't be remotely provable or defensible.

The stimulus clearly indicates some downsides of the elephants, but it's not telling us what to do to address those downsides. Just because there's a problem doesn't mean we *have to* do anything to solve it. But we do know that a problem exists. So why not just make the problem our Inference?

Therefore... KILL THE ELEPHANTS. Sorry, had to get that out of my system. KILL THE ELEPHANTS is how I complete the blank in my head every time, even though I've done this question approximately 1,200 times and know that KILL THE ELEPHANTS is in no way correct.

By making the Inference this broad, we're more likely to get a hit in the answer choices.

**INFERENCE**    Elephants in East Africa have some downsides.

Remember that the correct answer is going to complete the last sentence of the stimulus. It will be something illustrated by the elephant example, a rephrase of our Inference that makes sense in the blank.

**A)** [This example illustrates that] the preservation of wildlife *may* endanger human welfare

*So preserving wildlife may endanger humans. This is the downside we were talking about!* **A** *sounds like our Inference! Elephants are "wildlife," and elephants eating the humans' food would, indeed, endanger human welfare. Also, notice that provable "may" in the middle to soften* **A** *up.* **A** *is a provable choice.*

**B)** [This example illustrates that] it is time to remove elephants from the list of endangered species

*So we should take elephants off the endangered species list. First off, the stimulus doesn't even tell us elephants are on the endangered species list. Second, we don't know that stealing food from East African farms would be enough to take elephants off the list, if they were on it.* **B**'s *not close to provable.*

**C)** [This example illustrates that] television documentaries are *incapable* of doing more than reiterating accepted pieties

*So TV documentaries can't do more than say pieties. Wasn't the TV documentary mentioned in the stimulus saying more than pieties? That's what the first sentence said.* **C** *is the opposite of provable; it's literally contradicting the stimulus.*

**D)** [This example illustrates that] farmers and agricultural agents should work closely with wildlife conservationists before taking measures to control elephants

*So farmers and wildlife people should work together before trying to control the elephants. The stimulus is pointing toward the threat, not emphasizing caution with the elephants.* **D** *is going in the opposite direction. Also, notice that dangerous "should" in* **D***; there's no recommendation language in the stimulus, so we're on thin ice in terms of provability. Definitely not a provable choice.*

**E)** [This example illustrates that] it is unfair that people in any country should have to endure food shortages

*So it's unfair that people have to endure food shortages. While this may be true in real life, it's not what the stimulus is proving. There's no mention of fairness in the stimulus, so we can't prove anything fair or unfair from what we have to work with.* **E** *has too much judgment, not enough ties to the stimulus. Not provable.*

I added [This example illustrates that] to the beginning of every answer choice to remind you of the phrase before the blank as we evaluate each answer.

**A** is the correct answer. It's the only answer choice that doesn't go too far outside the provable realm of the stimulus.

## Controversy

| QUESTION STEM KEYWORDS | | POPULARITY | About 0-2 questions per section |
|---|---|---|---|
| • point at issue <br> • point of disagreement <br> • disagree <br> • differing opinions | | WHAT YOU'RE LOOKING FOR | The thing you can prove the two speakers disagree about |
| | | ROLE OF THE CONTROVERSY | It's the correct answer. YAY! |
| **QUESTION STEM EXAMPLES** | | TL;DR STRATEGY | You already have a Controversy. <br><br> Go choose it. |
| Max and Shirin disagree over whether <br><br> The statements above provide the most support for holding that Sandra would disagree with Yul about which one the following statements? <br><br> Which one of the following is the point at issue between Aubry and Tai? <br><br> The exchange between JT and Carolina most strongly supports the view that they disagree as to | | BACK-UP PLAN | Does the first speaker have to believe this is true/false? Does the second speaker have to believe this is true/false? <br><br> • If you get different answers to each question, choose it. <br> • If you get the same answer to each question or can't prove what one of the speakers believes, cross it off. <br> • If you're not sure, leave it for later. |

If you are having trouble with Controversy questions and skipped to this section, read the Controversy section of Chapter 8, The CLIR, now. Controversy design is discussed in detail there.

### CONTROVERSY GAME PLAN

The correct answer to a Controversy question is your CLIR Controversy! Yay!

If your Controversy doesn't appear in the answer choices, ask your Back-Up Plan question of every answer choice. You want to find something that you can prove the two speakers disagree about.

### TINY TIPS

- Don't hastily eliminate answer choices that state your Controversy in more specific or general terms than you originally designed. If it's referencing the same idea you are, it's a match.

- Sometimes, the correct Controversy answer is based on one of the speaker's necessary assumptions. They have to believe that necessary assumption, so it substantiates the disagreement. It's totally normal for the Controversy to not be spelled out word for word in both speakers. That's what the Second Speaker Inference is for.

## REAL CONTROVERSY EXAMPLE

*20.1.13*

Yolanda: Gaining access to computers without authorization and manipulating the data and programs they contain is comparable to joyriding in stolen cars; both involve breaking into private property and treating it recklessly. Joyriding, however, is the more dangerous crime because it physically endangers people, whereas only intellectual property is harmed in the case of computer crimes.

Arjun: I disagree! For example, unauthorized use of medical records systems in hospitals could damage data systems on which human lives depend, and therefore computer crimes also cause physical harm to people.

An issue in dispute between Yolanda and Arjun is

(A) whether joyriding physically endangers human lives
(B) whether the unauthorized manipulation of computer data involves damage to private property
(C) whether damage to physical property is more criminal than damage to intellectual property
(D) whether the unauthorized use of computers is as dangerous to people as is joyriding
(E) whether treating private property recklessly is ever a dangerous crime

First, translate.

*Yolanda: Hacking computers is comparable to joyriding because they are both about breaking into things and messing around. Joyriding is more dangerous though because it physically endangers people. Hacking only hurts intellectual property.*

*Arjun: No, hacking hospital records could put people in danger, so hacking also causes physical harm.*

Let's take our Second Speaker Inference, inferring something about what Yolanda said from Arjun's statements. We'll start with Arjun's conclusion: hacking also causes physical harm. Why bring this up? What's Arjun getting at and how does it relate to Yolanda?

Yolanda mentions physical harm too; that could be our link. She says joyriding is more dangerous than hacking because joyriding causes physical harm. Arjun takes a different perspective in his conclusion; he equals out hacking and joyriding in terms of danger (since you can cause physical harm hacking hospital records). This means he doesn't think joyriding is necessarily more dangerous, which leads us to our Second Speaker Inference:

Notice that Possibility ≠ Certainty classic flaw in Arjun's argument? Could Premises ≠ Must Conclusions.

**SECOND SPEAKER INFERENCE**    Therefore... hacking is just as dangerous as joyriding.

This points us straight to our Controversy:

**CONTROVERSY**    whether hacking is just as dangerous as joyriding

Yolanda disagrees with the Controversy; she believes that joyriding is more dangerous than hacking. Arjun agrees with the Controversy; he thinks that joyriding isn't necessarily more dangerous than hacking. Awesome, we're ready to find our Controversy in the answer choices.

**A)** whether joyriding physically endangers human lives

*So whether joyriding is physically dangerous. Arjun never comments on joyriding, and there's no reason to believe he disputes how dangerous it is. Plus, it's not close to our Controversy. Not provable.*

**B)** whether the unauthorized manipulation of computer data involves damage to private property

*So whether hacking damages property. Yolanda basically says this, so she agrees with it. But Arjun doesn't give us enough information to assume he believes hacking doesn't damage private property. If anything, I'd guess that he agrees. Not provable.*

<table>
<tr>
<td>

**C)** whether damage to physical property is more criminal than damage to intellectual property

</td>
<td>

*So whether damaging physical property is more criminal than damaging intellectual property. OK, characterizing things as "more criminal" is generally silly and not in the stimulus — it's not remotely provable. **C** is a tempting wrong answer if you're skimming though; it looks like it has the potential to make sense even though it's borderline gibberish. Not provable.*

</td>
</tr>
<tr>
<td>

**D)** whether the unauthorized use of computers is as dangerous to people as is joyriding

</td>
<td>

*So whether hacking is as dangerous as joyriding. That's our Controversy! We inferred that Arjun thinks hacking is just as dangerous as joyriding, and we know that Yolanda thinks the opposite. We can prove both these things, meaning **D** is a provable Controversy.*

</td>
</tr>
<tr>
<td>

**E)** whether treating private property recklessly is ever a dangerous crime

</td>
<td>

*So whether treating property recklessly is ever dangerous. Yolanda and Arjun agree on **E**. Yolanda says joyriding is dangerous and Arjun says hacking is dangerous. That overlap means they both agree that some form of treating property recklessly is dangerous. **E** isn't a provable Controversy.*

</td>
</tr>
</table>

**D** is the correct answer. It's the only answer that we can prove Yolanda and Arjun disagree on.

## CONTROVERSY CHALLENGE

*20.4.21*

Wirth:   All efforts to identify a gene responsible for predisposing people to manic-depression have failed. In fact, nearly all researchers now agree that there is no "manic-depression gene." Therefore, if these researchers are right, any claim that some people are genetically predisposed to manic-depression is simply false.

Chang:   I do not dispute your evidence, but I take issue with your conclusion. Many of the researchers you refer to have found evidence that a set of several genes is involved and that complex interactions among these genes produce a predisposition to manic-depression.

The point at issue between Wirth and Chang is whether

(A) efforts to identify a gene or set of several genes responsible for predisposing people to manic-depression have all failed

(B) it is likely that researchers will ever be able to find a single gene that predisposes people to manic-depression

(C) nearly all researchers now agree that there is no manic-depression gene

(D) current research supports the claim that no one is genetically predisposed to manic-depression

(E) the efforts made to find a gene that can produce a predisposition to manic-depression were thorough

*Where's the answer key?*

You'll find the answer key for all the Challenge Questions at the end of the chapter on page 357.

# Agreement

| QUESTION STEM KEYWORDS | | POPULARITY | About 0-1 questions per section |
|---|---|---|---|
| | | **WHAT YOU'RE LOOKING FOR** | The thing you can prove the two speakers agree about |
| • agree on<br>• point of agreement<br>• committed to agreeing | | **ROLE OF THE CONTROVERSY** | Agreement questions *hate* Controversies. Anything resembling the Controversy is incorrect. |
| **QUESTION STEM EXAMPLES** | | | You already have a Controversy. |
| | | **TL;DR STRATEGY** | Eliminate any answer choices resembling your Controversy.<br><br>Find something you can infer both speakers believe is true. |
| On the basis of their statements, Jim and Pam are committed to agreeing about which one of the following?<br><br>If Retta and Han are both sincere in what they say, then it can be properly concluded that they agree that | | **BACK-UP PLAN** | Does the first speaker *have to* believe this? Does the second speaker *have to* believe this?<br><br>• If yes to both, choose it.<br>• If no to either, cross it off.<br>• If you're not sure, leave it for later. |

*That "have to believe" part of the Back-Up Plan is really important. You may only know the speakers' opinions on an issue through an Inference.*

## AGREEMENT GAME PLAN

Agreement questions are the Controversy's evil twin. Well, maybe not evil, but they are rare, which makes them kinda startling. They're simple though: The correct answer is just something you can prove the two speakers agree on.

Agreement questions ask you to infer what *both* speakers must believe is true, which means identifying an overlapping belief between the two speakers. Only very rarely will the correct Agreement answer be explicitly stated by both speakers. **The speakers' shared necessary assumption is often the correct answer to an Agreement question.** Sometimes, the correct answer will be stated by one speaker, and you'll be asked to deduce that the other speaker must believe it as well.

I honestly think Agreement questions exist to trick people who aren't reading the question stem closely and will assume it's a Controversy question. Agreement questions are usually differentiated from Controversy questions through the subtraction of three letters (agree vs. **dis**agree, agreement vs. **dis**agreement) in the question stem, so the mistake is super easy to make.

To keep myself from falling for their trap, after reading the question stem, I'll repeat the phrase "Agree… what they agree on" to myself. This burns Agreement into my head. Then I underline the word "agree" in the question stem just to be extra sure. You may call this level of carefulness insane, but I know myself. I'll make a mistake if I coast, and so will you.

**The test makers know Agreement is a more rare question type and that skimmers will see "disagree" instead of "agree." This is why they usually put a Controversy in the answer choices on Agreement questions.** They're hoping you'll choose it because you forget the question type. You'll already have the Controversy on hand when you see it's an Agreement question, so eliminate any answer choices resembling your Controversy.

### TINY TIPS

- As with Controversy questions, you should be careful not to hastily eliminate answer choices because the answer isn't explicitly stated in both speakers. Always try to see the underlying necessary assumptions in each speaker's statement.

### REAL AGREEMENT EXAMPLE

*13.4.7*

Murray:   You claim Senator Brandon has accepted gifts from lobbyists. You are wrong to make this criticism. That it is motivated by personal dislike is shown by the fact that you deliberately avoid criticizing other politicians who have done what you accuse Senator Brandon of doing.

Jane:   You are right that I dislike Senator Brandon, but just because I have not criticized the same failing in others doesn't mean you can excuse the senator's offense.

If Murray and Jane are both sincere in what they say, then it can properly be concluded that they agree that

(A)   Senator Brandon has accepted gifts from lobbyists
(B)   it is wrong for politicians to accept gifts from lobbyists
(C)   Jane's criticism of Senator Brandon is motivated only by personal dislike
(D)   Senator Brandon should be criticized for accepting gifts from lobbyists
(E)   one or more politicians have accepted gifts from lobbyists

**CONTROVERSY**   whether Jane is wrong to criticize Senator Brandon

Don't you get the vibe that Murray is like Brandon's Chief of Staff? And Jane is a young hotshot reporter? I feel like I can picture them having this heated argument in a smoke-filled DC backroom.

First, translate.

*Murray: You say Senator Brandon took gifts, but you're wrong to criticize. You're obviously motivated by personal dislike because you don't call out other politicians who take gifts.*

*Jane: I don't like Senator Brandon, but just because I don't call out other people doesn't mean you can let Senator Brandon slide.*

We have to find the Controversy. For our Second Speaker Inference, what can we infer from Jane's statements about what Murray said? She admits that she doesn't like Senator Brandon, but she doesn't think he's excused by her not criticizing other people. She thinks she's still right to call Senator Brandon out. Taking this one step further, we can infer that Jane doesn't believe she's wrong to criticize. She disagrees with Murray's conclusion ("You are wrong to make this criticism"). That's the Controversy — Murray believes Jane is wrong to criticize; Jane doesn't believe she's wrong.

Now we see that it's an Agreement question. We have to find the unifying necessary assumption underlying both Murray and Jane. We need to find something super basic here — Murray and Jane are pretty firmly at odds.

Where's their common ground? Let's move beyond Senator Brandon. Murray says that it's wrong for Jane to single out Senator Brandon when the problem is widespread. And that widespread problem is our link. Murray says other politicians are taking gifts. Jane says Senator Brandon takes gifts. So according to both of them, *somebody* in politics is taking gifts.

**AGREEMENT**    Some politicians are taking gifts.

Now we're ready to find an approximation of our Agreement in the answer choices. Remember to cross out the Controversy. If either speaker disagrees with an answer choice, it's wrong.

**A)** Senator Brandon has accepted gifts from lobbyists

*So Senator Brandon has taken gifts. While Jane believes Senator Brandon takes gifts, Murray never admits it. We don't have the goods to assume Murray believes Senator Brandon takes gifts, so* **A** *is not a provable agreement.*

**B)** it is wrong for politicians to accept gifts from lobbyists

*So it's wrong for politicians to take gifts. There's nothing in the stimulus about wrongness. The closest we get is Jane calling accepting gifts a "failing," but if you look closely at Murray, he never even uses negatively-charged language to describe accepting gifts. We can't prove they agree on* **B**.

**C)** Jane's criticism of Senator Brandon is motivated only by personal dislike

*So Jane is criticizing only because she doesn't like Senator Brandon. The biggest problem with* **C** *is the word "only." Murray says Jane is motivated by personal dislike, but he never claims that's her* **only** *motivation. Jane admits that she dislikes, but she doesn't concede that the dislike is motivating her. They both believe that Jane dislikes Senator Brandon, but don't be fooled.* **C** *doesn't say "Jane dislikes Senator Brandon." It says that the dislike is her* **only** *motivation, and that's way too powerful.*

**D)** Senator Brandon should be criticized for accepting gifts from lobbyists

*So Senator Brandon should be criticized for taking gifts. This is the closest answer choice to our Controversy. Even though it's not exactly the same, it's close enough to eliminate quickly. Jane thinks Senator Brandon should be criticized, and Murray would likely err on the side of saying he shouldn't be criticized. It's not a perfect Controversy, but it's definitely not a provable agreement.*

**E)** one or more politicians have accepted gifts from lobbyists

*So some politicians are taking gifts. Awesome! We found the common ground between the speakers. Jane thinks Senator Brandon (and likely others) are taking gifts and Murray admits there are "other politicians who have done what you accuse the Senator of doing." It's a provable agreement.*

**E** is the correct answer. It's the only answer choice that we can prove both speakers agree on.

## Necessary Assumption (NA)

| QUESTION STEM KEYWORDS | | |
|---|---|---|
| • Any necessary condition indicator: <br> • necessary / depends / required / relies <br> • assumes / assumption <br> • the conclusion does not follow unless | | |

| | POPULARITY | About 2-4 questions per section |
|---|---|---|
| | WHAT YOU'RE LOOKING FOR | The thing you can prove **must** be true, if the conclusion is true |
| | ROLE OF THE LOOPHOLE | The correct answer is the negated version of the Loophole. |

| QUESTION STEM EXAMPLES | | |
|---|---|---|
| The argument assumes which one of the following? | | You already have a Loophole. |
| Which one of the following is an assumption required by the argument? | TL;DR STRATEGY | Negate your Loophole. It is now a necessary assumption. |
| Which one of the following is an assumption on which the argument relies? | | Go find it in the answer choices. |
| The argument depends on assuming that | BACK-UP PLAN | If the conclusion is true, does this **have to be true**? <br> • If yes, choose it. <br> • If no, cross it off. <br> • If you're not sure, leave it for later. |

If you're having trouble with Necessary Assumption questions and skipped here looking for help, head back to Chapter 5, Assumptions & the Loophole, now! There's a ton of content there to help you out.

### NECESSARY ASSUMPTION GAME PLAN

You'll already have the Loophole ready, so you're in a great spot when you see it's NA. Negate your Loophole to form a necessary assumption, look for that necessary assumption in the answer choices, and choose it!

But what if your Loophole isn't the one they decided to test in this particular set of answer choices? You can still get the question right. **Just ask every answer choice, "Does this have to be true?"** I do this on literally every necessary assumption answer choice I read and it never steers me wrong. When I cross something out on NA, I always say, "That doesn't have to be true" as my justification for crossing it out. NA really is that simple.

NA is my favorite question type. It's the most elegant, exacting form of argumentative critique. It's perfect.

### TINY TIPS

- Look for necessary indicators in the question stem to tell you it's an NA question.

- NA fills in gaps in the premises. The conclusion needs those premises to add up.

### BIGGEST TRAPS

- Mixing up sufficient and necessary assumptions is a super common error. **I want to keep you from choosing sufficient assumptions in NA questions.** So, I'm going to show you how NA questions have much more in common with Inference questions than with Sufficient Assumption (SA) questions. That way, if you confuse NA with something else, at least it will be something that won't lure you into wrong answers.

## 3 REASONS INFERENCE AND NECESSARY ASSUMPTION ARE BEST BUDS

**1.** Both their correct answers live in the *provable* necessary condition.

*The correct answer to an Inference question lives in the necessary condition:*

$$\text{stimulus true} \longrightarrow \text{Inference true}$$

*The correct answer to an NA question also lives in the necessary condition:*

$$\text{conclusion valid} \longrightarrow \text{NA true}$$

**2.** Both their conditional diagrams are activated in almost exactly the same way.

*On the Inference diagram, we always activate the sufficient condition of "stimulus true." Since we always assume the facts of the stimulus are true, we don't really think about it much. That's why we just say, "What has to be true?" when we talk about Inferences. But we're also assuming the stimulus is true on NA questions. So really the diagram for NA is:*

$$\begin{array}{c}\text{stimulus true} \\ + \\ \text{conclusion valid}\end{array} \longrightarrow \text{NA true}$$

*The real difference between NA and Inference: NA cares about the conclusion.*

**3.** NA is Inference's more mature sibling.

*NA is like Inference+. It's a hyper-Inference. An Inference for arguments. It's got extra baggage, but, at its core, NA is something that must be true given a particular sufficient condition, just like an Inference.*

So! I have subjected you to this list for one reason (actually two, the second reason is that I think it's cool): **If you are going to confuse NA with something, confuse it with its best bud Inference, not SA.** If you confuse NA with Inference, you will still get the question right. If you confuse NA with SA, you will likely get the question wrong.

## REAL NECESSARY ASSUMPTION EXAMPLE

*15.2.23*

No computer will ever be able to do everything that some human minds can do, for there are some problems that cannot be solved by following any set of mechanically applicable rules. Yet computers can only solve problems by following some set of mechanically applicable rules.

Which one of the following is an assumption on which the argument depends?

 (A) At least one problem solvable by following some set of mechanically applicable rules is not solvable by any human mind.

 (B) At least one problem not solvable by following any set of mechanically applicable rules is solvable by at least one human mind.

 (C) At least one problem solvable by following some set of mechanically applicable rules is solvable by every human mind.

(D) Every problem that is solvable by following more than one set of mechanically applicable rules is solvable by almost every human mind.

(E) Every problem that is solvable by following at least one set of mechanically applicable rules is solvable by at least one human mind.

First, translate.

*Computers are never going to be able to do everything some human minds can. This is because some problems can't be solved with mechanical rules and computers can only solve with mechanical rules.*

There's a big hole here. They never specify what "some human minds" can do; that's the dangling variable in the conclusion. They're just saying that since computers can only do this mechanistic rule stuff, they'll never be able to do what some human minds can do. But where did some human minds come from? They're assuming that some humans are capable of more than mechanical rules. Don't let them get away with this thought crime.

What if human minds can only solve problems with mechanical rules too? That would be a devastating; it would means computers and humans could be equal.

Circle the dangling variable in this stimulus before reading the accompanying explanation. What's the new idea in the conclusion?

**LOOPHOLE**     What if human minds can only solve mechanical problems?

Since it's an NA question, we negate the Loophole to get our necessary assumption. Our devastating Loophole can't be true, so it can't be true that the humans are only capable of mechanical stuff. That means that we need at least some humans to be capable of more. We need some humans to be able to solve more than just mechanical problems. Awesome, got it:

**NECESSARY**       Some human minds can solve more than just mechanical problems.
**ASSUMPTION**

This has to be true. If this weren't true, humans and computers would be equal, and the argument would fall apart. Now that we have our necessary assumption locked down, let's head to the answer choices. Some of these answer choices are really wordy, but once you translate them, their fate will become clear.

**A)** *At least one* problem solvable by following *some* set of mechanically applicable rules is not solvable by *any* human mind.

*So there's a mechanical problem out there that no human can solve. Does this have to be true? No, we need non-mechanical problems that humans can solve.* **A** *is talking about human limitation when we need human ability.* **A** *doesn't have to be true.*

**B)** *At least one* problem not solvable by following *any* set of mechanically applicable rules is solvable by *at least one* human mind.

*So there's a non-mechanical problem that a human can solve. Does this have to be true? Yes! This is telling us that some humans are capable of more than computers, exactly what we need. It's almost exactly our negated Loophole, and it's got the "at least one"s at the beginning and end of the answer choice, which are major provability boosts.* **B** *has to be true.*

**C)** *At least one* problem solvable by following *some* set of mechanically applicable rules is solvable by *every* human mind.

*So there's a mechanical problem that every human mind can solve. Does this have to be true? No,* **C** *says humans can do mechanical problems, and we need humans solving non-mechanical problems. We need to place human ability above computer ability.* **C** *isn't provable.*

**D)** *Every* problem that is solvable by following more than one set of mechanically applicable rules is solvable by *almost every* human mind.

*So almost every human can solve every mechanical problem that uses more than one set of rules. Does this have to be true? No, it's way too powerful. That "more than one set of rules" thing pushes* **D** *even further outside of what the stimulus can prove. And again, we don't need humans to be able to solve mechanical problems. Not a provable choice.*

**E)** *Every* problem that is solvable by following *at least one* set of mechanically applicable rules is solvable by *at least one* human mind.

*So at least one human can solve every mechanical problem. Does this have to be true? No, it's still linking humans to the wrong kind of problems.* **E** *is the more provable version of* **D**, *but it's still misdirected. We don't need humans to solve mechanical problems; we need them solving non-mechanical problems. Not provable.*

These first three answer choices are difficult because of their wordiness, but once you translate them and see what they're actually saying, **A** and **C** become a lot less attractive.

**B** is the correct answer. It is the only answer that *has to be true.*

## NECESSARY ASSUMPTION CHALLENGE

*16.3.12*

The retina scanner, a machine that scans the web of tiny blood vessels in the retina, stores information about the pattern formed by the blood vessels. This information allows it to recognize any pattern it has previously scanned. No two eyes have identical patterns of blood vessels in the retina. A retina scanner can therefore be used successfully to determine for any person whether it has ever scanned a retina of that person before.

The reasoning in the argument depends upon assuming that

 (A)   diseases of the human eye do not alter the pattern of blood vessels in the retina in ways that would make the pattern unrecognizable to the retina scanner

 (B)   no person has a different pattern of blood vessels in the retina of the left eye than in the retina of the right eye

(C)   there are enough retina scanners to store information about every person's retinas

(D)   the number of blood vessels in the human retina is invariant, although the patterns they form differ from person to person

(E)   there is no person whose retinas have been scanned by two or more different retina scanners

*15.3.12*

Proponents of organic farming claim that using chemical fertilizers and pesticides in farming is harmful to local wildlife. To produce the same amount of food, however, more land must be under cultivation when organic farming techniques are used than when chemicals are used. Therefore, organic farming leaves less land available as habitat for local wildlife.

Which one of the following is an assumption on which the author's argument depends?

(A)   Chemical fertilizers and pesticides pose no health threat to wildlife.

(B)   Wildlife living near farms where chemicals are used will not ingest any food or water containing those chemicals.

(C)   The only disadvantage to using chemicals in farming is their potential effect on wildlife.

(D)   The same crops are grown on organic farms as on farms where chemicals are used.

 (E)   Land cultivated by organic farming methods no longer constitutes a habitat for wildlife.

*Where's the answer key?*

You'll find the answer key for all the Challenge Questions at the end of the chapter on page 357.

## Method

| QUESTION STEM KEYWORDS | POPULARITY | About 0-2 questions per section |
| --- | --- | --- |
| | WHAT YOU'RE LOOKING FOR | A provable description of what happened in the stimulus |
| • argument proceeds by<br>• argumentative technique<br>• method of reasoning<br>• strategy of argumentation<br>• responds by<br>• describes | ROLE OF THE LOOPHOLE OR CONTROVERSY | You have to know what happened in the Argument to design your Loophole or Controversy. The correct answer to a Method question is just what happened in fancy words. |
| **QUESTION STEM EXAMPLES**<br><br>Which one of the following most accurately describes how the argument proceeds?<br><br>Of the following, which one most accurately describes Tom's strategy of argumentation? | TL;DR STRATEGY | You have a Loophole or a Controversy, so you know what happened.<br><br>Go find an answer choice that describes what happened. |
| The relationship of Denise's response to Malcolm's argument is that Denise's response<br><br>Wendell responds to Domenick's argument by | BACK-UP PLAN | Did this happen?<br><br>• If yes, choose it.<br>• If no, cross it off.<br>• If you're not sure, leave it for later. |

**METHOD GAME PLAN**

Method questions ask you to describe what happened in the stimulus in abstract terms. This is perfect! You already designed your Loophole, so you know the stimulus well enough to describe it.

When you see it's a Method question, bring your knowledge of the stimulus to the forefront. Look back over the stimulus and describe to yourself how the argument arrived at its conclusion. Method questions don't want you to be creative. **When you're choosing an answer, you have to be sure of one thing: It actually happened.**

You may be wondering, "I *really* just have to describe what happened in the stimulus? What's the catch?" The catch is one thing: language. **Method questions have some of the wordiest answer choices in all of LR.**

That's why there's a big word list on the next page. The Method Vocab List is filled with words you'll see in Method answer choices. If you're unsure about *any* of these words, memorize the definition. **You can't just "kinda get the gist" of these words.** You need to feel ultra-comfortable, like you could use the phrase in a sentence *easily*. If it's not *easy* to use, you don't know it well enough for the LSAT. As you go over this list, highlight the words you don't know to differentiate them from the rest.

# THE METHOD VOCAB LIST

| VEXING WORDS | WHAT THEY MEAN |
|---|---|
| qualify/qualified | to limit a claim, qualified claims are limited to make them more provable |
| implicit premise | assumption |
| suggests its conclusion is incorrect | says the facts of the conclusion are not true |
| questions the adequacy of a conclusion | says the conclusion has not been proven |
| inconsistent | contradicts |
| phenomenon/phenomena | a thing! or things! |
| drawing a distinction | pointing out a difference between two things |
| an instance | a specific example of something being discussed |
| refute | tear down someone else's argument |
| appeals to | looks to something to support their point |
| purported | something that is claimed to be true, but probably not true, usually used to throw shade |
| apply | to be relevant, if something doesn't apply, it shouldn't be used in the argument |
| significant | enough to matter |
| corresponding | a similar thing in another situation |
| disanalogous | not similar |
| (pre)supposition/(pre)suppose | assumption/assume |
| counterargument | an argument against a given point |
| counter assertions | make an argument against something |
| proposition | statement |
| supposed (pronounced *suppose-ED*, like "suppose" + the beginning of "education") | poorly assumed, usually used to throw shade |
| treats an X as a Y | pretends that X is Y |
| scope | the world of whatever you're talking about |

Believe it or not, this is the abridged version of the Method Vocab list. There are many more potentially confusing words. If you didn't *really* know three (or more) of the words listed here, visit elementalprep.com/bonus for the complete, uncut Method Vocab List.

Start using these words (at least in your head) throughout your daily life as you study for the LSAT. If you want this level of language to not feel foreign, you have to use it. These are all words you're going to be expected to use in law school, so you might as well internalize them now.

**Any ambiguity in the meaning of these words is an opening for the test makers to exploit you.** You must be very confident that you know what Method answer choices mean in order to resist the most tempting wrong answers. You may feel like you *basically* know what these phrases mean, but basically is not enough.

### TINY TIPS

- You are literally asking, "Did this happen?" to every answer choice. Method is that simple.

- You need confidence in your knowledge of the stimulus. When an answer choice says something happened in the stimulus and you don't remember it happening, you have to trust your memory instead of thinking, "Oh, maybe I'm wrong…" **You're probably not wrong. Any given answer choice has an 80% chance of being wrong. Unless you're missing 20+ questions per untimed LR section, you're mathematically more likely to be correct than any random answer choice. Trust yourself, not the answers.**

### BIGGEST TRAPS

- Wordy Method answers confuse test takers to lure them into bad decisions. Translate to avoid mistakes.

### REAL METHOD EXAMPLE

*16.3.25*

The government has no right to tax earnings from labor. Taxation of this kind requires the laborer to devote a certain percentage of hours worked to earning money for the government. Thus, such taxation forces the laborer to work, in part, for another's purpose. Since involuntary servitude can be defined as forced work for another's purpose, just as involuntary servitude is pernicious, so is taxing earnings from labor.

The argument uses which one of the following argumentative techniques?

(A) deriving a general principle about the rights of individuals from a judgment concerning the obligations of governments

(B) inferring what will be the case merely from a description of what once was the case

(C) inferring that since two institutions are similar in one respect, they are similar in another respect

(D) citing the authority of an economic theory in order to justify a moral principle

(E) presupposing the inevitability of a hierarchical class system in order to oppose a given economic practice

*Don't let the crazy vocab in this stimulus get to you. "Pernicious" just means harmful.*

OK, first translate.

*The government doesn't have the right to tax labor earning because the laborer has to work partly for the government. This means they're partly working for another's purpose. Involuntary servitude can be defined as working for another's purpose. Involuntary servitude is pernicious, so taxes are too.*

There's a lot going on here! First, identify the main conclusion. It's the first sentence ("The government has no right to tax earnings from labor"). That's what the rest of the argument is proving, despite the tricky conclusion indicators introducing the intermediate conclusions.

But there's a dangling variable! Notice how there's no mention of having a right to do anything in the premises. The closest we get is the last sentence calling taxes pernicious, but what if the government can still do pernicious things? That leads us straight to our Loophole:

**LOOPHOLE**    What if the government has the right to do pernicious things?

I see it's a Method question, so I have to describe the stimulus. The stimulus established similarities ("involuntary servitude" and "taxing earnings from labor") to say a quality of one thing must apply to the other (involuntary servitude is pernicious, so taxes are too). That's all we need heading into the answer choices — two things are similar, so a property of one applies to the other. Got it.

| | | |
|---|---|---|
| **A)** | deriving a general principle about the rights of individuals from a judgment concerning the obligations of governments | *So deriving a general rule about individual rights from judgments about government obligations. Did this happen? No. There's no general rule about the rights of individuals in the stimulus. The conclusion was about what the government doesn't have a right to do. That knocks **A** out. Not provable.* |
| **B)** | inferring what will be the case merely from a description of what once was the case | *So inferring what will happen from a description of what happened before. Did this happen? Nah, there's nothing about past to future in the stimulus. Not provable.* |
| **C)** | inferring that since two institutions are similar in one respect, they are similar in another respect | *Inferring that since two institutions are similar in one way they're similar in another way. Did this happen? Yeah, it matches what we said about similarity! It covers the two similar things and transferring a property from one to the other. It's conceptually provable.* |
| **D)** | citing the authority of an economic theory in order to justify a moral principle | *So referencing an economic theory's authority to justify a moral rule. Did this happen? No! Where was the economic theory? Where was the moral rule? Nowhere. Don't let them trick you into making **D** fit. None of this stuff happened.* |
| **E)** | presupposing the inevitability of a hierarchical class system in order to oppose a given economic practice | *So assuming an inevitable class hierarchy to go against an economic practice. **E** makes me so happy. It's wrong, but oh so right. Did this happen? No! Don't let yourself go off the deep end thinking about how labor and taxes could somehow relate to a hierarchical class system. **The correct answer works for you; you don't work for it. E** is so not provable. Cross it off and feel amazing about it.* |

*"derive" = conclusion*
*"from" = premises*

Break difficult answer choices into bite-sized pieces. Translate those pieces. Don't try to evaluate confusing answer choices all at once.

Was this particular Method example chosen just because of my irrational love for answer choice **E**? One guess.

**C** is the correct answer. It's the only answer choice that describes the stimulus.

## METHOD CHALLENGE

*18.2.5*

From a magazine article:    Self-confidence is a dangerous virtue: it often degenerates into the vice of arrogance. The danger of arrogance is evident to all who care to look. How much more humane the twentieth century would have been without the arrogant self-confidence of a Hitler or a Stalin!

The author attempts to persuade by doing all of the following EXCEPT

(A)    using extreme cases to evoke an emotional response
(B)    introducing value-laden terms, such as "vice"
(C)    illustrating the danger of arrogance
(D)    appealing to authority to substantiate an assertion
(E)    implying that Hitler's arrogance arose from self-confidence

*Where's the answer key?*

You'll find the answer key for all the Challenge Questions at the end of the chapter on page 357.

## Argument Part

| QUESTION STEM KEYWORDS | | POPULARITY | About 0-2 questions per section |
|---|---|---|---|
| • role in the argument<br>• functions in the argument<br>• argument part<br>• the reference to / the statement that<br>• quoting a phrase from the stimulus | | WHAT YOU'RE LOOKING FOR | A provable description of what the phrase is doing in the argument |
| | | ROLE OF THE LOOPHOLE | You already know the argument parts because you designed the Loophole. |
| QUESTION STEM EXAMPLES | | TL;DR STRATEGY | Go back up to the stimulus and bracket the phrase they mention in the question stem.<br><br>Identify the argument part before looking at the answer choices.<br><br>Find an approximation of the argument part in the answer choices. |
| The reference to the complaint of several centuries ago that powerful memory and extemporaneous eloquence were being destroyed plays which one of the following roles in the argument?<br><br>The statement that the law should require explicit safety labels on toys serves which one of the following functions in the consumer advocate's argument? | | BACK-UP PLAN | Is this what the phrase is doing?<br><br>• If yes, choose it.<br>• If no, cross it off.<br>• If you're not sure, leave it for later. |

**ARGUMENT PART GAME PLAN**

Argument Part question stems provide you with a phrase from the stimulus and ask which part of the argument that phrase is. You're totally prepared for Argument Part. It's your the opportunity to reap the rewards of all your CLIR argument part outlining.

Argument Part answer choices can go two directions. The answer choices could use the argument part category words we're used to, like premise and conclusion. It's awesome when this happens. But sometimes, the test makers use the formal descriptive language you'll find in Method answer choices instead. This means they want you to explain what the phrase was doing the long way. You'll see answer choices like:

| VEXING ANSWER LANGUAGE | WHAT IT MEANS |
|---|---|
| It is used to call into question... | It's given as evidence to call someone out... |
| It is offered as support for... | It's a premise or intermediate conclusion... |
| It functions as an analogue for... | It's similar to something else (half of an analogy)... |

**Stick close to the stimulus.** As you evaluate each answer choice, ask yourself, "Is this what the phrase is doing?"

1. **Look back up at the stimulus and bracket the quoted phrase. Figure out which argument part it is before reading the answer choices.**

   Skipping this step to "save time" will result in unnecessary wrong answers.

2. **Once you know the argument part, find an answer choice that describes that argument part.**

   Keep all the answer choices that look remotely reasonable. Two answers will often begin the same way (as in "It's a premise supporting the conclusion that...") and then differentiate themselves in the second half. You may have to identify a whole other argument part to make sure the second half of the answer matches as well.

## TINY TIPS

- **"For" is a premise indicator.** Everyone forgets about "for," but it can be a game changer on difficult Argument Part questions.

- Argument Part questions often quiz you on the difference between a main conclusion and an intermediate conclusion. If you are unclear on the difference between main conclusions and intermediate conclusions, take a second look at Chapter 2, Arguments & Inferences, now.

- Refer to the Method Vocab List for help decoding wordy Argument Part answer choices.

## BIGGEST TRAPS

- Students often get too creative on Argument Part. Don't critique how the author *should have* used the phrase. Describe what they actually did.

**REAL ARGUMENT PART EXAMPLE**

First, translate.

*15.3.11*

Consumer advocate:   The toy-labeling law should require manufacturers to provide explicit safety labels on toys to indicate what hazards the toys pose. The only labels currently required by law are labels indicating the age range for which a toy is intended. For instance, a "three and up" label is required on toys that pose a choking hazard for children under three years of age. Although the current toy-labeling law has indeed reduced the incidence of injuries to children from toys, parents could prevent such injuries almost entirely if toy labels provided explicit safety information.

The statement that the law should require explicit safety labels on toys serves which one of the following functions in the consumer advocate's argument?

(A)   It is a general principle supporting the conclusion of the argument.
(B)   It is a proposed compromise between two conflicting goals.
(C)   It is the conclusion of the argument.
(D)   It is evidence that must be refuted in order to establish the conclusion of the argument.
(E)   It is a particular instance of the general position under discussion.

*We should make toy safety labels say exactly what is dangerous. Right now, they just have to put an age range, like a 3+ label for toys that could choke kids under three. That's prevented some toy injuries, but if the labels provided specific information, parents could prevent injuries almost entirely.*

They're trying to prove that we should make these detailed labels mandatory. My issue with the stimulus is the jump from "parents could prevent such injuries almost entirely" to making the explicit safety information mandatory. Just because the parent *could* prevent almost all injuries with the information doesn't mean that they actually would. Some negligent parents may respond better to the age range labels because they don't watch their kids closely or read detailed labels. This leads us to our Loophole:

**LOOPHOLE**      What if some parents won't read the detailed safety warnings but do abide by the age range warnings?

The question stem is asking us which part of the argument "the law should require explicit safety labels on toys" is. Well, we already identified the conclusion, and this phrase matches! Look back up at the stimulus and bracket the first sentence if you haven't already. OK, awesome. We're going to look for an answer choice that says something approximating "main conclusion."

**A)**   It is a general principle supporting the conclusion of the argument.

*Is it a principle that supports the conclusion? No. It's the conclusion itself.*

**B)**   It is a proposed compromise between two conflicting goals.

*Is it a compromise between two goals? No, there are no conflicting goals in the stimulus and it's not a compromise.*

**C)**   It is the conclusion of the argument.

*Is it the conclusion? Yes! Exactly what we're looking for.*

**D)** It is evidence that must be refuted in order to establish the conclusion of the argument.

*Is it going against the conclusion? No, it is the conclusion.*

**E)** It is a particular instance of the general position under discussion.

*Is it an example of the general position we're talking about? No, it's the conclusion.*

**C** is the correct answer. It's the only answer that calls out the correct argument part.

## ARGUMENT PART CHALLENGE

*15.2.14*

Pedigreed dogs, including those officially classified as working dogs, must conform to standards set by organizations that issue pedigrees. Those standards generally specify the physical appearance necessary for a dog to be recognized as belonging to a breed but stipulate nothing about other genetic traits, such as those that enable breeds originally developed as working dogs to perform the work for which they were developed. Since dog breeders try to maintain only those traits specified by pedigree organizations, and traits that breeders do not try to maintain risk being lost, certain traits like herding ability risk being lost among pedigreed dogs. Therefore, pedigree organizations should set standards requiring working ability in pedigreed dogs classified as working dogs.

The phrase "certain traits like herding ability risk being lost among pedigreed dogs" serves which one of the following functions in the argument?

(A) It is a claim on which the argument depends but for which no support is given.
(B) It is a subsidiary conclusion used in support of the main conclusion.
(C) It acknowledges a possible objection to the proposal put forth in the argument.
(D) It summarizes the position that the argument as a whole is directed toward discrediting.
(E) It provides evidence necessary to support a claim stated earlier in the argument.

*Where's the answer key?*

You'll find the answer key for all the Challenge Questions at the end of the chapter on page 357.

## The Flaws   LET'S DESCRIBE BAD THINGS

Flaw is the most popular question type in Logical Reasoning. This is great because it's also probably the question type you're most prepared for (and also one of the most fun). There are *a lot* of Flaw questions, so it's worth investigating their nuances. Up to 10% of your LSAT score could be determined by your Flaw question performance.

**There are two flavors of Flaw question: Classic Flaw and Loophole Flaw. Both flavors ask you to describe a flaw in the argument, but they execute that mandate differently.**

**Classic Flaw questions ask for a *general* description of what the argument did wrong.** The correct answer is usually a description of a classic flaw, the ones you learned about in the Classic Flaws Chapter. You'll see language similar to what you find in Method answer choices, but Classic Flaw answer choices reliably translate to known classic flaws, like circular reasoning and overgeneralization. The answer choices are difficult to understand, but super predictable.

**Loophole Flaw questions ask for an *argument-specific* description of the Loophole.** Loophole Flaw doesn't use general descriptive language; it's specific to the language of the stimulus because it always references your stimulus-specific Loophole, not a general classic flaw. For example, in a stimulus about alligators, Loophole Flaw answer choices will likely mention the alligators instead of "presupposing what you seek to establish." Loophole Flaw is both a question type and an answer choice type. Loophole Flaw answer choices often invade Classic Flaw question stems.

The Loophole Flaw question stem is very similar to the Classic Flaw question stem, except for one key addition: a Loophole Flaw Prefix. The Loophole Flaw Prefix, which we'll explain in detail soon, tells you that the stimulus' problem was overlooking an argument-specific Loophole, not something cookie-cutter like Bad Conditional Reasoning.

Loophole Flaw Prefixes can also appear at the beginning of answer choices. When one is present at the start of an answer choice, you have the option to go the stimulus-specific Loophole route instead of the general Classic Flaw route.

# Classic Flaw

| QUESTION STEM KEYWORDS | POPULARITY | About 3-5 questions per section |
|---|---|---|

<table>
<tr><td rowspan="2">

**QUESTION STEM KEYWORDS**

- flaw / flawed
- most vulnerable to criticism on the grounds that it
- questionable technique employed
- the reasoning in the argument / the reasoning above
</td><td>

**WHAT YOU'RE LOOKING FOR**
</td><td>

A provable description of what the argument did wrong
</td></tr>
<tr><td>

**ROLE OF THE LOOPHOLE**
</td><td>

Classic flaws are just fancy, predictable Loopholes. The correct answer to a Classic Flaw question is your classic flaw Loophole.
</td></tr>
<tr><td rowspan="2">

**QUESTION STEM EXAMPLES**

The reasoning in the argument is most vulnerable to criticism on the grounds that the argument

Which one of the following most accurately describes a flaw in the reasoning of the argument?

Which one of the following is a questionable technique employed by the producer in responding to the critic?
</td><td>

**TL;DR STRATEGY**
</td><td>

You already have a Loophole; hopefully, it was formed around one of the classic flaws.

Go find an answer choice that describes this classic flaw.
</td></tr>
<tr><td>

**BACK-UP PLAN**
</td><td>

Is this what's wrong with the argument?

- If yes, choose it.
- If no, cross it off.
- If you're not sure, leave it for later.
</td></tr>
</table>

## CLASSIC FLAW GAME PLAN

**Classic Flaw is a seemingly omnipresent question type.** And you already know all about the classic flaws! The Classic Flaws Chapter incorporated them into your initial understanding of argumentation, so you have a natural leg up on the competition. You've been calling out classic flaws in your CLIR Loopholes, cementing Classic Flaw questions 100% into your wheelhouse.

The correct answer to a Classic Flaw question describes where the stimulus went wrong. You must find the argumentative choice that secured their downfall. If your Loophole did not identify a classic flaw, don't fret. Many Classic Flaw questions have Loophole Flaw answer choices mixed in. When you can't identify a classic flaw in the stimulus, your Loophole is often all you need.

One Classic Flaw curveball: recognizing how each of the classic flaws is expressed in the answer choices. Just like Method, the wordiness level on Classic Flaw answer choices can be high. Luckily, Classic Flaw is very predictable. The Amazing Flaw Chart is here to make Classic Flaw answer choices not half bad:

If you are having trouble with Classic Flaw questions, head back to Chapter 7, The Classic Flaws. All of the classic flaws are explained in detail there!

## THE AMAZING FLAW CHART

| CLASSIC FLAW | ANSWER CHOICE EXAMPLE | ANSWER CHOICE KEYWORDS |
|---|---|---|
| Bad Conditional Reasoning | "mistakes something that is necessary to bring about a situation for something that in itself is enough to bring about that situation" | • necessary / precondition / required <br> • sufficient / enough / ensure |
| Bad Causal Reasoning | "mistakes the cause of a particular phenomenon for the effect of that phenomenon" | • effect / result & cause / causal <br> • two things occur in conjunction <br> • one thing happens after another |
| Whole-to-Part / Part-to-Whole | "assuming that because something is true of each of the parts of a whole it is true of the whole itself" | • individual member of a group <br> • parts of a whole <br> • group as a whole |
| Overgeneralization | "makes a sweeping generalization... based on evidence drawn from a limited number of atypical cases" | • generalizing illegitimately <br> • few instances to all instances <br> • particular case / atypical cases |
| Survey Problems | "uses evidence drawn from a small sample that may well be unrepresentative" | • small / biased / unrepresentative sample |
| Possibility ≠ Certainty | "confuses an absence of evidence for a hypothesis with the existence of evidence against the hypothesis" | • merely possible... actual <br> • probably true... certainty <br> • has not been shown... not true |
| False Dichotomy | "assumes without warrant that a situation allows only two possibilities" | • excludes alternative explanation <br> • only two possibilities |
| Straw Man | "misdescribing the... position, thereby making it easier to challenge" | • misdescribes <br> • easier to challenge |
| Ad Hominem | "rejects a claim by attacking the proponents of the claim rather than addressing the claim itself" | • impugns / questions / attacks <br> • character / motives of proponents <br> • source argument |
| Circular Reasoning | "presupposes what it sets out to prove" | • presupposes what it seeks to establish <br> • restates claim / conclusion |
| Equivocation | "relies on two different uses of the term" | • term / word in two senses <br> • imprecise / ambiguous / vague |
| Appeal Fallacies | "cites the evidence... in direct support of a claim that lies outside their area of expertise" | • appeals to / cites <br> • outside area of expertise |
| Irrelevant! | "uses irrelevant facts to justify a claim" | • irrelevant / not relevant |
| Percentages ≠ Numbers | "takes no account of the relative frequency of... in the population as a whole" | • percentages / absolute numbers <br> • relative frequency |

## REAL CLASSIC FLAW EXAMPLE

*28.3.20*

Game show host: Humans are no better than apes at investing, that is, they do not attain a better return on their investments than apes do. We gave five stock analysts and one chimpanzee $1,350 each to invest. After one month, the chimp won, having increased its net worth by $210. The net worth of the analyst who came in second increased by only $140.

Each of the following describes a flaw in the game show host's reasoning EXCEPT:

(A)   A conclusion is drawn about apes in general on the basis of an experiment involving one chimpanzee.

~~(B)~~   No evidence is offered that chimpanzees are capable of understanding stock reports and making reasoned investment decisions.

(C)   A broad conclusion is drawn about the investment skills of humans on the basis of what is known about five humans.

(D)   Too general a conclusion is made about investing on the basis of a single experiment involving short-term investing but not long-term investing.

~~(E)~~   No evidence is considered about the long-term performance of the chimpanzee's portfolio versus that of the analysts' portfolios.

OK, first, relish the moment. This is probably the best LR question of all time (or at least my personal favorite). Now that you've relished, translate.

*Game show host: Humans aren't better at investing than apes; they don't get better returns on their investments. We gave $1,350 to five stock analysts and one chimp. The chimp made $210 after a month. The next best analyst made $140.*

Why not populate the New York Stock Exchange with apes in glasses? Well, look at the wording of the conclusion. It's extremely general and the sample is comically limited. They've concluded about "humans" and "apes" from one ape, five people, and one set of investments tracked for one month. This stimulus overgeneralizes in about a million different ways. Overgeneralization is the flaw here.

The ape could be unrepresentative of apes in general. The five analysts could be unrepresentative of humans in general. The month-long return could be unrepresentative of investment returns. Most people invest in things for far longer than a month. Remember, this was done **on a game show**.

Now, we're going to think really hard about whether apes are better at investing than humans. No wonder I turned down Harvard Law School to do this.

### LOOPHOLE          What if one should not overgeneralize all the things?

Since it's Classic Flaw **EXCEPT**, we want to choose the one answer that is *not* what's wrong with the stimulus. We're going to check off four flaws in the answer choices; those are the incorrect answers. We'll choose the one answer we can't check off.

**A)**   A conclusion is drawn about apes in general on the basis of an experiment involving one chimpanzee.

*So generalizes from one chimp to apes. Is this what's wrong with the argument? Yes! Awesome, it's one of the overgeneralizations. Flaw checked off.*

**B)**   No evidence is offered that chimpanzees are capable of understanding stock reports and making reasoned investment decisions.

*So they never offer evidence saying chimps are capable of investment reasoning. Is this what's wrong with the argument? No, the problem with B is that the chimp still gets better returns even if they don't understand how. It doesn't matter if they reasoned their way to those returns or chose them at random! They're making more, which is all the conclusion cares about. Since this is Classic Flaw **EXCEPT**, we want the one thing the argument didn't do wrong. B is out of left field, so we'll keep it around.*

EXCEPT questions are easiest to handle by process of elimination. For **EXCEPT**-specific strategy, check out the Answer Choice Strategy Section.

**C)** A broad conclusion is drawn about the investment skills of humans on the basis of what is known about five humans.

*So generalizes from five people to humans. Is this what's wrong with the argument? Yes! **C** mirrors **A**. Perfect, more overgeneralization. Flaw checked off.*

**D)** Too general a conclusion is made about investing on the basis of a single experiment involving short-term investing but not long-term investing.

*So generalizes from one short-term investing experiment to investing. Is this what's wrong with the argument? Yes! Another overgeneralization. Flaw checked off.*

**E)** No evidence is considered about the long-term performance of the chimpanzee's portfolio versus that of the analysts' portfolios.

*So it doesn't consider long-term performance of the chimp vs. the analysts. Is this what's wrong with the argument? Yes, but it's a little more difficult to see why. **E** doesn't use the word "general," but it's still calling out how the one-month timeline is unrepresentative of investing. Maybe the analysts would have gotten a higher return than the chimp in the long run. The conclusion would crumble. Flaw checked off.*

**B** is the correct answer. The four wrong answers are all flaws in the stimulus. We couldn't check **B** off, so it's correct.

## CLASSIC FLAW CHALLENGE

*20.4.18*

Dobson: Some historians claim that the people who built a ring of stones thousands of years ago in Britain were knowledgeable about celestial events. The ground for this claim is that two of the stones determine a line pointing directly to the position of the sun at sunrise at the spring equinox. There are many stones in the ring, however, so the chance that one pair will point in a celestially significant direction is large. Therefore, the people who built the ring were not knowledgeable about celestial events.

Which one of the following is an error of reasoning in Dobson's argument?

(A) The failure of cited evidence to establish a statement is taken as evidence that statement is false.

(B) Dobson's conclusion logically contradicts some of the evidence presented in support of it.

(C) Statements that absolutely establish Dobson's conclusion are treated as if they merely give some support to that conclusion.

(D) Something that is merely a matter of opinion is treated as if it were subject to verification as a matter of fact.

(E) Dobson's drawing the conclusion relies on interpreting a key term in two different ways.

Where's the answer key?

You'll find the answer key for all the Challenge Questions at the end of the chapter on page 357.

# Loophole Flaw

| | | |
|---|---|---|
| **QUESTION STEM KEYWORDS** | **POPULARITY** | About 0-1 questions per section |
| most vulnerable to criticism on the grounds that it + [Loophole Flaw Prefix] | **WHAT YOU'RE LOOKING FOR** | A provable description of how the argument overlooked your Loophole |
| **LOOPHOLE FLAW PREFIXES** <br><br> • mistakenly assumes <br> • fails to consider / establish <br> • presumes without providing sufficient justification <br> • takes for granted <br> • overlooks the possibility that | **ROLE OF THE LOOPHOLE** | The correct answer to Loophole Flaw calls the argument out for ignoring your Loophole. |
| **QUESTION STEM EXAMPLES** <br><br> The scholar's reasoning is flawed because the scholar **presumes without giving sufficient justification that** <br><br> The reasoning in the researcher's argument is questionable in that the argument **overlooks the possibility that** <br><br> The advertisement's reasoning is most vulnerable to criticism on the grounds that it **fails to consider whether** | **TL;DR STRATEGY** | You already have a Loophole. <br><br> Go find the answer choice that calls out the argument for assuming your Loophole isn't a factor. |
| | **BACK-UP PLAN** | Was it bad that the argument overlooked this? <br><br> • If yes, choose it. <br> • If no, cross it off. <br> • If you're not sure, leave it for later. |

## LOOPHOLE FLAW GAME PLAN

You're exceedingly ready for Loophole Flaw. You've been calling out authors all throughout your training and Loophole Flaw is just another opportunity.

The key to Loophole Flaw is the Loophole Flaw Prefix. That's what makes question stems and individual answer choices Loophole Flaw, instead of Classic Flaw. **All of the Loophole Flaw prefixes boil down to one meaning: The stimulus assumed something dumb in service of its argument.** What's the dumbest thing the author can assume? That your Loophole isn't a factor.

## TINY TIPS

- Loophole Flaw is still asking you to describe something that the argument did wrong. Unlike Classic Flaw, the correct answer will use specific information from the stimulus in its description of what went wrong. This means the correct answer will likely reference the stimulus directly; it will talk about taxes or dentistry, not fancy argument words.

## BIGGEST TRAPS

- Don't choose answers that describe a reasonable assumption in the argument. Not all assumptions are bad.

### REAL LOOPHOLE FLAW EXAMPLE

*23.3.7*

Studies indicate that the rate at which water pollution is increasing is leveling off: the amount of water pollution caused this year is almost identical to the amount caused last year. If this trend continues, the water pollution problem will no longer be getting more serious.

The reasoning is questionable because it ignores the possibility that

(A)  some types of water pollution have no noticeable effect on organisms that use the water

(B)  the types of water pollution caused this year are less dangerous than those caused last year

(C)  the leveling-off trend of water pollution will not continue

(D)  air and soil pollution are becoming more serious

(E)  the effects of water pollution are cumulative

**First, translate.**

*The amount of water pollution we create every year is no longer increasing; we polluted about the same amount this year as we did last year. If it stays this way, the water pollution problem won't get more serious.*

They think adding the same amount of pollution every year means the pollution problem isn't getting more serious... but we're still adding pollution to the water! That adds up. A polluted ecosystem gets worse the more pollution you add.

Like cool, we aren't adding even more than we did last year, but imagine we added 50 tons of pollution to the water system every year. After 10 years, we've added 500 tons total, and the year after that we will have added 550 tons total. 550 is more serious than 500; we can't assume that the water pollution will dissipate. This leads us straight to our Loophole:

**LOOPHOLE**   What if the water pollution problem grows more serious as pollution accumulates?

It's Loophole Flaw, so we're going to look for a description of our Loophole in the answer choices.

**A)**  *some* types of water pollution have no noticeable effect on organisms that use the water

*So some types of pollution don't have a noticeable effect on marine organisms. Is this what the argument did wrong? No, we don't even know that the "some types of water pollution" mentioned here are the types being used in the stimulus. Not provable.*

**B)**  the types of water pollution caused this year are less dangerous than those caused last year

*So this year's pollution is less dangerous than last year's pollution. Is this what the argument did wrong? No, the conclusion refers to the amount of pollution, not the type. Plus, **B** actually helps the stimulus. If water pollution isn't as dangerous this year, the conclusion is more likely. Not what we're looking for.*

**C)**  the leveling-off trend of water pollution will not continue

*So the water pollution will not actually level off. Is this what the argument did wrong? No, they guard the conclusion with "if this trend continues," so the conclusion only applies to the world in which the trend does continue. **C** can't be correct if it doesn't address the conclusion. Not provable.*

| | | |
|---|---|---|
| **D)** | air and soil pollution are becoming more serious | *So air and soil pollution are getting more serious. Is this what the argument did wrong? Come on, LSAT. Who cares about air and soil? The stimulus is about water; this isn't what they did wrong. Not provable.* |
| **E)** | the effects of water pollution are cumulative | *So water pollution is cumulative. Is this what the argument did wrong? Yes! It's our Loophole. This is the big hole they foolishly assumed wasn't an issue. Water pollution can get more serious even if the rate doesn't increase because its effects are cumulative, meaning they add up.* **E** *is provable.* |

**E** is the correct answer. It is the only answer choice that describes the argument's misstep.

## LOOPHOLE FLAW CHALLENGE

*19.4.3*

The number of calories in a gram of refined cane sugar is the same as in an equal amount of fructose, the natural sugar found in fruits and vegetables. Therefore, a piece of candy made with a given amount of refined cane sugar is no higher in calories than a piece of fruit that contains an equal amount of fructose.

The reasoning in the argument is flawed because the argument

(A)     fails to consider the possibility that fruit might contain noncaloric nutrients that candy does not contain

(B)     presupposes that all candy is made with similar amounts of sugar

(C)     confuses one kind of sugar with another

(D)     presupposes what it sets out to establish, that fruit does not differ from sugar-based candy in the number of calories each contains

(E)     overlooks the possibility that sugar might not be the only calorie-containing ingredient in candy or fruit

*

This Loophole Flaw Challenge question contains Loophole Flaw Prefixes in the answer choices, not the question stem.

*

*Where's the answer key?*

You'll find the answer key for all the Challenge Questions at the end of the chapter on page 357.

---

### PROVABLE QUESTIONS GAME PLAN

- Always look for provable language in the answer choices. **SOME, COULD,** and **MAY** are your provable friends.

- Never get rid of an answer to a Provable Question because it's too "easy," "simple," or "straightforward." Safe answers are the whole point of Provable Questions.

- Use the Provable Questions Road Map to consolidate the information in this chapter.

- Memorize the question stem keywords for the Provable Questions now.

## Quiz 10    PROVABLE QUESTIONS

### INSTRUCTIONS

*Answer these questions based on your knowledge of the chapter. Attempt to answer without looking back at the chapter first. If you don't know the answer, circle the question number and go find the answer in the chapter. Study the sections of the chapter that you couldn't remember at first.*

### Word Bank

| | | |
|---|---|---|
| NA | Argument Part | scope |
| qualify | presuppose | Inference |
| supposed | Classic Flaw | Controversy |
| Agreement | Conclusion | phenomenon |
| Loophole Flaw | implicit premise | Fill In |
| Method | MSS | |

**1.**    Complete the table using the word bank.

| PROVABLE QUESTION TYPE | CORRECT ANSWER |
|---|---|
| Agreement | The thing you can prove the two speakers agree about |
| Conclusion | A provable translation of the conclusion |
| Method | A provable description of what happened in the stimulus |
| FN1 | The thing you can prove completes the author's thought |
| Loophole Flaw | A provable description of how the argument overlooked your Loophole |
| MSS | The thing you can prove is very, very, very likely to be true |
| (Controversy) disagreement | The thing you can prove the two speakers disagree about |
| Necessary [illegible] | The thing you can prove must be true, if the conclusion is true |
| Classic Flaw | A provable description of what the argument did wrong |
| Argument Part | A provable description of what the phrase is doing in the argument |
| [illegible] | The thing you can prove definitely must be true |
| Inference | |

**2.** Complete the table using the word bank.

| METHOD VOCAB TERM | | MEANING |
|---|---|---|
| *Quality* | to limit a claim | |
| *Response* Implicit *pnml* | assumption | |
| *Phenomenon* | thing | |
| *Presuppose* | assume | |
| *Supposed* | poorly assumed | |
| *Scope* | the world of whatever you're talking about | |

*Circle the correct answer to the following questions.*

**3.** TRUE OR ~~FALSE~~     Conclusion questions are asking for the main conclusion, but the intermediate conclusion can also be correct.

**4.** ~~TRUE~~ OR FALSE     The correct answer to an MSS question does not have to be mathematically proven.

**5.** ~~TRUE~~ OR FALSE     On a Necessary Assumption question, you should evaluate answer choices by asking, "Does this have to be true?"

**6.** TRUE OR ~~FALSE~~     In Agreement questions, the speakers' shared sufficient assumption is the correct answer.

**7.** ~~TRUE~~ OR FALSE     "For" is a premise indicator.

**8.**   Circle the correct classic flaw in the table below.

| ANSWER CHOICE EXAMPLE | CIRCLE THE CORRECT CLASSIC FLAW | | |
|---|---|---|---|
| "confuses an absence of evidence for a hypothesis with the existence of evidence against the hypothesis" | (Possibility ≠ Certainty) | False Dichotomy | Straw Man |
| "relies on two different uses of the term" | Appeal Fallacies | Irrelevant! | (Equivocation) |
| "rejects a claim by attacking the proponents of the claim rather than addressing the claim itself" | False Dichotomy | Possibility ≠ Certainty | (Ad Hominem) |
| "mistakes something that is necessary to bring about a situation for something that in itself is enough to bring about that situation" | (Bad Conditional Reasoning) | (Bad Causal Reasoning) | Percentage ≠ Numbers |
| "assumes without warrant that a situation allows only two possibilities" | Bad Causal Reasoning | (False Dichotomy) | Circular Reasoning |
| "uses evidence drawn from a small sample that may well be unrepresentative" | Ad Hominem | (Survey Problems) | Appeal Fallacies |
| "takes no account of the relative frequency of… in the population as a whole" | Possibility ≠ Certainty | False Dichotomy | (Percentage ≠ Numbers) |
| "presupposes what it sets out to prove" | Bad Causal Reasoning | (Circular Reasoning) | Equivocation |

*Where's the answer key?*

You'll find the answer key at the end of the chapter on page 358.

## Provable Challenge Questions ANSWER KEY

| | | |
|---|---|---|
| Conclusion | 18.4.2 | B |
| Inference | 18.4.6 | D |
| | 18.4.10 | A |
| Most Strongly Supported | 18.4.24 | D |
| | 20.1.6 | D |
| Controversy | 20.4.21 | D |
| Necessary Assumption | 16.3.12 | A |
| | 15.3.12 | E |
| Method | 18.2.5 | D |
| Argument Part | 15.2.14 | B |
| Classic Flaw | 20.4.18 | A |
| Loophole Flaw | 19.4.3 | E |

*

Looking for a little extra help on these Challenge Questions?

You'll find explanations for each of the Challenge Questions online at elementalprep.com/bonus.

## Quiz 10 ANSWER KEY

### 1.

| PROVABLE QUESTION TYPE | CORRECT ANSWER |
| --- | --- |
| Agreement | The thing you can prove the two speakers agree about |
| Conclusion | A provable translation of the conclusion |
| Method | A provable description of what happened in the stimulus |
| Fill In | The thing you can prove completes the author's thought |
| Loophole Flaw | A provable description of how the argument overlooked your Loophole |
| MSS | The thing you can prove is very, very, very likely to be true |
| Controversy | The thing you can prove the two speakers disagree about |
| NA | The thing you can prove must be true, if the conclusion is true |
| Classic Flaw | A provable description of what the argument did wrong |
| Argument Part | A provable description of what the phrase is doing in the argument |
| Inference | The thing you can prove definitely must be true |

### 2.

| METHOD VOCAB TERM | MEANING |
| --- | --- |
| qualify | to limit a claim |
| implicit premise | assumption |
| phenomenon | thing |
| presuppose | assume |
| supposed | poorly assumed |
| scope | the world of whatever you're talking about |

### 3.

False. *Only* the main conclusion is the correct answer to a Conclusion question.

### 4.

True.

**5.**      True.

**6.**      False. In Agreement questions, the speakers' shared *necessary* assumption is the correct answer.

**7.**      True.

**8.**

| ANSWER CHOICE EXAMPLE | CIRCLE THE CORRECT CLASSIC FLAW |
|---|---|
| "confuses an absence of evidence for a hypothesis with the existence of evidence against the hypothesis" | Possibility ≠ Certainty |
| "relies on two different uses of the term" | Equivocation |
| "rejects a claim by attacking the proponents of the claim rather than addressing the claim itself" | Ad Hominem |
| "mistakes something that is necessary to bring about a situation for something that in itself is enough to bring about that situation" | Bad Conditional Reasoning |
| "assumes without warrant that a situation allows only two possibilities" | False Dichotomy |
| "uses evidence drawn from a small sample that may well be unrepresentative" | Survey Problems |
| "takes no account of the relative frequency of... in the population as a whole" | Percentage ≠ Numbers |
| "presupposes what it sets out to prove" | Circular Reasoning |

# OMMMM.

chapter ten. moment of zen.

# Chapter Breather    HOW DID YOU LEARN TO NOT FREAK OUT ABOUT THE TIME?

**VEENA**

I told myself that time spent worrying about the time is the worst usage of the time.

**CHRIS**

Practice. Just doing questions and getting familiar with the test.

**LAUREN**

Once I accepted the fact that some questions naturally take longer than others, there was less pressure on how long each individual question took to complete. What helped the most was when I finally internalized that just because a question was taking longer than I expected didn't mean that I was necessarily doing anything wrong. Taking practice tests also helped because I was able to become familiar with my own testing tendencies. Once I knew my time tendencies, I could better gauge if I had reason to freak out or not.

**KELLY**

I had some ridiculous time goals, and trying to hold myself to those standards ended up hindering me during the test and breaking my confidence down. The more I tried to speed through the test at the pace I thought I should be going at, the more nervous I became when I hit harder questions that I needed to spend more time on. I could've saved myself a lot of headache if I had just relaxed and spent more time with the harder questions on the first read!

## Principle & Parallel Questions Road Map

Remember, Principle Conform, Parallel Reasoning, and Parallel Flaw are all Provable Questions.

Principle Conform, Parallel Reasoning, and Parallel Flaw all play on one simple mechanic: matching. Analyze the stimulus and find its matching pair in the answer choices. Exactly how you the match the stimulus forms the difference between these question types.

Principle and Parallel are still Provable Questions, but they execute on that mandate a little differently. Provability here is all about matching; any answer choice that matches the stimulus is provable. For this reason, I'm not powerful/provable styling the answer choices in Chapter 11. You shouldn't be generally wary of powerful language on Principle Conform and Parallel Reasoning/Flaw.

| QUESTION TYPE | CORRECT ANSWER | BACK-UP PLAN | QUESTION STEM KEYWORDS |
|---|---|---|---|
| **Principle Conform** | Matching example <br><br> *or* <br><br> Matching principle | Does this embody the principle? <br><br> *or* <br><br> Does this underlie the example? | • principle / propositions <br> • most closely conforms <br> • illustrate <br> • situation / example |
| **Parallel Reasoning** | The answer that's built around the same Skeleton as the stimulus | Does this match the stimulus? | • parallel <br> • most similar <br> • pattern of reasoning <br> • analogy |
| **Parallel Flaw** | The answer that exhibits the same flaw as the stimulus | Does this match the flaw in the stimulus? | • parallel <br> • flawed / dubious <br> • pattern of reasoning <br> • analogy |

PRINCIPLE
& PARALLEL
QUESTIONS

## Principle Conform

❋

Remember, a principle is a general rule.

| QUESTION STEM KEYWORDS | POPULARITY | About 0-2 questions per section |
|---|---|---|
| | WHAT YOU'RE LOOKING FOR | Matching example<br><br>or<br><br>Matching principle |

| QUESTION STEM KEYWORDS | ROLE OF THE INFERENCE OR LOOPHOLE | |
|---|---|---|
| • principle / propositions<br>• most closely conforms<br>• illustrate<br>• situation / example | | **Principle Stimulus**<br><br>Your Inference puts the principle into action. This is exactly what the correct answer does as well.<br><br>**Example Stimulus**<br><br>Your Loophole blows up the gap in the example's reasoning. The principle in the correct answer bridges that gap. |

❋

Principle Conform questions are not the same as Strengthen and SA questions that use the word "principle" in the question stem and list a bunch of principles in the answer choices. In those questions, you should follow the advice provided in the Strengthen and SA sections.

| QUESTION STEM EXAMPLES | TL;DR STRATEGY | |
|---|---|---|
| Which one of the following conforms most closely to the principle illustrated above?<br><br>Which one of the following propositions is best illustrated by the situation described in the passage?<br><br>The reasoning above conforms most closely to which one of the following propositions?<br><br>Which one of the following propositions is best illustrated by the passage? | | You already have a Inference/Loophole.<br><br>If it's a Principle Stimulus, burn the principle into your head. Activate the principle with an example for your CLIR Inference.<br><br>If it's an Example Stimulus, come up with a principle that bridges the gap exposed by the Loophole.<br><br>Go choose the matching principle or example. |
| | BACK-UP PLAN | **Principle Stimulus**<br><br>Does this embody the principle?<br><br>**Example Stimulus**<br><br>Does this underlie the example?<br><br>• If yes, choose it.<br>• If no, cross it off.<br>• If you're not sure, leave it for later. |

### PRINCIPLE CONFORM GAME PLAN

Principle Conform asks you to match general principles to specific examples. But Principle Conform is a switch hitter: The general principle could reside in the stimulus or the answer choices. Either way, you find the match.

But what does it mean to "match" a principle and its example? Let's explore the two sides of Principle Conform:

|  | STIMULUS | ANSWER CHOICES | STRATEGY |
|---|---|---|---|
| **Principle to Example** | Principle | Example | • You'll read about a general rule in the stimulus and choose which example best follows that rule.<br>• Imagine the principle is a drawing in a coloring book. **You must color in the principle with an example.** Replace those generalities of the principle with colorful specifics, but make sure you get color in as many of the lines as possible. Don't go outside the lines. |
| **Example to Principle** | Example | Principle | • You'll read about a specific situation in the stimulus and choose which general rule substantiates its reasoning.<br>• **You must draw out the principle.** In this case, you have a bunch of color on the page, but it doesn't have any structure holding it up. You draw out the lines of a principle to provide the necessary structure to support the example's judgments. |

Let's explore what it really means for an example to conform to a principle. Once you understand this on an intuitive level, it won't matter if they give you the example or the principle in the stimulus. You'll know what a match looks like. Imagine you're telling a story to a friend. You start it off with "People who flake are the worst." Your friend is like "Why?" So you tell a few classic stories about your girl Natalie:

| PRINCIPLE | EXAMPLE STORIES |
|---|---|
| **People who flake are the worst.** | *Natalie left you alone eating bread at a restaurant an hour away from your apartment. She's "stuck at work :(" and not coming. So, Natalie's the worst.*<br><br>*Natalie didn't show up to bar trivia even though she confirmed, meaning no one on the team knows anything about sports now and there's no way you're winning free drinks. So, Natalie's the worst.*<br><br>*Natalie was supposed to take care of your plants while you're on a trip. When you get back home, even your aloe plant is somehow dead. Natalie went last-minute rafting without telling you. So, Natalie's the worst.* |

We illustrated a principle in our stories about Natalie. In order to illustrate this principle about flaking, we needed a story about someone who flaked. It wouldn't have made sense to illustrate a principle about flaking with an example about someone who is not a flake.

**Keep in mind that the matching principle and its example are interchangeable. If one of them is the stimulus, the other one is the correct answer and vice versa.** They are a corresponding pair. If the answer choice is correct, the stimulus and the answer choice should be able to switch places.

Beware of answer choices that prove the opposite of what you have evidence for.

**TINY TIPS**

- Never assume the word "principle" in the question stem necessarily means it's Principle Conform. Skimming the question stem is an invitation for disaster.

- It's helpful to think of principles conditionally. If our principle is "People who flake are the worst," you can think of it like **flake ⟶ worst**. Setting it up conditionally clarifies exactly what is (and is not) provable. This principle can prove that someone is the worst (**flake ⟶ worst**), or, if you take the contrapositive, it can prove that someone does not flake all the time (**~worst ⟶ ~flake**). **This works because both worst and ~flake live in the necessary condition.** An answer choice claiming **~worst** or **flake** is not provable.

- Be on the lookout for correct answer choices that activate the contrapositive of the principle.

> **REMEMBER!**   *You can only prove things that live in the necessary condition.*
>
> *If you struggle with time, pay attention to the following: Any answer choice claiming to prove something you can't get into the necessary condition is automatically wrong.*

**REAL PRINCIPLE CONFORM EXAMPLE**

23.3.24

A person's failure to keep a promise is wrong only if, first, doing so harms the one to whom the promise is made and, second, all those who discover the failure to keep the promise lose confidence in the person's ability to keep promises.

Which one of the following judgments most closely conforms to the principle above?

(A) Ann kept her promise to repay Felicia the money she owed her. Further, this convinced everyone who knew Ann that she is trustworthy. Thus, Ann's keeping her promise was not wrong.

(B) Jonathan took an oath of secrecy concerning the corporation's technical secrets, but he sold them to a competitor. His action was wrong even though the corporation intended that he leak these secrets to its competitors.

(C) George promised to repay Reiko the money he owed her. However, George was unable to keep his promise to Reiko and as a result, Reiko suffered a serious financial loss. Thus, George's failure to keep his promise was wrong.

(D) Because he lost his job, Carlo was unable to repay the money he promised to Miriam. However, Miriam did not need this money nor did she lose confidence in Carlo's ability to keep promises. So, Carlo's failure to keep his promise to Miriam was not wrong.

(E) Elizabeth promised to return the book she borrowed from Steven within a week, but she was unable to do so because she became acutely ill. Not knowing this, Steven lost confidence in her ability to keep a promise. So, Elizabeth's failure to return the book to Steven was wrong.

First, translate. In this case, we're going to translate by diagramming the conditional.

**Note what's in the necessary condition of the original statement and its contrapositive. Those necessary conditions are all we can prove.** Any answer choice concluding **failing wrong** (the sufficient condition) will be incorrect. We have a Premise Set, so let's activate the conditional for our Inference:

**INFERENCE**   Someone broke her promise to another person, but she didn't harm them when she did it. So it wasn't wrong for her to fail.

As we go through the answer choices, remember the examples can only prove **harms promise maker + everyone loses confidence**, or, if we go with the contrapositive, we can prove **~failing wrong**. Those are the principle's two necessary conditions. **Be suspicious of any answer claiming something other than those two things.**

**A)** Ann kept her promise to repay Felicia the money she owed her. Further, this convinced everyone who knew Ann that she is trustworthy. Thus, Ann's keeping her promise was not wrong.

*So Ann kept her promise, and everyone thinks she's trustworthy, so it's not wrong for Ann to have kept the promise. This is a classic terrible Principle Conform answer choice. They are trying to lure you into choosing the opposite. The stimulus is all about failing to keep a promise. Ann keeping her promise doesn't activate any part of the conditional; in fact, it sidesteps the principle entirely.* **A** *is the opposite of provable.*

**B)** Jonathan took an oath of secrecy concerning the corporation's technical secrets, but he sold them to a competitor. His action was wrong even though the corporation intended that he leak these secrets to its competitors.

*So Jonathan broke his secrecy promise and it was wrong, even though the promiser intended for Jonathan to break the promise. Another terrible answer. Remember, it's impossible to prove* **failing wrong** *with this principle.* **Failing wrong** *is the sufficient, not the necessary.* **B** *doesn't follow the conditional; it's not provable.*

**C)** George promised to repay Reiko the money he owed her. However, George was unable to keep his promise to Reiko and as a result, Reiko suffered a serious financial loss. Thus, George's failure to keep his promise was wrong.

*So George broke his promise to Reiko, and it was wrong because Reiko suffered. Just like in* **B**, *we can't prove* **failing wrong**; *that's the sufficient condition, not the necessary.* **C** *is trying to tempt you into reading the conditional backwards without negating. Not provable.*

**D)** Because he lost his job, Carlo was unable to repay the money he promised to Miriam. However, Miriam did not need this money nor did she lose confidence in Carlo's ability to keep promises. So, Carlo's failure to keep his promise to Miriam was not wrong.

*So Carlo broke his promise to Miriam. But he didn't harm Miriam and she didn't lose confidence in him; so, Carlo's failure wasn't wrong. We can actually prove* **D**! *It follows the principle's contrapositive perfectly.* **D** *says both necessary conditions (**harms promise maker** and **everyone loses confidence**) were not met; therefore, we know that the sufficient condition didn't happen (**~failing wrong**). We can prove* **D**.

**E)**   Elizabeth promised to return the book she borrowed from Steven within a week, but she was unable to do so because she became acutely ill. Not knowing this, Steven lost confidence in her ability to keep a promise. So, Elizabeth's failure to return the book to Steven was wrong.

*So Elizabeth broke her promise to Steven, and Steven lost confidence in her; so, her promise-breaking was wrong.* **E** *is very similar to* **C**. ***When two answers are this similar, they are both wrong. The correct answer is necessarily unique.*** *They are trying to play the same exact trick they did in* **C**; *they want you to read the conditional backwards. But we can't prove* **failing wrong**. **E** *isn't provable.*

**D** is the correct answer. It is the only answer choice that follows the stimulus' principle exactly.

### PRINCIPLE CONFORM CHALLENGE

*23.2.13*

Committee member:   We should not vote to put at the top of the military's chain of command an individual whose history of excessive drinking is such that that person would be barred from commanding a missile wing, a bomber squadron, or a contingent of fighter jets. Leadership must be established from the top down.

The committee member's argument conforms most closely to which one of the following principles?

 No one who would be barred from important jobs in an organization should lead that organization.
(B)   Whoever leads an organization must have served at every level in the organization.
(C)   Whoever leads an organization must be qualified to hold each important job in the organization.
(D)   No one who drinks excessively should hold a leadership position anywhere along the military's chain of command.
(E)   No one who cannot command a missile wing should be at the top of the military's chain of command.

*Where's the answer key?*

You'll find the answer key for all the Challenge Questions at the end of the chapter on page 387.

# Parallel Reasoning

| | | |
|---|---|---|
| **QUESTION STEM KEYWORDS** | **POPULARITY** | About 1 question per section |
| | **WHAT YOU'RE LOOKING FOR** | The answer that's built around the same Skeleton as the stimulus |
| • parallel<br>• most similar<br>• pattern of reasoning<br>• analogy | **ROLE OF THE LOOPHOLE** | Your Loophole forces you to analyze how the argument is operating. You need this information to come up with a Skeleton. |
| **QUESTION STEM EXAMPLES** | **TL;DR STRATEGY** | You already have a Loophole, so you are familiar with the argument.<br><br>Abstract a Skeleton from the stimulus. Basically, say what happened in the stimulus while cutting out as many specific nouns and verbs from the stimulus as possible. It should sound like "Thing 1 is a consequence of thing 2."<br><br>Overlay the Skeleton on each answer choice and see if it fits.<br><br>Choose the answer choice that fits the Skeleton. |
| • The reasoning in which one of the following is most similar to the reasoning above?<br>• The pattern of reasoning in the argument above is most similar to that in which one of the following?<br>• The pattern of reasoning in the argument above is most closely paralleled in which one of the following? | **BACK-UP PLAN** | Does this match the stimulus?<br><br>• If yes, choose it.<br>• If no, cross it off.<br>• If you're not sure, leave it for later. |

When I first started prepping for the LSAT, I loved about 95% of Logical Reasoning from day one. The other 5%? Parallel. But about a year ago, I had an epiphany. I realized why Parallel is on the test.

Parallel is here to test your ability to reason by analogy, which is a goal I totally buy into. Lawyers often use analogies as a reasoning tool; it's important to be able to tell a good analogy (where the two halves actually are similar) from a not-so-good one (where the two halves are not actually similar). Now that I think of Parallel as an analogy seek and find, I'm so down for them.

## BIG TIPS

You're reuniting analogy soulmates on Parallel Reasoning. It's one question with essentially six stimuli, one up top and five in the answer choices. Two of those stimuli are a matching pair; they're the ones you're tasked with reuniting with your awesome powers of logical reasoning. One half of the match is the stimulus and the other half of the match is the correct answer. The other four orphaned stimuli are the incorrect answers.

Our strategy on Parallel Reasoning is twofold. We've got a low-effort strategy for Standard Parallel questions and then we've got a chainsaw to cut through the more difficult Wordy Parallel questions. How do you know if a Parallel stimulus is wordy or not? One simple test: Were you able to understand the stimulus on the first read? If the answer is "NO, send help," it's wordy. We'll get to Wordy Parallel in a hot second, but let's start with Standard Parallel.

The key to Standard Parallel is the Skeleton. **The Skeleton is the story of the stimulus with as few words from the stimulus as possible.** It's the encapsulation of only the most basic elements of the stimulus. Abstracting a Skeleton from the stimulus is what you'll do on most Parallel questions.

**HOW TO ROCK STANDARD PARALLEL QUESTIONS**

1. **Read and understand the stimulus. Translate it and CLIR it.**

2. **Abstract a Skeleton from your translation.**

   Replace the flashy words in your translation with boring placeholders. You'll end up with something like, "Thing 1 causes thing 2. We don't want thing 2, so we won't do thing 1."

3. **Overlay the Skeleton on each answer choice to see if it matches. If an answer matches, choose it.**

Let's examine how to shift from specific to skeletal in a few examples:

**SPECIFIC**   Running is one way to torture yourself.

*First step, translate: "OK, so running is one way to torture." No worries, the sentence is already simple.*

*Now, strip away all the words with any personality. These are flashy words, like "running" and "torture." The boring connector words, like "is," are the ones you want to leave in your Skeleton.*

*So if I strip away "running" and "torture," what am I going to replace them with? Bland placeholders: "Running" becomes "thing 1" and "torture" becomes "thing 2." I like to use "thing 1" and "thing 2" as my personal bland placeholders because they sound the most natural to me. It's fine if you want to use **A** and **B**, 1 and 2, or "thing" and "other thing," as long as you can easily keep track of them. **You want this Skeleton to be something you can commit to memory easily, so it has to be in your language.***

**SKELETON**   Thing 1 is one way of doing thing 2.

*Alright, so my replacement yields: "Thing 1 is one way to thing 2." This sounds kind of clunky and hard to remember. I'll make it a little more intuitive: "Thing 1 is one way of doing thing 2."*

**QUICK SKELETON FAQ**

**Q.**  *What are flashy words?*

**A.**  Flashy words are specific nouns and verbs from the stimulus that will be replaced in the correct Parallel answer choice. Words like "Sammy," "hamstring," and "abbreviate" are flashy words. You want to filter flashy words out of the Parallel stimulus and replace them with bland placeholders when you design your Skeleton.

**Q.** *What's a bland placeholder?*

**A.** A bland placeholder is a word that's general enough to apply to any answer choice. Things like "thing 1," "**A**," or "a reason" apply equally to answer choices about balance beams or marine life. That's why we use them. Here's a list of frequently used bland placeholders:

| | | | |
|---|---|---|---|
| *thing* | *group member* | *category* | *consequence* |
| *group* | *property* | *reason* | *cause* |

**Q.** *What are boring connector words?*

**A.** If you don't know a word's part of speech, it's probably a boring connector word. Words like "of," "could," and "that" are boring connector words. You don't need to replace them with bland placeholders when you design your Skeleton. They're already pretty bland.

Alright, now that we have our bearings, let's take apart another example.

| | | |
|---|---|---|
| **SPECIFIC** | Cardiovascular exercise could produce feelings closely corresponding to either extreme happiness or extreme sadness, or, strangely, both. | *First, read this slowly enough that you understand what happened in a non-pretend way. Next, translate: "OK, so cardio could make you happy or sad or both."*<br><br>*Look how "produce feelings closely corresponding to either extreme happiness or extreme sadness, or, strangely, both" shrunk to "make you happy or sad or both"! This is going to make the Skeleton so much easier!* **If you skip translating, you only make your life harder.** |
| **SKELETON** | Thing 1 could cause thing 2, thing 3, or both. | *Now, strip out the flashy words: Our flashy words here are "cardio" and "make you happy or sad." We'll replace them with "thing 1" and "cause thing 2 or thing 3." That leaves us with: "Thing 1 could cause thing 2 or thing 3 or both."* |

Awesome! Let's try a slightly more complex example.

| | | |
|---|---|---|
| **SPECIFIC** | Ultra-marathoners have something wrong with them. | *First, translate: "OK, so ultra-marathoners have something wrong."*<br><br>*Now, cut the flashy words: The flash here is "ultra-marathoners" and "something wrong." "Ultra-marathoners" are more like a group than a thing, so I'll go with that and replace "ultra-marathoners" with "group." Then we have "something wrong." What's "something wrong" doing in this sentence? It's telling us a quality the group has, right? We can replace "something wrong" with "property."* |
| **SKELETON** | This group has this property. | *After subbing in the replacements, our sentence reads, "Group has a property." And with a little grammatical smoothing we get: "This group has this property."* |

One more example, complete with archaic writing:

| | | |
|---|---|---|
| **SPECIFIC** | All of the above was written out of jealousy. | *First, translate: "OK, so everything was written because of jealousy." "Everything" is just an easier way of saying "all of the above," and "because of" is a more modern way of saying "out of."* |
| | | *Now, flashy words out: The flash left in the translation is "written" and "jealousy." "Written" is just a random pastish tense verb that's doing nothing but specifying what "was." Since I don't want specifics, I can just delete it and stick with "was." Now what's "jealousy" doing in the sentence? It's giving me a reason why I did something. Let's just change it to "reason." With my substitutions in the translation, I get "Everything was because of reason," which smooths out to "Everything was because of this reason."* |
| **SKELETON** | Everything was because of this reason. | |

> "Out of" was in there because I like to write like I'm living in the 1890's.

## SKELETON RECAP

Skeleton design quickly becomes intuitive, just like with the CLIR. Don't stress too much about having a perfect Skeleton. If it gets the job done, meaning it is general enough to be easily applied to the answer choices, it is a good Skeleton. When I created these examples, I wasn't conscious of any of the steps I was taking. I filled in that process for you to help illustrate what is behind the automatic. You'll get there too. You just have to practice.

## REAL STANDARD PARALLEL EXAMPLE

15.3.13

Reptiles are air-breathing vertebrates with completely ossified skeletons; so alligators must be air-breathing vertebrates with completely ossified skeletons.

In terms of its logical features, the argument above most resembles which one of the following?

(A) Green plants take in carbon dioxide and release oxygen back into the air; so it follows that grass takes in carbon dioxide and releases oxygen into the air.
(B) Some red butterflies are poisonous to birds that prey on them; so this particular red butterfly is poisonous to birds that prey on it.
(C) Knowledge about the empirical world can be gained from books; so Virginia Woolf's book *A Room of One's Own* must provide knowledge about the empirical world.
(D) Dierdre has seen every film directed by Rainer Werner Fassbinder; so Dierdre must have seen *Ali: Fear Eats the Soul*, a film directed by Fassbinder.
(E) Skiers run a high risk of bone fracture; so it is likely that Lindsey, who has been an avid skier for many years, has suffered a broken bone at some point.

First, translate:

*Reptiles are air-breathing vertebrates with ossified skeletons. Therefore, alligators are air-breathing vertebrates with ossified skeletons.*

The only possible Loophole here is "What if alligators aren't reptiles?" The author is assuming alligators are reptiles. It turns out alligators actually are reptiles, and whether that fact counts as common knowledge is debatable. Otherwise, we've found our diamond in the rough... a valid argument on the LSAT. *\*gasp\**

So let's design our Skeleton. I won't go through every step, since you've seen the process already. If I actually hit this question during the test I'd just think: "OK, so a category has this quality; so, this thing they think is in the category has the quality."

**SKELETON**  A category has a quality. So, an assumed category member has this quality.

Alright, now I'm ready to apply my Skeleton to the answer choices and look for a match.

**A)** Green plants take in carbon dioxide and release oxygen back into the air; so it follows that grass takes in carbon dioxide and releases oxygen into the air.

*So green plants take in CO₂ and release oxygen; therefore, grass takes in CO₂ and releases oxygen. Alright, let's check our Skeleton: Green plants are our category and we've got some qualities. Grass is our assumed category member and it has the same qualities. Notice how we have to use our outside knowledge to deduce that grass is part of the green plants category. This is exactly what we had to do with the stimulus. Looks like a provable match!*

**B)** Some red butterflies are poisonous to birds that prey on them; so this particular red butterfly is poisonous to birds that prey on it.

*So some red butterflies are poisonous to predators; therefore, this particular red butterfly is poisonous to predators. This doesn't match our Skeleton. There's no category offered. They try to trick us with the "some red butterflies" thing, but that's not a category — that's a characterization of some category members. Not a provable match.*

**C)** Knowledge about the empirical world can be gained from books; so Virginia Woolf's book *A Room of One's Own* must provide knowledge about the empirical world.

*So knowledge can be gained from books; therefore, this particular Woolf book must provide knowledge. The problem here is the jump from **CAN** in the premises to **MUST** in the conclusion. The stimulus doesn't have this mismatch. The stimulus says the category has these qualities, not that it **can** have them. **C** isn't a provable match.*

**D)** Dierdre has seen every film directed by Rainer Werner Fassbinder; so Dierdre must have seen *Ali: Fear Eats the Soul*, a film directed by Fassbinder.

*So Dierdre has seen every film by Fassbinder; therefore, Dierdre's seen this particular film by Fassbinder. Close, but no cigar. The stimulus **assumed** that alligators were reptiles and there's no parallel assumption in **D**. **D** spells everything out for us; it tells us Ali is a film by Fassbinder, no assumption needed. The stimulus didn't tell us alligators are reptiles. **D** just isn't a provable match.*

**E)** Skiers run a high risk of bone fracture; so it is likely that Lindsey, who has been an avid skier for many years, has suffered a broken bone at some point.

*So skiers are likely to fracture; therefore, it's likely that Lindsey, a veteran skier, has had a fracture. Even though Lindsey is an example of the skier category, all the likelihood stuff has no analogue in the Skeleton. Our Skeleton was much more cut and dry than **E**; a category has qualities and that's it. Not a provable match.*

**A** is the correct answer. It's the only answer choice that matches our Skeleton.

## RUNNING THE NUMBERS ON WORDY PARALLEL

Wordy Parallel is a special breed of linguistic *schadenfreude*. It happens when the stimulus repeats the same phrases in many different combinations. Seem innocent? It's not. Here are a few wordy examples to give you a feel:

### THIS IS WHAT WORDINESS HELL LOOKS LIKE.

*Some magazines are uninteresting. All uninteresting reading material is about dogs. Therefore, some magazines are about dogs.*

*We know that backwards baseball caps cause red flags. For backwards baseball caps cause people to be untrustworthy and unwholesome, and untrustworthy and unwholesome behavior puts people in danger. Anything that could endanger a given person produces red flags.*

If you're anything like me, you were just like, "Uhh… what?" in response to these. I wrote those examples and every time I read them I *still* have that response. But many stimuli closely resemble these examples, and they require a comprehension aid for most of us to understand them in a timely fashion. Taking notes and making flashcards are comprehension aids. The numbers are your comprehension aid for Wordy Parallel.

The numbers will give you the correct answer to very difficult questions with mathematical certainty. Once you get used to them, they're awesome.

---

### HOW TO RUN THE NUMBERS

1. **Recognize that the stimulus is wordy. Normally, you'd translate next, but the numbers will be your translation on overdrive.**

2. **Go to the beginning of the stimulus and write a 1 on your scratch paper. This will stand for the first term they're playing around with. You will continue to use a 1 to refer to this term.**

   Number each new and repeated term as you go. If the stimulus is conditional, start diagramming after the **1**. If it's not conditional, just write a simple translation between your numbers. If you see a negated term, give it a number and then squiggle it **(~)**, just like negated terms in conditional reasoning. For instance, "pachyderms **(1)** are not packing **(~2)**."

3. **Once you hit the end of the stimulus, read the whole thing back to yourself with just the numbers translation.**

4. **Number the answer choices. Choose the answer that matches the pattern in the stimulus.**

   Survey each answer choice before you start numbering; if the answer choice is totally off the rails, you don't even have to number it.

   Always number the answer choices in the same argument part order as the stimulus.

   Stop numbering when you realize the pattern is not the same as the stimulus. Incorrect answers add/delete numbers or use the numbers differently than the stimulus.

---

Let's number one of our examples together:

*Some magazines **(1)** are uninteresting **(~2)**. All uninteresting **(~2)** reading material is about dogs **(3)**. Therefore, some magazines **(1)** are about dogs **(3)**.*

How did the numbers happen? It's super similar to Skeleton design. I just replaced the flashy words with numbers instead of boring placeholders.

| | |
|---|---|
| **Some magazines are uninteresting.** | *The flashy words here are "magazines" and "uninteresting." We'll make "magazines" a **1** and make "uninteresting" a **~2**.* |
| **All uninteresting reading material is about dogs.** | *The flashy words here are "uninteresting reading material" and "dogs." We've already numbered "uninteresting" with a **~2**, so we can repeat that here. Now we have "dogs," a new flashy word. We'll make it a **3**.* |
| **Some magazines are about dogs.** | *We've already seen both flashy words here, "magazines" and "dogs." "Magazines" is a **1** and "dogs" is a **3**, so we'll write those numbers in.* |

The asterisk sidebar note:

I developed the numbers to help Alex, one particular student who *really* struggled with Parallel. He had tried and failed to implement basically every Parallel methodology on the market. After Alex learned the numbers, Parallel was simple. The numbers were so useful that I personally never went back to doing Wordy Parallels any other way.

Now, let's read the example just using the numbers and deleting the words that underlie them.

*Some **(1)**s are **(~2)**s. All **(~2)**s are **(3)**s. Therefore, some **(1)**s are **(3)**s.*

**PREMISES**    $1 \xleftrightarrow{s} {\sim}2 \longrightarrow 3$

**CONCLUSION**    $1 \xleftrightarrow{s} 3$

Now, check out the same pattern of numbers written out with different subjects. Both of these examples match. They would be correct answers, if this were a real question.

**CORRECT MATCH**
**SAME ORDER OF ARGUMENT PARTS**

*Some wallets **(1)** are not made of plastic **(~2)**. All things that are not made of plastic **(~2)** are cheap **(3)**. Therefore, some wallets **(1)** are cheap **(3)**.*

**PREMISES**    $1 \xleftrightarrow{s} {\sim}2 \longrightarrow 3$

**CONCLUSION**    $1 \xleftrightarrow{s} 3$

**CORRECT MATCH**
**DIFFERENT ORDER OF ARGUMENT PARTS**

*We know that some scenic vistas **(1)** are very exciting **(2)**. After all, some scenic vistas **(1)** are not boring **(~3)**, and all non-boring objects **(~3)** are very exciting **(2)**.*

**PREMISES**    $1 \xleftrightarrow{s} {\sim}3 \longrightarrow 2$

**CONCLUSION**    $1 \xleftrightarrow{s} 2$

Notice how the exact numbers and negations differed between these two examples, but the pattern remained the same. That's what matters for the correct answer.

I wanted you to see what a match looks like when the numbers and negations aren't exactly the same, so I purposefully did not label the second example in the same argument part order (breaking my own rules!). It's a little harder to see like this, but the two arguments still match. Reasoning from the first to the last number in the **SOME** chain is the core of the reasoning. That's what absolutely needs to happen for the answer to be correct.

**TOP 4 NUMBERS PRO TIPS**

1. **It's the pattern that has to match, not the individual 1s and 2s.**

    Imagine all your numbers were replaced by "this" and "that." Would the answer sound similar to the stimulus? If so, you have the correct answer.

2. **They will sometimes switch the order of the argument parts between the stimulus and the correct answer.**

    Number the answer choices in the same argument part order as the stimulus to make it easier to see the match. For instance, if the stimulus has the conclusion first, number it first in the answers too.

3. **You can eliminate most answers as soon as the pattern of reasoning diverges. Stop numbering once you realize it's wrong.**

    For example, if you have a pure if/then stimulus, you can quickly eliminate answer choices using **SOME/MOST**.

Another!

*We know that backwards baseball caps (**1**) cause red flags (**2**). For backwards baseball caps (**1**) cause people to be untrustworthy (**~3**) and unwholesome (**~4**), and untrustworthy (**~3**) and unwholesome (**~4**) behavior puts people in danger (**5**). Anything that could endanger (**5**) a given person produces red flags (**2**).*

This time we're facing causal reasoning. Let's see how the numbers can help us.

| | |
|---|---|
| **Backwards baseball caps cause red flags.** | *This is our conclusion. Our flashy words are "backwards baseball caps" and "red flags." We'll give "backwards baseball caps" a **1** and "red flags" a **2**.* |
| **Backwards baseball caps cause people to be untrustworthy and unwholesome.** | *We have one repeat and two new numbers. "Backwards baseball caps" is a **1**, so we'll pencil that in. "Untrustworthy" and "unwholesome" get new numbers. Since both words are negative, I'm going to give "untrustworthy" a **~3** and "unwholesome" a **~4**.* |
| **Untrustworthy and unwholesome behavior puts people in danger.** | *We already labeled "untrustworthy" a **~3** and "unwholesome" a **~4**, so let's write those again here. "Danger" is new, so let's give it a **5**.* |
| **Anything that could endanger a given person produces red flags.** | *The flashy words are "red flags" and "endanger a given person." "Red flags" is a repeat, so we just label it a **2** again. "Endanger" sounds a lot like "danger" from the previous phrase, so it's a repeat too. We'll label it with a **5**.* |

Here's the number translation:

*We know that **(1)**s cause **(2)**s. Because **(1)**s cause **(~3)** and **(~4)**, and **(~3)** and **(~4)** cause **(5)**. **(5)**s cause **(2)**s.*

Let's see how some correct matches look:

**CORRECT MATCH**
**SAME ORDER OF ARGUMENT PARTS**

*We know that potato chips **(1)** cause feelings of deliciousness **(2)**. Potato chips **(1)** cause a lack of despair **(~3)** and a lack of cheating **(~4)**, and a lack of despair **(~3)** and a lack of cheating **(~4)** cause one to become unhealthy **(5)**. Unhealthiness **(5)** produces feelings of deliciousness **(2)**.*

**CORRECT MATCH**
**DIFFERENT ORDER OF ARGUMENT PARTS**

*Painting a mural **(1)** causes us to waste time **(~3/4)**. Wasting time **(~3/4)** causes you to ignore your planner **(5)**. Bad ideas **(2)** result from ignoring your planner **(5)**. Therefore, painting a mural **(1)** causes bad ideas **(2)**.*

> I labeled the conclusion first (even when the order was different) because it was first in the original argument.

**Did you notice how ~3 and ~4 are combined in the second example? It is still a match despite this.** The test makers combine **AND/OR** statements like this in the correct answers to some particularly difficult Parallel questions. I don't love this trick, but you have to be ready for it because it could happen on your LSAT.

Here's why it works: "Untrustworthy **(~3)** and unwholesome **(~4)**" always operated together, as a unit, in the original argument. Go back and check it out. "Untrustworthy **(~3)** and unwholesome **(~4)**" were always one block. The pattern of reasoning treated them as one thing — so it's not a big leap to actually make them one thing in the correct answer. It's still the same pattern.

## TINY TIPS

- Some students strongly prefer using letters instead of numbers when designing their Skeleton and running the numbers. This is totally cool! You should do whatever works for you. The one downside of using letters: What if one of the letters you randomly use to represent things happens to correspond to a part of the stimulus that you don't intend? For example, say you always use **A**, **B**, **C**, **D** as placeholders, and then the first term you want to label is "dalmatians." It is literally a **D**, but you would want to use **A** because that's the order you typically go in. This is potentially confusing, so I avoid it altogether by going with the numbers instead.

- I hear this all the time: "But Parallel is soooooooooooo long…" OK, so Parallel is seriously not that long. Parallel questions tend to be longer than most other LR questions, but that does not mean that they are oppressively long to the point of unavoidable mental fatigue. An average-ish Parallel question is something like 250 words. (Did I manually count the number of words on ten Parallel questions to figure this out? Yes, yes I did.) If you scroll through Facebook/Twitter/Instagram for more than 10 minutes, you are reading thousands of words. **The difference between Parallel Reasoning and Facebook isn't the number of words; it's the level of attention that's required to understand the words.** Strengthen your attention and the length of the question won't be a problem.

> On average it takes between 6-11 Facebook statuses to equal one Parallel question.

Alright, let's see how the numbers work on a real Wordy Parallel question.

$1 \rightarrow \cancel{2} \rightarrow \cancel{3}$
$1 \rightarrow \cancel{3}$

## REAL WORDY PARALLEL EXAMPLE

*23.2.25*

I chose this Wordy Parallel example because, amongst the contenders, this was the question I personally could not easily do without the numbers. I found myself being lazy and evaluating a few Wordy Parallels without the numbers, but when I hit this one, I picked up my pencil and numbered it myself to peel back the thick layer of wordiness guarding relatively simple reasoning.

**Economist:** No economic system that is centrally planned can efficiently allocate resources, and efficient allocation of resources is a necessary condition for achieving a national debt of less than 5 percent of Gross Domestic Product (GDP). It follows that any nation with a centrally planned economy has a national debt that is at least 5 percent of GDP.

The pattern of reasoning exhibited by the economist's argument is most similar to that exhibited by which one of the following?

(A) Not all mammals are without wings, because bats are mammals and bats have wings.

(B) All of the rural districts are free of major air pollution problems because such problems occur only where there is a large concentration of automobiles, and there are no such places in the rural districts.

(C) All of the ungulates are herbivores, and most herbivores would not attack a human being. It follows that any animal that would attack a human being is unlikely to be an ungulate.

(D) All rock stars who are famous have their own record companies, and all rock stars with their own record companies receive company profits over and above their regular royalties. This implies that receiving large regular royalties is a necessary condition for being a famous rock star.

(E) Every mutual fund manager knows someone who trades on inside information, and no one who trades on inside information is unknown to every mutual fund manager. One must conclude that no mutual fund manager is unknown to everyone who trades on inside information.

$1 \xdashrightarrow{} 2 \rightarrow \cancel{3}$

First, let's translate each statement and number as we go. The first premise isn't so bad once you translate out the "no" from the conditional.

| First Premise Translation | If you're centrally planned **(1)**, then you can't efficiently allocate **(~2)**. |
|---|---|

Write the numbers **1 ⟶ ~2** on your scratch paper. Awesome. Let's translate the next statement.

| Second Premise Translation | If national debt is less than 5% of GDP **(3)**, then you're efficiently allocating **(2)**. |
|---|---|

That was a big simplification in translation. In fact, that bit about GDP is really what makes this question difficult. You have to spend enough time on this statement to really understand what it means. The phrase "is a necessary condition" helps because it tells you exactly where "efficiently allocating" goes on the diagram. From there, we just have that phrase about GDP. All it means is that the national debt is less than 5% of GDP.

Write the numbers **3 ⟶ 2** on your scratch paper. Alright, on to the conclusion.

| Conclusion Translation | If you're centrally planned **(1)**, then you have national debt at 5%+ of GDP **(~3)**. |
|---|---|

Beware of Parallel answer choices that use the same flashy words as the stimulus. They are almost always wrong.

The key to getting these numbers on the conclusion is the realization that the bit about GDP in the conclusion is the negated form of what we saw in the second premise. Once you make that connection, the conditional logic becomes clear and the chain comes together. Here's how the numbers and the diagram look:

| PREMISE | 1 ⟶ ~2 |
|---|---|
| PREMISE | 3 ⟶ 2 |
| CONCLUSION | 1 ⟶ ~3 |

*Economist: No economic system that is centrally planned (1) can efficiently allocate resources (~2), and efficient allocation of resources (2) is a necessary condition for achieving a national debt of less than 5 percent of Gross Domestic Product (GDP) (3). It follows that any nation with a centrally planned economy (1) has a national debt that is at least 5 percent of GDP (~3).*

Looks like the premises chain, right? Just gotta take the contrapositive of the second premise and link them up.

**PREMISE CHAIN**        **1 ⟶ ~2 ⟶ ~3**

We can read the chain from first term to last term and see the **1 ⟶ ~3** conclusion is valid. That's our pattern of reasoning: three-part premise chain and a conclusion that reads from the first to the last term. That's the pattern we want to find in the answer choices.

**A)** Not all mammals are without wings, because bats are mammals and bats have wings.

*So some mammals have wings because bats are mammals and have wings. I don't even have to number this answer choice. The NOT ALL (which I translated to SOME) is not a pure conditional; it's SOME/MOST. There is no SOME/MOST in the stimulus, so A isn't a provable match.*

**B)** All of the rural districts are free of major air pollution problems because such problems occur only where there is a large concentration of automobiles, and there are no such places in the rural districts.

*Alright, no obvious red flags here. Let's number it. Looks like the conclusion is the first sentence, but it was last in the stimulus, so I'll number it last. I'll start with translating "because such problems occur only where there is a large concentration of automobiles." What are "such problems"? I'll translate in "air pollution" as the "problem" to make things easier later.*

| **First Premise Translation** | air pollution (1) ⟶ car concentration (2) |
|---|---|

*Next, "there are no such places in the rural districts."*

| **Second Premise Translation** | car concentration (2) ⟶ NOT rural district (~3) |
|---|---|

*Ahhh… I'm seeing a much prettier version of our chain from the stimulus. So far the premises add up to: **1 ⟶ 2 ⟶ ~3**! Let's see if the conclusion messes it up:*

| **Conclusion Translation** | rural district (3) ⟶ NOT air pollution (~1) |
|---|---|

*So the conclusion (**3 ⟶ ~1**) is a correct reading of the chain! We have a three-part chain and a correct reading involving the first and the last term. **B**'s a match!*

You might be like, "But **B** used the contrapositive in the conclusion and the stimulus didn't! Riot!" It's OK that **B** used the contrapositive. Remember, the contrapositive is the same idea as the original statement, just read differently.

**C)** All of the ungulates are herbivores, and most herbivores would not attack a human being. It follows that any animal that would attack a human being is unlikely to be an ungulate.

*We've got SOME/MOST here too. That MOST in the second premise ("most herbivores") is deadly for **C**'s chances. I'm not eliminating **C** because "one word isn't right" or "it's not perfect." That MOST means there's an entirely different form of reasoning going on here. It's impossible for **C** to match.*

**D)** All rock stars who are famous have their own record companies, and all rock stars with their own record companies receive company profits over and above their regular royalties. This implies that receiving large regular royalties is a necessary condition for being a famous rock star.

*OK, no obvious red flags here. Time to number.*

| **First Premise Translation** | famous rock star (1) ⟶ star owns record (2) |

*Good so far.*

| **Second Premise Translation** | star owns record (2) ⟶ company profits (3) |

*Great. We have a three-part chain.*

| **Conclusion Translation** | famous rock star (1) ⟶ large royalties (4) |

*Boooooooooooo.* **D** *went rogue. There's a* **4** *in the conclusion here and no* **4** *in the stimulus. Notice, "receiving large regular royalties* **(4)***" ≠ "receive company profits over and above their regular royalties* **(3)***." There's something about the way* **D** *is worded that makes it really hard to see this difference at first, but* **D**'s *not a match.*

---

*You don't pull out a chainsaw to cut a piece of paper, just like you don't run the numbers when a Skeleton works. But, when you have an answer choice like* **E** *to cut through, you're glad you have the chainsaw, even if it's a pain to dig it out of the garage.*

*Check out the personalized if/then action on that second premise translation.*

**E)** Every mutual fund manager knows someone who trades on inside information, and no one who trades on inside information is unknown to every mutual fund manager. One must conclude that no mutual fund manager is unknown to everyone who trades on inside information.

*Nothing obviously wrong because who knows what that gibberish even means! Let's number one of the wordiest answers of all time.*

| **First Premise Translation** | mutual manager (1) ⟶ know insider (2) |

*Good so far, but now the second premise is exceptionally wordy. Let's break it down piece by piece: "No one who trades on inside information is unknown to every mutual fund manager." What does that actually mean? No insider trader is unknown to every mutual fund manager. OK, so if I'm an insider trader, then I'm not unknown to every fund manager. But what does it mean to be "not unknown to every mutual fund manager"? It means that you are known to some mutual fund manager. So I'm left with: If I'm an insider trader, I'm known to some mutual fund manager.*

| **Second Premise Translation** | insider (3) ⟶ known to mutual manager (4) |

*Now that we have the numbers, we can see that they aren't even chaining. Being an insider trader in the second premise is not the same term as knowing an insider trader in the first premise. Being known to a mutual fund manager is not the same thing as knowing an insider trader.* **E** *is done, so there's no point continuing to number. The conclusion introduces even more new terms, taking* **E** *even further from a provable match.*

**B** is the correct answer. It's the only one that executes a three-part chain and reads it like the stimulus.

## PARALLEL REASONING CHALLENGE

*18.2.13*

Because some student demonstrations protesting his scheduled appearance have resulted in violence, the president of the Imperialist Society has been prevented from speaking about politics on campus by the dean of student affairs. Yet to deny anyone the unrestricted freedom to speak is to threaten everyone's right to free expression. Hence, the dean's decision has threatened everyone's right to free expression.

The pattern of reasoning displayed above is most closely paralleled in which one of the following?

(A) Dr. Pacheco saved a child's life by performing emergency surgery. But surgery rarely involves any risk to the surgeon. Therefore, if an act is not heroic unless it requires the actor to take some risk, Dr. Pacheco's surgery was not heroic.

(B) Because anyone who performs an act of heroism acts altruistically rather than selfishly, a society that rewards heroism encourages altruism rather than pure self-interest.

(C) In order to rescue a drowning child, Isabel jumped into a freezing river. Such acts of heroism performed to save the life of one enrich the lives of all. Hence, Isabel's action enriched the lives of all.

(D) Fire fighters are often expected to perform heroically under harsh conditions. But no one is ever required to act heroically. Hence, fire fighters are often expected to perform actions they are not required to perform.

(E) Acts of extreme generosity are usually above and beyond the call of duty. Therefore, most acts of extreme generosity are heroic, since all actions that are above and beyond the call of duty are heroic.

*20.4.15*

Rhonda will see the movie tomorrow afternoon only if Paul goes to the concert in the afternoon. Paul will not go to the concert unless Ted agrees to go to the concert. However, Ted refuses to go to the concert. So Rhonda will not see the movie tomorrow afternoon.

The pattern of reasoning displayed above is most closely paralleled in which one of the following?

(A) If Janice comes to visit, Mary will not pay the bills tomorrow. Janice will not come to visit unless she locates a babysitter. However, Janice has located a babysitter, so she will visit Mary.

(B) Gary will do his laundry tomorrow only if Peter has to go to work. Unless Cathy is ill, Peter will not have to go to work. Since Cathy is not ill, Gary will not do his laundry tomorrow.

(C) Kelly will barbecue fish tonight if it does not rain and the market has fresh trout. Although the forecast does not call for rain, the market does not have fresh trout. So Kelly will not barbecue fish tonight.

(D) Lisa will attend the family reunion next week only if one of her brothers, Jared or Karl, also attends. Karl will not attend the reunion, but Jared will. So Lisa will attend the reunion.

(E) George will not go to the museum tomorrow unless Mark agrees to go. Mark will go to the museum only if he can postpone most of his appointments. Mark has postponed some of his appointments, so he will go to the museum.

*Where's the answer key?*

*You'll find the answer key for all the Challenge Questions at the end of the chapter on page 387.*

## Parallel Flaw

| QUESTION STEM KEYWORDS | | POPULARITY | About 1 question per section |
|---|---|---|---|
| • parallel <br> • pattern of reasoning <br> • flawed / dubious / questionable / faulty <br> • analogy | | **WHAT YOU'RE LOOKING FOR** | The answer choice that exhibits the same flaw as the stimulus |
| | | **ROLE OF THE LOOPHOLE** | Your Loophole identifies the flaw to match. Choose the answer that has the same Loophole as the stimulus. |
| **QUESTION STEM EXAMPLES** | | **TL;DR STRATEGY** | You already have a Loophole. It should reveal a flaw. <br><br> Go find that same flaw exhibited in an answer choice. |
| • Which one of the following arguments exhibits flawed reasoning that is most parallel to that in the argument above? <br> • The flawed reasoning in which one of the following arguments most closely resembles the flawed reasoning in the argument above? <br> • Which one of the following is most appropriate as an analogy demonstrating that the reasoning in the argument above is flawed? | | **BACK-UP PLAN** | Does this match the flaw in the stimulus? <br><br> • If yes, choose it. <br> • If no, cross it off. <br> • If you're not sure, leave it for later. |

**I'm overjoyed when I see that one of the Parallel-looking questions is Parallel Flaw instead of Parallel Reasoning. Parallel Flaw usually requires a lot less detail work to answer.**

### PARALLEL FLAW GAME PLAN

Parallel Flaw is similar to Parallel Reasoning, but not *exactly* the same. In Parallel Flaw, your task is to literally find the parallel flaw. Meaning, your Loophole finds the stimulus' flaw and you go find the same flaw in the answer choices.

I really struggled with Parallel Flaw when I first started prepping for the LSAT. I was holding the answer choices in Parallel Flaw to the same standard I was using on Parallel Reasoning. When I didn't see that exact premise-for-premise match, I would get frustrated and recheck my work over and over again, thinking I was missing something. Often, Parallel Flaw provides a lot more leeway on its parallelness. Trust me, I learned this one the hard way. **As long as the flaw matches, it's the correct answer.**

If you think that two answer choices are both displaying the same matching flaw, use the tactics described in the Parallel Reasoning section. They will work to narrow things down. The danger is that those tactics may make you too picky, if applied generally and with zeal.

### TINY TIPS

• Find the Loophole in the stimulus and then in each answer choice. When an answer choice Loophole matches the stimulus Loophole, choose it. That's Parallel Flaw.

- Watch out for the valid version of the reasoning in the stimulus. For instance, if the stimulus contains a conditional flaw, there will almost certainly be at least one valid conditional answer choice. Do not choose that answer choice. Be absolutely sure that the answer you choose is flawed.

## REAL PARALLEL FLAW EXAMPLE

*18.2.17*

Biographer:    Arnold's belief that every offer of assistance on the part of his colleagues was a disguised attempt to make him look inadequate and that no expression of congratulations on his promotion should be taken at face value may seem irrational. In fact, this belief was a consequence of his early experiences with an admired older sister who always made fun of his ambitions and achievements. In light of this explanation, therefore, Arnold's stubborn belief that his colleagues were duplicitous emerges as clearly justified.

The flawed reasoning in the biographer's argument is most similar to that in which one of the following?

(A)   The fact that top executives generally have much larger vocabularies than do their subordinates explains why Sheldon's belief, instilled in him during his childhood, that developing a large vocabulary is the way to get to the top in the world of business is completely justified.

(B)   Emily suspected that apples are unhealthy ever since she almost choked to death while eating an apple when she was a child. Now, evidence that apples treated with certain pesticides can be health hazards shows that Emily's long-held belief is fully justified.

(C)   As a child, Joan was severely punished whenever she played with her father's prize Siamese cat. Therefore, since this information makes her present belief that cats are not good pets completely understandable, that belief is justified.

(D)   Studies show that when usually well-behaved children become irritable, they often exhibit symptoms of viral infections the next day. The suspicion, still held by many adults, that misbehavior must always be paid for is thus both explained and justified.

(E)   Sumayia's father and mother were both concert pianists, and as a child, Sumayia knew several other people trying to make careers as musicians. Thus Sumayia's opinion that her friend Anthony lacks the drive to be a successful pianist is undoubtedly justified.

First, translate and enjoy.

*Biographer: Arnold thinks that whenever someone helps him or congratulates him, they're really just trying to make him look inadequate. He thinks this way because his sister made fun of his ambitions when he was a kid. His belief is justified because of this past explanation.*

The conclusion is that Arnold's belief about his colleagues is justified. But why would an explanation necessarily justify his current belief? There's a difference between explanation and justification. "Justified" is the dangling variable in the conclusion.

Arnold's sister making fun of his ambition explains why Arnold is a paranoid crazy, but that doesn't mean Arnold's justified to think his colleagues are out to get him. The explanation just shows why he's viewing their actions through that lens. Our Loophole needs to highlight this difference between explanation and justification.

**LOOPHOLE**   What if the past explanation for a current belief doesn't justify that belief?

So now that we see it's Parallel Flaw, we'll look for an answer with this same Loophole. If we run into trouble, we can always Skeleton the stimulus. Let's head to the answer choices and find our Loophole in action.

This question is phenomenal, and it only gets better in the answer choices. Welcome to law firm life, where everything that seems nice is actually an elaborate ploy to destroy you.

**A)** The fact that top executives generally have much larger vocabularies than do their subordinates explains why Sheldon's belief, instilled in him during his childhood, that developing a large vocabulary is the way to get to the top in the world of business is completely justified.

*So executives have better vocabularies, and this explains Sheldon's childhood belief that large vocabularies send you straight to the top. So Sheldon's childhood belief is justified. This doesn't match our Loophole. The timeline is backwards. We want a past experience to erroneously justify a present belief. **A** has a present fact erroneously explaining and then justifying a past belief. It also has some false causation thrown in for good measure. Not a match.*

**B)** Emily suspected that apples are unhealthy ever since she almost choked to death while eating an apple when she was a child. Now, evidence that apples treated with certain pesticides can be health hazards shows that Emily's long-held belief is fully justified.

*So Emily has a childhood belief that apples are unhealthy because she almost choked to death on an apple. The current fact that pesticides on apples are unhealthy justifies Emily's childhood belief. **B** is very similar to **A**; the timeline is still backwards. We don't want to justify a childhood belief. We want to erroneously justify a current belief with a past explanation. In this case, Emily has believed apples are unhealthy forever, and she's using this new information to justify that past belief. Not the same Loophole. Not a match.*

**C)** As a child, Joan was severely punished whenever she played with her father's prize Siamese cat. Therefore, since this information makes her present belief that cats are not good pets completely understandable, that belief is justified.

*So Joan was punished for playing with a cat as a child. This makes her current belief that cats are bad pets understandable, and therefore, justified. But what if a past explanation doesn't make a current belief justified? The Loophole works here too! While Joan's childhood experience makes her belief more understandable (just like Arnold), we can't equate an explanation with justification. The timeline matches. We've got a past explanation and a justified present belief. Perfect match.*

**D)** Studies show that when usually well-behaved children become irritable, they often exhibit symptoms of viral infections the next day. The suspicion, still held by many adults, that misbehavior must always be paid for is thus both explained and justified.

*So studies show that when normally good children are bad, they get sick the next day. So the adults' belief that you always pay for being bad is explained and justified. The problem here is that they aren't equating explanation with justification. The Loophole doesn't hold because the conclusion contains both explained and justified. There's no jump from one to the other. **D's** not a match.*

⁕ Also, **D** is for real arguing that kids get sick as a punishment for misbehaving, like illness karma. WHAT.

**E)** Sumayia's father and mother were both concert pianists, and as a child, Sumayia knew several other people trying to make careers as musicians. Thus Sumayia's opinion that her friend Anthony lacks the drive to be a successful pianist is undoubtedly justified.

*So Sumayia grew up around professional pianists. Therefore, her opinion that her friend Anthony doesn't have what it takes to be a successful pianist is justified. Notice that there's nothing about explaining anything in* **E**. *They basically just qualify Sumayia to have an opinion and then say that her opinion is justified. There's no jump from explanation to justification. The same Loophole doesn't apply. Not a match.*

## PARALLEL FLAW CHALLENGE

*15.2.4*

A recent study monitored the blood pressure of people petting domestic animals in the laboratory. The blood pressure of some of these people lowered while petting the animals. Therefore, for any one of the people so affected, owning a pet would result in that person having a lower average blood pressure.

The flawed pattern of reasoning in the argument above is most similar to that in which one of the following?

 (A) Because a single dose of a drug acts as a remedy for a particular ailment, a healthy person can ward off that ailment by taking single doses regularly.

 (B) Because buying an automobile is very expensive, people should hold on to an automobile, once bought, for as long as it can be maintained in running condition.

 (C) Since pruning houseplants is enjoyable for some people, those people should get rid of houseplants that do not require frequent pruning.

 (D) Since riding in a boat for a few minutes is relaxing for some people, those people would be more relaxed generally if those people owned boats.

 (E) Since giving a fence one coat of white paint makes the fence white, giving it two coats of white paint would make it even whiter.

**C** is the correct answer. It's the only answer that has the exact same Loophole as the stimulus.

*Where's the answer key?*

You'll find the answer key for all the Challenge Questions at the end of the chapter on page 387.

---

### PRINCIPLE & PARALLEL QUESTIONS GAME PLAN

- Always look for the provable match in the answer choices. Mimic the linguistic structures from the stimulus when you get to the answer choices.

- Never skip translation on Principle & Parallel.

- Focus on matching the pattern, not the exact numbers, on Wordy Parallel.

- Memorize the question stem keywords for the Principle & Parallel Questions now.

## Quiz 11  PRINCIPLE & PARALLEL QUESTIONS

### INSTRUCTIONS

*Answer these questions based on your knowledge of the chapter. Attempt to answer without looking back at the chapter first. If you don't know the answer, circle the question number and go find the answer in the chapter. Study the sections of the chapter that you couldn't remember at first.*

### Word Bank

Parallel Flaw              Parallel Reasoning              Principle Conform

**1.**  Complete the table using the word bank. Each question type will be used exactly once.

| QUESTION TYPE | CORRECT ANSWER |
|---|---|
| PR | The answer that's built around the same Skeleton as the stimulus |
| PC | The matching example or matching principle |
| PF | The answer that exhibits the same flaw as the stimulus |

*Circle the correct answer to the following questions.*

**2.**  TRUE OR ~~FALSE~~  Parallel Reasoning and Parallel Flaw questions are Powerful Questions.

**3.**  ~~TRUE~~ OR ~~FALSE~~  The principle and its example are interchangeable.

**4.**  ~~TRUE~~ OR FALSE  You can only prove things that live in the necessary condition.

**5.**  ~~TRUE~~ OR ~~FALSE~~  A Skeleton should keep all the flashy words from the stimulus.

**6.**  ~~TRUE~~ OR FALSE  When Running the Numbers, you should be most concerned with whether the *pattern* of numbers matches, not whether the individual numbers match.

**7.**  TRUE OR ~~FALSE~~  Parallel Flaw is exactly the same as Parallel Reasoning.

*Where's the answer key?*

You'll find the answer key at the end of the chapter on page 388.

# Principle & Parallel Challenge Questions     ANSWER KEY

| Principle Conform | 23.2.13 | A |
|---|---|---|
| Standard Parallel | 18.2.13 | C |
| Wordy Parallel | 20.4.15 | B |
| Parallel Flaw | 15.2.4 | D |

＊

Looking for a little extra help on these Challenge Questions?

You'll find explanations for each of the Challenge Questions online at elementalprep.com/bonus.

## Quiz 11   ANSWER KEY

### 1.

| QUESTION TYPE | CORRECT ANSWER |
| --- | --- |
| Parallel Reasoning | The answer that's built around the same Skeleton as the stimulus |
| Principle Conform | The matching example or matching principle |
| Parallel Flaw | The answer that exhibits the same flaw as the stimulus |

### 2.

False. Parallel Reasoning and Parallel Flaw questions are *Provable* Questions.

### 3.

True.

### 4.

True.

### 5.

False. A Skeleton should *strip out* all the flashy words from the stimulus.

### 6.

True.

### 7.

False. Parallel Flaw just wants you to match the *flaw* from the stimulus with the same flaw in the correct answer.

# OMMMM.

chapter eleven. in your possession.

## Chapter Breather  THE FAST AND THE QUESTION STEM QUIZ

### INSTRUCTIONS

*For each of the following question stems, identify the question type and circle the correct Powerful/Provable identification.*

| | QUESTION STEM | QUESTION TYPE | POWERFUL/PROVABLE |
|---|---|---|---|
| 1. | Which one of the following, if true, most helps to resolve the apparent paradox? | Resolve | (Powerful) or Provable? |
| 2. | The reasoning in the researcher's argument is questionable in that the argument overlooks the possibility that | Loophole Fran | Powerful or (Provable)? |
| 3. | Which one of the following is a questionable technique employed by the producer in responding to the critic? | Classic Flaw | Powerful or (Provable)? |
| 4. | The information above, if accurate, can best be used as evidence against which one of the following hypotheses? | Contradiction | (Powerful) or Provable? |
| 5. | The information above provides the most support for which one of the following statements? | MSS | Powerful or (Provable)? |
| 6. | Which one of the following most accurately describes how the argument proceeds? | Method | Powerful or (Provable)? |
| 7. | Which one of the following, if true, most tends to undermine the argument? | Weaken | (Powerful) or Provable? |
| 8. | The conclusion drawn above follows logically if which one of the following is assumed? | SA | (Powerful) or Provable? |
| 9. | The argument assumes which one of the following? | Necessary | Powerful or (Provable)? |
| 10. | Which one of the following conforms most closely to the principle illustrated above? | Principle Conform | Powerful or (Provable)? |
| 11. | Which one of the following can properly be concluded from the information given above? | Inferred | Powerful or (Provable)? |
| 12. | Which one of the following, if true, provides the most support for the argument? | Strengthen | (Powerful) or Provable? |

❋

*Where's the answer key?*

You'll find the answer key after the next Breather on page 421.

CHAPTER

# 12

# THE
# ANSWER
# CHOICES

## Powerful or Provable?  THE SPECTRUM OF ANSWER CHOICE SUCCESS

> If you skipped the Powerful-Provable Primer, **go back to page 257 and read it now.** You will not be well served reading this chapter without reading the Powerful-Provable Primer first.

All correct answer choices are either powerful or provable.

We're finally moving to the answer choices, you guys! The hardest part of Logical Reasoning is here!

Why'd it take so long to get here? The test writers are *really* good at crafting devious wrong answers; that's why we needed to master the stimulus and the question types first. To quickly and intuitively see through the wrong answer traps, you need a strong defense against their power of suggestion.

Now we're placing the answer choice types on the Powerful-Provable Spectrum, just like we did with the question types. This will vastly simplify your Logical Reasoning approach. Pay close attention to the next page. The Complete Powerful-Provable Spectrum shows which answer choice types are great for which question types, summarizing a couple hundred pages (and a couple years of research). It's the ultimate Logical Reasoning cheat sheet.

❋

The Complete Powerful-Provable Spectrum is also known as "The Entirety of Ellen Cassidy's Late Twenties."

> **Flip your book and study The Complete Powerful-Provable Spectrum on the next page.** Everything you need to know about the question types and the answer choice types is summarized here.

Throughout this chapter, we'll discuss each of these answer choice types in the context of the Powerful-Provable Spectrum. We'll start with the Red Flags, generally dangerous answer choices on any question. These answers land in the middle of the Powerful-Provable Spectrum, meaning they're neither powerful nor provable. Then we'll move to Powerful Answers (great on Powerful Questions) and Provable Answers (great on Provable Questions).

❋

You always have to play the cards you're dealt — many answer choice sets aren't going to contain a mythically perfect correct answer. You just want the most Powerful/Provable Answer out of what you have to work with.

The answer choice types represent the generalizations I've gleaned from thousands of Logical Reasoning answer choices. But they are just that: generalizations. Logical Reasoning tests both reasoning ability (more of a science) and your facility with language (more of an art). That artistic side does not lend itself to hard and fast rules, so there will always be exceptions. **Let the answer choice types give you a baseline level of skepticism and favor,** but if you have a good reason to believe that something I've cautioned you against is correct, choose it.

# PROVABLE

CONCLUSION

INFERENCE

MSS

FILL IN

CONTROVERSY

AGREEMENT

NA

METHOD

ARGUMENT PART

CLASSIC FLAW

LOOPHOLE FLAW

PRINCIPLE CONFORM

PARALLEL REASONING

PARALLEL FLAW

PROVABLE CONDITIONALS

WEAK ANSWERS

## ANSWER CHOICE TYPES

RED FLAGS

OPPOSITE CLAIM

DORMANT CONDITIONALS

COMPARATIVES & ABSOLUTES

ALLLLLLMOST

GROUPED EXTREME

IMPORTANT

CRAZY NONSENSE

BEST WAY

GROUPED OPPOSITE

POWERFUL CONDITIONALS

STEPLADDER

STRONG ANSWERS

## THE COMPLETE POWERFUL-PROVABLE SPECTRUM

# POWERFUL

STRENGTHEN

WEAKEN

SA

COUNTER

CONTRADICTION

EVALUATE

RESOLUTION

# Best Way    RED FLAG

**POWERLFUL** ↓↑ **PROVABLE**

**WHAT'S BEST WAY?**

Best Way literally uses the words "best way" or a Best Way keyword.

**REAL LSAT EXAMPLE:** *June 2007.3.24*

Sociologist:    Romantics who claim that people are not born evil but may be made evil by the imperfect institutions that they form cannot be right, for they misunderstand the causal relationship between people and their institutions. After all, institutions are merely collections of people.

**BEST WAY ANSWER**

A society's institutions are the **surest gauge** of that society's values.

The following answer choices reside near the middle of The Complete Powerful-Provable Spectrum. They are suspect on all the question types.

Answer choice types are mostly consistent regardless of the question type (meaning a Best Way is always a Best Way regardless of what question it's attached to). I won't list the question type of the answer choice type examples, unless the question type matters for the classification.

Best Way is the best precisely because it is so the worst. It's a prevalent incorrect answer, falling into the mediocre middle of our Powerful-Provable Spectrum. Why is it so bad? Best Way has two things that are dangerous on their own but deadly when combined: superlatives and value judgments. This combination is what renders Best Way neither powerful nor provable.

Here are a few examples of how Best Way and its keywords look:

Best Way

The **best way** to milk a cow is to shout at it.

The **least harmful** method for digging a ditch is harmonizing with your friends.

The **most efficient way** to remedy the budget deficit is to increase spending.

**Best Way is not powerful.**

Deeming something "the best" isn't powerful when we don't know why it's the best. The reason it's the best is what would make the answer powerful. Powerful Answers are specific, concrete, and applicable to the stimulus. Best Way is none of those things.

**Best Way is not provable.**

Best Way claims something is superior to literally every other option; a claim that extreme has a ton of potential Loopholes to account for. It's *really* hard to prove.

Best Way has a few friends to be cautious about as well: the Best Way keywords. They're all constructed like this: **[superlative]** + **[value judgment]**. Keep in mind, this list of keywords is not exhaustive. The **[superlative]** + **[value judgment]** combinations are virtually endless.

**A FEW BEST WAY KEYWORDS**

*most effective*          *most efficient*          *least harmful*          *least damaging*

**IS THERE ANY TIME WHEN BEST WAY COULD BE OK?**

When the stimulus is literally about the best way to do something, you're safe to choose Best Way.

Seriously, there is a Parallel Reasoning question in PrepTest 58 that has "The best way..." in every single answer choice. I feel so trolled.

# Important     RED FLAG

**POWERFUL** ←———————————↓———————————→ **PROVABLE**
                          ↑

| WHAT'S IMPORTANT? | REAL LSAT EXAMPLE: *24.2.22* | IMPORTANT ANSWER | |
|---|---|---|---|

**Important identifies something as "important" or an Important keyword.**

Copernicus's astronomical system is superior to Ptolemy's and was so at the time it was proposed, even though at that time all observational evidence was equally consistent with both theories. Ptolemy believed that the stars revolved around the earth at great speeds. This struck Copernicus as unlikely; he correctly thought that a simpler theory is that the earth rotates on its axis.

Other things being equal, the simpler of two competing theories is the more ***scientifically important*** theory.

Spoiler: Important is not actually important.

Important is the squishiest faker out there. Arguments are built and destroyed with facts, and Important has nothing to do with facts; it's a vague adjective. Just like with Best Way, we don't know why this thing is being labeled important, and those reasons are what could be powerful or provable. This lands Important stranded in the middle of our Powerful-Provable Spectrum. Basically, don't choose Important, unless you have a good reason.

**Important is not powerful.**

Just calling something important isn't powerful. To be powerful, we need the facts behind *why* the thing is important. Cool it with the judgments.

**Important is not provable.**

Important is too vague to be provable. There's no universal definition of what makes something "important," meaning we can't really prove anything "important" without a ton of specific stimulus ammunition.

The word "important" reeks of snake oil.

Important has friends too: the Important keywords. All of the caution for Important also applies to these guys.

### A FEW IMPORTANT KEYWORDS

| | | | | |
|---|---|---|---|---|
| *primary* | *primarily* | *foremost* | *crucial* | *critical* |
| *imperative* | *paramount* | *significant* | *pressing* | *vital* |

They like to glue the word "factor" after Important and its keywords.

### IS THERE ANY TIME WHEN IMPORTANT COULD BE OK?

Important becomes viable if the stimulus has explicitly mentioned something being important. An answer choice that mirrors language from the stimulus is always promising.

## Crazy Nonsense    RED FLAG

POWERFUL ←→ PROVABLE

**WHAT'S CRAZY NONSENSE?**

**Crazy Nonsense has nothing to do with anything in the stimulus.**

**REAL LSAT EXAMPLE:** *June 2007.2.14*

A cup of raw milk, after being heated in a microwave oven to 50 degrees Celsius, contains half its initial concentration of a particular enzyme, lysozyme. If, however, the milk reaches that temperature through exposure to a conventional heat source of 50 degrees Celsius, it will contain nearly all of its initial concentration of the enzyme. Therefore, what destroys the enzyme is not heat but microwaves, which generate heat.

**CRAZY NONSENSE ANSWER**

Milk that has been heated in a microwave oven does not *taste noticeably different* from milk that has been briefly heated by exposure to a conventional heat source.

Crazy Nonsense is exactly what it sounds like: crazy and nonsense. The subject of Crazy Nonsense is never mentioned in the stimulus. They make you think, "What? This has nothing to do with anything." Crazy Nonsense is the easiest answer choice to get rid of, if you accept the fact that the LSAT will purposefully put stupid things in the answer choices (you should accept this because they *definitely* do). Their craziness is neither powerful nor provable.

What's Crazy Nonsense look like? Here are a few examples:

| STIMULUS SUBJECT | CRAZY NONSENSE ANSWER CHOICE | DON'T WORK FOR IT! |
|---|---|---|
| **bacteria X causes liver disease** | Bacteria X doesn't cause hair loss. | Don't stretch your mind to try to connect liver disease to hair loss just because they happened to include an answer choice with hair loss. |
| **embroiderers in 16th century England** | Dressmakers in 16th century England had high mortality rates. | Don't start overthinking. Don't consider, "But maybe dressmakers and embroiderers are the same people? Sometimes?" |
| **amount of leisure time for factory workers** | The average American spends 10% of their income on leisure activities. | Don't start the imagination train: "Maybe if they are working less they have less money to spend? Then they wouldn't spend that money on leisure? Right?" |

You may wonder why I even include Crazy Nonsense in a discussion of the answer choices. I mean I named it Crazy Nonsense, and these are supposedly the easiest to eliminate. Why waste the page space and your valuable time? Well, I include it because brilliant students choose Crazy Nonsense in real life. They use their brilliant minds to make a million excuses for Crazy Nonsense, but this needs to stop. **Stop making excuses for answer choices.**

Why do we choose Crazy Nonsense? Lack of confidence. Trust yourself. There's an 80% chance that any given answer choice is wrong. **Unless you are literally missing 20 questions per section (80% wrong), you are statistically better off trusting yourself instead of an answer choice.** Students often say, "This is hard. Let me see if the answer choices can help." The answer choices are not there to help. 80% of the answer choices are designed to destroy you. Don't let your guard down.

## Crazy Nonsense is not powerful.

You have to target the stimulus to be powerful. Crazy Nonsense is out of left field; it's not doing what a Powerful Question needs.

## Crazy Nonsense is not provable

Provability requires a firm stimulus link. This is exactly what Crazy Nonsense doesn't have.

**REMEMBER!**    *Your mantra against Crazy Nonsense:* ***The answer choices work for me; I don't work for them.***

### IS THERE ANY TIME WHEN CRAZY NONSENSE COULD BE OK?

In the hardest of questions, the correct answer could initially look like Crazy Nonsense. Here are the times to entertain what may seem like Crazy Nonsense:

| | |
|---|---|
| **You've gotten rid of every answer choice.** | In this case, do an Answer Choice Reset (fully explained on page 256). You're still in control. Don't let the answer choices suggest at you. Make a Mission and see which answer completes it. |
| **It could be a Loophole in the argument.** | Sometimes Loopholes can initially look off-topic, but they're linked to the argument in a powerful way. |
| **It could be an Omitted Option.** | One of the Omitted Options is New Factor Causing One or Both. And new factors are... well... new. They have to introduce new information that could look like it's from out of nowhere. But it will be linked to something from the stimulus. This link is what separates Crazy Nonsense from a potentially Powerful Answer. |
| **It's a specific example of a category from the stimulus.** | Sometimes the stimulus will be about a large category, like mammals or emporiums. Potentially Powerful/Provable Answers may mention a category member as long as they link it to the stimulus. |
| | Imagine a stimulus about emporiums and an answer that begins, "Rudy's, a successful local emporium..." That clause defining Rudy's as an emporium makes all the difference. Without it, we don't know what Rudy's is. But with that link, we're talking about something potentially powerful or provable. |

## Grouped Extreme    RED FLAG

**POWERFUL** ← | → **PROVABLE**

**WHAT'S A GROUPED EXTREME?**

A Grouped Extreme centers on the most extreme part of the group discussed in the stimulus.

**REAL LSAT EXAMPLE:** *June 2007.3.14*

Commentator:   In academic scholarship, sources are always cited, and methodology and theoretical assumptions are set out, so as to allow critical study, replication, and expansion of scholarship. In open-source software, the code in which the program is written can be viewed and modified by individual users for their purposes without getting permission from the producer or paying a fee. In contrast, the code of proprietary software is kept secret, and modifications can be made only by the producer, for a fee. This shows that open-source software better matches the values embodied in academic scholarship, and since scholarship is central to the mission of universities, universities should use only open-source software.

**GROUPED EXTREME ANSWER**

*Whatever software tools are most advanced* and can achieve the goals of academic scholarship are the ones that should alone be used in universities.

Grouped Extremes talk about the best/worst part of the group from the stimulus. They really say, "A small part of the group referred to in the stimulus has this quality." But we unconsciously cut Grouped Extremes a lot more slack than we would give to this phrasing. Why? Because extremes sound important. In real life, we pay attention to the people who are the best/worst at something. On the LSAT, you have to protect against this tendency. Here's how Grouped Extremes look:

**Grouped Extremes**

The boxers who punch the **hardest**...

The boxers with the **fewest** blocks...

The **best** boxers in the league...

**Grouped Extremes are not powerful.**

The best/worst part of any group is necessarily a small part of that group. Assigning a characteristic to an outlier doesn't necessarily affect anything else in the group. Powerful Answers affect the stimulus, which isn't in the cards for Grouped Extreme.

**Grouped Extremes are not provable.**

Provable Answers find direct support in the stimulus. Since Grouped Extremes are about a necessarily small (and unrepresentative) part of the stimulus, they are super tough to prove.

**IS THERE ANY TIME WHEN GROUPED EXTREMES COULD BE OK?**

When the stimulus hinges on the quality mentioned in the Grouped Extreme, you must consider these answer choices. As always, the stimulus is king.

# Allllllllmost   RED FLAG

**POWERFUL** ←→ **PROVABLE**

## WHAT'S ALLLLLLLMOST?

An Allllllllmost is *totally* right except for one word or phrase that is off-the-rails wrong.

## REAL LSAT EXAMPLE: *24.3.24*

Ethicist:   A society is just when, and only when, first, each person has an equal right to basic liberties, and second, inequalities in the distribution of income and wealth are not tolerated unless these inequalities are to everyone's advantage and are attached to jobs open to everyone.

## ALLLLLLLMOST ANSWER

Society S guarantees everyone an equal right to basic liberties, while allowing inequalities in the distribution of income and wealth that are to the advantage of everyone. Further, the jobs to which these inequalities are attached are open to **most people**. Thus, society S is just.

Analyze this example stimulus and think through why the "most people" sinks the Allllllllmost's chances. The question type is Principle Conform.

In your heart of hearts, you know that one word in Allllllllmost is **wrong**. It's not non-ideal; it's **WRONG**. It shouldn't be there, but the rest of the answer choice looks so good that you still want to choose Allllllllmost. Allllllllmost is an especially enticing option if none of the other answer choices look particularly good. However, the word that you know is wrong renders the rest of the answer choice neither powerful nor provable.

## Allllllllmost is not powerful.

The one wrong word throws Allllllllmost off its target, neutralizing any power it would have had otherwise.

## Allllllllmost is not provable.

It's impossible to prove that one wrong word in Allllllllmost, so the whole answer choice becomes impossible to prove. You have to be able to prove the *entire* answer choice for it to be a provable option.

**Every single word in the correct answer has to be passable.** You can't take an average on an answer that is 95% great and 5% completely wrong and call it pretty good. That 95-5 answer is out 100% of the time. **Choose an inoffensive, mediocre-sounding answer over an Allllllllmost.**

It's better to choose an answer you don't completely understand than to choose an answer you know has major problems, even if those problems revolve around just one word.

Allllllllmost illustrates the importance of reading and considering every answer *in its entirety* before choosing it or crossing it off. Many students consider the beginning or end of an answer choice more than its other half; this leads to avoidable errors. One word at the end (or beginning) can tank an answer's chances. **There are no "important parts" of answer choices. The entire answer is the most important part.**

## Opposite Claim    RED FLAG

POWERFUL                                                                                          PROVABLE

### WHAT'S OPPOSITE CLAIM?

An **Opposite Claim**
is about the opposite
of the argument's
conclusion.

### REAL LSAT EXAMPLE: *24.2.24*

No mathematical proposition can be proven true by
observation. It follows that it is impossible to know
any mathematical proposition to be true.

### OPPOSITE CLAIM ANSWER

If a proposition can
be proven true by
observation, then it
*can be known to be true.*

Opposite Claim
answer choices are
especially prevalent
when stimuli contain a
recommendation, usually
using the word "should."
This is especially
common on Principle
Conform.

Opposite Claim negates the conclusion of the stimulus and characterizes that negation. It's a little more complicated
than the other Red Flags, which is why it's slightly closer to the powerful side of The Complete Powerful-Provable
Spectrum. But Opposite Claim is still dangerous on most questions. Check out a couple examples:

### CONCLUSION

The land baron **should be** fined.

Therefore, Theodore **is a liar.**

### OPPOSITE CLAIM

Land barons **should not be** fined for mistreating their underlings.

People are **not liars** when we cannot incontrovertibly prove their ideas false.

**Opposite Claim can be powerful on Weaken and
Counter... it just doesn't happen often.**

Since Opposite Claim is about the opposite of the
conclusion, it's hard to choose on most Powerful
Questions.

That said, Opposite Claim is powerful when you want to
prove the opposite of the conclusion. It can be ideal in
really simple Weaken and Counter questions.

**Opposite Claim is not provable.**

You can't prove anything about the world where the
opposite of the conclusion is true. That's not the world
you have information about. Opposite Claim is an
especially bad idea on Principle Conform.

### WHEN CAN OPPOSITE CLAIM BE POWERFUL?

If you think a conditional
is Opposite Claim,
make sure you're taking
the contrapositive into
account.

**Opposite Claim can say the premises lead to the opposite of the conclusion.** This would, indeed, cast doubt on
the validity of the conclusion, which is what we want on Weaken and Counter. Check out this example:

> The novelist **should not be** blamed for the poor sales of her last book. The publisher's marketing strategy
> was flawed from the start. Without a marketing campaign, it didn't matter how epic the novel was.

### OPPOSITE CLAIM

Novelists should be blamed for the consequences of marketing campaigns for
their books.

This Opposite Claim makes the conclusion less likely, right? If this were a Weaken or Counter question, this Opposite
Claim would be powerful. Otherwise, Opposite Claim is suspicious on Powerful Questions.

# Dormant Conditionals   RED FLAG

**POWERFUL**                                                                                                          **PROVABLE**

Back in the Conditional Reasoning Chapter, we talked about how the absence of the sufficient condition lets you ignore the conditional. If this doesn't sound familiar, re-read the Sufficient Condition section on page 108.

### WHAT'S A DORMANT CONDITIONAL?

**A Dormant Conditional is never activated by premises in the stimulus.**

**REAL LSAT EXAMPLE**: *June 2007.2.22*

Editorialist:   News media rarely cover local politics thoroughly, and local political business is usually conducted secretly. These factors each tend to isolate local politicians from their electorates. This has the effect of reducing the chance that any particular act of resident participation will elicit a positive official response, which in turn discourages resident participation in local politics.

### DORMANT CONDITIONAL ANSWER

Particular acts of resident participation would be likely to elicit a positive response from local politicians *if those politicians were less isolated from their electorate.*

If you can activate the contrapositive of a conditional, it is not Dormant.

Dormant Conditionals are useless. In general, conditional answers are only powerful/provable when their sufficient condition (of the original statement or its contrapositive) is activated by facts from the stimulus. This is precisely what doesn't happen in Dormant Conditionals, which is why they're so satisfying to eliminate.

Let's explore Dormant Conditionals with an example:

*Cats enjoy watercolors above all other rainy day activities. This includes judging humans from the tops of bookcases and worshiping their dark god. Therefore, no cat is a cynic.*

**Dormant Conditionals**

**If cats don't enjoy watercolors,** no cat is a cynic.

**If cats prefer worshiping their dark god to painting watercolors,** no cat is a cynic.

**If cats had great painting skills,** cats would successfully reanimate their dark god.

Look closely at the bolded sufficient conditions. None of them happened in the stimulus. We can't activate any contrapositives either. That's why each of these potential answer choices is Dormant; the sufficient conditions aren't activated. And, as you know, inactive conditionals might as well not exist. They don't do anything. **It's called conditional reasoning precisely because it's only relevant under certain conditions.** Each of these potential answer choices might as well not exist, which means they can't exert power over the reasoning in the stimulus and they can't be proven.

*Why can't the conclusion activate the conditional?*

Good question, imaginary friend! In order to activate the conditional, we need a fact, something we assume is true. We never assume the conclusion is true because we're not dirty circular reasoners. Conditionals activated by the conclusion are still Dormant (except in one narrow case outlined in the Provable Conditionals section).

### Dormant Conditionals are not powerful.

Dormant Conditionals are the opposite of powerful. They can't get anything done.

### Dormant Conditionals are not provable.

We can't prove a Dormant Conditional because we don't know what happens in the Dormant Conditional shadow universe.

Dormant Conditionals are easy wins — you know they're wrong on a mathematical level. That's why you have to learn to identify them. The upside is too great to ignore.

## Comparatives & Absolutes    RED FLAG

**POWERFUL** ⟶ ⟵ **PROVABLE**

| WHAT ARE COMPARATIVES & ABSOLUTES? | ABSOLUTE STIMULUS: *June 2007.3.19* | COMPARATIVE ANSWER |
|---|---|---|
| A **Comparative** states a relative relationship between two things. (Like saying X is *more* than Y.)<br><br>An **Absolute** attaches an adjective to a thing. (Like saying X is great. No mention of Y.) | Editor:   Many candidates say that if elected they will reduce governmental intrusion into voters' lives. But voters actually elect politicians who instead promise that the government will provide assistance to solve their most pressing problems. Governmental assistance, however, costs money, and money can only come from taxes, which can be considered a form of governmental intrusion. Thus, governmental intrusion into the lives of voters will rarely be substantially reduced over time in a democracy. | Governmental intrusion into the lives of voters is no *more burdensome in nondemocratic countries than it is in democracies.* |

**The mismatch of Comparatives and Absolutes between the stimulus and the answer choices is the Red Flag.** Most sentences on the LSAT are Absolutes; statements are Absolutes when they're not examining their subject in relation to something else. Comparatives literally compare two things. But Comparatives and Absolutes are like oil and water. They don't mix. **Comparative Answers are only powerful/provable when there's a Comparative relationship established (or assumed) in the stimulus.** This means Comparative Answers are neither powerful nor provable when combined with an Absolute stimulus.

Comparatives have a few keyword friends too. Each of these words indicates a Comparative relationship is afoot:

**A FEW COMPARATIVE KEYWORDS**

| *more* | *less* | *better* | *worse* | *-er endings* |
|---|---|---|---|---|

Now, check out a few examples to illustrate the difference between Comparatives & Absolutes:

<table>
<tr><th>COMPARATIVES</th><th>ABSOLUTES</th></tr>
<tr><td>Khan makes **worse** coffee than Dolores.</td><td>Khan makes **bad** coffee.</td></tr>
<tr><td>Khan's plans for galactic domination are **more grandiose** than Kevin's.</td><td>Khan's plans for galactic domination are **grandiose**.</td></tr>
<tr><td>Khan makes **better** French toast than Tim.</td><td>Khan makes **great** French toast.</td></tr>
</table>

These pairs seem similar at first glance, right? They're each saying nice things about Khan. But, in reality, the Comparatives and the Absolutes are leagues apart. Why?

*Notice the bolded Comparative Keywords in the Comparatives column. These words tip you off that a Comparative relationship is being described.*

*Notice the lack of Comparative Keywords in the Absolutes column. The lack of Comparative Keywords tips you off that the statement is an Absolute.*

> You can always be great (Absolute), but not better than someone else (Comparative).

> You can always be worse than someone else (Comparative), but not bad (Absolute).

Comparatives depend too much on an unknown (who you're comparing against) to reliably translate to an Absolute. That's why we can never prove anything across the Comparative and Absolute chasm. The same Loopholes apply every time.

**WHEN COULD A COMPARATIVE ANSWER BE POWERFUL AGAINST AN ABSOLUTE STIMULUS?**

When the Comparative relationship in the stimulus is assumed, a Comparative Answer could be powerful/provable. In this case, you're not actually mixing Comparatives and Absolutes as much as you are sensing a Comparative that's not explicitly stated. Comparative Answers can be powerful because they point out a difference between two things that the stimulus assumed were the same. Here's an example of a stealth Comparative:

> *We should build the new opera house in our town. Shadeville built a new opera house and they have been met with unmatched prosperity ever since.*

They're assuming that our town will have the same reaction to the new opera house that Shadeville did, a stealth comparison between our town and Shadeville. But what if there are significant differences between our town and Shadeville? What if Shadeville is a large metropolis full of wealthy opera lovers and we're a tiny rural town with only a stop sign and a Taco Bell? The opera house probably wouldn't work out as well for us.

| Potentially Powerful Loopholes | What if Shadeville is much larger and wealthier than our town? |
| | What if Shadeville has a higher population of opera lovers than our town? |

For Comparative Answers to be powerful, the Comparative relationship needs to matter to the argument in the stimulus, even if it only matters for an assumption.

## Strong Answers    POWERFUL ANSWER

POWERFUL ↓↑                                                                    PROVABLE

**WHAT'S A STRONG ANSWER?**

Strong Answers contain **bold language** and **Certainty Power Players.**

**REAL LSAT EXAMPLE:** *June 2007.2.13*

Standard aluminum soft-drink cans do not vary in the amount of aluminum that they contain. Fifty percent of the aluminum contained in a certain group (M) of standard aluminum soft-drink cans was recycled from another group (L) of used, standard aluminum soft-drink cans. Since all the cans in L were recycled into cans in M and since the amount of material other than aluminum in an aluminum can is negligible, it follows that M contains twice as many cans as L.

**STRONG ANSWER**

***All*** of the aluminum in an aluminum can is recovered when the can is recycled.

The following answer choices reside on the powerful side of The Complete Powerful-Provable Spectrum. They are preferable on Powerful Questions.

Strong Answers contains bold, vibrant, armored words. They are powerful, but not provable. They make big claims.

**Strong Answers are powerful.**

Powerful Questions ask you to do big things to the stimulus. They want you to affect the stimulus' validity; you can use all the tools at your disposal. You aren't constrained by what's reasonable or what we know for sure. You just want to get things done as effectively as possible. Strong Answers are built for that.

**Strong Answers are not provable.**

Provable Questions don't respond well to going big. They require the right answer to meet a burden of proof. Sometimes, the stimulus will be strong enough to prove a strong correct answer, but it's not very common. As with every recommendation made in this section, **use this as a guidepost, not a replacement for evaluating individual answer choices in the context of the stimulus.**

Remember **MUST** and **CANNOT**, your Certainty Power Players? Strong Answers often contain these powerful Power Players.

**A FEW STRONG ANSWER KEYWORDS**

| *all* | *every(time)* | *none* | *never* | *always* |
|---|---|---|---|---|
| *only* | *required* | | | |

**WHEN COULD A STRONG ANSWER WORK ON A PROVABLE QUESTION?**

It sometimes seems like correct Necessary Assumption answers are Strong Answers. They may contain Strong Answer keywords, but conceptually, they're just ruling out a Loophole. Saying that one disastrous edge case can't happen isn't particularly powerful on a conceptual level. While this answer sounds linguistically strong, in reality, it's super provable.

**POWERFUL** ↓
        ↑                                                                           **PROVABLE**

**REAL LSAT EXAMPLE:** *June 2007.2.19*

**STEPLADDER ANSWER**

A Stepladder
outlines a directly
proportional
relationship
between two things.

↑
Steps!

Historian:   The Land Party achieved its only
national victory in Banestria in 1935. It
received most of its support that year in
rural and semirural areas, where the bulk of
Banestria's population lived at the time. The
economic woes of the years surrounding that
election hit agricultural and small business
interests the hardest, and the Land Party
specifically targeted those groups in 1935. I
conclude that the success of the Land Party
that year was due to the combination of the
Land Party's specifically addressing the
concerns of these groups and the depth of the
economic problems people in these groups
were facing.

*The greater* the degree
of economic distress
someone is in, *the more*
likely that person is to vote.

Stepladders are crazy powerful; directly proportional relationships are rad. Check out a couple examples:

**Stepladders**

**The more** work experience she gains, **the more** disillusioned she becomes.

**The less** we invest in infrastructure, **the smaller** the chance of a renaissance.

**Stepladders are powerful.**

Stepladders super connect two things. They're the
perfect response to a dangling variable. If you're trying
to fix an argument, Stepladders are powerful allies. They
create the ultimate link between two things.

**Stepladders are not provable.**

Stepladders are a bad call on Provable Questions.
**Their provability is intrinsically flawed**: They always
collapse at their endpoints. Stepladders imply that
even the smallest increase/decrease in the first object
will yield a corresponding increase/decrease in the
second object. This is essentially impossible to prove.

✳ Stepladders are
especially desirable in
Strengthen and SA
questions. They're
the ultimate dangling
variable solve.

Let's explore how a Stepladder's provability is at odds with common sense:

*The more caffeine one ingests, the more alert one is.*

At first glance, this sounds pretty provable, right? Caffeine does tend to make one more alert. However, "tend to"
is much more provable than a true Stepladder. Let's look at the extremes: Is someone who's had 500 cups of coffee
going to be more alert than someone who's had 499 cups? Is someone who's had 0.01 grams of coffee more alert
than someone who's had none? Probably not. The Stepladder claims there's *always* a difference no matter where
you are on the ladder. This is why Stepladders are almost impossible to prove.

✳ Both the 500 and the
499 coffee people are
probably dead, so clearly
there's some point of
diminishing returns.

## Powerful Conditionals   POWERFUL ANSWER

POWERFUL ↓↑ ――――――――――――――――――――――――――――――――――――――― PROVABLE

**WHAT'S A POWERFUL CONDITIONAL?**

**REAL LSAT EXAMPLE:** *June 2007.2.6*

**POWERFUL CONDITIONAL ANSWER**

*Powerful Conditionals never have the conclusion in the sufficient condition. They are only ever activated by a premise.*

**A Powerful Conditional connects premises to the conclusion or to other premises.**

An undergraduate degree is necessary for appointment to the executive board. Further, no one with a felony conviction can be appointed to the board. Thus, Murray, an accountant with both a bachelor's and a master's degree, cannot be accepted for the position of Executive Administrator, since he has a felony conviction.

*Only* candidates eligible for appointment to the executive board can be accepted for the position of Executive Administrator.

Powerful Conditionals bridge the conditional gap in the stimulus. Check out the two ways to build that bridge:

1. Link a premise to another premise

   premise 1 ⟶ premise 2 (~premise 2 ⟶ ~premise 1)

   Linking two premises is powerful if **premise 2 (or ~premise 1)** is already super linked to the conclusion. With the gap between the premises fixed, the argument is set.

*Be on the lookout for IF OUR PREMISES, THEN OUR CONCLUSION — it's a highly common correct answer. For more info on IF OUR PREMISES, THEN OUR CONCLUSION, check back to page 169.*

2. Link a premise to the conclusion

   premise ⟶ conclusion (~conclusion ⟶ ~premise)

   This is the ultimate win for an answer choice. IF OUR PREMISES, THEN OUR CONCLUSION constructions are super powerful and surprisingly common.

On Powerful Questions, choose Powerful Conditionals whenever you can. There's no better ally.

# Grouped Opposite   POWERFUL ANSWER

**POWERFUL** ↓ ↑ **PROVABLE**

**WHAT'S A GROUPED OPPOSITE?**

A Grouped Opposite is about the opposite of the group discussed in the stimulus.

**REAL LSAT EXAMPLE:** *16.2.21*

Several years ago, as a measure to reduce the population of gypsy moths, which depend on oak leaves for food, entomologists introduced into many oak forests a species of fungus that is poisonous to gypsy moth caterpillars. Since then, the population of both caterpillars and adult moths has significantly declined in those areas. Entomologists have concluded that the decline is attributable to the presence of the poisonous fungus.

**GROUPED OPPOSITE**

A strain of *gypsy moth whose caterpillars are unaffected by the fungus* has increased its share of the total gypsy moth population.

Grouped Opposites are about the opposite of the stimulus. If you have a stimulus about runners with bad knees, a Grouped Opposite is about runners who don't have bad knees. Essentially, Grouped Opposites add a "not" in front of the subject of the stimulus. **Grouped Opposites can be powerful, but mostly just with causal stimuli.** That's why they're closer to the middle of The Complete Powerful-Provable Spectrum. Let's see how Grouped Opposites affect a causal argument:

*Runners with bad knees often retire. Therefore, bad knees are the cause of retirement in runners.*

Now check out how these Grouped Opposites (runners without bad knees) can affect the argument.

| **GROUPED OPPOSITE** | **DOES THIS MEAN BAD KNEES CAUSE RETIREMENT?** |
|---|---|
| **Runners without bad knees retire at the same rate as runners with bad knees.** | This makes bad knees sound like not that big a deal. If everyone's retiring at the same rate, it seems like bad knees probably don't cause much. |
| **Runners without bad knees retire less than runners with bad knees.** | This makes it sound like bad knees are a big deal. If you keep running without bad knees, they might cause retirement. |

These were both Grouped Opposites, but they had different powerful effects on the causal claim!

**Grouped Opposites are powerful in causal reasoning, but not much else.**

The stimulus is, by definition, not about the Grouped Opposite. That separation makes power a tough sell, except in causal reasoning.

**Grouped Opposites are not provable.**

Since the stimulus is not about the Grouped Opposite, it's almost impossible to prove anything about the Grouped Opposite necessarily true.

**IS THERE ANY TIME WHEN GROUPED OPPOSITES COULD BE PROVABLE?**

In stupid simple conditionals, yes. Imagine a premise says, "Only cypress trees have leaves." This diagrams to **leaves ⟶ cypress.** You can prove the contrapositive **(~cypress ⟶ ~leaves)**: Trees that are not cypresses don't have leaves. Sounds like a Grouped Opposite, right? Answers this simple only appear once in a blue moon, but it's a great example of when to choose the obvious correct answer regardless of general guidelines.

Bad knees = cause
Retirement = effect

Notice how these Grouped Opposites don't definitively prove or disprove the causal relationship. They just nudge it in different directions.

Grouped Opposites work better on Weaken and Strengthen than SA for this exact reason.

## Weak Answers    PROVABLE ANSWER

**POWERFUL** ————————————————————————————→ **PROVABLE**

### WHAT'S A WEAK ANSWER?

**Weak Answers contain flexible language and Possibility Power Players.**

### REAL LSAT EXAMPLE: *June 2007.3.6*

Jablonski, who owns a car dealership, has donated cars to driver education programs at area schools for over five years. She found the statistics on car accidents to be disturbing, and she wanted to do something to encourage better driving in young drivers. Some members of the community have shown their support for this action by purchasing cars from Jablonski's dealership.

### WEAK ANSWER

Altruistic actions ***sometimes*** have positive consequences for those who perform them.

Weak Answers are cautious. They use words directly from the stimulus. They rule out an edge case. They state possibilities instead of certainties. Obviously, you aren't going to find the Strong Answer keywords (all, every, never, etc…) here. Weak Answers are provable, not powerful. They make tiny, qualified claims.

### A FEW WEAK ANSWER KEYWORDS

| | | | | |
|---|---|---|---|---|
| *could* | *(at least) one* | *varies* | *not necessarily* | *may* |
| *can* | *tend to* | *usually* | *possibly* | *does not depend on* |
| *(at least) some* | *not all* | *possible* | *sometimes* | *a chance* |

### Weak Answers are not powerful.

Powerful Questions want you to make an impact on the stimulus. Obviously, Weak Answers aren't going to have a huge impact.

### Weak Answers are provable.

Provable Questions want safe answers. The correct answer has to be able to handle the provable burden. The smaller the answer choice, the easier it will be for it to stand up to that burden. Weak Answers don't require a lot to be true, making them perfect choices on Provable Questions.

# Provable Conditionals    PROVABLE ANSWER

**POWERFUL** ←————————————————————————————→ **PROVABLE**

### WHAT'S A PROVABLE CONDITIONAL?

A Provable Conditional reads the conditional chain from the stimulus or states a necessary assumption.

**REAL LSAT EXAMPLE**: *June 2007.3.22*

If the price it pays for coffee beans continues to increase, the Coffee Shoppe will have to increase its prices. In that case, either the Coffee Shoppe will begin selling noncoffee products or its coffee sales will decrease. But selling noncoffee products will decrease the Coffee Shoppe's overall profitability. Moreover, the Coffee Shoppe can avoid a decrease in overall profitability only if its coffee sales do not decrease.

### PROVABLE CONDITIONAL ANSWER

The Coffee Shoppe's overall profitability will decrease *if the price it pays for coffee beans continues to increase.*

Provable Conditionals restate what the stimulus has already given you. They can do this in two ways:

1. **Read your chain**

   Provable Conditionals often follow a conditional stimulus, usually containing a chain. Once you have that chain diagrammed, the correct answer is any correct reading of your chain or its contrapositive.

2. **State a necessary assumption**

   Luckily, you're already quite familiar with one Provable Conditional: the necessary assumption. The Assumption Chain (**SA ⟶ Conclusion True ⟶ NA**) is baaaaack.

   Necessary assumptions place the conclusion in the sufficient condition, a special privilege that none of the other Powerful or Provable Conditionals get to take advantage of. Necessary assumptions are the only time you'll ever see the conclusion in the sufficient condition of a correct answer. This makes sense; if the conclusion is true, the necessary assumption must be true. Necessary assumptions are provable, meaning they're great answers on Provable Questions.

⁎ Inference and MSS questions are typically where you'll find necessary assumption answer choices stated as Provable Conditionals.

---

## THE ANSWER CHOICES GAME PLAN

- Know the answer choice types well enough to use them in context. Once you really know them, you'll see Logical Reasoning answer choice sets fundamentally more clearly.

- Rely on the Powerful-Provable Spectrum when you're stumped in the answer choices.

- Play the hand you're dealt in the answer choices. Don't reject the best answer available because you're frustrated that there isn't a perfect answer in the set.

- Let the answer choices survive on their own merits. You are not authorized to add or subtract elements from the answer choices to make them correct or incorrect.

---

## Quiz 12 THE ANSWER CHOICES

### INSTRUCTIONS

Answer these questions based on your knowledge of the chapter. Attempt to answer without looking back at the chapter first. If you don't know the answer, circle the question number and go find the answer in the chapter. Study the sections of the chapter that you couldn't remember at first.

### Word Bank

| | | |
|---|---|---|
| Grouped Opposite | Allllllmost | Provable Conditionals |
| Strong Answers | Best Way | Powerful Conditionals |
| Opposite Claim | Grouped Extreme | Comparatives & Absolutes |
| Weak Answers | Crazy Nonsense | Dormant Conditionals |
| Stepladder | | Important |

**1.** Complete the table using the word bank and circle the correct answer choice category. Each answer choice type will be used exactly once.

| ANSWER CHOICE TYPE | DESCRIPTION | CIRCLE THE CORRECT CATEGORY |
|---|---|---|
| Grouped extreme | Centers on the most extreme part of the group in stimulus | (Red Flag) Powerful Provable |
| Powerful conditionals | A conditional that connects premises to the conclusion or other premises | Red Flag (Powerful) Provable |
| Allllllmost | Is totally right except for one word or phrase | (Red Flag) Powerful Provable |
| Stepladder | Outlines a directly proportional relationship between two things | Red Flag (Powerful) Provable |
| Weak | Contains flexible language and Possibility Power Players | Red Flag Powerful (Provable) |
| Opposite claim | Centers on the opposite of argument's conclusion | (Red Flag) Powerful Provable |
| Strong | Contains bold language and Certainty Power Players | Red Flag (Powerful) Provable |

410

| | | | | |
|---|---|---|---|---|
| *dormant conditional* | A conditional that is never activated by premises from stimulus | (Red Flag) | Powerful | Provable |
| *provable conditional* | A conditional that reads a chain from the stimulus or states a necessary assumption | Red Flag | Powerful | (Provable) |
| *crazy reversal* | Has nothing to do with anything in the stimulus | (Red Flag) | Powerful | Provable |
| *Important* | Identifies something as "important" or an Important keyword | (Red Flag) | Powerful | Provable |
| *Comparatives – absolutes* | Mismatches Comparatives and Absolutes between the stimulus and the answer choices | (Red Flag) | Powerful | Provable |
| *best way* | Literally uses the words "best way" or a Best Way keyword. | (Red Flag) | Powerful | Provable |
| *grouped opposites* | Centers on the opposite of the group discussed in the stimulus | Red Flag | (Powerful) | Provable |

*Circle the correct answer to the following questions.*

**2.** **TRUE OR (FALSE)**   Grouped Extremes can be powerful with causal stimuli, but are undesirable in pretty much all non-causal reasoning scenarios.

**3.** **TRUE OR (FALSE)**   Comparative answer choices are powerful with Absolute stimuli.

**4.** Seek and find!   Circle only the Strong Answer keywords in the word cloud.

could        sometimes        (must)        (only)

tends        (required)        (every)        some

none         (all)             (never)       conclusion

**5.** Seek and find!   Circle only the Weak Answer keywords in the word cloud.

every        (sometimes)       (usually)        only

required     (tends)           (may)            (at least some)

not all      (could)           conclusion       (not necessarily)

*Where's the answer key?*

You'll find the answer key at the end of the chapter on page 412.

## Quiz 12 ANSWER KEY

### 1.

| ANSWER CHOICE TYPE | DESCRIPTION | PROVABLE / POWERFUL / RED FLAG |
|---|---|---|
| Grouped Extreme | Centers on the most extreme part of the group in stimulus | Red Flag |
| Powerful Conditionals | A conditional that connects premises to the conclusion or other premises | Powerful |
| Alllllllmost | Is totally right except for one word or phrase | Red Flag |
| Stepladder | Outlines a directly proportional relationship between two things | Powerful |
| Weak Answers | Contains flexible language and Possibility Power Players | Provable |
| Opposite Claim | Centers on the opposite of argument's conclusion | Red Flag |
| Strong Answers | Contains bold language and Certainty Power Players | Powerful |
| Dormant Conditionals | A conditional that is never activated by premises from stimulus | Red Flag |
| Provable Conditionals | A conditional that reads a chain from the stimulus or states a necessary assumption | Provable |
| Crazy Nonsense | Has nothing to do with anything in the stimulus | Red Flag |
| Important | Identifies something as "important" or an Important keyword | Red Flag |
| Comparatives & Absolutes | Mismatches Comparatives and Absolutes between the stimulus and the answer choices | Red Flag |
| Best Way | Literally uses the words "best way" or a Best Way keyword. | Red Flag |
| Grouped Opposite | Centers on the opposite of the group discussed in the stimulus | Powerful |

### 2.

False. *Grouped Opposites* can be powerful with causal stimuli, but are undesirable in pretty much all non-causal reasoning scenarios.

### 3.

False. Comparative answer choices are powerful only when you have a *comparative* relationship established (or assumed) in the stimulus.

### 4.

You should have circled the following Strong Answer keywords and no other words: all, every, must, none, never, only, required.

### 5.

You should have circled the following Weak Answer keywords and no other words: could, not necessarily, usually, not all, at least some, sometimes, tends, may.

# ANSWER CHOICE STRATEGY

## Time-Saving Tricks for Fun and Profit

## The Answer Choice Ratings

The answer choices are just like restaurants on Yelp. They live to be ruthlessly judged. The answer choice ratings turn your intuitive reaction into a planned response to each answer choice.

| RATING | RESPONSE | ACTION | RHYME |
|--------|----------|--------|-------|
| 5 | Perfection incarnate. | Draw an arrow next to **5s**. | **5s** have lives. |
| 4 | It's fine. Could be right. | Draw a dash next to **4s**. | **4s** have chores. |
| 3 | Not actively offensive. | Leave **3s** open. | **3s** have fleas. |
| 2 | Pretty bad, but maybe? | Leave **2s** open. | **2s** have blues. |
| 1 | Never in a million years. | Cross off **1s**. | **1s** don't get a rhyme because they're garbage. |

You're only crossing out **1s** on your first pass through the answer choices. Every other answer choice stays in the running until your second pass through. This keeps you from crossing out potentially good answers hastily. **It's perfectly fine to read an answer choice, say, "I don't know," and leave it for the next one.** If the answer choice is better than "never in a million years," leave it open.

> You should never spend more than ten seconds on an answer choice on the first read through. If you can't decide if you like it in that amount time, it's totally cool; leave the answer choice open.

### BUT WHAT IF I CROSS OFF ALL THE ANSWER CHOICES?

**Perform an Answer Choice Reset. Erase all of your cross-outs and re-evaluate the answer choices from scratch.** This time, lower your standards for a positive rating (anything above **1**). Only cross out the answer choices that are *never* going to work. If you've crossed everything off, two problems are possibly afoot:

1. **You missed something in the stimulus.** This is not an epic screw up. We all miss something in the stimulus sometimes. This is because we're human, not because we're bad at LR. You just have to keep your cool, re-evaluate the stimulus, and return to the answer choices.

2. **The answer choices are tricky and unfortunate.** Return to the stimulus to make a Mission. Look closely at the answer choices in the context of the Mission. Puzzle out what the remaining answer choices mean and whether they're accomplishing your Mission.

Both of these situations are good candidates for hyper-skipping!

---

※ 3 is also the rating when you have no idea what an answer choice means.

※ Yes, all eight *Community* fans reading this book, the Rhyme column is from the "App Development and Condiments" episode of *Community*. Credit goes to Jordan Blum, Parker Deay, and Dan Harmon.

※ I know marking up the answer choices with ratings is a different animal/impossible on the Digital LSAT. However, by the time you get to digital PTs, these sorting impulses will become intuitive.

# Hyper-Skipping    A MUCH-IMPROVED COUSIN OF SKIPPING

**Hyper-skipping is crucial to finishing Logical Reasoning in time.** Here's how to hyper-skip:

1. **You hit a question and, for whatever reason, you find it extremely difficult.**

   Maybe you've re-read the stimulus three times and still have no idea what it means. Maybe you've crossed out every answer and cannot see how any of them could possibly be right. Maybe you have it down to two answers and they both look right. You're likely repeating expletives in your head.

2. **Answer the question *immediately*.**

   Go with your gut. Choose something fast. Use Powerful-Provable.

3. **Flag the hyper-skipped question so you can return to it easily, if you have time at the end.**

   The accuracy of hyper-skipped questions is about the same as the accuracy of the section as a whole. For instance, if you tend to miss 10% of questions, you'll miss about 10% of your hyper-skipped questions as well. This means you shouldn't rush the end of the section just to get back to the hyper-skips.

There is no guessing penalty on the LSAT. Make sure to answer every question.

Hyper-skipping authorizes you to just go with your gut instinct. Trust yourself. Once you've hit a mental block with a question, you aren't going to magically see something new; frustration is getting in the way. Fresh eyes are the only path toward epiphany.

You may be laughing at me right now, thinking, "Getting back to questions? *Time at the end?!* Girl, you don't know me." **But you know *why* most people don't have time at the end? Because they're not hyper-skipping.**

Never read the answer choices or the question type before the stimulus. There is no advantage to doing this.

## HOW TO CHOOSE YOUR HYPER-SKIP ANSWER

1. Use the answer choice Red Flags from the previous section to narrow it down. Rely on the Powerful-Provable Spectrum. Remember that each answer choice you eliminate increases your probability of getting the question right, so this is totally worth it.

2. Once you've (hopefully) gotten rid of some of the answer choices, go with your freaking gut. Don't second guess yourself and choose something you crossed out in the previous step. Make a split-second decision.

## DON'T SACRIFICE THE FOREST FOR A STUPID TREE

Test takers spend a significant amount of time fixating on a small number of difficult questions. I'm talking more than three minutes on one question. This is catastrophic, and not just because of the time cost. The worst part of fixating on one question for that long is the mental exhaustion of trying and trying (and trying) to find the answer and failing. This feels even worse when you know there are more questions to come. Hyper-skipping enables you to spend your time more wisely and pleasantly.

From a strategic perspective, Logical Reasoning is drastically different than Logic Games and Reading Comprehension. It's a much higher stakes decision to just blow off a game or a passage because it will cost you five questions minimum, but even the highest scorers often have a cushion of one or two wrong per LR section. These are questions they're allowing and expecting themselves to get wrong! You can blow off some questions in LR and it's not even a big deal.

Individual LR questions don't actually matter that much. There are 50 or 51 of them, and they are all islands.

You should hyper-skip when your inner monologue starts repeating itself as you're doing the question.

**If you hit a hard question and really don't know the answer, hyper-skip it and move on.** That one question doesn't matter. All the time you save by not holding onto that hard question will allow you to reach more questions. The best-case scenario is that you save enough time to come back to those hyper-skipped questions and approach them with fresh eyes. **You'll often find that, with a fresh perspective, you will quickly see what you were missing.**

### DO I HAVE TO READ ALL THE ANSWER CHOICES?

Yes, you have to give yourself the chance to read the correct answer. Sometimes I'm sure that, for instance, **B** is correct until I get to **E**. Then I realize I'm wrong. Actually, **E** is correct for sure. If I hadn't read **E**, I would have chosen **B** and gotten the question wrong. **If you don't read all the answer choices, you will fall prey to avoidable errors.**

The one situation where you don't have to read all the answer choices is when you're at the end of a section, running out of time (less than two minutes left), and you find an obviously correct answer early on. In this situation, just take the risk and move on to the next question. Reading the rest of the answer choices could prevent you from attempting another question before time is called.

### WHEN YOU SHOULD(N'T) CHANGE YOUR ANSWER

On average, test takers lose points by changing their answers late in the game. This is because the original answer usually represents their gut feeling and the new answer is typically an expression of doubt. That doubt causes students to make reckless decisions that cost them points. You must fulfill *both* of the following criteria in order to change your answer:

If you can't tell me why your original choice is wrong, you should not change your answer. If you can't tell me why your new choice is right, you should not change your answer.

1. You must know that your original answer is **wrong**.

This means you realize that the original answer is unequivocally a huge mistake. This mistake is now obvious to you.

**Should Change Reaction**     "Oh my god, no no no no no no. I NEED to change this."

**Shouldn't Change Reaction**     "But it still might be wrong..."

2. You must know that your new answer is **right**.

This means you realize that the new answer is *obviously* right.

**Should Change Reaction**     "Duh, of course it's **D**. How did I not see this. I'm such an idiot."

**Shouldn't Change Reaction**     "But this one could be good too..."

Notice that I did not use the words "worse" and "better" to describe your old and new answer. Don't compare answer choices with such murky value judgments. **One of the answer choices you're considering is correct. The other answer choice is incorrect. There is no gray area.**

# The Except Mark

An **EXCEPT** question turns your answer choice process upside down. **In an EXCEPT question, the four wrong answers fulfill the Mission of the question and the correct answer fails to do so.** This doesn't mean that the correct answer does the opposite of what the question asks; it means that it doesn't do as it's told.

| **EXCEPT Question Prompts** | Each of the following helps to resolve the apparent discrepancy **EXCEPT**: |
| | Each of the following, if true, would strengthen the argument **EXCEPT**: |
| | Which one of the follow, if true, **LEAST** strengthens the argument? |

**LEAST** means the same thing as **EXCEPT**. You're totally free to use the **EXCEPT MARK** when you see **LEAST** as well.

**Students often forget the EXCEPT.** This results in picking an answer that perfectly fulfills the Mission of the question. There are four wrong answers that fulfill the Mission in an **EXCEPT** question, so it's a real embarrassment of riches if you forget the question is **EXCEPT**. To avoid this error, always use the **EXCEPT MARK**.

> Always complete **EXCEPT** questions through process of elimination using the **EXCEPT MARK**.

As soon as you finish reading the question stem and realize it's **EXCEPT**:

1. Select the orange highlighter at the top of the screen. This is your trusty **EXCEPT** highlighter. Do not use the orange highlighter for any other purpose.

2. Highlight the **EXCEPT** in the question stem.

3. If an answer choice completes the question type's Mission, highlight its first word. This is your **EXCEPT MARK**.

4. When you hit an answer choice that doesn't fulfill the question type's Mission, do not highlight it. Leave it blank.

5. Once you've read through all the answer choices, more than one answer choice will be highlighted with an **EXCEPT MARK**. Since the correct answer is unique, you won't be tempted to choose any of the orange highlighted answers.

6. Choose the answer without an orange **EXCEPT MARK**.

**EXCEPT** is much easier through process of elimination. Our brains process "Which one is strengthening?" much more efficiently than "Which one is not strengthening?" You can just affirm that four answers are doing what the question type wants and choose whichever answer is left. **EXCEPT** is no harder than a normal question if you stick to the **EXCEPT MARK**.

# OMMMM.

chapter twelve. brought by elves.

## Chapter Breather   ADVANCED TRANSLATION DRILL

You've graduated from the Basic Translation Drill to the Advanced Translation Drill! This is where all our skills come together for practice and refinement.

### INSTRUCTIONS

**1.**   Grab a clean LR section.

**2.**   Read the stimulus well once. You can go back and re-read sentences as you go, as much as you want. Once you hit the last period at the end of the stimulus, you're done.

**3.**   Say, "OK, so…" and tell yourself what happened in the stimulus. Do it casually, like you're explaining a story to a friend.

**4.**   This explanation is your translation of the stimulus. **Say the translation out loud**, if you have a tutor or a study buddy, say it to them. Your goal is to reduce the stimulus to things that actually matter. By hearing the stimulus in your own words, you forget about the distracting jargon and focus more clearly.

**5.**   Design your CLIR. Say it out loud.

**6.**   Read the question stem and identify whether it's powerful or provable. Rephrase your CLIR to exactly what you're looking for. Say the following out loud, "So I'm looking for something that's going to… **[spin on your CLIR]**."

**7.**   Translate each answer choice out loud. Rate the answer choices on a scale of 1-5 as you go. Write the mark associated with your rating next to each answer choice.

**8.**   Choose an answer.

### ADVANCED TRANSLATION DRILL FAQ

**Q.**   *Say it out loud? Girl, you don't know me.*

**A.**   We're switching away from writing the translation to saying it out loud here. The reasons we switch are:

1.   Saying it is faster.

2.   Saying it is less tedious.

3.   Saying it is a step closer to how you'll do the translation on the actual test.

**Q.**   *Why can't I just do the translation in my head starting now?*

**A.**   Because I want you to actually do it. I want you to commit to every step of the process. Jumping to doing it in your head before you build the translation and CLIR habit leads to skipping translation and CLIR. **Committing to process is how we build intuition. If you do it one way enough times, that becomes the way you do it.**

*Do not use the June 2007 LR for the Advanced Translation Drill. You can use any other LR section, but the questions should be fresh.*

*Don't worry about time on the Advanced Translation Drill.*

**Q.** *When do I get to start doing it in my head?*

**A.** When this drill becomes easy for you. When you're familiar enough with this process that it's no longer difficult and external. When there's no chance you'll cut out steps in a misguided attempt to save time.

**Q.** *What if I'm studying in a library or library-like environment where I can't make noise?*

**A.** Ideally, don't do this drill there. If the space is unavoidable, do the steps in your head, but be strict with yourself to make sure you're consciously doing each step. Make a list of each step of the process (Translation, CLIR, flipping the CLIR) and physically check off each objective as you complete it on each question. At the end, you should have 25 or 26 check marks next to your objectives.

The Advanced Translation Drill is a great opportunity to start Camouflage Review!

Learn more about this awesome technique for reviewing your practice sections at elementalprep.com/camo

Since you will answer the questions in the Advanced Translation Drill and you won't record your translation on paper, there's no answer key on this one. Use your correct and incorrect answers to judge your progress. If you get a question wrong, **use your Wrong Answer Journal (page 456) to track the reason why the question was wrong and what your proposed solution is.**

### DO I HAVE TO DO THE TRANSLATION DRILLS? I WANT TO DO TIMED SECTIONS.

I recommend the Basic & Advanced Translation Drills for everyone. But I insist upon repeated use of these drills for students who relate to any of the following:

1.  You've done previous LR studying before picking up this book and have been stalled on improvement.

2.  You feel like you've plateaued and will never get any better.

3.  You think you get the mechanics of LR and can't understand why you're getting so many wrong.

4.  When you look at your wrong answers after doing a section, you think, "This is such an easy question. Why would I ever have chosen that? How could I get this wrong?"

The Translation Drills were created for a specific student who embodied this profile. They benefit everyone, but they *must* be done repeatedly if you relate to that characterization. (Seriously, if you skipped the Basic Translation Drill, go back and do it.) It works for this type of student because the wrong answer profile associated with them is predicated strongly on misreads. By relying on your translation, you diminish the possibility of repeated misreads.

**Translation Drills have single-handedly taken students from -10+ per section to -1.** And that -10+ is *after* months of significant LSAT prep. Honestly, you only hurt yourself by skipping Translation Drills and doing timed sections instead.

# The Fast and the Question Stem Quiz    ANSWER KEY

| | QUESTION STEM | QUESTION TYPE | POWERFUL/PROVABLE |
|---|---|---|---|
| 1. | Which one of the following, if true, most helps to resolve the apparent paradox? | Resolution | Powerful |
| 2. | The reasoning in the researcher's argument is questionable in that the argument overlooks the possibility that | Loophole Flaw | Provable |
| 3. | Which one of the following is a questionable technique employed by the producer in responding to the critic? | Classic Flaw | Provable |
| 4. | The information above, if accurate, can best be used as evidence against which one of the following hypotheses? | Contradiction | Powerful |
| 5. | The information above provides the most support for which one of the following statements? | Most Strongly Supported (MSS) | Provable |
| 6. | Which one of the following most accurately describes how the argument proceeds? | Method | Provable |
| 7. | Which one of the following, if true, most tends to undermine the argument? | Weaken | Powerful |
| 8. | The conclusion drawn above follows logically if which one of the following is assumed? | Sufficient Assumption (SA) | Powerful |
| 9. | The argument assumes which one of the following? | Necessary Assumption (NA) | Provable |
| 10. | Which one of the following conforms most closely to the principle illustrated above? | Principle Conform | Provable |
| 11. | Which one of the following can properly be concluded from the information given above? | Inference | Provable |
| 12. | Which one of the following, if true, provides the most support for the argument? | Strengthen | Powerful |

FULL LOGICAL REASONING

SECTION PRACTICE

## It's Showtime

Take your time with these sections. Use Powerful-Provable.

You're ready! You know your question types. You know your answer choice types. You know to translate and CLIR. This is your chance to put it all together with some training wheels to guide you.

Since we're using the sections we translated and CLIRed here, the only ambiguity left in these questions is the question stem and the answer choices. If you still get questions wrong in these two sections, despite reviewing the stimuli twice in the Basic Translation Drill and CLIR Drill, you know your issue is with the answer choices, not the stimulus. That will make identifying the Reason Missed in your Wrong Answer Journal a lot easier.

To make it even easier to identify why you missed questions, we'll incorporate a question stem identification quiz into these sections as well. **As you go, write the question type to the side of each question stem.** Each question's type is listed alongside the correct answer in the answer key. When you check your answers, you'll also see whether your question stem identification was right. If the question stem identification was wrong, you may have a clue as to why you missed the question.

*Do the questions get harder later in the section?*

In my experience, the first 10 or so questions are *on average* easier. The difficulty ramps up from #11-21 and tapers off after that. There are often easy-medium questions at the end of the section. This is, of course, a **huge generalization**. It isn't always true. There are plenty of difficult #4s and easy #19s in the history of the LSAT.

If you're having trouble with a question, don't psyche yourself out because it's in the beginning of the section and you "must be stupid." Easier questions can seem impossible when you misread them; this makes them feel just as hard as a real difficult question. You're not stupid.

**This is a great time to start Camouflage Reviewing your practice sections on elementalprep.com/camo.**

**Camouflage Review is a new way to review your practice sections for maximum score improvement.** After completing a section (and before looking at the answer key), input your answers into the Camouflage Review system and it will return a list of questions for you to revisit. **Some of these Camouflage Review questions are wrong answers, but some of them are camouflaged correct answers lurking to test your confidence.** On your second pass through these questions you won't know how many you missed, so you'll be challenged to change your answer or stay with your previous answer.

Obviously, not fully completing questions because of time pressure also leads to wrong answers. But time pressure is really a subsection of misreads. Time pressure is causing you to not fully read the questions.

Based on how you perform on your second pass through the camouflaged questions, the system will present your unique wrong answer profile. There are three main reasons students miss questions: conceptual gaps, misreads, and self-doubt. Here's how Camouflage Review helps you analyze what's causing your wrong answers:

- Wrong answers you miss again in Camouflage Review indicate conceptual gaps.

- Wrong answers you correct in Camouflage Review indicate a misread.

- Correct answers that you switch away from in Camouflage Review indicate self-doubt.

Seeing these differences between your wrong answers helps you improve as much as possible from each practice section. There's no point in obsessing over a question you simply misread and quickly corrected; those misses result from translation issues. But **the questions you miss twice are gold mines**. They represent the gaps in your understanding of the test; dive into these twice-missed questions and find out what conceptual gap is tripping you up. You can ensure that you never make that same mistake again.

**And remember, start your Wrong Answer Journal on these sections!**

*As you answer these questions, write the question type to the side of each question stem. Check your question type identification when you grade the section.*

1.   Economist:   Every business strives to increase its productivity, for this increases profits for the owners and the likelihood that the business will survive. But not all efforts to increase productivity are beneficial to the business as a whole. Often, attempts to increase productivity decrease the number of employees, which clearly harms the dismissed employees as well as the sense of security of the retained employees.

Which one of the following most accurately expresses the main conclusion of the economist's argument?

(A)   If an action taken to secure the survival of a business fails to enhance the welfare of the business's employees, that action cannot be good for the business as a whole.

(B)   Some measures taken by a business to increase productivity fail to be beneficial to the business as a whole.

(C)   Only if the employees of a business are also its owners will the interests of the employees and owners coincide, enabling measures that will be beneficial to the business as a whole.

(D)   There is no business that does not make efforts to increase its productivity.

(E)   Decreasing the number of employees in a business undermines the sense of security of retained employees.

2.   All Labrador retrievers bark a great deal. All Saint Bernards bark infrequently. Each of Rosa's dogs is a cross between a Labrador retriever and a Saint Bernard. Therefore, Rosa's dogs are moderate barkers.

Which one of the following uses flawed reasoning that most closely resembles the flawed reasoning used in the argument above?

(A)   All students who study diligently make good grades. But some students who do not study diligently also make good grades. Jane studies somewhat diligently. Therefore, Jane makes somewhat good grades.

(B)   All type A chemicals are extremely toxic to human beings. All type B chemicals are nontoxic to human beings. This household cleaner is a mixture of a type A chemical and a type B chemical. Therefore, this household cleaner is moderately toxic.

(C)   All students at Hanson School live in Green County. All students at Edwards School live in Winn County. Members of the Perry family attend both Hanson and Edwards. Therefore, some members of the Perry family live in Green County and some live in Winn County.

(D)   All transcriptionists know shorthand. All engineers know calculus. Bob has worked both as a transcriptionist and as an engineer. Therefore, Bob knows both shorthand and calculus.

(E)   All of Kenisha's dresses are very well made. All of Connie's dresses are very badly made. Half of the dresses in this closet are very well made, and half of them are very badly made. Therefore, half of the dresses in this closet are Kenisha's and half of them are Connie's.

3. A century in certain ways is like a life, and as the end of a century approaches, people behave toward that century much as someone who is nearing the end of life does toward that life. So just as people in their last years spend much time looking back on the events of their life, people at a century's end _____.

Which one of the following most logically completes the argument?

(A) reminisce about their own lives
(B) fear that their own lives are about to end
(C) focus on what the next century will bring
(D) become very interested in the history of the century just ending
(E) reflect on how certain unfortunate events of the century could have been avoided

4. Consumer: The latest *Connorly Report* suggests that Ocksenfrey prepackaged meals are virtually devoid of nutritional value. But the *Connorly Report* is commissioned by Danto Foods, Ocksenfrey's largest corporate rival, and early drafts of the report are submitted for approval to Danto Foods' public relations department. Because of the obvious bias of this report, it is clear that Ocksenfrey's prepackaged meals really are nutritious.

The reasoning in the consumer's argument is most vulnerable to criticism on the grounds that the argument

(A) treats evidence that there is an apparent bias as evidence that the Connorly Report's claims are false
(B) draws a conclusion based solely on an unrepresentative sample of Ocksenfrey's products
(C) fails to take into account the possibility that Ocksenfrey has just as much motivation to create negative publicity for Danto as Danto has to create negative publicity for Ocksenfrey
(D) fails to provide evidence that Danto Foods' prepackaged meals are not more nutritious than Ocksenfrey's are
(E) presumes, without providing justification, that Danto Foods' public relations department would not approve a draft of a report that was hostile to Danto Foods' products

5. Scientist: Earth's average annual temperature has increased by about 0.5 degrees Celsius over the la[st] century. This warming is primarily the result of t[he] buildup of minor gases in the atmosphere, blockin[g] the outward flow of heat from the planet.

Which one of the following, if true, would count as evidence against the scientist's explanation of Earth's warming?

(A) Only some of the minor gases whose presence in the atmosphere allegedly resulted in the phenomenon described by the scientist were produced by industrial pollution.
(B) Most of the warming occurred before 1940, while most of the buildup of minor gases in the atmosphere occurred after 1940.
(C) Over the last century, Earth received slightly more solar radiation in certain years than it di[d] in others.
(D) Volcanic dust and other particles in the atmosphere reflect much of the Sun's radiation back into space before it can reach Earth's surface.
(E) The accumulation of minor gases in the atmosphere has been greater over the last century than at any other time in Earth's histo[ry].

6. An undergraduate degree is necessary for appointment to the executive board. Further, no one with a felony conviction can be appointed to the board. Thus, Murra[y,] an accountant with both a bachelor's and a master's degree, cannot be accepted for the position of Executiv[e] Administrator, since he has a felony conviction.

The argument's conclusion follows logically if which o[ne] of the following is assumed?

(A) Anyone with a master's degree and without a felony conviction is eligible for appointment to the executive board.
(B) Only candidates eligible for appointment to the executive board can be accepted for the positio[n] of Executive Administrator.
(C) An undergraduate degree is not necessary for acceptance for the position of Executive Administrator.
(D) If Murray did not have a felony conviction, he would be accepted for the position of Executive Administrator.
(E) The felony charge on which Murray was convicted is relevant to the duties of the positio[n] of Executive Administrator.

426

7.  Ethicist:  The most advanced kind of moral motivation is based solely on abstract principles. This form of motivation is in contrast with calculated self-interest or the desire to adhere to societal norms and conventions.

The actions of which one of the following individuals exhibit the most advanced kind of moral motivation, as described by the ethicist?

(A)  Bobby contributed money to a local charity during a charity drive at work because he worried that not doing so would make him look stingy.

(B)  Wes contributed money to a local charity during a charity drive at work because he believed that doing so would improve his employer's opinion of him.

(C)  Donna's employers engaged in an illegal but profitable practice that caused serious damage to the environment. Donna did not report this practice to the authorities, out of fear that her employers would retaliate against her.

(D)  Jadine's employers engaged in an illegal but profitable practice that caused serious damage to the environment. Jadine reported this practice to the authorities out of a belief that protecting the environment is always more important than monetary profit.

(E)  Leigh's employers engaged in an illegal but profitable practice that caused serious damage to the environment. Leigh reported this practice to the authorities only because several colleagues had been pressuring her to do so.

8.  Proponents of the electric car maintain that when the technical problems associated with its battery design are solved, such cars will be widely used and, because they are emission-free, will result in an abatement of the environmental degradation caused by auto emissions. But unless we dam more rivers, the electricity to charge these batteries will come from nuclear or coal-fired power plants. Each of these three power sources produces considerable environmental damage. Thus, the electric car _____.

Which one of the following most logically completes the argument?

(A)  will have worse environmental consequences than its proponents may believe

(B)  will probably remain less popular than other types of cars

(C)  requires that purely technical problems be solved before it can succeed

(D)  will increase the total level of emissions rather than reduce it

(E)  will not produce a net reduction in environmental degradation

Where's the answer key?

You'll find the answer key for this section on page 442.

9. Although video game sales have increased steadily over the past 3 years, we can expect a reversal of this trend in the very near future. Historically, over three quarters of video games sold have been purchased by people from 13 to 16 years of age, and the number of people in this age group is expected to decline steadily over the next 10 years.

Which one of the following, if true, would most seriously weaken the argument?

(A) Most people 17 years old or older have never purchased a video game.
(B) Video game rentals have declined over the past 3 years.
(C) New technology will undoubtedly make entirely new entertainment options available over the next 10 years.
(D) The number of different types of video games available is unlikely to decrease in the near future.
(E) Most of the people who have purchased video games over the past 3 years are over the age of 16.

10. Double-blind techniques should be used whenever possible in scientific experiments. They help prevent the misinterpretations that often arise due to expectations and opinions that scientists already hold, and clearly scientists should be extremely diligent in trying to avoid such misinterpretations.

Which one of the following most accurately expresses the main conclusion of the argument?

(A) Scientists' objectivity may be impeded by interpreting experimental evidence on the basis of expectations and opinions that they already hold.
(B) It is advisable for scientists to use double-blind techniques in as high a proportion of their experiments as they can.
(C) Scientists sometimes neglect to adequately consider the risk of misinterpreting evidence on the basis of prior expectations and opinions.
(D) Whenever possible, scientists should refrain from interpreting evidence on the basis of previously formed expectations and convictions.
(E) Double-blind experimental techniques are often an effective way of ensuring scientific objectivity.

11. It is now a common complaint that the electronic media have corroded the intellectual skills required and fostered by the literary media. But several centuries ago the complaint was that certain intellectual skills, such as the powerful memory and extemporaneous eloquence that were intrinsic to oral culture, were being destroyed by the spread of literacy. So, what awaits us is probably a mere alteration of the human mind rather than its devolution.

The reference to the complaint of several centuries ago that powerful memory and extemporaneous eloquence were being destroyed plays which one of the following roles in the argument?

(A) evidence supporting the claim that the intellectual skills fostered by the literary media are being destroyed by the electronic media
(B) an illustration of the general hypothesis being advanced that intellectual abilities are inseparable from the means by which people communicate
(C) an example of a cultural change that did not necessarily have a detrimental effect on the human mind overall
(D) evidence that the claim that the intellectual skills required and fostered by the literary media are being lost is unwarranted
(E) possible evidence, mentioned and then dismissed, that might be cited by supporters of the hypothesis being criticized

12. Suppose I have promised to keep a confidence and someone asks me a question that I cannot answer truthfully without thereby breaking the promise. Obviously, I cannot both keep and break the same promise. Therefore, one cannot be obliged both to answer all questions truthfully and to keep all promises.

Which one of the following arguments is most similar in its reasoning to the argument above?

(A) It is claimed that we have the unencumbered right to say whatever we want. It is also claimed that we have the obligation to be civil to others. But civility requires that we not always say what we want. So, it cannot be true both that we have the unencumbered right to say whatever we want and that we have the duty to be civil.

(B) Some politicians could attain popularity with voters only by making extravagant promises; this, however, would deceive the people. So, since the only way for some politicians to be popular is to deceive, and any politician needs to be popular, it follows that some politicians must deceive.

(C) If we put a lot of effort into making this report look good, the client might think we did so because we believed our proposal would not stand on its own merits. On the other hand, if we do not try to make the report look good, the client might think we are not serious about her business. So, whatever we do, we risk her criticism.

(D) If creditors have legitimate claims against a business and the business has the resources to pay those debts, then the business is obliged to pay them. Also, if a business has obligations to pay debts, then a court will force it to pay them. But the courts did not force this business to pay its debts, so either the creditors did not have legitimate claims or the business did not have sufficient resources.

(E) If we extend our business hours, we will either have to hire new employees or have existing employees work overtime. But both new employees and additional overtime would dramatically increase our labor costs. We cannot afford to increase labor costs, so we will have to keep our business hours as they stand.

13. Standard aluminum soft-drink cans do not vary in the amount of aluminum that they contain. Fifty percent of the aluminum contained in a certain group (M) of standard aluminum soft-drink cans was recycled from another group (L) of used, standard aluminum soft-drink cans. Since all the cans in L were recycled into cans in M and since the amount of material other than aluminum in an aluminum can is negligible, it follows that M contains twice as many cans as L.

The conclusion of the argument follows logically if which one of the following is assumed?

(A) The aluminum in the cans of M cannot be recycled further.

(B) Recycled aluminum is of poorer quality than unrecycled aluminum.

(C) All of the aluminum in an aluminum can is recovered when the can is recycled.

(D) None of the soft-drink cans in group L had been made from recycled aluminum.

(E) Aluminum soft-drink cans are more easily recycled than are soft-drink cans made from other materials.

14. A cup of raw milk, after being heated in a microwave oven to 50 degrees Celsius, contains half its initial concentration of a particular enzyme, lysozyme. If, however, the milk reaches that temperature through exposure to a conventional heat source of 50 degrees Celsius, it will contain nearly all of its initial concentration of the enzyme. Therefore, what destroys the enzyme is not heat but microwaves, which generate heat.

Which one of the following, if true, most seriously weakens the argument?

(A) Heating raw milk in a microwave oven to a temperature of 100 degrees Celsius destroys nearly all of the lysozyme initially present in that milk.

(B) Enzymes in raw milk that are destroyed through excessive heating can be replaced by adding enzymes that have been extracted from other sources.

(C) A liquid exposed to a conventional heat source of exactly 50 degrees Celsius will reach that temperature more slowly than it would if it were exposed to a conventional heat source hotter than 50 degrees Celsius.

(D) Milk that has been heated in a microwave oven does not taste noticeably different from milk that has been briefly heated by exposure to a conventional heat source.

(E) Heating any liquid by microwave creates small zones within it that are much hotter than the overall temperature that the liquid will ultimately reach.

15. A new government policy has been developed to avoid many serious cases of influenza. This goal will be accomplished by the annual vaccination of high-risk individuals: everyone 65 and older as well as anyone with a chronic disease that might cause them to experience complications from the influenza virus. Each year's vaccination will protect only against the strain of the influenza virus deemed most likely to be prevalent that year, so every year it will be necessary for all high-risk individuals to receive a vaccine for a different strain of the virus.

Which one of the following is an assumption that would allow the conclusion above to be properly drawn?

(A) The number of individuals in the high-risk group for influenza will not significantly change from year to year.
(B) The likelihood that a serious influenza epidemic will occur varies from year to year.
(C) No vaccine for the influenza virus protects against more than one strain of that virus.
(D) Each year the strain of influenza virus deemed most likely to be prevalent will be one that had not previously been deemed most likely to be prevalent.
(E) Each year's vaccine will have fewer side effects than the vaccine of the previous year since the technology for making vaccines will constantly improve.

16. Taylor: Researchers at a local university claim that 61 percent of the information transferred during a conversation is communicated through nonverbal signals. But this claim, like all such mathematically precise claims, is suspect, because claims of such exactitude could never be established by science.

Sandra: While precision is unobtainable in many areas of life, it is commonplace in others. Many scientific disciplines obtain extremely precise results, which should not be doubted merely because of their precision.

The statements above provide the most support for holding that Sandra would disagree with Taylor about which one of the following statements?

(A) Research might reveal that 61 percent of the information taken in during a conversation is communicated through nonverbal signals.
(B) It is possible to determine whether 61 percent of the information taken in during a conversation is communicated through nonverbal signals.
(C) The study of verbal and nonverbal communication is an area where one cannot expect great precision in one's research results.
(D) Some sciences can yield mathematically precise results that are not inherently suspect.
(E) If inherently suspect claims are usually false, then the majority of claims made by scientists are false as well.

17. Hospital executive: At a recent conference on nonprofit management, several computer experts maintained that the most significant threat faced by large institutions such as universities and hospitals is unauthorized access to confidential data. In light of this testimony, we should make the protection of our clients' confidentiality our highest priority.

The hospital executive's argument is most vulnerable to which one of the following objections?

(A) The argument confuses the causes of a problem with the appropriate solutions to that problem.
(B) The argument relies on the testimony of experts whose expertise is not shown to be sufficiently broad to support their general claim.
(C) The argument assumes that a correlation between two phenomena is evidence that one is the cause of the other.
(D) The argument draws a general conclusion about a group based on data about an unrepresentative sample of that group.
(E) The argument infers that a property belonging to large institutions belongs to all institutions.

18. Modern science is built on the process of posing hypotheses and testing them against observations–in essence, attempting to show that the hypotheses are incorrect. Nothing brings more recognition than overthrowing conventional wisdom. It is accordingly unsurprising that some scientists are skeptical of the widely accepted predictions of global warming. What is instead remarkable is that with hundreds of researchers striving to make breakthroughs in climatology, very few find evidence that global warming is unlikely.

The information above provides the most support for which one of the following statements?

(A) Most scientists who are reluctant to accept the global warming hypothesis are not acting in accordance with the accepted standards of scientific debate.
(B) Most researchers in climatology have substantial motive to find evidence that would discredit the global warming hypothesis.
(C) There is evidence that conclusively shows that the global warming hypothesis is true.
(D) Scientists who are skeptical about global warming have not offered any alternative hypotheses to explain climatological data.
(E) Research in global warming is primarily driven by a desire for recognition in the scientific community

19.  Historian:  The Land Party achieved its only national victory in Banestria in 1935. It received most of its support that year in rural and semirural areas, where the bulk of Banestria's population lived at the time. The economic woes of the years surrounding that election hit agricultural and small business interests the hardest, and the Land Party specifically targeted those groups in 1935. I conclude that the success of the Land Party that year was due to the combination of the Land Party's specifically addressing the concerns of these groups and the depth of the economic problems people in these groups were facing.

Each of the following, if true, strengthens the historian's argument EXCEPT:

(A)  In preceding elections the Land Party made no attempt to address the interests of economically distressed urban groups.
(B)  Voters are more likely to vote for a political party that focuses on their problems.
(C)  The Land Party had most of its successes when there was economic distress in the agricultural sector.
(D)  No other major party in Banestria specifically addressed the issues of people who lived in semirural areas in 1935.
(E)  The greater the degree of economic distress someone is in, the more likely that person is to vote.

20.  Gamba:  Muñoz claims that the Southwest Hopeville Neighbors Association overwhelmingly opposes the new water system, citing this as evidence of citywide opposition. The association did pass a resolution opposing the new water system, but only 25 of 350 members voted, with 10 in favor of the system. Furthermore, the 15 opposing votes represent far less than 1 percent of Hopeville's population. One should not assume that so few votes represent the view of the majority of Hopeville's residents.

Of the following, which one most accurately describes Gamba's strategy of argumentation?

(A)  questioning a conclusion based on the results of a vote, on the grounds that people with certain views are more likely to vote
(B)  questioning a claim supported by statistical data by arguing that statistical data can be manipulated to support whatever view the interpreter wants to support
(C)  attempting to refute an argument by showing that, contrary to what has been claimed, the truth of the premises does not guarantee the truth of the conclusion
(D)  criticizing a view on the grounds that the view is based on evidence that is in principle impossible to disconfirm
(E)  attempting to cast doubt on a conclusion by claiming that the statistical sample on which the conclusion is based is too small to be dependable

21.  Driver:  My friends say I will one day have an accident because I drive my sports car recklessly. But I have done some research, and apparently minivans and larger sedans have very low accident rates compared to sports cars. So trading my sports car in for a minivan would lower my risk of having an accident.

The reasoning in the driver's argument is most vulnerable to criticism on the grounds that this argument

(A)  infers a cause from a mere correlation
(B)  relies on a sample that is too narrow
(C)  misinterprets evidence that a result is likely as evidence that the result is certain
(D)  mistakes a condition sufficient for bringing about a result for a condition necessary for doing so
(E)  relies on a source that is probably not well-informed

22. Editorialist: News media rarely cover local politics thoroughly, and local political business is usually conducted secretively. These factors each tend to isolate local politicians from their electorates. This has the effect of reducing the chance that any particular act of resident participation will elicit a positive official response, which in turn discourages resident participation in local politics.

Which one of the following is most strongly supported by the editorialist's statements?

(A) Particular acts of resident participation would be likely to elicit a positive response from local politicians if those politicians were less isolated from their electorate.

(B) Local political business should be conducted less secretively because this would avoid discouraging resident participation in local politics.

(C) The most important factor influencing a resident's decision as to whether to participate in local politics is the chance that the participation will elicit a positive official response.

(D) More-frequent thorough coverage of local politics would reduce at least one source of discouragement from resident participation in local politics.

(E) If resident participation in local politics were not discouraged, this would cause local politicians to be less isolated from their electorate.

23. Philosopher: An action is morally right if it would be reasonably expected to increase the aggregate well-being of the people affected by it. An action is morally wrong if and only if it would be reasonably expected to reduce the aggregate well-being of the people affected by it. Thus, actions that would be reasonably expected to leave unchanged the aggregate well-being of the people affected by them are also right.

The philosopher's conclusion follows logically if which one of the following is assumed?

(A) Only wrong actions would be reasonably expected to reduce the aggregate well-being of the people affected by them.

(B) No action is both right and wrong.

(C) Any action that is not morally wrong is morally right.

(D) There are actions that would be reasonably expected to leave unchanged the aggregate well-being of the people affected by them.

(E) Only right actions have good consequences.

24. Car companies solicit consumer information on such human factors as whether a seat is comfortable or whether a set of controls is easy to use. However, designer interaction with consumers is superior to survey data; the data may tell the designer why a feature on last year's model was given a low rating, but data will not explain how that feature needs to be changed in order to receive a higher rating.

The reasoning above conforms most closely to which one of the following propositions?

(A) Getting consumer input for design modifications can contribute to successful product design.

(B) Car companies traditionally conduct extensive postmarket surveys.

(C) Designers aim to create features that will appeal to specific market niches.

(D) A car will have unappealing features if consumers are not consulted during its design stage.

(E) Consumer input affects external rather than internal design components of cars.

25. During the nineteenth century, the French academy of art was a major financial sponsor of painting and sculpture in France; sponsorship by private individuals had decreased dramatically by this time. Because the academy discouraged innovation in the arts, there was little innovation in nineteenth century French sculpture. Yet nineteenth century French painting showed a remarkable degree of innovation.

Which one of the following, if true, most helps to explain the difference between the amount of innovation in French painting and the amount of innovation in French sculpture during the nineteenth century?

(A) In France in the nineteenth century, the French academy gave more of its financial support to painting than it did to sculpture.

(B) The French academy in the nineteenth century financially supported a greater number of sculptors than painters, but individual painters received more support, on average, than individual sculptors.

(C) Because stone was so much more expensive than paint and canvas, far more unsponsored paintings were produced than were unsponsored sculptures in France during the nineteenth century.

(D) Very few of the artists in France in the nineteenth century who produced sculptures also produced paintings.

(E) Although the academy was the primary sponsor of sculpture and painting, the total amount of financial support that French sculptors and painters received from sponsors declined during the nineteenth century.

# Start Your Wrong Answer Journal Now

Remember the Wrong Answer Journal from way back in the Introduction? Here's a mini-reminder:

| TEST.SECTION.# | STIMULUS TYPE | QUESTION TYPE | REASON MISSED | SOLUTION |
|---|---|---|---|---|
| 62.4.24 | PS → I | Fill In | Didn't understand stimulus, went into answers blind | Translate stimulus, break it down. What is it saying and what does that mean? |

*Your Wrong Answer Journal is ready to go on page 456!*

That's a Wrong Answer Journal! To start *your* Wrong Answer Journal, go back to your wrong answers in June 2007, Section 2 now. Analyze your mistakes. Get specific about what *exactly* your errors were.

Your first major step will be filling in the "Reason Missed" column. When you're reviewing, ask "Why?" of the first Reason Missed you identify. Your first Reason Missed idea may be a cop-out like "Down to 2!" or "Misread." It's not that these ideas are *wrong*; it's just that they won't help you improve that much. You need to get much more specific and actionable to make your Wrong Answer Journal useful! An actionable Reason Missed leads to a real Solution.

For example, say you missed a question and you're trying to fill in the Reason Missed column. Your first idea is "I misread the right answer." Push yourself harder. Ask yourself, "Why did I misread the right answer?" This gets you closer to the root cause of why you're missing questions. Your answer to the "Why?" may be "Because I was going too fast in the answer choices." This is much better. Now your Solution is obvious: Don't rush the answer choices.

Next, you'll fill in the Solution column. Your Solution has to be an action you can control. You can control whether you rush the answer choices way more than you can control "stop misreading." We'd all like to stop misreading, but it's not exactly an achievable goal without concrete steps. These concrete steps go in the Solution column.

## SECTION REVIEW PRO TIPS

1. **Camouflage Review *every single section*.**

   This is really the only Section Review Pro Tip of any note. **You will get so much more out of the section if you Camo it.**

   *Go to elementalprep.com/camo for all the joy your body can handle.*

2. **Do not go straight to the answer key when you are done with the section.**

   Camouflage Review requires you to not know which questions are wrong in order to provide value. Do not spoil the Camo.

3. **Never mark the correct answer when you check.**

   Allow yourself the opportunity to redo the question without knowing. Take a short break if you remember the answer key.

4. **Never erase the wrong answer you chose.**

   You want to get inside your own head and figure out why you chose that incorrect answer.

5. **Re-attempt incorrect questions.**

   Fill in your Wrong Answer Journal after your second attempt at the question.

*As you answer these questions, write the question type to the side of each question stem. Check your question type identification when you grade the section.*

1.  Situation:   Someone living in a cold climate buys a winter coat that is stylish but not warm in order to appear sophisticated.

    Analysis:   People are sometimes willing to sacrifice sensual comfort or pleasure for the sake of appearances.

    The analysis provided for the situation above is most appropriate for which one of the following situations?

    (A)   A person buys an automobile to commute to work even though public transportation is quick and reliable.
    (B)   A parent buys a car seat for a young child because it is more colorful and more comfortable for the child than the other car seats on the market, though no safer.
    (C)   A couple buys a particular wine even though their favorite wine is less expensive and better tasting because they think it will impress their dinner guests.
    (D)   A person sets her thermostat at a low temperature during the winter because she is concerned about the environmental damage caused by using fossil fuels to heat her home.
    (E)   An acrobat convinces the circus that employs him to purchase an expensive outfit for him so that he can wear it during his act to impress the audience.

2.  After replacing his old gas water heater with a new, pilotless, gas water heater that is rated as highly efficient, Jimmy's gas bills increased.

    Each of the following, if true, contributes to an explanation of the increase mentioned above EXCEPT:

    (A)   The new water heater uses a smaller percentage of the gas used by Jimmy's household than did the old one.
    (B)   Shortly after the new water heater was installed, Jimmy's uncle came to live with him, doubling the size of the household.
    (C)   After having done his laundry at a laundromat, Jimmy bought and started using a gas dryer when he replaced his water heater.
    (D)   Jimmy's utility company raised the rates for gas consumption following installation of the new water heater.
    (E)   Unusually cold weather following installation of the new water heater resulted in heavy gas usage.

3.  Carolyn:   The artist Marc Quinn has displayed, behind a glass plate, biologically replicated fragments of Sir John Sulston's DNA, calling it a "conceptual portrait" of Sulston. But to be a portrait, something must bear a recognizable resemblance to its subject.

    Arnold:   I disagree. Quinn's conceptual portrait is a maximally realistic portrait, for it holds actual instructions according to which Sulston was created.

    The dialogue provides most support for the claim that Carolyn and Arnold disagree over whether the object described by Quinn as a conceptual portrait of Sir John Sulston

    (A)   should be considered to be art
    (B)   should be considered to be Quinn's work
    (C)   bears a recognizable resemblance to Sulston
    (D)   contains instructions according to which Sulston was created
    (E)   is actually a portrait of Sulston

4.  Many corporations have begun decorating their halls with motivational posters in hopes of boosting their employees' motivation to work productively. However, almost all employees at these corporations are already motivated to work productively. So these corporations' use of motivational posters is unlikely to achieve its intended purpose.

    The reasoning in the argument is most vulnerable to criticism on the grounds that the argument

    (A)   fails to consider whether corporations that do not currently use motivational posters would increase their employees' motivation to work productively if they began using the posters
    (B)   takes for granted that, with respect to their employees' motivation to work productively, corporations that decorate their halls with motivational posters are representative of corporations in general
    (C)   fails to consider that even if motivational posters do not have one particular beneficial effect for corporations, they may have similar effects that are equally beneficial
    (D)   does not adequately address the possibility that employee productivity is strongly affected by factors other than employees' motivation to work productively
    (E)   fails to consider that even if employees are already motivated to work productively, motivational posters may increase that motivation

5. Atrens: An early entomologist observed ants carrying particles to neighboring ant colonies and inferred that the ants were bringing food to their neighbors. Further research, however, revealed that the ants were emptying their own colony's dumping site. Thus, the early entomologist was wrong.

Atrens's conclusion follows logically if which one of the following is assumed?

(A) Ant societies do not interact in all the same ways that human societies interact.
(B) There is only weak evidence for the view that ants have the capacity to make use of objects as gifts.
(C) Ant dumping sites do not contain particles that could be used as food.
(D) The ants to whom the particles were brought never carried the particles into their own colonies.
(E) The entomologist cited retracted his conclusion when it was determined that the particles the ants carried came from their dumping site.

6. Jablonski, who owns a car dealership, has donated cars to driver education programs at area schools for over five years. She found the statistics on car accidents to be disturbing, and she wanted to do something to encourage better driving in young drivers. Some members of the community have shown their support for this action by purchasing cars from Jablonski's dealership.

Which one of the following propositions is best illustrated by the passage?

(A) The only way to reduce traffic accidents is through driver education programs.
(B) Altruistic actions sometimes have positive consequences for those who perform them.
(C) Young drivers are the group most likely to benefit from driver education programs.
(D) It is usually in one's best interest to perform actions that benefit others.
(E) An action must have broad community support if it is to be successful.

7. Antonio: One can live a life of moderation by never deviating from the middle course. But then one loses the joy of spontaneity and misses the opportunities that come to those who are occasionally willing to take great chances, or to go too far.

Marla: But one who, in the interests of moderation, never risks going too far is actually failing to live a life of moderation: one must be moderate even in one's moderation.

Antonio and Marla disagree over

(A) whether it is desirable for people occasionally to take great chances in life
(B) what a life of moderation requires of a person
(C) whether it is possible for a person to embrace other virtues along with moderation
(D) how often a person ought to deviate from the middle course in life
(E) whether it is desirable for people to be moderately spontaneous

8. Advertisement: Fabric-Soft leaves clothes soft and fluffy, and its fresh scent is a delight. We conducted a test using over 100 consumers to prove Fabric-Soft is best. Each consumer was given one towel washed with Fabric-Soft and one towel washed without it. Ninety-nine percent of the consumers preferred the Fabric-Soft towel. So Fabric-Soft is the most effective fabric softener available.

The advertisement's reasoning is most vulnerable to criticism on the grounds that it fails to consider whether

(A) any of the consumers tested are allergic to fabric softeners
(B) Fabric-Soft is more or less harmful to the environment than other fabric softeners
(C) Fabric-Soft is much cheaper or more expensive than other fabric softeners
(D) the consumers tested find the benefits of using fabric softeners worth the expense
(E) the consumers tested had the opportunity to evaluate fabric softeners other than Fabric-Soft

9.   Naturalist:   The recent claims that the Tasmanian tiger is not extinct are false. The Tasmanian tiger's natural habitat was taken over by sheep farming decades ago, resulting in the animal's systematic elimination from the area. Since then naturalists working in the region have discovered no hard evidence of its survival, such as carcasses or tracks. In spite of alleged sightings of the animal, the Tasmanian tiger no longer exists.

Which one of the following is an assumption on which the naturalist's argument depends?

(A)   Sheep farming drove the last Tasmanian tigers to starvation by chasing them from their natural habitat.
(B)   Some scavengers in Tasmania are capable of destroying tiger carcasses without a trace.
(C)   Every naturalist working in the Tasmanian tiger's natural habitat has looked systematically for evidence of the tiger's survival.
(D)   The Tasmanian tiger did not move and adapt to a different region in response to the loss of habitat.
(E)   Those who have reported sightings of the Tasmanian tiger are not experienced naturalists.

10.   Advertisers have learned that people are more easily encouraged to develop positive attitudes about things toward which they originally have neutral or even negative attitudes if those things are linked, with pictorial help rather than exclusively through prose, to things about which they already have positive attitudes. Therefore, advertisers are likely to _____.

Which one of the following most logically completes the argument?

(A)   use little if any written prose in their advertisements
(B)   try to encourage people to develop positive attitudes about products that can be better represented pictorially than in prose
(C)   place their advertisements on television rather than in magazines
(D)   highlight the desirable features of the advertised product by contrasting them pictorially with undesirable features of a competing product
(E)   create advertisements containing pictures of things most members of the target audience like

11.   Feathers recently taken from seabirds stuffed and preserved in the 1880s have been found to contain only half as much mercury as feathers recently taken from living birds of the same species. Since mercury that accumulates in a seabird's feathers as the feathers grow is derived from fish eaten by the bird, these results indicate that mercury levels in saltwater fish are higher now than they were 100 years ago.

The argument depends on assuming that

(A)   the proportion of a seabird's diet consisting of fish was not as high, on average, in the 1880s as it is today
(B)   the amount of mercury in a saltwater fish depends on the amount of pollution in the ocean habitat of the fish
(C)   mercury derived from fish is essential for the normal growth of a seabird's feathers
(D)   the stuffed seabirds whose feathers were tested for mercury were not fully grown
(E)   the process used to preserve birds in the 1880s did not substantially decrease the amount of mercury in the birds' feathers

12.   Novel X and Novel Y are both semiautobiographical novels and contain many very similar themes and situations, which might lead one to suspect plagiarism on the part of one of the authors. However, it is more likely that the similarity of themes and situations in the two novels is merely coincidental, since both authors are from very similar backgrounds and have led similar lives.

Which one of the following most accurately expresses the conclusion drawn in the argument?

(A)   Novel X and Novel Y are both semiautobiographical novels, and the two novels contain many very similar themes and situations.
(B)   The fact that Novel X and Novel Y are both semiautobiographical novels and contain many very similar themes and situations might lead one to suspect plagiarism on the part of one of the authors.
(C)   The author of Novel X and the author of Novel Y are from very similar backgrounds and have led very similar lives.
(D)   It is less likely that one of the authors of Novel X or Novel Y is guilty of plagiarism than that the similarity of themes and situations in the two novels is merely coincidental.
(E)   If the authors of Novel X and Novel Y are from very similar backgrounds and have led similar lives, suspicions that either of the authors plagiarized are very likely to be unwarranted.

13.	Therapist:	Cognitive psychotherapy focuses on changing a patient's conscious beliefs. Thus, cognitive psychotherapy is likely to be more effective at helping patients overcome psychological problems than are forms of psychotherapy that focus on changing unconscious beliefs and desires, since only conscious beliefs are under the patient's direct conscious control.

Which one of the following, if true, would most strengthen the therapist's argument?

(A)	Psychological problems are frequently caused by unconscious beliefs that could be changed with the aid of psychotherapy.

(B)	It is difficult for any form of psychotherapy to be effective without focusing on mental states that are under the patient's direct conscious control.

(C)	Cognitive psychotherapy is the only form of psychotherapy that focuses primarily on changing the patient's conscious beliefs.

(D)	No form of psychotherapy that focuses on changing the patient's unconscious beliefs and desires can be effective unless it also helps change beliefs that are under the patient's direct conscious control.

(E)	All of a patient's conscious beliefs are under the patient's conscious control, but other psychological states cannot be controlled effectively without the aid of psychotherapy.

14.	Commentator:	In academic scholarship, sources are always cited, and methodology and theoretical assumptions are set out, so as to allow critical study, replication, and expansion of scholarship. In open-source software, the code in which the program is written can be viewed and modified by individual users for their purposes without getting permission from the producer or paying a fee. In contrast, the code of proprietary software is kept secret, and modifications can be made only by the producer, for a fee. This shows that open-source software better matches the values embodied in academic scholarship, and since scholarship is central to the mission of universities, universities should use only open-source software.

The commentator's reasoning most closely conforms to which one of the following principles?

(A)	Whatever software tools are most advanced and can achieve the goals of academic scholarship are the ones that should alone be used in universities.

(B)	Universities should use the type of software technology that is least expensive, as long as that type of software technology is adequate for the purposes of academic scholarship.

(C)	Universities should choose the type of software technology that best matches the values embodied in the activities that are central to the mission of universities.

(D)	The form of software technology that best matches the values embodied in the activities that are central to the mission of universities is the form of software technology that is most efficient for universities to use.

(E)	A university should not pursue any activity that would block the achievement of the goals of academic scholarship at that university.

15.    A consumer magazine surveyed people who had sought a psychologist's help with a personal problem. Of those responding who had received treatment for 6 months or less, 20 percent claimed that treatment "made things a lot better." Of those responding who had received longer treatment, 36 percent claimed that treatment "made things a lot better." Therefore, psychological treatment lasting more than 6 months is more effective than shorter-term treatment.

Which one of the following, if true, most seriously weakens the argument?

(A)    Of the respondents who had received treatment for longer than 6 months, 10 percent said that treatment made things worse.
(B)    Patients who had received treatment for longer than 6 months were more likely to respond to the survey than were those who had received treatment for a shorter time.
(C)    Patients who feel they are doing well in treatment tend to remain in treatment, while those who are doing poorly tend to quit earlier.
(D)    Patients who were dissatisfied with their treatment were more likely to feel a need to express their feelings about it and thus to return the survey.
(E)    Many psychologists encourage their patients to receive treatment for longer than 6 months.

16.    Philosopher:    Nations are not literally persons; they have no thoughts or feelings, and, literally speaking, they perform no actions. Thus they have no moral rights or responsibilities. But no nation can survive unless many of its citizens attribute such rights and responsibilities to it, for nothing else could prompt people to make the sacrifices national citizenship demands. Obviously, then, a nation _____.

Which one of the following most logically completes the philosopher's argument?

(A)    cannot continue to exist unless something other than the false belief that the nation has moral rights motivates its citizens to make sacrifices
(B)    cannot survive unless many of its citizens have some beliefs that are literally false
(C)    can never be a target of moral praise or blame
(D)    is not worth the sacrifices that its citizens make on its behalf
(E)    should always be thought of in metaphorical rather than literal terms

17.    When exercising the muscles in one's back, it is important, in order to maintain a healthy back, to exercise the muscles on opposite sides of the spine equally. After all, balanced muscle development is needed to maintain a healthy back, since the muscles on opposite sides of the spine must pull equally in opposing directions to keep the back in proper alignment and protect the spine.

Which one of the following is an assumption required by the argument?

(A)    Muscles on opposite sides of the spine that are equally well developed will be enough to keep the back in proper alignment.
(B)    Exercising the muscles on opposite sides of the spine unequally tends to lead to unbalanced muscle development.
(C)    Provided that one exercises the muscles on opposite sides of the spine equally, one will have a generally healthy back.
(D)    If the muscles on opposite sides of the spine are exercised unequally, one's back will be irreparably damaged.
(E)    One should exercise daily to ensure that the muscles on opposite sides of the spine keep the back in proper alignment.

18.    Editorialist:    In all cultures, it is almost universally accepted that one has a moral duty to prevent members of one's family from being harmed. Thus, few would deny that if a person is known by the person's parents to be falsely accused of a crime, it would be morally right for the parents to hide the accused from the police. Hence, it is also likely to be widely accepted that it is sometimes morally right to obstruct the police in their work.

The reasoning in the editorialist's argument is most vulnerable to criticism on the grounds that this argument

(A)    utilizes a single type of example for the purpose of justifying a broad generalization
(B)    fails to consider the possibility that other moral principles would be widely recognized as overriding any obligation to protect a family member from harm
(C)    presumes, without providing justification, that allowing the police to arrest an innocent person assists rather than obstructs justice
(D)    takes for granted that there is no moral obligation to obey the law
(E)    takes for granted that the parents mentioned in the example are not mistaken about their child's innocence

19.   Editor:   Many candidates say that if elected they
             will reduce governmental intrusion into voters'
             lives. But voters actually elect politicians who
             instead promise that the government will provide
             assistance to solve their most pressing problems.
             Governmental assistance, however, costs money,
             and money can come only from taxes, which can
             be considered a form of governmental intrusion.
             Thus, governmental intrusion into the lives of
             voters will rarely be substantially reduced over
             time in a democracy.

Which one of the following, if true, would most
strengthen the editor's argument?

(A)   Politicians who win their elections usually keep
      their campaign promises.
(B)   Politicians never promise what they really intend
      to do once in office.
(C)   The most common problems people have are
      financial problems.
(D)   Governmental intrusion into the lives of voters
      is no more burdensome in nondemocratic
      countries than it is in democracies.
(E)   Politicians who promise to do what they actually
      believe ought to be done are rarely elected.

20.   We should accept the proposal to demolish the old
      train station, because the local historical society, which
      vehemently opposes this, is dominated by people who
      have no commitment to long-term economic well-being.
      Preserving old buildings creates an impediment to new
      development, which is critical to economic health.

The flawed reasoning exhibited by the argument above
is most similar to that exhibited by which one of the
following arguments?

(A)   Our country should attempt to safeguard
      works of art that it deems to possess national
      cultural significance. These works might not
      be recognized as such by all taxpayers, or even
      all critics. Nevertheless, our country ought to
      expend whatever money is needed to procure all
      such works as they become available.
(B)   Documents of importance to local heritage should
      be properly preserved and archived for the sake
      of future generations. For, if even one of these
      documents is damaged or lost, the integrity of the
      historical record as a whole will be damaged.
(C)   You should have your hair cut no more than once
      a month. After all, beauticians suggest that their
      customers have their hair cut twice a month, and
      they do this as a way of generating more business
      for themselves.
(D)   The committee should endorse the plan to
      postpone construction of the new expressway.
      Many residents of the neighborhoods that
      would be affected are fervently opposed to that
      construction, and the committee is obligated to
      avoid alienating those residents.
(E)   One should not borrow even small amounts of
      money unless it is absolutely necessary. Once
      one borrows a few dollars, the interest starts to
      accumulate. The longer one takes to repay, the
      more one ends up owing, and eventually a small
      debt has become a large one.

21. Ethicist: On average, animals raised on grain must be fed sixteen pounds of grain to produce one pound of meat. A pound of meat is more nutritious for humans than a pound of grain, but sixteen pounds of grain could feed many more people than could a pound of meat. With grain yields leveling off, large areas of farmland going out of production each year, and the population rapidly expanding, we must accept the fact that consumption of meat will soon be morally unacceptable.

Which one of the following, if true, would most weaken the ethicist's argument?

(A) Even though it has been established that a vegetarian diet can be healthy, many people prefer to eat meat and are willing to pay for it.

(B) Often, cattle or sheep can be raised to maturity on grass from pastureland that is unsuitable for any other kind of farming.

(C) If a grain diet is supplemented with protein derived from non-animal sources, it can have nutritional value equivalent to that of a diet containing meat.

(D) Although prime farmland near metropolitan areas is being lost rapidly to suburban development, we could reverse this trend by choosing to live in areas that are already urban.

(E) Nutritionists agree that a diet composed solely of grain products is not adequate for human health.

22. If the price it pays for coffee beans continues to increase, the Coffee Shoppe will have to increase its prices. In that case, either the Coffee Shoppe will begin selling noncoffee products or its coffee sales will decrease. But selling noncoffee products will decrease the Coffee Shoppe's overall profitability. Moreover, the Coffee Shoppe can avoid a decrease in overall profitability only if its coffee sales do not decrease.

Which one of the following statements follows logically from the statements above?

(A) If the Coffee Shoppe's overall profitability decreases, the price it pays for coffee beans will have continued to increase.

(B) If the Coffee Shoppe's overall profitability decreases, either it will have begun selling noncoffee products or its coffee sales will have decreased.

(C) The Coffee Shoppe's overall profitability will decrease if the price it pays for coffee beans continues to increase.

(D) The price it pays for coffee beans cannot decrease without the Coffee Shoppe's overall profitability also decreasing.

(E) Either the price it pays for coffee beans will continue to increase or the Coffee Shoppe's coffee sales will increase.

23. Political candidates' speeches are loaded with promises and with expressions of good intention, but one must not forget that the politicians' purpose in giving these speeches is to get themselves elected. Clearly, then, these speeches are selfishly motivated and the promises made in them are unreliable.

Which one of the following most accurately describes a flaw in the argument above?

(A) The argument presumes, without providing justification, that if a person's promise is not selfishly motivated then that promise is reliable.

(B) The argument presumes, without providing justification, that promises made for selfish reasons are never kept.

(C) The argument confuses the effect of an action with its cause.

(D) The argument overlooks the fact that a promise need not be unreliable just because the person who made it had an ulterior motive for doing so.

(E) The argument overlooks the fact that a candidate who makes promises for selfish reasons may nonetheless be worthy of the office for which he or she is running.

24. Sociologist: Romantics who claim that people are not born evil but may be made evil by the imperfect institutions that they form cannot be right, for they misunderstand the causal relationship between people and their institutions. After all, institutions are merely collections of people.

Which one of the following principles, if valid, would most help to justify the sociologist's argument?

(A) People acting together in institutions can do more good or evil than can people acting individually.

(B) Institutions formed by people are inevitably imperfect.

(C) People should not be overly optimistic in their view of individual human beings.

(D) A society's institutions are the surest gauge of that society's values.

(E) The whole does not determine the properties of the things that compose it.

25. Some anthropologists argue that the human species could not have survived prehistoric times if the species had not evolved the ability to cope with diverse natural environments. However, there is considerable evidence that *Australopithecus afarensis*, a prehistoric species related to early humans, also thrived in a diverse array of environments, but became extinct. Hence, the anthropologists' claim is false.

The reasoning in the argument is most vulnerable to criticism on the grounds that the argument

(A) confuses a condition's being required for a given result to occur in one case with the condition's being sufficient for such a result to occur in a similar case

(B) takes for granted that if one species had a characteristic that happened to enable it to survive certain conditions, at least one related extinct species must have had the same characteristic

(C) generalizes, from the fact that one species with a certain characteristic survived certain conditions, that all related species with the same characteristic must have survived exactly the same conditions

(D) fails to consider the possibility that *Australopithecus afarensis* had one or more characteristics that lessened its chances of surviving prehistoric times

(E) fails to consider the possibility that, even if a condition caused a result to occur in one case, it was not necessary to cause the result to occur in a similar case

*Where's the answer key?*

You'll find the answer key for this section on page 443.

| | CORRECT ANSWER | QUESTION TYPE |
|---|---|---|
| 1 | B | Conclusion |
| 2 | B | Parallel Flaw |
| 3 | D | Fill In |
| 4 | A | Classic Flaw |
| 5 | B | Weaken |
| 6 | B | SA |
| 7 | D | Principle Conform |
| 8 | A | Fill In |
| 9 | E | Weaken |
| 10 | B | Conclusion |
| 11 | C | Argument Part |
| 12 | A | Parallel Reasoning |
| 13 | C | SA |
| 14 | E | Weaken |
| 15 | D | SA |
| 16 | D | Controversy |
| 17 | B | Classic Flaw |
| 18 | B | MSS |
| 19 | A | Strengthen |
| 20 | E | Method |
| 21 | A | Classic Flaw |
| 22 | D | MSS |
| 23 | C | SA |
| 24 | A | Principle Conform |
| 25 | C | Resolution |

# June 2007, Section 3 ANSWER KEY

| | CORRECT ANSWER | QUESTION TYPE |
|---|---|---|
| 1 | C | Principle Conform |
| 2 | A | Resolution |
| 3 | E | Controversy |
| 4 | E | Classic Flaw (all Loophole Flaw answer choices) |
| 5 | C | SA |
| 6 | B | Principle Conform |
| 7 | B | Controversy |
| 8 | E | Loophole Flaw |
| 9 | D | NA |
| 10 | E | Fill In |
| 11 | E | NA |
| 12 | D | Conclusion |
| 13 | B | Strengthen |
| 14 | C | Principle Conform |
| 15 | C | Weaken |
| 16 | B | Fill In |
| 17 | B | NA |
| 18 | B | Classic Flaw |
| 19 | A | Strengthen |
| 20 | C | Parallel Flaw |
| 21 | B | Weaken |
| 22 | C | Inference |
| 23 | D | Classic Flaw |
| 24 | E | Strengthen |
| 25 | A | Classic Flaw |

EPILOGUE

me:    Dude! You finished the book!

you:   Yeah, but now I have to...

me:    Wait a second though! You just did something awesome. It takes serious dedication to finish this monster. You just achieved something massive.

you:   But I haven't really studied LR yet...

me:    You have though! Reading this book is studying LR. You needed to know this stuff before beginning full practice sections. Now you know it! And you can start rocking out. That's huge.

you:   Yeah, I guess it's just like the LSAT never ends. Until I have the score I want on the actual test, it feels like I've done nothing.

me:    It's a process though. Take a second to appreciate how much progress you've made so far. Are you a better critical thinker today than you were a month ago? I bet you are. That makes you a baller. Also, a granter of dreams.

you:   Granter of dreams?

me:    Well, you bought this book, read it, and it hopefully improved your life in some way. That's been my dream for the past five years. And you just made it real. So thank you. So much. For that.

you:   You're welcome? Wow, you're like really into this. All I wanted was an LSAT prep book that didn't suck.

me:    Yeah, I know, and hopefully you got that! If you have any questions, comments, concerns, or sayings of "hi," don't hesitate to shoot me an email at ellen@elementalprep.com. I promise you won't annoy me. LSAT students make my life.

you:   It's really ok?

me:    It's REALLY ok.

you:   I only believe that because you are clearly so weird.

me:    I buy that. This whole LSAT thing is going to be ok though. Don't be afraid to come back to this book if you can't remember certain concepts. It's intended to be reread — there are lots of easter eggs you probably didn't catch on the first read.

you:   Yeah, I can believe that.

me:    But you should know that I'm in your corner, reader. You can do this. That's the one conclusion in your LSAT journey you don't need to question.

*Check out all these solo stimuli from throughout the book reprinted as full questions! They are here for your unfettered practice enjoyment.*

1. Chronic fatigue syndrome, a condition that afflicts thousands of people, is invariably associated with lower-than-normal concentrations of magnesium in the blood. Further, malabsorption of magnesium from the digestive tract to the blood is also often associated with some types of fatigue. These facts in themselves demonstrate that treatments that raise the concentration of magnesium in the blood would provide an effective cure for the fatigue involved in the syndrome.

   The argument is most vulnerable to which one of the following criticisms?

   (A)   It fails to establish that lower-than-normal concentrations of magnesium in the blood are invariably due to malabsorption of magnesium.
   (B)   It offers no evidence that fatigue itself does not induce lowered concentrations of magnesium in the blood.
   (C)   It ignores the possibility that, even in people who are not afflicted with chronic fatigue syndrome, concentration of magnesium in the blood fluctuates.
   (D)   It neglects to state the exact concentration of magnesium in the blood which is considered the normal concentration.
   (E)   It does not specify what methods would be most effective in raising the concentration of magnesium in the blood.

2. A survey of alumni of the class of 1960 at Aurora University yielded puzzling results. When asked to indicate their academic rank, half of the respondents reported that they were in the top quarter of the graduating class in 1960.

   Which one of the following most helps account for the apparent contradiction above?

   (A)   A disproportionately large number of high-ranking alumni responded to the survey.
   (B)   Few, if any, respondents were mistaken about their class rank.
   (C)   Not all the alumni who were actually in the top quarter responded to the survey.
   (D)   Almost all of the alumni who graduated in 1960 responded to the survey.
   (E)   Academic rank at Aurora University was based on a number of considerations in addition to average grades.

3. Student representative:   Our university, in expelling a student who verbally harassed his roommate, has erred by penalizing the student for doing what he surely has a right to do: speak his mind!

   Dean of students:   But what you're saying is that our university should endorse verbal harassment. Yet surely if we did that, we would threaten the free flow of ideas that is the essence of university life.

   Which one of the following is a questionable technique that the dean of students uses in attempting to refute the student representative?

   (A)   challenging the student representative's knowledge of the process by which the student was expelled
   (B)   invoking a fallacious distinction between speech and other sorts of behavior
   (C)   misdescribing the student representative's position, thereby making it easier to challenge
   (D)   questioning the motives of the student representative rather than offering reasons for the conclusion defended
   (E)   relying on a position of power to silence the opposing viewpoint with a threat

4. Herbalist:   Many of my customers find that their physical coordination improves after drinking juice containing certain herbs. A few doctors assert that the herbs are potentially harmful, but doctors are always trying to maintain a monopoly over medical therapies. So there is no reason not to try my herb juice.

   The reasoning in the herbalist's argument is flawed because the argument

   (A)   attempts to force acceptance of a claim by inducing fear of the consequences of rejecting that claim
   (B)   bases a conclusion on claims that are inconsistent with each other
   (C)   rejects a claim by attacking the proponents of the claim rather than addressing the claim itself
   (D)   relies on evidence presented in terms that presuppose the truth of the claim for which the evidence is offered
   (E)   mistakes the observation that one thing happens after another for proof that the second thing is the result of the first

5. The Volunteers for Literacy Program would benefit if Dolores takes Victor's place as director, since Dolores is far more skillful than Victor is at securing the kind of financial support the program needs and Dolores does not have Victor's propensity for alienating the program's most dedicated volunteers.

The pattern of reasoning in the argument above is most closely paralleled in which one of the following?

(A) It would be more convenient for Dominique to take a bus to school than to take the subway, since the bus stops closer to her house than does the subway and, unlike the subway, the bus goes directly to the school.

(B) Joshua's interest would be better served by taking the bus to get to his parent's house rather than by taking an airplane, since his primary concern is to travel as cheaply as possible and taking the bus is less expensive than going by airplane.

(C) Belinda will get to the concert more quickly by subway than by taxi, since the concert takes place on a Friday evening and on Friday evenings traffic near the concert hall is exceptionally heavy.

(D) Anita would benefit financially by taking the train to work rather than driving her car, since when she drives she has to pay parking fees and the daily fee for parking a car is higher than a round-trip train ticket.

(E) It would be to Fred's advantage to exchange his bus tickets for train tickets, since he needs to arrive at his meeting before any of the other participants and if he goes by bus at least one of the other participants will arrive first.

6. Each of the elements of Girelli's recently completed design for a university library is copied from a different one of several historic libraries. The design includes various features from Classical Greek, Islamic, Mogul, and Romanesque structures. Since no one element in the design is original, it follows that the design of the library cannot be considered original.

Which one of the following is a reasoning error made in the argument?

(A) assuming that because something is true of each of the parts of a whole it is true of the whole itself

(B) generalizing illegitimately from a few instances of a certain kind to all instances of that kind

(C) concluding that an unknown instance of a phenomenon must have all the properties of the known instances

(D) presupposing that alternatives that can be true separately cannot be true together

(E) deriving a factual conclusion from evidence derived from reports of aesthetic preferences

7. Politician: Those economists who claim that consumer price increases have averaged less than 3 percent over the last year are mistaken. They clearly have not shopped anywhere recently. Gasoline is up 10 percent over the last year; my auto insurance, 12 percent; newspapers, 15 percent; propane, 13 percent; bread, 50 percent.

The reasoning in the politician's argument is most vulnerable to criticism on the grounds that the argument

(A) impugns the character of the economists rather than addressing their arguments

(B) fails to show that the economists mentioned are not experts in the area of consumer prices

(C) mistakenly infers that something is not true from the claim that it has not been shown to be so

(D) uses evidence drawn from a small sample that may well be unrepresentative

(E) attempts to persuade by making an emotional appeal

8. Consumer activist: By allowing major airlines to abandon, as they promptly did, all but their most profitable routes, the government's decision to cease regulation of the airline industry has worked to the disadvantage of everyone who lacks access to a large metropolitan airport.

Industry representative: On the contrary, where major airlines moved out, regional airlines have moved in and, as a consequence, there are more flights into and out of most small airports now than before the change in regulatory policy.

The industry representative's argument will not provide an effective answer to the consumer activist's claim unless which one of the following is true?

(A) No small airport has fewer flights now than it did before the change in policy regarding regulation of the airline industry.

(B) When permitted to do so by changes in regulatory policy, each major airline abandoned all but large metropolitan airports.

(C) Policies that result in an increase in the number of flights to which consumers have easy access do not generally work to the disadvantage of consumers.

(D) Regional airlines charge less to fly a given route now than the major airlines charged when they flew the same route.

(E) Any policy that leads to an increase in the number of competitors in a given field works to the long-term advantage of consumers.

9. Many people do not understand themselves, nor do they try to gain self-understanding. These people might try to understand others, but these attempts are sure to fail, because without self-understanding it is impossible to understand others. It is clear from this that anyone who lacks self-understanding will be incapable of understanding others.

The reasoning in the argument is flawed because the argument

(A) mistakes something that is necessary to bring about a situation for something that in itself is enough to bring about that situation

(B) fails to take into account the possibility that not everyone wants to gain a thorough understanding of himself or herself

(C) blames people for something for which they cannot legitimately be held responsible

(D) makes use of the inherently vague term "self-understanding" without defining that term

(E) draws a conclusion that simply restates a claim given in support of that conclusion

10. Ethicist: A society is just when, and only when, first, each person has an equal right to basic liberties, and second, inequalities in the distribution of income and wealth are not tolerated unless these inequalities are to everyone's advantage and are attached to jobs open to everyone.

Which one of the following judgments most closely conforms to the principle described above?

(A) Society S guarantees everyone an equal right to basic liberties, while allowing inequalities in the distribution of income and wealth that are to the advantage of everyone. Further, the jobs to which these inequalities are attached are open to most people. Thus, society S is just.

(B) Society S gives everyone an equal right to basic liberties, but at the expense of creating inequalities in the distribution of income and wealth. Thus, society S is not just.

(C) Society S allows inequalities in the distribution of income and wealth, although everyone benefits, and these inequalities are attached to jobs that are open to everyone. Thus, society S is just.

(D) Society S distributes income and wealth to everyone equally, but at the expense of creating inequalities in the right to basic liberties. Thus, society S is not just.

(E) Society S gives everyone an equal right to basic liberties, and although there is an inequality in the distribution of income and wealth, the jobs to which these inequalities are attached are open to all. Thus, society S is just.

11. Director of Ace Manufacturing Company: Our management consultant proposes that we reassign staff so that all employees are doing both what they like to do and what they do well. This, she says, will "increase productivity by fully exploiting our available resources." But Ace Manufacturing has a long-standing commitment not to exploit its workers. Therefore, implementing her recommendations would cause us to violate our own policy.

The director's argument for rejecting the management consultant's proposal is most vulnerable to criticism on which one of the following grounds?

(A) failing to distinguish two distinct senses of a key term

(B) attempting to defend an action on the ground that it is frequently carried out

(C) defining a term by pointing to an atypical example of something to which the term applies

(D) drawing a conclusion that simply restates one of the premises of the argument

(E) calling something by a less offensive term than the term that is usually used to name that thing

12. Cafeteria patron: The apples sold in this cafeteria are greasy. The cashier told me that the apples are in that condition when they are delivered to the cafeteria and that the cafeteria does not wash the apples it sells. Most fruit is sprayed with dangerous pesticides before it is harvested, and is dangerous until it is washed. Clearly, the cafeteria is selling pesticide-covered fruit, thereby endangering its patrons.

Which one of the following is an assumption on which the argument depends?

(A) The apples that the cafeteria sells are not thoroughly washed after harvest but before reaching the cafeteria.

(B) Most pesticides that are sprayed on fruit before harvest leave a greasy residue on the fruit.

(C) Many of the cafeteria's patrons are unaware that the cafeteria does not wash the apples it sells.

(D) Only pesticides that leave a greasy residue on fruit can be washed off.

(E) Fruits other than apples also arrive at the cafeteria in a greasy condition.

13. At Happywell Inc., last year the average annual salary for dieticians was $50,000, while the average annual salary for physical therapists was $42,000. The average annual salary for all Happywell employees last year was $40,000.

If the information above is correct, which one of the following conclusions can properly be drawn on the basis of it?

(A) There were more physical therapists than dieticians at Happywell last year.

(B) There was no dietician at Happywell last year who earned less than the average for a physical therapist.

(C) At least one Happywell employee earned less than the average for a physical therapist last year.

(D) At least one physical therapist earned less than the lowest-paid Happywell dietician last year.

(E) At least one dietician earned more than the highest-paid Happywell physical therapist last year.

14. There is strong evidence that the cause of migraines (severe recurrent headaches) is not psychological but instead is purely physiological. Yet several studies have found that people being professionally treated for migraines rate higher on a standard psychological scale of anxiety than do people not being professionally treated for migraines.

Which one of the following, if true, most helps to resolve the apparent discrepancy in the information above?

(A) People who have migraine headaches tend to have relatives who also have migraine headaches.

(B) People who have migraine headaches often suffer these headaches when under emotional stress.

(C) People who rate higher on the standard psychological scale of anxiety are more likely to seek professional treatment than are people who rate lower on the scale.

(D) Of the many studies done on the cause of migraine headaches, most of those that suggest that psychological factors such as anxiety cause migraines have been widely publicized.

(E) Most people who have migraines and who seek professional treatment remain in treatment until they stop having migraines, whether their doctors consider the cause to be physiological or psychological.

15. A fundamental illusion in robotics is the belief that improvements in robots will liberate humanity from "hazardous and demeaning work." Engineers are designing only those types of robots that can be properly maintained with the least expensive, least skilled human labor possible. Therefore, robots will not eliminate demeaning work—only substitute one type of demeaning work for another.

The reasoning in the argument is most vulnerable to the criticism that it

(A) ignores the consideration that in a competitive business environment some jobs might be eliminated if robots are not used in the manufacturing process
(B) assumes what it sets out to prove, that robots create demeaning work
(C) does not specify whether or not the engineers who design robots consider their work demeaning
(D) attempts to support its conclusion by an appeal to the emotion of fear, which is often experienced by people faced with the prospect of losing their jobs to robots
(E) fails to address the possibility that the amount of demeaning work eliminated by robots might be significantly greater than the amount they create

16. Legislator: Your agency is responsible for regulating an industry shaken by severe scandals. You were given funds to hire 500 investigators to examine the scandals, but you hired no more than 400. I am forced to conclude that you purposely limited hiring in an attempt to prevent the full extent of the scandals from being revealed.

Regulator: We tried to hire the 500 investigators but the starting salaries for these positions had been frozen so low by the legislature that it was impossible to attract enough qualified applicants.

The regulator responds to the legislator's criticism by

(A) shifting the blame for the scandals to the legislature
(B) providing information that challenges the conclusion drawn by the legislator
(C) claiming that compliance with the legislature's mandate would have been an insufficient response
(D) rephrasing the legislator's conclusion in terms more favorable to the regulator
(E) showing that the legislator's statements are self-contradictory

17. No mathematical proposition can be proven true by observation. It follows that it is impossible to know any mathematical proposition to be true.

The conclusion follows logically if which one of the following is assumed?

(A) Only propositions that can be proven true can be known to be true.
(B) Observation alone cannot be used to prove the truth of any proposition.
(C) If a proposition can be proven true by observation, then it can be known to be true.
(D) Knowing a proposition to be true is impossible only if it cannot be proven true by observation.
(E) Knowing a proposition to be true requires proving it true by observation.

18. Until recently it was thought that ink used before the sixteenth century did not contain titanium. However, a new type of analysis detected titanium in the ink of the famous Bible printed by Johannes Gutenberg and in that of another fifteenth-century Bible known as B-36, though not in the ink of any of numerous other fifteenth-century books analyzed. This finding is of great significance, since it not only strongly supports the hypothesis that B-36 was printed by Gutenberg but also shows that the presence of titanium in the ink of the purportedly fifteenth-century Vinland Map can no longer be regarded as a reason for doubting the map's authenticity.

The reasoning in the passage is vulnerable to criticism on the ground that

(A) the results of the analysis are interpreted as indicating that the use of titanium as an ingredient in fifteenth-century ink both was, and was not, extremely restricted

(B) if the technology that makes it possible to detect titanium in printing ink has only recently become available, it is unlikely that printers or artists in the fifteenth century would know whether their ink contained titanium or not

(C) it is unreasonable to suppose that determination of the date and location of a document's printing or drawing can be made solely on the basis of the presence or absence of a single element in the ink used in the document

(D) both the B-36 Bible and the Vinland Map are objects that can be appreciated on their own merits whether or not the precise date of their creation or the identity of the person who made them is known

(E) the discovery of titanium in the ink of the Vinland Map must have occurred before titanium was discovered in the ink of the Gutenberg Bible and the B-36 Bible

19. Most people believe that yawning is most powerfully triggered by seeing someone else yawn. This belief about yawning is widespread not only today, but also has been commonplace in many parts of the world in the past, if we are to believe historians of popular culture. Thus, seeing someone else yawn must be the most irresistible cause of yawning.

The argument is most vulnerable to which one of the following criticisms?

(A) It attempts to support its conclusion solely by restating that conclusion in other words.

(B) It cites the evidence of historians of popular culture in direct support of a claim that lies outside their area of expertise.

(C) It makes a sweeping generalization about yawning based on evidence drawn from a limited number of atypical cases.

(D) It supports its conclusion by appealing solely to opinion in a matter that is largely factual.

(E) It takes for granted that yawns have no cause other than the one it cites.

20. Office manager:   I will not order recycled paper for this office. Our letters to clients must make a good impression, so we cannot print them on inferior paper.

Stationery supplier:   Recycled paper is not necessarily inferior. In fact, from the beginning, the finest paper has been made of recycled material. It was only in the 1850s that paper began to be made from wood fiber, and then only because there were no longer enough rags to meet the demand for paper.

In which one of the following ways does the stationer's response fail to address the office manager's objection to recycled paper?

(A) It does not recognize that the office manager's prejudice against recycled paper stems from ignorance.

(B) It uses irrelevant facts to justify a claim about the quality of the disputed product.

(C) It assumes that the office manager is concerned about environmental issues.

(D) It presupposes that the office manager understands the basic technology of paper manufacturing.

(E) It ignores the office manager's legitimate concern about quality.

21. A commonly accepted myth is that left-handed people are more prone to cause accidents than are right-handed people. But this is, in fact, just a myth, as is indicated by the fact that more household accidents are caused by right-handed people than are caused by left-handed people.

The reasoning is flawed because the argument

(A) makes a distinction where there is no real difference between the things distinguished
(B) takes no account of the relative frequency of left-handed people in the population as a whole
(C) uses the word "accidents" in two different senses
(D) ignores the possibility that some household accidents are caused by more than one person
(E) gives wholly irrelevant evidence and simply disparages an opposing position by calling it a "myth"

22. In a recent study, each member of two groups of people, Group A (composed of persons sixty-five to seventy-five years old) and Group B (composed of college students), was required to make a telephone call to a certain number at a specified time. The time when each call was initiated was recorded electronically. Group A proved far better at remembering to make a telephone call precisely at a specified time than did Group B. There were fourteen lapses in Group B but only one lapse in Group A. Clearly, at least one type of memory does not suffer as a person ages.

Which one of the following, if all of them are true, is LEAST helpful in establishing that the conclusion above is properly drawn?

(A) There was the same number of people in each group.
(B) The same group of researchers answered the calls made by the callers in both study groups.
(C) Among the college students there were no persons more than forty years old.
(D) Both groups had unrestricted access to telephones for making the required calls.
(E) The members of the two groups received their instructions approximately the same amount of time before they were to make their telephone calls.

23. Despite the best efforts of astronomers, no one has yet succeeded in exchanging messages with intelligent life on other planets or in other solar systems. In fact, no one has even managed to prove that any kind of extraterrestrial life exists. Thus, there is clearly no intelligent life anywhere but on Earth.

The argument's reasoning is flawed because the argument

(A) fails to consider that there might be extraterrestrial forms of intelligence that are not living beings
(B) confuses an absence of evidence for a hypothesis with the existence of evidence against the hypothesis
(C) interprets a disagreement over a scientific theory as a disproof of that theory
(D) makes an inference that relies on the vagueness of the term "life"
(E) relies on a weak analogy rather than on evidence to draw a conclusion

24. Copernicus's astronomical system is superior to Ptolemy's and was so at the time it was proposed, even though at that time all observational evidence was equally consistent with both theories. Ptolemy believed that the stars revolved around the earth at great speeds. This struck Copernicus as unlikely; he correctly thought that a simpler theory is that the earth rotates on its axis.

The argument most closely conforms to which one of the following principles?

(A) Simplicity should be the sole deciding factor in choosing among competing scientific theories.
(B) If one theory is likely to be true, and another competing theory is likely to be false, then the one likely to be true is the superior of the two.
(C) If all observational evidence is consistent with two competing theories, the one that is more intuitively true is the more practical theory to adopt.
(D) Other things being equal, the more complex of two competing theories is the inferior theory.
(E) Other things being equal, the simpler of two competing theories is the more scientifically important theory.

25. Unplugging a peripheral component such as a "mouse" from a personal computer renders all of the software programs that require that component unusable on that computer. On Fred's personal computer, a software program that requires a mouse has become unusable. So it must be that the mouse for Fred's computer became unplugged.

The argument is most vulnerable to which one of the following criticisms?

(A) It contains a shift in the meaning of "unusable" from "permanently unusable" to "temporarily unusable."
(B) It treats an event that can cause a certain result as though that event is necessary to bring about that result.
(C) It introduces information unrelated to its conclusion as evidence in support of that conclusion.
(D) It attempts to support its conclusion by citing a generalization that is too broad.
(E) It overlooks the possibility that some programs do not require a peripheral component such as a mouse.

26. Bank deposits are credited on the date of the transaction only when they are made before 3 P.M. Alicia knows that the bank deposit was made before 3 P.M. So, Alicia knows that the bank deposit was credited on the date of the transaction.

Which one of the following exhibits both of the logical flaws exhibited by the argument above?

(A) Journalists are the only ones who will be permitted to ask questions at the press conference. Since Marjorie is a journalist, she will be permitted to ask questions.
(B) We know that Patrice works only on Thursday. Today is Thursday, so it follows that Patrice is working today.
(C) It is clear that George knows he will be promoted to shift supervisor, because George will be promoted to shift supervisor only if Helen resigns, and George knows Helen will resign.
(D) John believes that 4 is a prime number and that 4 is divisible by 2. Hence John believes that there is a prime number divisible by 2.
(E) Pat wants to become a social worker. It is well known that social workers are poorly paid. Pat apparently wants to be poorly paid.

27. Commentator: Because of teacher hiring freezes, the quality of education in that country will not improve. Thus, it will surely deteriorate.

The flawed reasoning in which one of the following is most similar to that in the commentator's argument?

(A) Because Raoul is a vegetarian, he will not have the pepperoni pizza for lunch. It follows that he will have the cheese pizza.
(B) Given that over 250 years of attempts to prove the Goldbach conjecture have failed, it will probably never be proved. Hence, it is more likely to be disproved than proved.
(C) Since funding levels for social programs are being frozen, our society will not become more harmonious. Thus, it may become more discordant.
(D) Since there is a storm moving in, the outside temperature cannot rise this afternoon. Therefore, it must fall.
(E) The starter in Mary's car gave out weeks ago, and so it is impossible for the car to start. Therefore, it will not start.

*Where's the answer key?*

You'll find the answer key for this section on page 454.

## Real LSAT Practice Extravaganza   ANSWER KEY

| | CORRECT ANSWER | WHICH PREPTEST? |
|---|---|---|
| 1 | B | 15.3.9 |
| 2 | A | 5.1.14 |
| 3 | C | 7.4.9 |
| 4 | C | 19.2.14 |
| 5 | A | 16.2.19 |
| 6 | A | 17.3.16 |
| 7 | D | 42.2.12 |
| 8 | C | 14.2.17 |
| 9 | E | 17.2.2 |
| 10 | D | 24.3.24 |
| 11 | A | 19.2.1 |
| 12 | A | 17.2.10 |
| 13 | C | 12.1.8 |
| 14 | C | 19.4.20 |
| 15 | E | 16.2.10 |
| 16 | B | 19.2.6 |
| 17 | E | 24.2.24 |
| 18 | A | 12.1.24 |
| 19 | D | 15.2.17 |
| 20 | B | 7.1.17 |
| 21 | B | 19.2.7 |
| 22 | B | 42.4.9 |
| 23 | B | 16.3.2 |
| 24 | D | 24.2.22 |
| 25 | B | 27.4.10 |
| 26 | C | 31.2.21 |
| 27 | D | 39.4.26 |

# Appendix B    A LIST OF ALL THE REAL LSAT QUESTIONS IN THIS BOOK

| PREPTEST | SECTION | QUESTIONS |
|---|---|---|
| PT 4 | 1 | 1 |
| PT 5 | 1 | 14 |
| PT 7 | 1 | 17, 22 |
|  | 4 | 9 |
| PT 11 | 2 | 2 |
| PT 12 | 1 | 8, 24 |
| PT 13 | 4 | 7 |
| PT 14 | 2 | 17 |
| PT 15 | 2 | 4, 14, 17, 23 |
|  | 3 | 9, 11,12, 13, 20 |
| PT 16 | 2 | 10, 19, 21 |
|  | 3 | 2, 5, 10, 12, 25 |
| PT 17 | 2 | 2, 6, 7, 10, 13 |
|  | 3 | 12, 14, 15, 16, 18 |
| PT 18 | 2 | 5, 13, 17, 18 |
|  | 4 | 2, 6, 7, 10, 12, 15, 23, 24 |
| PT 19 | 2 | 1, 6, 7, 14 |
|  | 4 | 3, 13, 20, 26 |
| PT 20 | 1 | 6, 13 |
|  | 4 | 6, 15, 18, 21 |
| PT 23 | 2 | 13, 25 |
|  | 3 | 7, 24 |
| PT 24 | 2 | 22, 24 |
|  | 3 | 24 |
| PT 27 | 4 | 10 |
| PT 28 | 3 | 20 |
| PT 31 | 2 | 21 |
| PT 39 | 4 | 26 |
| PT 42 | 2 | 12 |
|  | 4 | 9 |
| JUNE 2007 | 2 | All Questions |
|  | 3 | All Questions |

Powrful AND Prenease

Start your Wrong
Answer Journal here!

| TEST.SECTION.# | STIMULUS TYPE | QUESTION TYPE | REASON MISSED | SOLUTION |
|---|---|---|---|---|
| 39.2.1 | | MC | rushed to AC, didn't breakdown stimulus | Slow down, when reading, handle |
| 39.2.13 | | Disagree | Took something as likely as being certain. | Read key words in AL carefully |
| 39.2.21 | | SA | didn't diagram correctly | take more time on these types of questions |
| 39.2.24 | | MBF | didn't diagram correctly | when there is conditional language, diagram. |
| CLIR #1 | | | - identify MC stimulus<br>- identify type of stimulus<br>- develop CLIR | |
| 39.4.16 | L | SA | - went to questions too fast before understanding stimulus | - make sure I have a clear transition develop CLIR before reading SA |
| 38.4.21 | L | CF | - overthought didn't trust gut. | - if facilitating between AC go with gut answer |
| 39.4.11 | L | LFLAW | - overthought didn't trust S.T. didn't | |
| 39.4.19 | L | NA | - recognize that NA is pervasive QT those of powerful answer | whenever I enter a question type is powerful or pervasive flag |
| 39.4.20 | L | FLAW | - didn't think about causation and the possibility of a third factor | - when you see causation recognize and think about the omitted this |
| 39.2.23 | L | FLAW | - didn't understand the stimulus and energy | - make sure I have a clear transition before reading to QT & AC |
| 40.1.4 | C | Method | - didn't identify that as pervasive QT. led me to choosing a powerful | - whether I am looking for powerful or pervasive AC before jumping into the |
| 40.3.6 | L | Argument Part | - answer didn't identify a premise indicator and as a result misrelated the conclusion | - pay attention to premise and conclusion indicators |
| 40.3.14 | L | LFLAW | - fell for a dormant condition | - do not choose a condition in the AC if it is not addressed by the stimulus |

BT
↓
CLIR
↓
QT → Powrful or Prevease → AL

456

LA → II → MT → BH

MT → II

LA →

LA → II

∅ → R
―――――
LA → R

| TEST.SECTION.# | STIMULUS TYPE | QUESTION TYPE | REASON MISSED | SOLUTION |
|---|---|---|---|---|
| 40.3.15 | L | SA | mistaken *only* to sufficient when it is a necessary and the *only* is a group 1 indicator | recognize "only" as necessary and "the only" as sufficient |
| 40.3.22 | L | NA | - didn't spend enough time even then<br>- didn't recognize causation like I should have | - when encountering causation immediately think of omitted factors |
| 40.3.25 | L | Parallel Method | - didn't break down each AC as carefully as I should | - paraphrasing of method of reasoning more generally, case attention to words and how the argument is structured |
| 40.3.26 | L | Weaken | - lost sight of what I was attempting to weaken | - with weaken except reliably try weaken and, process of elimination instead of thinking absence that, |
| 41.1.05 | L | MC | - misread stimulus | Be honest with yourself doesn't weaken about your basic transition — understand the stimulus before moving |
| 41.1.13 | C | Weaken | - chose an answer that I was not 100% comfortable with | - If a AC feels like N may be correct it probably isn't, be able to use the stimulus is involved |
| 41.1.16 | L | Weaken | - eliminated correct AC early on b/c it didn't have parallel language | - recognize that sure for AC are conceptually parallel necessary quotes even longest yet correct |
| 41.1.21 | I | MBT | - rely in stimulus justified that being ___ just about ____ | - don't make ____ assumptions about the apparent core of the stimulus especially when the stimulus doesn't address it |
| 41.1.22 | L | Flaw | - didn't accurately identify the loophole | - Find a definite loophole before moving onto the question |
| 41.1.23 | L | Parallel Flaw | - did not breakdown stimulus, did not look for "reasons" of the stimulus | - For ___ parallel Flaw questions breakdown stimulus |
| 42.2.11 | C | MSS | - did not read stimulus thoroughly | - Slow down and be honest w/ yourself on basic transition |
| 42.2.17 | L | FLAW | - misunderstood Flaw | - go w/ gut |
| 42.2.21 | L | Principle | - didn't find exact match, almost right | realize that w/ principle conform it does not have to conform perfectly |
| 42.2.22 | L | Parallel Method | - did not read AC carefully enough | - do not eliminate unless you have read carefully and are 100% sure it is wrong. |
| 42.4.19 | L | NA | - made an assumption I chose AC that involved wording not in stimulus | - make sure AC is supported by the stimulus |

Q17, 19
PT 42 sec 4

SI → EG → word leader coop
slow thought when too optimistic

| TEST.SECTION.# | STIMULUS TYPE | QUESTION TYPE | REASON MISSED | SOLUTION |
|---|---|---|---|---|
| 42.4.17 | RC/L | MBT | Confused "Rather" with "Latter" | – Read Stimulus carefully! |
| 43.2.17 | L | MBT | made an invalid same inference | – when you see any same *word* asked *about* value same relationships |
| 43.3.25 | L | Parallel method | did not eliminate AC thoroughly *enough* | – Parallel method – think about *what went* wrong in *question* SS |
| 44.2.13 | L | SA | – didn't *trace* *arg* conclusion | – If *there* is confusing *language* make sure you *trace* |
| 44.2.14 | I | MSS | – didn't pay *attention* to the *direction* of causal /conclusion | – If A → B *so then* C Not *necessary* causes A |
| 44.2.22 | L | PF | – *was* *agreed* to *support* *that* the *theory*, but the *authority* was an *expert* | – *appeal* to authority *does* not *have* to be *expert* |
| 44.2.24 | L | AP | – didn't *pay* *attention* to *surrounding* *context* | – *See* *context* *follows* and *preceding* *argument* *parts* to *determine* *their* *role* |
| 44.4.19 | L | PF | – didn't *map* out *the* *flaw* | – *on flaws* *try* 2 1st *of* *conditional* *language* *map* out *on scrap* |
| 44.4.20 | L | F | – passed an *illicit* *notion* | – read AC carefully |
| 44.4.22 | L | F | – didn't *notice* the false *dichotomy* | – when *distinguishing* *between* *two* *purely* *force apart* the *middle* *ground* |
| 44.4.26 | L | SA | – *was* *disregarded* AC on *account* of *personal* *language* | – AC w/ *personal* *language* can be *considered* *personal* *point*. |
| 45.1.03 | L | NA | – did not correctly *identify* *required* | – *eliminate* AC that *are* *sufficient*, ask if *required* if *true* does *this* *hold* |
| 45.1.08 | I | MBT | – did not recognize the *wording* in *the* AC | – *Read* AC *to* *be* *true* *especially* *when* *carefully* *two* *then* *are* *used* *interchangeably* |
| 45.1.12 | L | Weak | – didn't *eliminate* *an* AC *and* *just* *chose* *one* | – *when* AC *talks* *about* *doesn't* *or* *might* *See* *Stimulus* *also* *discusses* *it* |
| 45.1.16 | L | weak | – didn't have a *clear* understanding *of* the *conclusion* | – *make* *sure* *you* *know* *the* *conclusion* |

| TEST.SECTION.# | STIMULUS TYPE | QUESTION TYPE | REASON MISSED | SOLUTION |
|---|---|---|---|---|
| 45.1.18 | L | Weak | didn't correctly identify conclusion | • If something is not used for one purpose it does not necessarily mean it won't be used for another purpose |
| 45.1.20 | L | Flaw | - chose an answer I did not like | - chose make sure the answer you chose is one that you can support |
| 45.1.25 | L | Parallel method | - didn't correctly identify the logical structure | - when saying heavy PM, make sure you map it out |
| 45.1.26 | L | S | - Ran out of time | • go fast on Qustions 1-10 |
| 46.2.11 | L | Flaw | - missed that they were talking about managers they that humans not employees | - If you are unsure of AC, reread the stimulus |
| 16.2.20 | L | PF | - didn't follow stimulus, followed career | - PF will memory have a trap w/ similar choice matter, be wary of such traps |
| 16.2.23 | L | SA | - discounted correct AC just because it sound wrong | - diagram out the logic on these problems |
| 5.4.04 | L | weak | - attacked a small part of the purpose | - Don't attack purpose |
| 15.4.17 | L | Flaw | - attacked the conclusion not the relation between premises and conclusion | - don't attack conclusion |
| 5.4.18 | I | MSS | - didn't look at connection between premises and focused on answer | - pay attention to referenced parody - don't necessary eliminate AC based on strong language |
| 5.4.20 | L | PF | - chose an answer that appeared attractive but was incorrect | - concentrate the specific form is instead of just the stimulus |
| 5.4.22 | L | SA | - confused sufficient and necessary conditions | - recognize "the only" is a sufficient indicator |
| 5.4.24 | L | Flaw | - didn't fully focus on Davis' flaws but would the opposite | - Make sure you distinguish who's argument you are evaluating for a flaw |
| 5.3.15 | L | NA | - Didn't treat what I thought our thought | - were unsure true if - If it is to success evidence and they require some certainty then NA damages |
| 7.1.2 | L | weak | - attacked the wrong part of the stimulus and in doing so I guessed and was wrong | - Don't get TOO caught up in equivocation, especially if it's not the focal part of the stimulus |

| TEST.SECTION.# | STIMULUS TYPE | QUESTION TYPE | REASON MISSED | SOLUTION |
|---|---|---|---|---|
| 47.1.16 | MJI | NASS | drew a conclusion that is not discussed in the stimulus | for NASS if it is not addressed expands campus may not be answer |
| 47.1.22 | L | Weak | *[illegible]* the main conclusion | *[illegible]* focus on main & not *[illegible]* conclusion |
| 47.1.24 | L | mWeak | *[illegible]* the assump being made, that *[illegible]* are necessary | to *[illegible]* a *[illegible]* show just the necessary *[illegible]* is *[illegible]* necessary |
| 47.1.26 | L | Strength | argument suggests *[illegible]* - need scrutiny to *[illegible]* conclusion | when *[illegible]* is suggested - to strengthen eliminate *[illegible]* |
| 47.3.14 | L | Weak | chose E, *[illegible]* had any AC in head | If I go through AC, had part, skip. |
| 47.3.20 | L | Method | let the confusing language lead me to a confusing language | *[illegible]* confusing language go slow and break down what its saying |
| 47.3.21 | L | SA | missed the gap in reasoning | *[illegible]* is fed after *[illegible]* the assumed |
| 60.3.06 | L | PM | missed the number of students, talks about *[illegible]* chose AC w/ TWO | in PM, make sure # of people/*[illegible]* are similar *[illegible]* of the |
| 66.3.07 | L | AP | *[illegible]* stimulus | *[illegible]* *[illegible]* could *[illegible]* one another |
| 60.3.12 | I | MBT | *[illegible]* stimulus | *[illegible]* don't speed through stimulus, *[illegible]* are *[illegible]* in conditional *[illegible]* |
| 60.3.22 | L | NA | did not check to see if this has to be true, also skipped through it *[illegible]* time | *[illegible]* trying all NA AC always see if "conclusion is *[illegible]*" does this have to *[illegible]* |
| | | | | |
| | | | | |
| | | | | |
| | | | | |

| TEST.SECTION.# | STIMULUS TYPE | QUESTION TYPE | REASON MISSED | SOLUTION |
|---|---|---|---|---|
| | | | | |
| | | | | |
| | | | | |
| | | | | |
| | | | | |
| | | | | |
| | | | | |
| | | | | |
| | | | | |
| | | | | |
| | | | | |
| | | | | |
| | | | | |
| | | | | |

| TEST.SECTION.# | STIMULUS TYPE | QUESTION TYPE | REASON MISSED | SOLUTION |
|---|---|---|---|---|
| | | | | |
| | | | | |
| | | | | |
| | | | | |
| | | | | |
| | | | | |
| | | | | |
| | | | | |
| | | | | |
| | | | | |
| | | | | |
| | | | | |
| | | | | |
| | | | | |

462